Middleware Networks

Concept, Design and Deployment of Internet Infrastructure

The Kluwer International Series on ADVANCES IN DATABASE SYSTEMS

Series Editor
Ahmed K. Elmagarmid

Purdue University
West Lafayette, IN 47907

Other books in the Series:

ADVANCED DATABASE INDEXING, *Yannis Manolopoulos, Yannis Theodoridis, Vassilis J. Tsotras;* ISBN: 0-7923-7716-8
MULTILEVEL SECURE TRANSACTION PROCESSING, *Vijay Atluri, Sushil Jajodia, Binto George* ISBN: 0-7923-7702-8
FUZZY LOGIC IN DATA MODELING, *Guoqing Chen* ISBN: 0-7923-8253-6
INTERCONNECTING HETEROGENEOUS INFORMATION SYSTEMS, *Athman Bouguettaya, Boualem Benatallah, Ahmed Elmagarmid* ISBN: 0-7923-8216-1
FOUNDATIONS OF KNOWLEDGE SYSTEMS: With Applications to Databases and Agents, *Gerd Wagner* ISBN: 0-7923-8212-9
DATABASE RECOVERY, *Vijay Kumar, Sang H. Son* ISBN: 0-7923-8192-0
PARALLEL, OBJECT-ORIENTED, AND ACTIVE KNOWLEDGE BASE SYSTEMS, *Ioannis Vlahavas, Nick Bassiliades* ISBN: 0-7923-8117-3
DATA MANAGEMENT FOR MOBILE COMPUTING, *Evaggelia Pitoura, George Samaras* ISBN: 0-7923-8053-3
MINING VERY LARGE DATABASES WITH PARALLEL PROCESSING, *Alex A. Freitas, Simon H. Lavington* ISBN: 0-7923-8048-7
INDEXING TECHNIQUES FOR ADVANCED DATABASE SYSTEMS, *Elisa Bertino, Beng Chin Ooi, Ron Sacks-Davis, Kian-Lee Tan, Justin Zobel, Boris Shidlovsky, Barbara Catania* ISBN: 0-7923-9985-4
INDEX DATA STRUCTURES IN OBJECT-ORIENTED DATABASES, *Thomas A. Mueck, Martin L. Polaschek* ISBN: 0-7923-9971-4
DATABASE ISSUES IN GEOGRAPHIC INFORMATION SYSTEMS, *Nabil R. Adam, Aryya Gangopadhyay* ISBN: 0-7923-9924-2
VIDEO DATABASE SYSTEMS: Issues, Products, and Applications, *Ahmed K. Elmagarmid, Haitao Jiang, Abdelsalam A. Helal, Anupam Joshi, Magdy Ahmed* ISBN: 0-7923-9872-6
REPLICATION TECHNIQUES IN DISTRIBUTED SYSTEMS, *Abdelsalam A. Helal, Abdelsalam A. Heddaya, Bharat B. Bhargava* ISBN: 0-7923-9800-9
SEARCHING MULTIMEDIA DATABASES BY CONTENT, *Christos Faloutsos* ISBN: 0-7923-9777-0
TIME-CONSTRAINED TRANSACTION MANAGEMENT: Real-Time Constraints in Database Transaction Systems, *Nandit R. Soparkar, Henry F. Korth, Abraham Silberschatz* ISBN: 0-7923-9752-5
DATABASE CONCURRENCY CONTROL: Methods, Performance, and Analysis, *Alexander Thomasian, IBM T. J. Watson Research Center* ISBN: 0-7923-9741-X

MIDDLEWARE NETWORKS

Concept, Design and Deployment of Internet Infrastructure

Michah Lerner, *AT&T Labs*
George Vanecek, *AT&T Labs*
Nino Vidovic, *AT&T Labs*
Dado Vrsalovic, *Intel Corp.*

SPRINGER SCIENCE+BUSINESS MEDIA, LLC

ISBN 978-1-4757-8364-3 ISBN 978-0-306-47022-6 (eBook)
DOI 10.1007/978-0-306-47022-6

Library of Congress Cataloging-in-Publication Data

A C.I.P. Catalogue record for this book is available
from the Library of Congress.

Printed on acid-free paper.

Table of Contents

List of Figures

List of Tables

Preface

Long ago, when the computer industry was young, software was built - and rebuilt - from the "ground up". Each application was custom designed and built for a given machine, and interacted directly with the hardware of that particular machine only. The idea of a common operating system - let alone middleware upon which to rapidly develop new applications - was a mere flicker of a dream in the minds of a few visionaries. The applications for a particular computer were usually built by its vendor. Needless to say, software was scarce and expensive.

Gradually, computer vendors began to recognize that software applications would become the driving force of their industry. In their quest to satisfy customer demands for unerring software rapidly delivered, the vendors sought new ways to develop software more quickly and at a lower cost. From these roots, the Independent Software Vendor (ISV) industry emerged. In order to make the building of applications cheaper and easier, ISVs, often in partnership with computer vendors, endeavored to create an "environment" that would assure more or less "common" functionality for all applications. As a result, various operating systems were born.

Much later, the breakneck rise in the Internet created a situation of ubiquitous connectivity between fully autonomous components. Collectively, this may comprise the largest and most complex distributed system ever developed by a civilization. Operating on an international scale, Internet needs to provide reliable services to billions of people around the world. Today many companies are competing to provide these services. Again, an ability to quickly and economically build various IP[1] services, or outsource their building, is crucial to attract and retain customers. A parallel with the past and the need for an independent service vendor (ISV) community is quite obvious.

1. Internet Protocol

This led to the idea of a common IP service platform and the creation of GeoPlex, conceived, developed and deployed at AT&T Labs, and referenced in this book. GeoPlex is the "project codeword" for generations of Advanced Networking Middleware. This middleware strives towards fully integrated global connectivity. To date, this has provided important deployments of service architecture, and further it has infused the community with leading-edge ideas. Many of these ideas have been incorporated into ongoing standards and evolution of the Internet industry. The GeoPlex principles will likely survive many generations of evolutionary deployments.

GeoPlex is not an operating system, nor does it attempt to compete with one. It is *networking middleware* that uses one or more operating systems running on computers connected to the Internet. Unlike an operating system which manages resources of a given machine such as users, files, and processes, GeoPlex is a service platform that manages networks and on-line services. Contrasted to a process-oriented operating system such as Unix, GeoPlex maps all of the IP network activities into one or more *services*.

There are several basic design principles GeoPlex designers adhered to. As a service platform, above all else, it abstracts the low-level network fabric while offering values to on-line services; values that help in their ability to scale to support very large number of customers or assume security and privacy. These include the ability to support any well behaved client-server IP application unmodified, the ability to map any system activity to a service, and the ability to present the same interface to any client independent of his role as an end-user, an administrator, a customer care agent, or a sales representative.

This book describes one approach in the telecommunication industry's transition to IP data networks. It offers a case study, an exercise if you like, of how to organize and build a complex system with simple, off-the shelf components. It does this by offering an introductory reference to the GeoPlex project of AT&T Labs. This project defined, designed and developed innovative Platform Infrastructure Software that pioneered a vision of an IP Service Platform. GeoPlex was the predecessor for the emerging Internet infrastructure and services of the new AT&T.

We note that, although the complete platform deployed in a production network would require the support of many proprietary components, this book describes the kernel that consists only of standard components and protocols.

This book does not offer a complete coverage of related work in the telecommunication industry nor does it intend to be a complete guide to GeoPlex. It is, however, a goal of the authors to present a thorough picture of what GeoPlex is, its Application Programming Interfaces (APIs), and the impact of deploying an IP Service Platform on the telecommunications industry.

Dalibor "Dado" Vrsalovic

Book Outline

The material in this book is presented in three major parts: *IP Technology Fundamentals, IP Service Platform Fundamentals,* and *Building the IP Platform.* Part I of *IP Technology Fundamentals* presents key technologies and issues that lay the foundation for building IP service platforms. Chapter One reviews present telecommunications and the Internet timelines, and describes the metamorphosis occurring in the telecommunications industry and its impact on network vendors and the software industry. Next we look at the emergence of the Internet Protocol (IP) as the convergence mechanism; the changing role of the network; and ubiquity of access devices. This leads to the section on the "civilizing" of data networks and customers' expectations of what data networks should and should not be. The chapter finishes with challenges for 21st century networks and a summary of the current state of the Internet. This discussion concludes with a question:

> *What is missing in the way things are done today, and why does this impel the industry towards IP service platforms?*

Chapter Two provides a brief technology overview and gives a broad perspective on related technologies as a means of demonstrating the parallels between present developments in the Internet and the Public Switched Telephone Network (PSTN). The chapter starts with a high level description of the PSTN technologies and services. Here we introduce the Intelligent Network (IN) and the Advanced Intelligent Network (AIN), and look at TINA-C, JAIN, and Parlay as examples of middleware efforts to bridge PSTN and data services. Next we briefly describe data network mechanisms consisting of frame relays, ATMs, gigabit ethernets, and wireless systems. The rest of the chapter describes a broad range of current and emerging services and applications such as Quality of Service (QoS) and Virtual Private Networks (VPNs). Included are sections on the client/server model, network security, data encryption, certificates and authorities. Higher up in the abstraction it consists of Unified Messaging (UM) support, Electronic Commerce (EComm), and IP Telephony and Voice-over-IP. At the highest level of abstraction, the chapter describes the services offered by the World Wide Web and the emerging support of Java, XML, and HTTP/1.1.

Part II of this book outlines the IP platform fundamentals. Chapter Three looks at the current market of network-enabled and online services. It first looks at the issues dealing with the development and delivery of services along with the opportunities for the telecommunications carriers that are essential in addressing these issues. It is here that we look more closely at the benefits of network middleware. The chapter finishes with the several lengthy provisioning scenarios through which we attempt to describe the challenges and opportunities.

Chapter Four addresses IP platform requirements such as security, scalability, and interoperability that are driving the movement towards IP service platforms. It then presents design principles on which an IP platform architecture and a subsequent implementation can be based. The implementations follow the evolution in Internet Architectures, from client-server through multi-layered systems. This leads directly to the IP platform capabilities that were designed into the GeoPlex system. We begin exploration of these capabilities, in Chapter Five, by extending the architecture into an edge gateway supporting service nodes, called S-Nodes.

In Chapter Five, we outline the reengineering of the underlying network infrastructure in order to enable the deployment of the service platform. Here we look at the physical architecture and the relationship between the different hardware components.

Part III of the book plunges into the technical details for the system. Beginning in Chapter Six with a detailed discussion of security fundamentals, it proceeds to discuss the application of these fundamentals to a variety of practical security problems. These include authentication, security over open networks, and single sign on (SSO).

Chapter Seven describes middleware as the methodology that unites diverse standards in internetworking as well as application support. This builds upon open APIs as a fundamental principle of software engineering, with platform support that integrates multiple layers. Chapter Seven also introduces the development kits that embody the design principles. Detailed discussion of the components, found in Chapter Eight and Nine, describes the layered software environment through discussions as well as examples.

Then, in Chapter 10, we describe the monitoring and management requirements that are unique to IP service platforms, particularly as they seamlessly integrate multiple distributed components. Chapter 11 describes sample services, including virtual worlds integrated with networking.

We conclude the book with Chapter 12 by mapping the proposed systems onto the new and emerging application service provider sector. It is pleasing to note that what may have started five years ago as a attempt to rejuvenate the aging telecommunication infrastructure is now finding its acceptance in the Internet space of Application Service Providers (ASPs).

Audience

This is not just another book about Internet protocols. This book has something unique to offer. Anyone – whether a University student, an engineer in the Telecommunications or Software industry, or the people charting the future of the Internet – is provided with all the elements to understand the complex issues of design and deployment of emerging systems.

We envisioned this book as a starting place to acquire an overall picture of the issues and topics of platform technologies, what exists *right now* as well as *where things are going*. Thus we describe the background, APIs, and a working reference architecture.

This book is intended for technical people interested in the next generation of data networks. It assumes working knowledge of Internetworking, including network protocols, network fabric basics, and software development. While Parts I and II contain a general text on the technology that require little programming experience, Part III is intended for developers and technology managers with its emphasis on architecture and APIs.

Thus if we combine the slightly different audiences of Parts I, II and III, one should read this book if he or she is

- An administrator of an Internet Service Provider (ISP) and wants to learn what service support the industry will likely offer in the future
- Someone interested in contributing to the growth of the ASP market
- An application designer and wants to learn what new capabilities the network may offer
- A software developer and wants to preview the APIs that will link applications and services with the network infrastructure
- A professional who wants to understand network middleware, or
- One who wants to keep up with the emerging telecommunications infrastructure

Contacting the Authors

Michah receives email sent to **michah@ieee.org.** George is best contacted directly through **george@vanecek.com**. Nino reads **v_nino@hotmail.com.** Dado can be reached at **dalibor.f.vrsalovic@intel.com**. The contributors can also be reached through the main AT&T Labs IP Technology Organization (IPTO) main number at **(408) 576-1300.**

Acknowledgements

This book is based largely on the collective experiences of the authors and the entire IPTO team of AT&T Labs in designing and developing the GeoPlex system. It offers our perspective on the five years of seminal design leading to the new infrastructure. As such the authors recognize the commitments and contributions of the entire team and in a small way, this book serves as a tribute to all the people who conceived the idea of an IP service platform. This group survived all the ups and downs of this project, including constant change in the industry, trivestiture of AT&T, and the breath taking rate of innovation.

The authors are representatives of a much larger group that designed and implemented the GeoPlex system, leading to this book. The effort started with a small group of techies, visionaries, and their supports in the early part of 1995, and grew to more than several hundred persons in and outside the Labs. This small group consisted of Dado, Nino, Partha Dutta, Jerry Le Donne, George, Nelu Mihai, Tom London, Tim Thompson, Steve Klinkner, Karen Jensen-Parish, Dave Witkowski and Dan Zenchelsky. Later on, important contributions were made by Ed Bilove and David Bernstein.

Partha Dutta and Karl Siil provided much of the security infrastructure. Likewise, Mohamed Aganagic, Nelu, and Sinisia Srbljic did the original domain design and offered support in the service scalability designs found in Chapter Four. Dino Hodzic implemented much of the GMMS and authored a document that we took to make up much of Chapter 10. Rajiiv Maheshwari supported much of the work on the APIs which in detail were put together by a many others, namely, Tim Thompson, Steve Klinkner, Jay Perry, Bill Bouma, Lutz Lennemann, Gary Timus and Neelesh Thakur. Collaboration with Igor Balabine, Igor Kobzar, Mahesh Kumar, Vishwa Prasad, Peter Brown, Chris Marty, Patrick Sullivan and countless others were essential. These are by no means the only people who contributed, but they are the ones whose work found its way into this book.

We thank Scott Perry ("the Skipper") for the wisdom and management expertise he provided during part of the project. Finally, we thank John Petrillo for his initial vision about the need for the transformation of the communications industry, constant encouragement, and support during these last five years.

George Vanecek
Castro Valley, California

PART I

IP Technology Fundamentals

This first part of this book reviews network technology fundamentals, in particular key technologies and issues pertinent to the building of IP service platforms. We take the position that the Internet is not just a client-server application which merely exploits available transport technologies, as the school of "dumb network" supports. Rather, the Internet is simultaneously a shaping-force for the new telecommunications infrastructure, and the subject of innovations that continue to change it in fundamental ways. At this time, the industry needs to embrace change and not be afraid of radical revision to the infrastructure. The Internet is adapting as its infrastructure changes; and the adoption of the IP service platform approach is moving to support many different types of devices, transport mechanisms, user communities and services. Think of the IP service platform as an adaptive distributed-computing substrate. This book demonstrates that an open and standard IP platform can indeed provide a stable platform necessary for service development and deployment during and after this adaptation. Upon completion of this part, you should understand why an IP service platform is necessary, and you should appreciate the many ramifications to the changes underway within the circuit-switched network.

CHAPTER 1 Introduction

The genesis of an IP service platform is rooted in the many different technologies that rapidly matured and became commonplace during the second half of the 1990's. The discussion of next-generation networks based on common IP service platforms cannot easily be made without first establishing the framework of how it fits in with emerging technologies, as well as users' expectations of what those technologies should deliver. The chapter begins with the first "opening" of the network upon expiration of Bell's patents. It progresses rapidly to the end of the 20th century telecommunications era and onto expectations for the burgeoning 21st century data communication and information revolution. Along the way, we point out the major evolutions in technology, as well as the essential relationship between business and technology.

1.1 The Golden Age of the Telecommunication Industry

The late eighties were "golden years" for the telecommunications industry. Since the beginning of the telegraph and the telephone revolution at the turn of the 20th century, the industry has worked diligently to achieve global communications at affordable rates. The successes can arguably be attributed to the fact that for most of the century, AT&T and the Bell System functioned as a legally sanctioned, regulated monopoly. Driven by the fundamental principles set forth in 1907 by Theodore Vail, AT&T's first president, the company worked hard to offer "one system, one policy, and universal service."

When the Bell patents expired circa 1894, hundreds of independent local firms began to compete (but not cooperate) with the Bell company, eventually causing great frustration to customers. Vail argued that "the telephone, by the nature of its technology, would operate most efficiently as a monopoly providing universal service". Government regulation, "provided it is independent, intelligent, considerate, thorough and just," was an appropriate and acceptable substitute for the competitive marketplace.[1] The federal government directed the nascent industry to offer universal services for the benefit of all customers, regardless of their location. Thanks in part to the monopoly that made it economically feasible, the Bell Telephone Company succeeded in creating a telephony infrastructure that met these goals.

It is illuminating to consider the words of Vail in 1910, in light of the current revolution surrounding the Internet,

> *"...One system with a common policy, common purpose, and common action; comprehensive, universal, interdependent, intercommunicating like the highway system of the country, extending from every door to every other door affording electrical communication of every kind, from everyone at every place to everyone at every other place."*[2]

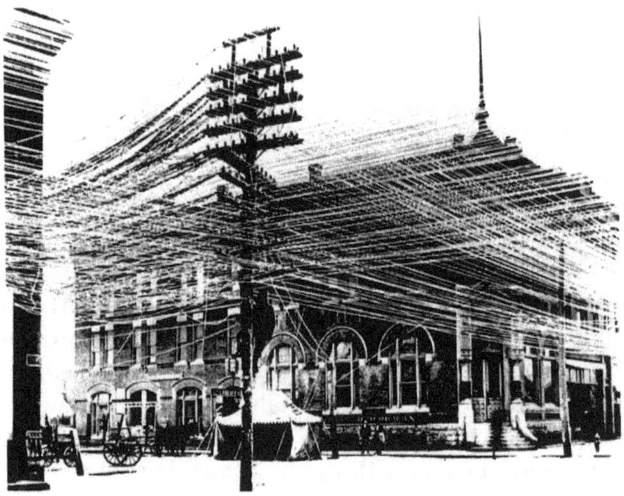

Figure 1-1: Kansas, 1909 – *The Wages of Competition*

and compare this to the vision offered by William Gates, founder and Chairman of Microsoft, the world's most successful software company:

> *... company vision that will focus on customers and the power of the Internet, offering people and businesses the ability to be connected and empowered any time, anywhere, and on any device."*[3]

The Internet of 2000 – like the Universal Service of 1910 – builds upon innovations and new technologies. As with Universal Service, the Internet has significant impact upon the existing infrastructure. Perhaps this explains the views of both Vail and Gates.

1. From the "Background on Divestiture", http://www.att.com/corporate/restructure/hist2.html
2. Theodore Vail, AT&T Annual Report, 1910.
3. Microsoft Corporate Profile: **http://www.microsoft.com/presspass/cpIntro.htm**

The current infrastructure revolution can be traced to the emergence of new network technologies during the 1980s. These innovations galvanized the industry toward developing a whole new field of services. New consumer devices proliferated in tandem with rising computing power at astonishingly lower prices. The telephone became only one of many different ways of accessing information. To the benefit of us all, the telecommunications industry perceived an opportunity – and an obligation, perhaps – to bring these innovations to the masses. Mike Armstrong, the current CEO and president of AT&T, is overseeing and vigorously pursuing changes to the industry in much the same way that Theodore Vail did a century ago.

1.2 Internet - The New Kid on the Block

It is difficult to find anyone who does not recognize the term *Internet.* Although it had its beginnings in the early 1970s, public awareness started more recently in 1991. At that time, the National Science Foundation (NSF) privatized and commercialized its NSFnet, allowing the first commercial use of the Internet. Soon the first Commercial Internet Exchange was launched. Initially, government contracts were given to BBN Planet, MCI, and Sprint; and commercial services were launched by UUNet and PSINet. By 1992, the number of Internet hosts rocketed to *one million* – mostly academic and military users. In 1993, the World Wide Web (WWW) and the Mosaic web browser from NCSA were introduced. The number of users and the amount of traffic flowing over the Internet has grown exponentially ever since, reaching 10 million users in 1995, and 100 million in 1998.

Since its infancy, the Internet has served as a "model" for Internetworking and online systems development – a model in the sense that it responds rapidly to consumer needs, spurring technological advances and vast increases in committed resources. From the point-of-view of a network provider, a major challenge for the next-generation network is to properly administer its resources. For example, who – or what – will be using them, and who – or what – will be controlling them? The network and its end point devices should mutually communicate control and policy information so as to better utilize distributed network resources. To the consumer, or network client, the resources should be simply seen as a managed space over which the clients have some advisory control.

This perspective extends the telecommunication industry's observations that the full functionality and usefulness of the data networks have, thus far, been greatly underutilized. This functional underutilization tends to move all costs, management, and complexity to the end points and casts the burden upon the end point devices. This arguably increases the overall complexity of the end-devices and potentially reduces the user's ability to manage and operate the devices. It also reduces their useful life as their deployment and obsolescence almost coincide! Such scenarios cannot compete in the current information-centric world, with its focus upon unique functionality, simplicity, reliability, and of course competitive cost. Instead, industry scrutiny now discerns the unique advantages of each element in the communication infrastructure and strives to develop these to their full potential. Rather than obsolescence, the industry makes a concerted effort to fully leverage all resources.

We may observe this trend from its birth in 1978 with Vincent Cerf's *Catenet*, and the subsequent publication of "DOD Standard IP" as RFC-760 in January 1980. These paved the way for the Internet, a packet-delivery, connectionless, best-effort, network of networks. The Internet mushroomed out of the idea that individual computers could talk to each other and that essential network services (such as Domain Name Service) should be implemented at the application level and not tied to the protocol architecture. Over the following decade or so, the IP-networking industry exerted most of its efforts on achieving higher bandwidth, faster access, lower cost, and greater participation while stemming the tide of increasing control and legislation from the federal government. The basic framework remained largely unchanged up through the early 1990's, relegated mostly to research laboratories and halls of academia.

Then, during the mid 1990's, the ripening Internet technology flourished into a dominant technology. Embraced by business, enhanced through innovation, and nourished through massive investment, the Internet now serves as the favored basis for 21st Century telecommunications. The Internet must now satisfy many high-performance demands. Businesses want security, reliability, reduced operational costs, and customer reach. Consumers want ease of use and advanced features. Everyone wants the reliability and the simplicity of the global telephone network. Equally important are the hybrid services and the move towards convergence of the telephone network, the Internet, the wireless networks, broadcast networks, and many enterprise networks.

Interestingly, the Internet was not designed to support many of today's telecommunication requirements. For example, the pure client-server architecture does not scale. It is difficult to secure rigorously. It provides little or no support for network-based services. For instance, the network's essential services run on machines that are distinguished only by size or user's preferences, and it is a mere artifact that they are owned and operated by the network providers. The Internet still depends on distributed control. This complicates traffic engineering although it insulates the network against certain failures. Indeed, many of the original contributors, including Bob Metcalfe who invented Ethernet, find continued bewilderment and awe in the continued use of the Internet, particularly given its present capacity. In spite of all this, there is a general agreement that the Internet – with all its flaws – is the best we have and that emerging networks will retain many of its basic features.

There is growing realization that the Internet should evolve towards an aggregation of smart, service-supporting and cooperating networks. Moreover, these networks should interoperate with other types of networks and a wide range of clients. Network function should thrive in a heterogeneous environment of multiple providers and domains. To this end, the basic fabric of packet delivery and Domain Name Services functions needs to be supplemented with additional service-supporting capabilities that are intrinsic to the support of the above objectives.

1.3 Metamorphosis of the Telecommunications Industry

In spite of the focus upon the Internet, many people may not be aware of the guiding influence that the telecommunication industry had on the early realization and deployment of the Internet and, conversely, of the profound changes that took place in the industry as a result.

At the beginning of the 21st century, the Telcos are aggressively making profound changes to enable hybrid network technology and become global information and knowledge providers. This refutes the pundits who would claim the Telcos are captives of history, destined to move slowly, like some dinosaur on its way to extinction. On the contrary, the Telcos understand the profound lessons that have been learned by other industries, such as the railroads, and are moving aggressively to reshape their networks and their businesses. In a few brief lines, let's review what happened to the Railroads, and why the Telcos are not repeating history's errors.

> *A century ago, the railroad industry, then the comparative equivalent of the telecommunications industry today, owned not only most of the long distance transportation, but exerted a major influence on the affairs of the state. Few affairs dealing with transportation or commerce were outside the influence of the railroads. At that time, two seemingly insignificant technologies emerged. The first was a self-propelled ground vehicle, free of geographical restrictions imposed by rails, called the automobile. The second was the self-propelled air vehicle, free of restrictions imposed by gravity, called the aeroplane. The automobile was weak and frail and subject to frequent mishaps as well as poor road conditions, exacerbated by poor weather conditions. The early aeroplane was but a toy that could fly short distances, carry only a few persons or small, light cargo, and was greatly affected by even minor weather conditions.*
>
> *At this point the railroad barons, through a lack of vision and the hubris of their position, failed to understand the significance and the potential of these new technologies. They reasoned that they were in the railroad business and not the transportation business. They failed to envision heavy cargo moving long distances efficiently and cost effectively over their rail lines; then unloaded at depots onto trucks for dispersal to local distribution centers. Neither did they imagine the automobiles' efficient high-speed delivery of items over the last mile, providing material directly to the point of demand. Nor did they fore-*

see the diversity of cargo with its need for multiple classifications. They did not grasp that aeroplanes, no matter how small, could nevertheless fly very long distances to deliver high-priority items in a fraction of a locomotive's delivery time.

Such a transportation network – built from hybrid services and utilizing heterogeneous technologies – eluded the barons. Consequently, they elected to lay more iron and upgrade their locomotives and cars while undermining or at best ignoring the new transportation intruders. The rest, as we say, is history.

Unlike the railroads, the U.S. auto industry faced overseas competition during the 1970s and 1980s. The Japanese auto industry refined the production of automobiles, thereby reducing cost and improving quality. The hard-hit U.S. industry staggered, tens of thousands of auto workers were laid off, and then recovered thanks to an eagerness to change. This change involved close collaboration on the part of the auto industry players and their entire supply chains. It required that the "Big Three" develop new understanding of various corporate roles as they think and act globally[1]. Sometimes they compete, and at other times they must collaborate – this being called *"coopetition" (sic.)*. The U.S. auto industry now manages change in response to developing technology, and once again leads the world.

These lessons have not been lost on the telecommunications industry. AT&T, as well as most of the major Telcos, began to restructure their core business based on the notion that the industry is fundamentally in the *communications business* – not merely a provider of telephony services. As we will later point out, telephony is seen as a service that transports specific "cargo" over data networks. Compared to the century it took to build the Plain Old Telephony Service (POTS) network as we know it today, it took less than a decade for the industry to reorganize itself in much the same way that the aging U.S. auto industry did a decade ago.

1.4 Rising Intelligence in the Network

"Intelligence" in telephone networks has been evolving since the 1960's when the concept of stored program control (SPC) was added to the telephone switch. To those unfamiliar with telephony jargon, the term "intelligence" may raise visions of human cognition and reasoning with science fiction overtones. Given the actual meaning, the use of the term is unfortunate. Network intelligence actually means the ability to provide services to users by means of standardized and reusable software modules. The primary example is the switched network known as the Intelligent Network (IN),

1. The "Big Three" were Chrysler, Ford, and General Motors (GM). Chrysler recently merged with the major European automobile firm Mercedes to become DaimlerChrysler.

which we analyze in Chapter 2. The switched network demonstrates the substantial value realized by creating an enhanced network that does more than offer end-to-end communication to the users.

Four decades later, intelligence (in the IN/AIN sense) is being introduced into data networks, and slowly, but with an increasing rate, into the Internet itself. These data networks are also "smart" in the sense that middleware is gradually appearing in the data networks. One can describe general properties of this yet-unbuilt network: it will be more functional and essential than the present-day Internet, and it will be less complex and more open than the current PSTN. Beyond these general properties, one can only speculate whether the next-generation network will be active or passive, smart, dumb, or intelligent; open or proprietary. It will likely provide each of these where appropriate.

To understand the move to place the intelligence into the network, reflect on the rise of electronic commerce (so-called "eCommerce") and consider a key problem you will face adding new services as a service provider. Ultimately, you succeed or fail based on how well you deliver network services to users.

Suppose your task is to add a new eCommerce wine buying service, **ninovino.com**, to your existing service offering. **Ninovino.com**, like any network service, has two distinct aspects: content and infrastructure. Users care about content. They come to **ninovino.com** because they are interested in wine. On the other hand, the infrastructure connects users to content and supports all the operational details of the services. Infrastructure is everything from the physical wiring to the login screen to the billing system. Users notice the infrastructure only when it does not work, such as when they cannot log on or their bill is wrong.

But you must care a lot, even without knowing the first thing about wine. Your partners at **ninovino.com** have Merlots and Sauvignon Blancs down cold. You, on the other hand, have to worry about the infrastructure. If you have a typical network, adding **ninovino.com** will involve creating a whole new set of infrastructure functions. You will have to create a user database for those who join **ninovino.com**. Then you'll need to design and implement a registration system. Don't forget to track user sessions, decide how much to charge, design an order-entry system and deploy a billing system. You *might* be able to borrow the user database from your calling application, the usage tracking from your distance learning package, and adapt the billing system from another eCommerce application. Don't forget to test all of this and develop the operational procedures, both for normal and abnormal operations. Bringing up **ninovino.com** means a lot of work that has nothing to do with wine and everything to do with infrastructure. The reader will observe this follows the regular system-development model, and does not leverage any intrinsic network functions other than reliable delivery.

We call this a "smokestack" network model, because each new service requires that you develop a complete vertical slice of each needed network function. Smokestack development is expensive, slow, and frustrating. It adds unnecessary complexity to your network and delays the introduction of revenue-generating services. The smokestack development model simply cannot support the next generation of full-featured, media-rich networks.

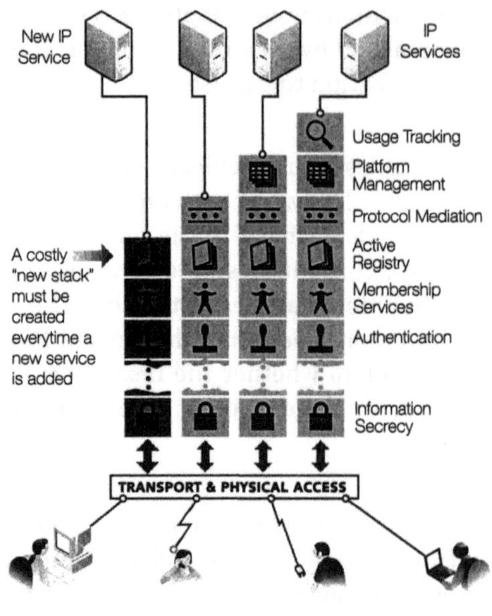

Figure 1-2: Identical Smokestacks

One clever way out of this bind is to integrate essential functions and outsource as much of the service support as possible. Why duplicate membership management, authentication, access control, usage recording, and security? What if those functions were *integrated*, available to any new service, the same way that a PC operating system provides essential functions to application programs?

Look deeper into the system and you find intelligent clients, intelligent services, and yet, ironically, a dumb network. It is ironic because the network is the one common element that touches everything. In most cases the network just transports data from one point to another. Your job would be substantially easier if you could take advantage of a smarter network. Instead of battling a hodge-podge of incompatible programs and technology, you could take advantage of an integrated, flexible communications framework. Supported by such a network, you would be free to develop profitable new services faster and more reliably.

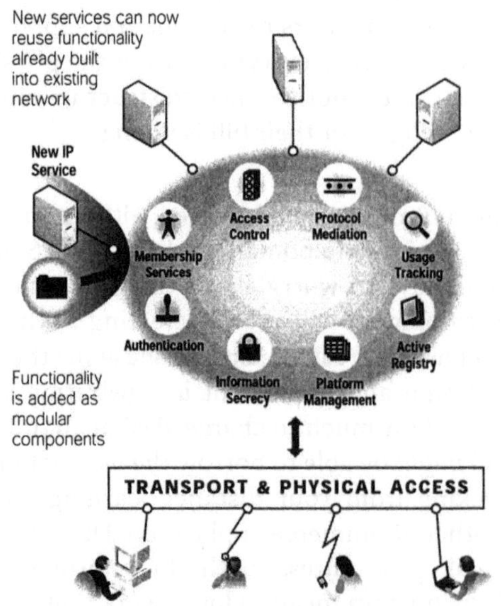

Figure 1-3: Middleware Model

To this end, there is a collective movement within the network-related industries to enhance their network infrastructures and enable support of new services. The collective movement consists of fairly separate efforts. Each one addresses a key challenge within the network infrastructure. To list only three of these:

- **Virtual Private Networks** (VPNs) to allow private and secure communication over public networks
- **Quality of Service** (QoS) to add control over network resources to the packet deliver mechanisms of packet networks
- **Voice on the Network** (VoN) to allow voice communication over data networks

No network innovation can remain a technology "island" onto itself. There are interdependent areas with each solution depending on the connection to others. This results in necessary interoperability, with a dependence on a common set of features. Common functionality and network intelligence can be engineered directly into the network, providing a powerful form of networking middleware.

1.5 Civilizing Data Networks

Much effort is still required in building a network that offers extended function to include interoperability, last-mile convergence, security and quality of service. There is, however, little debate focused on the question of what kind of a network we really want, should have, or need. Sometimes we get so caught up with new technology that we do not pause to consider how best to utilize it.

In relation to the provisioning of emerging networks, technologists typically espouse two schools of thought. One comes from the Internet side that advocates keeping the network as simple as possible and placing all the intelligence outside, within the hosts. The other comes from the telecommunications side that advocates high intelligence in the network, while keeping the end point devices as simple as possible. Despite compelling arguments in both camps, it is clear that neither is completely right nor completely wrong. This is demonstrated by Internet2 and Next Generation Internet (NGI) on the academic side, and by Virtual Private Networks (VPNs) and Voice over IP (VoIP) efforts on the Telco sides. Internet2 is a project supported by the University Corporation for Advanced Internet Development (UCAID) with over 170 U.S. university participants working with corporate and affiliate members to research and develop advanced Internet technologies vital to higher education. Internet2 is complementary to the federally-led NGI through contributions and demonstrations.

The diversity of these two schools seems to ensure that both the technical and social aspects of the future networks will be thoroughly explored. What is clear is that the future networks will be smarter, active, and more capable than the first generation Internet, but less complex and more open than the typical PSTN. These networks should also evolve in a way that neither infringes on our privacy, nor creates a global monopoly. In a way, if you consider the innovation and re-engineering of data networks, collectively the effort is directed towards civilizing data networks. It is an exercise in building the ideal digital society.

By way of comparison to early American history - when the settlers civilized the rocky terrain of New Hampshire, the fertile soils of California, and the wide expanse between the two - each settler depended on his own resources and abilities to settle and establish communities. The settlers had to carry all provisions, defend themselves against bandits, and fight for rights of passage. Their lawless West is the stuff of American legend, as is the survival of the rugged individuals settling on the East. Despite our origins as independent groups, today we live in a "civilized society" with a common law. Society - not individuals - builds roads, bridges, schools, and courts of law. We share this common infrastructure and the multitude of commercial benefits.

The future network will offer, similarly, a common infrastructure to enable digital presence in the network. Why build servers and applications to handle security and privacy in a proprietary way if the network is secure? Why pay for and maintain private lines out of the need for guaranteed performance and capacity when the public network offers both? Why deal with multiple forms of identification, passwords, accounts, phone numbers, and cards when the network manages our identities and orchestrates access?

1.6 End-point Devices and the Changing the Role of Networks

Data networks already support more at the periphery than just UNIX workstations and PCs running Microsoft Windows. Many other types of information devices are now and will increasingly become dominant. This includes personal data assistants (PDAs such as the Palm Pilot), network appliances (such as the Internet refrigerator), smart phones (such as Nokia's IP wireless device with built-in GPS), desktop boxes (such as WebTV), networked game stations, embedded systems (such as GM's OnStar), and game consoles (such as Sony Playstation or Nintendo). For some, like the smart phones, lack of local mass storage or low-end computing power will put the burden on network services to provide persistent state and computing resources. For others, like the next generation of game consoles, high-computing ability and broadband access will create opportunities for new services requiring the mediation and application support of the service providers. To the user, an intelligent network presence may support access to any device, at any time, and from anywhere with a wide range of supporting services.

Here an analogy to intelligence in the PSTN is appropriate. The telecommunication networks can historically be seen as moving from the telegraph, to the telephone, to the intelligent IN/AIN, and recently to the ubiquitous intelligent communications network. Presently, the telephone network can be characterized as offering a balance. On one hand, the PBX provides dedicated premises equipment. On the other hand, Centrex offers centralized network equipment with the same functionality as the PBX but without the cost and effort of operating one's own equipment. Regardless of deployment, both offer services which, when seen in their entirety, create the "PSTN experience".

These designs were specifically engineered to handle the limited capabilities of the first-generation telephone devices. Service providers could use either intelligence in the network or intelligence in the PBXs. They both offer services that are independent of the limitations of the end device. Today, there is a far greater opportunity to balance the service support inequality between the network and the end devices by taking full advantage of all the equipment.

1.7 Growing Dependency on Middleware

While putting intelligence into the telecommunication networks has been the goal of the PSTN for quite a while, in recent years a separate but in many ways a similar goal was followed by the software industry with its pursuit of middleware.

There are many definitions of middleware. Functionally, it embraces the full diversity of the software world enabling the interconnectivity and operability of applications, systems and devices. The Gartner Group calls it "runtime system software that enables application level interactions among programs". Some professionals have described it as "the odd bits of programs residing between the operating system and the application layer"[1]. From the network perspective, middleware is above the network layer, and below the applications layer. As such, it provides the common basis for the applications to share structure, framework, and common functionality. With middleware, software vendors are beginning to integrate, support, and enhance large complex applications.

As a taxonomy imposes structure upon the domain, one would expect a standard taxonomy for network middleware. Unfortunately, there are only partial taxonomies. We can categorize middleware loosely as being related to communication, security, or integration, where

- *Communication middleware* consists of protocols and architecture supporting distributed systems and computing based on the object-oriented paradigm and

1. From article by ADT Staff on Middleware [STAF99].

message passing, for example CORBA ORBs using IIOP/GIOP, or Java with RMI and JINI. DCOM, sponsored by Microsoft, is a third example

- *Security middleware*, which contains the essential functions of authentication, access control, data privacy and integrity, and encryption. It must navigate the complexities of multiple protocols, session keys and certificates, and administrative requirements
- *Integration middleware,* which constitutes the integration between a computing platform and enterprise-wide applications. These provide a management layer supporting multiple and complex application engines. It provides adapters between the concepts, details and frameworks of many application components. As an example, the next generation of middleware (as described by some) in the form of Enterprise Application Integration (EAI) falls into this category

The taxonomies can be application-specific as well, for example

- Data transform software
- Message-oriented middleware
- Object request brokers
- Application servers
- Transaction monitors
- Directories, and
- Publish-and-subscribe software

What is certain is that as network-enabled service and online applications grow in complexity, middleware will emerge as a key technology for offering solutions in this space. This trend is also finding its way into the network infrastructure of carriers, Internet Service Providers (ISP), and Application Service Providers (ASP). For these, middleware is considered to encompass a large set of services with the components needed to support them, thereby driving a common set of applications constructed within a networking computer environment. Such environments are typically distributed over a large geographical area.

1.8 Need for Protocol Mediation and Translation in the Network

Classically, network applications evolved around the client-server and the peer-to-peer models. The connectivity between the hosts is provide by a simple packet delivery mechanism. A more sophisticated model, long used by many industries, is based on the role of a mediator and a broker. This translates into a modified client-server model that is the client-network middleware-server model. These mediators are located at various points other than the end points. Indeed, network-located components to improve performance have been used in the web nearly from its inception. Cache proxies are one such example, since their presence in the network has many positive benefits. They reduce network traffic and improve the user experience.

There is, however, a much greater asset in the use of transparent proxies by service providers and enterprises for general protocol mediation and translation. The active network-based analysis of data can serve many roles:

1. Seamlessly deliver services and applications across a variety of different communications networks. For example, mediation can seamlessly integrate POTS and packet networks by automatically transforming traffic, signaling, and billing information from traditional POTS formats to IP-based protocols and vice-versa. The supporting mediation system can optimize traffic flow across networks according to service characteristics and leverage specific network strengths (e.g., database technology and content)
2. Transparently convert protocols and "render" media for different interfaces and for various emerging information appliances. Mediation can be offered as a virtual "proxy" capability to support "thin" client interfaces such as speech-activated telephony and device-independent graphical-browser interfaces. For pagers, mediation converts Network Signaling Protocol to Paging Network Protocol such as IP-TNPP (Telelocator Network Paging Protocol) and IP-Wireless Signaling such as SMS and CDPD. Mediation can also enable interoperability between incompatible NT and Unix LAN/WAN environments and client/server software
3. Compensate for different bandwidth capabilities by automatically providing caching, mirroring, and load distribution functionality
4. Provide a means for capabilities such as security, localization, and personalization by offering intelligent filters, proxies, and web-based self-provisioning of services

For service providers, economic benefit can be obtained in intercepting and manipulating protocols. The network can easily manage and manipulate all standard protocols to add value as necessary. Consider several examples of this. The first example relates to standard protocols used by World Wide Web such as HTTP and FTP. The network can transparently support a distributed cache architecture that intelligently monitors and caches documents flowing over the Web. For early-entry ISPs that oversubscribe their service, and have limited capacity at their peering routers, local caches may be the only way to reduce outgoing traffic and eliminate peak-hour bottlenecks. For these ISPs, this has the following benefits:

- Network congestion is reduced by eliminating repeated access to the servers holding commonly accessed information
- HTTP and FTP server loads are reduced by off-loading the content into the network caches

- Document usage recording can be handled by the network instead of the servers while guaranteeing that the service operators still hold the control and get paid for the documents given to the users
- The servers' document access rights are honored by the network, removing the responsibility from the service providers

The second example relates to streaming video protocols. Consider a video source streaming a live MPEG to a number of users. If the users are authenticated with the network, the network mediation system can know the hardware capabilities and therefore the limitations of the users' access devices and their bandwidth. MPEG proxies on the side of the streaming source can dynamically adjust the quality and size of the images to provide a stream that is optimally configured for the bandwidth and capability of the users' devices.

One can also envision putting virus scanners at the network edges to monitor mail, web and ftp protocols. Load balancing is a form of mediation. So is access control and tunnelling. Clearly the benefits of mediation as one of the basic features of a network has not been fully realized.

1.9 Emergence of IP as the Unifying Mechanism of Computing and Communication

The telecommunications industry has joined the software and operating system industries in accepting the Internet Protocol (IP) as its industry standard. Other competing standards such as Frame Relay and ATM have been specialized to enterprise and network core solutions. IP, on the other hand, is now embraced for all its consumer internetworking and internal services. That includes everything from telephony to Operations Support Systems (OSS). In an essence, IP has become the mechanism by which the industry can unify computing and communication.

The Vice President of AT&T Internet Services, Kathleen B. Early, said:

> *"AT&T strongly believes that IP is the unifying protocol for transforming the telecommunications industry worldwide."*

IP was invented by Vincent Cerf and Bob Kahn in 1974 as a communication protocol using a UNIX system. It emerged and partially owes it success to the prior invention of Ethernet by Bob Metcalfe at a Xerox laboratory in Palo Alto, California. In 1978, the Department of Defense mandated TCP/IP as the standard for its data networks, and by 1983 it became the protocol standard for the *A*dvanced *R*esearch *P*rojects *A*gency *NET*-work, or ARPANET. Over the next decade, ARPANET slowly grew into the Internet we know today, thanks to nurturing mostly by universities and research labs. Only since the mid-1990's has it "exploded" in commercial and consumer popularity, powered mainly by the invention of the World Wide Web (WWW) by Tim Berners-Lee at CERN in 1989.

Interestingly, IP success is based only partly on its technical merits. The best technology does not always succeed and IP is certainly not the ideal solution for every telecommunications need. The TCP/IP protocol suite was designed to address a very specific data network requirement, specifically a "bomb proof" network, or one that would operate despite outages in multiple components.

IP is a standard that enjoys wide coverage and acceptance, due primarily to the success of the Internet and the WWW; yet its adaptation in the telecommunications industry was initially greeted with much reservation. As it stands now, the Internet depends almost entirely on IP version 4 (IPv4), and this falls short of what the carriers expect in terms of quality and reliability. IPv4 is not secure, does not support isochronous streams or quality of service, and offers only a 32-bit address space that is already in danger of running out of host addresses.

The telecommunications industry recognizes these shortcomings and together with network vendors and the software industry is aggressively working on new solutions. This can be seen in what the Chief Executive Officer of AT&T, Mike Armstrong, recently committed to:

> *"We will do for [the Internet] what we have been doing for years with the telephone - make it safe, reliable, and secure."*

For telecommunication carriers, the move to IP means they must increase router capacity, eliminate excessive router hops, support multiple grades of services, and deliver QoS for multiple traffic classes. The traffic will include diverse classes, including real-time and bursty-data services. The carriers must also manage peering between other networks. These are formidable goals when achieved at global scale with carrier-grade quality and reliability.

So why is IP the winner? Consider IP in the company of the other technologies that are equal winners: IP, Ethernet, and the WWW. In all cases, the underlying technologies are very simple, easy to understand, and easy to implement. More importantly, they are open and ubiquitous. Everyone can both contribute to their growth and simultaneously benefit from their growth; and best of all, market forces dictate that problems are addressed and fixed.

John Backus, a computer-science pioneer and the author of several early high-level programming languages, speculated about future programming languages: "I don't know what the computer language will be, but I know it will be called `FORTRAN`", a sentiment echoed by Martin Greenfield's statement "The one central attribute of Fortran is its name"[1]. In a similar fashion we can postulate that we don't know what the future communication networks will be, but we now suspect that it will use IP.

1.10 From Protocols to Interfaces

The early Internet was primarily a network of wires connecting a set of routers, bridges, and hubs, that interconnected a set of hosts. The hosts were self-contained systems communicating with each other over a well-defined set of wire protocols. At the lowest level, a *protocol* defines the syntax of information and the semantics of its content so that a server and its clients can understand each other. By this nature, everything that happened outside the boundary of a host is based on protocols.

Internally, hosts are collections of hardware and software components, interconnected into subsystems. Various layers of hardware, firmware, and software utilize resources such as the CPU engine, the operating system kernel, the file system, the networking system, the graphics system, and the sound system. These subsystems, unlike the independent hosts, are highly interdependent on each other through a well-defined set of interfaces. These interfaces export a subsystem's functionality externally via Application Programming Interfaces (APIs). More importantly, the interfaces take on a natural horizontal layering in which the abstraction played a key role in simplifying both the programming effort and the ultimate user experience.

The two methods - network connected hosts on one hand, and single-chassis "chips and wire" machines on the other - arose as specific solutions given the underlying infrastructures. The first uses fully autonomous systems. These communicate over a single bandwidth-limited channel, and may be geographically dispersed. The second method combines smaller components into a collocated, tightly coupled, and interdependent device possessing many channels with unlimited capacity and bandwidth.

These systems must communicate to achieve their purposes. The "language" of communication therefore must receive considerable attention, specifically to distinguish between *protocols* and *interfaces*. One might speculate that the form of communication, be it protocol or interface, is relatively unimportant. However, the form of communication is actually very important. Were we to view the choice as a mere "implementation detail", then inevitably we would also find that the difference between the protocol and interface technologies must also be resolved as "implementation detail". This leads directly to a close association between the underlying technology and the level of abstraction that the infrastructure presents.

1. The fascinating development of this revolutionary language is described by John Backus in "The History of Fortran I, II, and III" in *IEEE Annals of the History of Computing*, Vol. 20, No. 4, 1998.

Such an approach may succeed for discrete systems designed to operate without any further change. It does not work well for large heterogeneous, distributed systems operating in a climate of constant change. Distributed systems need to manage constant change in the layers below and above. Protocols and interfaces take on very different roles. Protocols, better referred to here as wire protocols, operate at a very low level of abstraction. Interfaces, on the other hand, rise to a higher level of abstraction. Interfaces encapsulate activities and hide much of the underlying implementation detail.

This brings us once again to the notion of network middleware and the application program interfaces (APIs) that they offer. Presently, the Internet has yielded many attempts to offer middleware in the form of development platforms that hide the underlying diversity and complexity through interfaces. Examples include TINA, TINA-C, JTAPI, JAIN, Parlay, and APIs for H.323 and SIP. The hardware vendors have been using the concept of well defined interfaces (such as the PCI, ISA, USB, or the PCMCIA) for a long time to build components and assemble complete systems using third party components. It seems that the software industry is following suit and the carriers are more than ready to build their next-generation networks with middleware based on these interfaces. One must question the wisdom of such an approach, given the low-level abstraction of protocols. This contrasts with the high-level API abstraction, as required for distributed systems.

1.11 Challenges for the 21st Century Networks

In the broader picture, significant advancements are taking place in the way enterprises use information, which directly impacts consumers. Enterprises are expanding their use of global networks. Telephony services are being used in new, multimedia and integrated ways. Corporations are connecting to the Internet to reach broader customer bases while interconnecting their branch offices though Virtual Private Networks. Use of internal information technology networks ("Intranets") are being coordinated with the Internet, online services, and WANs. To conduct business in the fiercely competitive global market place, companies and end users need fast, reliable, and interoperable ways of communicating, accessing information, and doing business. With the merging of computing and communications, society is moving toward a "spaceless-timeless dimension". The technologies of the Internet, Multimedia, and Electronic Commerce are lowering the historical barriers of time, distance, and cost. Multinational business customers are looking to harness this convergence of telephony and computing in order to push back the barriers of geography and time. They are looking to build and access these networks as soon as possible.

It has been said that the Internet is a driving force behind profound changes to communications in the 21st century. The ensuing "global village" will likely change the perceptions of our individual and national identities. This statement is, however, based more on a vision of what the Internet can offer rather than what it currently offers. The beauty of our times is that the vision is readily attainable. We already have the enabling technologies and know-how to achieve most of what we can envision. Nevertheless, we do not have the luxury to solve every problem. We have to target and solve the right problems. One criterion for problem selection is the identification of the leading challenges.

Here we discuss several key challenges that are confronting future telecommunications networks.

1.11.1 Empowering Anyone to become a Service Provider?

From early human history up until a few years ago, only a few privileged elite could author and distribute information to the masses, particularly geographically distributed ones. Indeed, an official Imprimatur was, for much of Europe, a prerequisite for any publication; this had substantial and often repressive effects upon the content of printed materials. This is clearly no longer the case. Indeed, with the World Wide Web, anyone can publish anything in nearly any media.

The World Wide Web enabled anyone to distribute information to the masses; be they governments, large corporations, universities, special interest groups, or private individuals. All that is needed is a connection to the Internet through an Internet Service Provider (ISP) and a server to host the web content. The cost of the former is typically $19.95 a month and the latter is a PC for under $500.

If we adjust for the emerging times, a new challenge emerges as well: How do we enable anyone to be a service provider? A service provider is someone who offers services to subscribers and benefits economically by doing so. Consider the following example.

What if you are an individual and you had some content you want to advertise or sell on the Internet, say, grandma's secret recipes for *knedliky* (or *knaidloch*) from her village south of Prague. Each month you get charged the $19.95 by your ISP but instead of paying it, you receive a check for $9980.95. This comes from the 100,000 people who paid a dime each to access your content. For simplicity, let's not worry about FICA and federal and state taxes, nor the fee to the ISP for perhaps offering some outsourcing services.

What you need is a mechanism for advertising your content, an easy means of updating content, the ability to specify access rights, the means of monitoring usage, and the means to clear financial transactions. You want to do this preferably through standard, off-the-shelf applications, such as a common web browser and your email client, or third-party services. You do not want to learn all the latest technology and build a self-contained computing center, nor have lots of hardware and software and contracts for others to run and manage it.

This challenge requires that many problems be solved including two key ones. Service scalability is one. The second is outsourcing of the OSS and financial functions. ISPs and ASPs can provide these specialized functions.

This is, however, a non-trivial challenge as was already demonstrated by a fallacy that arose around the early Web that "on the Internet, everyone looks the same". This refers to the impression that one cannot tell how big or small the web content provider is since even the little guys' home pages can look like the big corporations'. The fallacy arose from the first impressions one got from the look and feel of the content presentation. Anyone can buy inexpensive tools or hire someone to create rich-looking dynamic web pages. Today, one does not have to be an engineer or a computer scientist with an art degree.

Where the fallacy quickly breaks down is in the ability to handle a large volume of requests. The fallacy completely falls apart under very high-volume bursts of requests that can flood even the largest of hosting services. In a somewhat explosive example during the early web days, the single T1 line that serviced Purdue University's main campus in West Lafayette was completely shut down for hours when a chemistry graduate student placed pictures and instructions on how to start a barbecue using liquid oxygen. Network congestion completely choked off the campus to any external network traffic.

Such problems plagued the first generation Internet. It was based on a simple access and transport role for the backbone, with a similarly simple client-server mechanism. It lacked any network middleware support. There are many problems with the simple model. First, the client-server model does not scale; no matter how large the server (or cluster of servers) is, the high-demand bursts will always outstrip the server's ability to handle the loads. Second, using the same argument, no amount of reasonable bandwidth will offer guaranteed access without causing a bottleneck. The imperfect solution of an over-engineered network is expensive. Worse, it can be shown that over-engineered systems will still fail to support the traffic peaks that result from multiple coincident interactions, even when the average load remains within the system's design parameters. As such, few service providers on the Internet today can offer fast, responsive services without the dependence on network middleware.

Thus consider again the question of whether it is possible to enable everyone to be a service provider. It is clear from the discussion above that few can do this alone, no matter how resourceful or affluent they may be. Ultimately, the approach fails, as scalability and operational costs increase with an expanding customer base. The answer is for the network to provide all necessary support, and thereby offset the functional insufficiency of those who do not have it. When designing networks and network infrastructure, we can build a common infrastructure that can support various groups based on their size and their ability to pay. Technically speaking, we could treat everyone the same (from a one-horse operation to the largest corporate giants) and build in capabilities that can be turned on or off as needed. This would create the ability to outsource many basic requirements to run a service and ultimately would enable anyone to be a service provider.

1.11.2 Enabling Faster Time to Market at Lower Cost

The above scenario of individuals as service providers falls at one end of a spectrum that spans the realm of possibilities. While the majority of users would prefer to outsource the entire infrastructure to someone else, other more resourceful individuals and corporations may prefer to control some part or the entire part of offering services. As we proceed along the spectrum, greater importance is placed upon the ability to interoperate, customize, extend and self-provision services outside the network infrastructure.

This presents two major challenges when bringing new services to market. First is the time required to develop the new services, and second is the cost of the development. Both challenges can be related to the number of developers it will take to write, test, and "productize" the code, and the level of abstraction that exists from which they can begin to create their service's value to differentiate themselves from everyone else. One goal of a network infrastructure is to create a sufficiently high level of abstraction without creating too much of a good thing. Ultimately, it should be possible to take an existing legacy system, integrate it with the network infrastructure, and implement it with half a dozen developers within a month of work. Similarly, it should be possible to take a new idea and, after creating the core of the system that offers the actual value of the service, take two developers and two weeks to create a world-class online service.

This is not a new challenge. The software industry offers solutions tailored specifically to these challenges. Such solutions unfortunately target very specific vertical markets. The challenge of network middleware is to offer general, lasting solutions for a wide-range of services that leverage the emergence of network intelligence. This means creating value in the network. This value must be easy to use. A fundamentally different data network emerges, one that facilitates the easy and productive use of network capabilities.

1.11.3 Reducing Complexity and Providing for Ease-of-use

Perhaps the most ambitious goal is embracing new and emerging technologies for the benefit of end users as quickly as they become available. This can bring the "latest and greatest" to market faster. The viability of this goal requires that our systems – and in particular the network that delivers the services – must keep technical complexity in check. Consider the dilemma found by the first users of any technology. New technology may be somewhat disruptive and may even impel its users to change their lifestyles. The personal usage-styles of the World Wide Web users are a case in point.

Yet even if consumers accept this change, they have to pay the associated costs. New technologies classically impose a cost on their initial users:

- A high learning curve to technical proficiency
- A high level of management and upkeep
- Poor user interfaces
- Functions incompatible with other existing products
- Poor documentation and service support

New products are rarely user friendly despite their functionality. They are typically developed by programmers for programmers, or by engineers for engineers. If the market expects consumers to accept major changes in their lifestyles, the producers and providers have to take on the responsibility of the stated challenge.

The 21st century will most likely be marked by a tight interdependence between man and machine. Increasingly complex technology needs to be reengineered for simplicity and ease-of-use. Businesses are finding out that customers are very receptive to highly functional systems, provided the technology does not get in the way and works as expected. The challenge is thus to find ways to maintain a high rate of innovation (and increasing system complexity) while presenting the users with a constant or even reduced learning curve.

1.11.4 Design for Seamless Interoperability and Mobility

The time in which users are willing to buy and operate a wide range of non-interoperable devices is quickly coming to an end. Answering machines, voice recorders, home PCs, TVs, phones, ATMs, credit cards, PDAs, and ISPs that do not communicate, share user identity and preferences, or exchange data will slowly be replaced by smart devices and service operators that interoperate and offer mobility.

Interestingly, the smarter devices get, the more intelligent the network must become to support these devices. This is not a technical but rather an economic necessity based on costs of ownership.

One aspect of this is the emergence of Public Key Infrastructures (PKIs) and Certificate Authorities (CA). Interoperability and mobility mean that users, service providers, merchants and businesses have to manage risks, identities and rights. For two carriers to interoperate their services, or for users to roam over foreign networks, credentials have to be presented and verified. Such mechanisms have to be built into the networks, standardized, and then made available for widespread use.

1.11.5 Working towards Reliable IP Networks

The telecommunications industry has expended great engineering efforts to achieve 99.999 percent reliable telephony. Today, the reliability and service availability of the telephone are taken for granted. The telephone network even has its own redundant power source so that when the local electrical grid fails, telephones still operate. Compare this to the slow and unreliable ISP and Internet services, and you see a wide gap between the reliability and availability of the telephone service and today's Internet services. That is not to say that IP is not reliable.

> *"IP is said to be 99.9 percent reliable, which may sound good to some people, but to me, that means 1,000 defects per million."* [KRAU99]

The challenge here is to make IP networks equal if not more reliable than the PSTN. Given the much larger demand on the Internet compared to the PSTN of the future, this reliability will be a necessity.

1.11.6 Consolidated Intelligence in Data Networks

When we consider the efforts of Virtual Private Networks (VPNs), Quality-of-Service (QoS), Voice-over-IP (VoIP), unified messaging, e-commerce, and online entertainment, we observe the wealth of supporting distributed systems spanning the entire network stack spectrum from the physical up to the application layer, from the en devices through the network and into supporting services. There is an healthy abundance of experimentation trying to resolve issues relating to how and where to put the pieces required to support the applications.

The challenge here is to recognize that data networks are getting more intelligent and that it is imperative to help in identifying the "how's" and "where's".

1.12 Summary

Many within the Industry perceive that IP has vanquished other networking technologies, and that it is now time to sit back and build on its established technology. Others, like us, however, see this as a transition time marked by a major readjustment driven by social, political, and market forces. Once this readjustment stabilizes, as will happen when the Internet becomes a common utility, we may find, "although unlikely", that the underlying technology may end up falling short of expectations.

Early on, at the beginning of the AT&T WorldNet offer, many in the industry wanted simply "to follow the vertical smokestack model and throw a bunch of servers into a big server farm in some complex and connect it to the world with fat pipes." [KRAU99] From the management and operational perspective, this is a valid solution, as it reduces the cost of operations and saves the company money while satisfying the short entry time requirement. From an infrastructure, extensibility and long-term value proposition perspective, this is very expensive and somewhat shortsighted. We have learned that many problems are much more complex than previously understood. Service-related issues need a generalized solution that can be customized - rather than custom solutions that cannot be generalized. Occasionally in our rush to conduct business and maintain a leadership role, we neglect the long term consequences. What we need now is to recreate ourselves in the same way that the auto industry did a decade ago; take account of our situation, look at the surroundings, and invest in our future. As part of such efforts, it also means that new ways and methods be tried, allowed to grow, with the proven successes incorporated while the mistakes recognized and learned from. Ignoring these considerations would repeat the errors of the railroad, steel, and other industries about whom the American philosopher and Harvard scholar might have anticipated:

> *"Those who cannot remember the past are condemned to fulfill it."*
>
> - George Santayana
> THE LIFE OF REASON, 1906

CHAPTER 2 **Technology Overview**

This chapter lays out the background needed to understand IP service platforms, and in particular the synergistic technological developments that are transforming the communications industries. The spectrum of the interrelated topics is very broad. We view them from the unifying perspective of network middleware that spans the gamut from the physical network fabric to the applications themselves. In this chapter we focus on the key technologies needed by the IP service platform, and how these technologies are directly impacted by such a platform. We also identify their significance and relationships to other technologies. Beginning with developments in the circuit-switched networks that make up our telephone systems, we then explore their relationship to packet networks – such as the Internet – that carry our data in a multitude of forms, and the services these networks offer. Coincident innovations in the software industries extend the client and server technologies and thus imbue the Internet with a dynamic and interactive presence. From this technological mosaic emerges the substrate for reliable systems enabling businesses and consumers through the 21st Century.

2.1 Public Switched Telephone Network (PSTN)

To most of us, the oldest and most pervasive communication network in the world is the Public Switched Telephone Network (PSTN). This is the familiar global voice telephone network that provides telephone to anyone with a telephone and access rights. Today, PSTN spans every country and territory in the world. Since the invention of the telephone in the late 1800's, PSTN has steadily grown out of the original Bell System network developed by AT&T. In the U.S., it is made up of 196 geographical local access and transport areas (LATAs) that are serviced by one or more Local Exchange Carriers (LECs). Some of the well known LECs are GTE, Ameritech, NYNEX, Bell Atlantic, Bell

South, and Southwestern Bell. Inter-LATA traffic is provided by the Interexchange Carriers (IXCs). Examples of IXCs are AT&T, MCI WorldCom, Sprint, and Interliant. The three-digit area codes are assigned to LECs within a given LATA.

This relationship between LATAs, LECs and IXCs is shown in Figure 2-1. Typical customers connect their premises equipment over a local loop to the LEC's closest central office (CO). The LEC connects its COs through a number of lines to its switching centers, called tandem offices (TA).

The inter-LATA calls are switched to an IXC's point of presence (POP) based on the customer's choice of long distance providers. Once the call leaves the LATA and enters the IXC network, it may get switched through multiple provider's networks based on their peering arrangements.

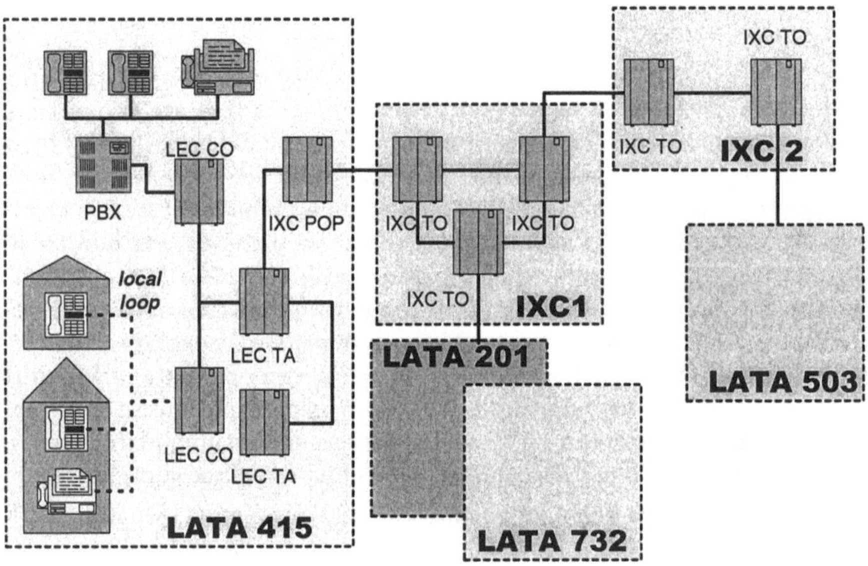

Figure 2-1: The LATA view of PSTN

As part of "our" telephone network we may also think of wireless cell phones (see Figure 2-2). This service is supported by a separate network using different technologies from the wireline PSTN; however, the two are closely peered and offer seamless exchange of voice services. Unfortunately, there are several competing service standards including different ones for analog and digital; these include the advanced mobile phone service (AMPS) for analog, digital AMPS (D-AMPS), global system for mobile communications (GSM), personal communications service (PCS), low-earth orbiting satellites (LEO), specialized mobile radio (SMR), and cellular digital packet data (CDPA). In the U.S., PCS is the dominant service with the large national PCS providers being AT&T Wireless and Sprint PCS; most local Bells support their own cellular networks. A service that runs well on one of these standards or networks may be of interest to the others as well; for example, the mobile "browser cell phone" merges desirable features that originated in separate networks.

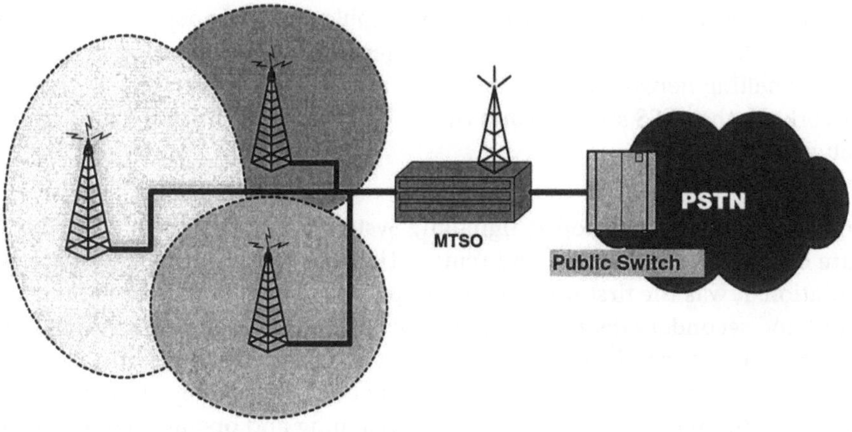

Figure 2-2: Connection Layers: Tower, MTSO Mobile Switch, PSTN Central Office

The PSTN is based on circuit-switching technology that establishes and maintains a single end-to-end circuit for each call placed. The management of the calls requires the support of three primary functions: switching, transmission, and signalling.

- *Switching.* This function handles automatic call routing by means of highly sophisticated computers such as the 4ESS switching machines. A national network has on the order of 100 such switches strategically located in major hubs. They were introduced in the mid-1970's and continue to be upgraded with state-of-the art switching technology. Today, a single 4ESS switch can handle upwards of 1.2 million calls per hour
- *Transmission.* These facilities are responsible for physical transport of the call's information, in a manner that permits satisfactory recovery of the source signal. The technologies include fiber-optic cables, microwaves, radio relays, and satellite communications. Most of today's traffic is carried over Synchronous Optical NETworks (SONET) and Dense Wave Division Multiplexing (DWDM) on fiber-optic cables. SONET operates at multiples of OC1 (51.84 Mb/s) and the European equivalent ITU-T SDH operating at OC3 and above
- *Signalling.* This function operates the out-of-band signalling which controls the flow of calls across the network and supports the enhanced telephony services such as toll-free calling including 800 service. We do not consider in-band signalling

2.1.1 Intelligent Network

The PSTN is actually composed of two networks. The first is the switched network that carries the calls over circuits, and the second is data network that carries signalling. This signalling network benefits greatly from reliable digital transport and processing. They improve the efficiency of network management, while operating at much lower cost. The signalling network also enables new and enhanced services. At the heart of this network are the 4ESS switches and the SS7 protocol that form the modern Intelligent Network.

In the mid-1970s, AT&T developed Signalling System 6 (SS6) for the old Bell System to automate calling-card validation, and remove the dependency on operators to handle this validation. It was the first use of new computer-controlled switching functions on an out-of-band secondary data network. The result was an all-in-one solution in which each switch also performed basic call processing and database processing for both services and control. These solutions were typically built and deployed by different vendors who used different approaches to the provisioning and operation of the switches. This required extensive and expensive coordination to synchronize and update both the software and the database contents in the entire network. Nevertheless, this enabled service providers to begin creating new services such as call forwarding. These services were custom built from scratch and required extensive patching to integrate into the existing systems.

As a side note, even with the later move to IN/AIN, this practice of building vertically integrated systems continued until the early 1990s. In much the same way, the early history of Internet services followed the same model. Yet in both industries, the telecommunication and the Internet models for building, provisioning, and operating services relied on a shared common infrastructure mainly out of economic necessity.

Ten years later, a faster and more capable Signalling System 7 (SS7) was developed as a layered protocol with signalling links of 64Kbs. Today it supports 1.54 megabit signalling links. This established a global standard based on Common Channel Interoffice Signalling architecture (CCIS), and was the beginning of the Intelligent Network (IN). With the introduction of SS7, services moved out of the switches and into Service Control Points (SCP).

The basic components of SS7 are the Signal Transfer Points, Service Control Points, and Service Switching Points, as shown in Figure 2-3.

- **STP – Signal Transfer Point**

  STPs are signal transfer points which route queries between central office switches and databases in SCPs. These are packet switches that forward SS7 messages from SSPs to SCPs based on the destination address of the SCPs.

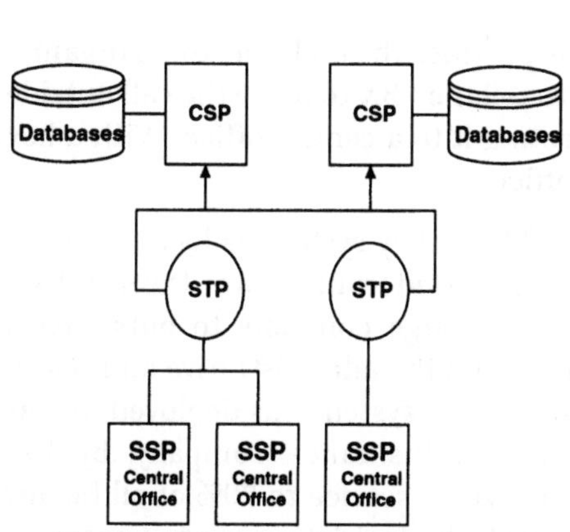

Figure 2-3: SS7 components of an IN/AIN

- **SCP – Service Control Point**

  SCPs are the databases that hold the call routing instructions and the enhanced services such as the network-based voice mail, or fax and IVR applications.
- **SSP – Service Switching Point**

  SSPs enable central offices to initiate queries to databases and specialized computers.

The model for the Intelligent Network was realized when the services moved from switches and into the SCPs, where these services could accept standardized messages. This standardization concept was well understood in the software industry, but it was not until the adaptation of SS7 and its common set of standardized messages that the model entered the telephone networks. The standard message and the well specified set of rules published by ITU-T and Bellcore created a very powerful platform on which to build the next generation of telephony services.

2.1.2 Private Branch Exchange, Key Systems, and Centrex

Businesses using telephony services depend on the use of Private Branch Exchanges (PBX), key systems, or Centrex systems; they support voice mail, service call centers, speed dialing, redial, and other advanced voice services. All of these systems provide connectivity between the members of the supported organization and the connectivity to the PSTN. They differ in the location of the equipment and the ownership of that equipment.

PBX and key systems are on-site privately owned systems. They differ mainly in the size with PBX supporting large organizations while key systems tend to support small businesses with only dozens of connections. Due to the large organizations supported by PBX, PBX's are connected to the central offices with T1 or PRI ISDN trunks. However, the big difference between the two lies in the control of the local telephones. PBX grounds all calls and thus provides the dial tone to its organization. To call outside, an outside access code has to tell the PBX to route the call outside. The PBX then has dedicated trunk lines connecting it to a central office. With a key system, the dial tone is provided by the central office.

Centrex, in contrast to a PBX or key system, is located in the central office of a telephone company; the term is derived from the words central and exchange. The motivation for a Centrex was for a large company to outsource its PBX services to the telephone company and save on the administrative and operational cost of managing their own PBXs. The first Centrex system was deployed in 1965 in Newark, New Jersey to support the Prudential Life Insurance Company. By 1982, according to a 1986 DataPro report, Centrex provided service to 70% of all business with over 1000 lines. Since the divestiture of 1984, the legislation made Centrex more applicable to both small and large businesses.

It is insightful to note that the Intelligent Network and the Centrex/PBX systems are targeting the same requirements but from different sides of the spectrum. IN/AIN offers telephone companies the infrastructure on which to build in-network services focused primarily on home subscribers; while the latter offers local services and control to organizations. As we explore next, the "new kid on the block" (i.e., Internet) offers these customers a captivating wealth of services common to both the PSTN and data networks.

2.1.3 Services Spanning both the PSTN and the Internet

Since the early days of data networks, many ventures have tried to interoperate services in the PSTN and the data networks. These span a spectrum from controlling telephone-based devices and services from Internet hosts, up through running large data and call centers in support of PSTN services. The results include Computer Telephony Integration (CTI) with Telephony APIs (e.g., TAPI/JTAPI/TSAPI) on one end, and carrier-class interoperability efforts such as TINA, Java AIN (JAIN), and Parlay API on the other end. Several of these convergence technologies strive to decouple the upper-layer services from the specific supporting technologies, and we describe several challenges introduced through this realization.

CTI and Telephony APIs

Some of the key CTI applications include Integrated Voice Response (IVR), predictive dialing, "faxback", call center management, and IP telephony. To address the growing demand by businesses to deploy CTI applications a number of competing standards developed. These include Lucent's Passageways, IBM's CallPath, SunXTL, Microsoft's TAPI, Sun's JTAPI, and Novell/Lucent's TSAPI. As an example, Microsoft's TAPI integrates multimedia stream control with legacy telephony and H.323 conferencing standard as part of its Windows platform. TAPI solutions use their COM API to integrate a TAPI Server, interoperating with a PBX or a PC modem for PSTN access or ATM/ISDN NIC for WAN access, with an LDAP directory and TAPI clients. TAPI uses RTP and RTCP for managing the synchronization and timing of its isochronous (i.e., fixed duration between events or signals) packets.

In October 1996, Sun developed Java Telephony API (JTAPI) in cooperation with IBM, Intel, Lucent, Nortel, and Novell in an effort to offer a Java-based open-specification for computer telephony standard. One of its goals was to bridge the gap between numerous proprietary, competing standards for CTI. With JTAPI, applications, regardless of the platform on which they were developed, are able to interoperate with JTAPI-compliant components built with the other standards.

TINA (Telecommunication Information Network Architecture)

In 1993, the TINA Consortium (TINA-C) was formed with 40 leading Telcos and software companies to cooperatively create a common architecture to address the communication industry's growing difficulty with the delivery of new services, or adaptation to changes within the infrastructure. In 1997 TINA-C delivered a set of validated architectural specifications that integrated all management, development and control functions into a unified, logical software architecture supported by a single distributed computing platform, the Distributed Processing Environment (DPE). TINA's DPE is based on OMG technology, CORBA, and extends CORBA to provide functions specific to telecommunication.

TINA's architecture is based on four principles, specifically:

- Object-oriented analysis and design
- Distribution
- Decoupling of software components, and
- Separation of concern

These principles address the telecommunication industry's requirements of interoperability, portability and reusability of software components, and achieves valuable independence from specific technologies. Creation and management of complex systems, formerly the burden of large vertically integrated corporations, can now be shared among different business stakeholders, such as consumers, service providers, and connectivity providers.

JAIN (Java APIs for Integrated Network)

JAIN is a set of Intelligent Network (IN) specific APIs developed by Sun Microsystems for the Java platform. JAIN targets the integration of PSTN, wireless, and IP networks, and specifically aims at some of the incompatibility between IN programs that use SS7. The JAIN APIs define interfaces for TCAP (SS7 database and switch interactions), ISUP (ISDN signalling) and MAP (cellular processing); its classes also support Operations Administration and Maintenance (OA&M) and Media Gateway Controller Protocol (MGCP). These capabilities parallel JAIN support for IP voice protocols (H.323 and SIP). Together, they enable service development that is independent of the underlying communications stacks and implementations.

At its core, the JAIN architecture defines a software component library, development tools, a service creation environment (SCE), and a carrier-grade service logic execution environment for building next-generation services for integrated PSTN, packet and wireless networks.

Parlay API

In May 1998, an industry consortium was formed to develop an open API standard that would allow 3rd party developers access to the Telcos' switches and which would support new IP-based telephony services. The consortium was spearheaded by British Telecom given the discussions with the AT&T GeoPlex project, and now also includes DGM&S Telecom, Microsoft, Nortel Networks, Siemens, Ericsson, Cisco and others. The Parlay API being standardized by the consortium would facilitate the internetworking of IP networks with the PSTN while maintaining its integrity, performance and security.

Parlay's philosophy closely parallels the approach taken in the GeoPlex project at AT&T. Due to the close interoperation with PSTN, however, the architecture does not subscribe to all the design principles described in this book. Specifically, it does not subscribe to the Routing Principle.

The Parlay API supports registration, security, discovery, event notification, QA&M, charging and billing, logging and auditing, load and fault management, and offers service interfaces for services such as call control and messaging.

Parlay-based applications are also intended to support TAPI-based applications developed by enterprises.

JAIN and Parlay APIs are complimentary and together will provide significant opportunities to expand the access and breadth of services available. Java provides the common mechanism that makes Parlay services available on the Internet. Parlay is a way to bring telecom models including security to the JAIN community, expanding the reach of the JAIN activity.

2.2 *Packet Networks*

This brings us to digital packet networks; these move data in small packets. Unlike the switched networks that dedicate a single circuit to a single session, these move many packets from many sessions over the same circuit simultaneously. The previous spanning services (Section 2.1.3) anticipated many of these interrelated developments.

Today with all the sophistication and complexity of the PSTN, many people perceive the telephone and the data networks as being two completely different technologies having little to do with each other. They perceive the use of modems to tunnel over POTS between our computers and the Internet as shown in Figure 2-4; or perhaps think of DSL or cable as offering direct broadband to the Internet through their ISP.

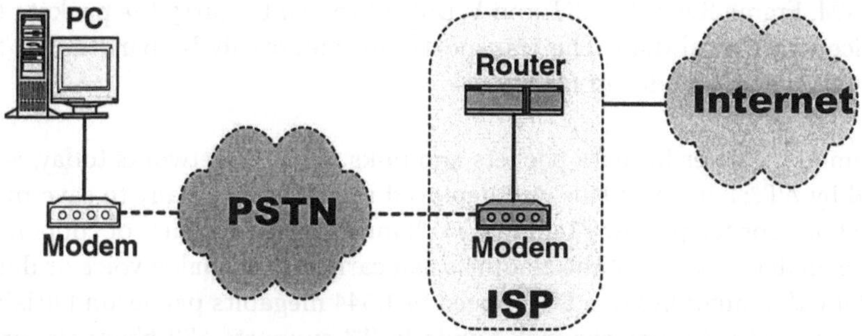

Figure 2-4: Tunneling to an ISP over POTS to reach the Internet

What many people do not realize is that parts of the PSTN have carried Internet traffic since the very beginning of digital signalling, and this rising trend builds upon the existing properties of the PSTN. Specifically: *the underlying network technologies for carrying voice and data are the same.* Their respective transport networks are therefore merging into one network. In some cases the all-digital voice circuits even bridge the "last mile" into the subscriber's business or home, thereby eliminating the remnant analog portion from their local loops. In other cases the customers retain analog equipment.

Due to the mix of premises technologies, the differences in this mix can be handled at local switches and associated programs. These edge components distinguish between analog and digital traffic. The ingress network adjusts to each kind of traffic, and for PSTN service the source signals are transparent to the transport network. For example, transmission impairments (i.e., noise) present different challenges to analog and data signals.

The classic case is echo on a two-wire connection. Only analog devices – such as the "black phone" – require echo cancellation to filter out the return signal inherent in the sharing of one wire-pair by both end points. The networks' echo canceller removes the return signal that arrives after one round-trip delay time. Whereas echo cancellation removes unwanted signals from analog voice, it must be disabled during digital transmission. Digital signals have different characteristics than analog ones. Modem devices actively maximize the useful bandwidth through signal-specific adjustments adapting to various kinds of line-noise, including echo. The network's echo-cancellation would drastically reduce the available digital bandwidth, and must be disabled during digital traffic. Digital packet phones could make the echo cancellers completely obsolete on all-digital loops, and thus eliminate the cost of these devices.

Another example of network convergence is in the use of T1 lines to simultaneously carry data as part of the Internet, while also carrying voice. A PBX supports these multiple traffic types over a single central-office connection. Network transports such as T1, T3, ATM, Frame Relay, SONET and WDM subsequently carry the packets for both PSTN voice and digital data. The transports can potentially be partitioned to carry other media, including video or fax.

T1 is a common carrier for data packets and links many IP networks today, yet it was developed by AT&T in the 1960s and deployed in 1983 specifically to save money on outside cabling for telephony. T1 allows 24 channels over two pairs of copper, fiber, or microwave media. Any one of the channels can carry either analog voice or data packets. For data, that amounts to a DS-1 speed of 1.544 megabits per second arising from the DS-0 speed of 64kb per channel. Similarly, T3 supports 672 channels, or a DS-3 speed of 44 megabits per second. The WAN that became the Internet was built largely as a result of the existence of T1s serving the PSTN. Early in its deployment, channel banks served the time-division muliplexing functions in connecting the T1 lines to PBXs and central offices. It was at these channel banks that external data connections could tap into the T1 lines along with audio lines from telephones and PBXs, and apportion some or all of the 24 channels for data packets.

It was not long before T1 offered companies the solution for their long-distance communication needs for the multiple medias of both voice and data. Corporations could lease private T1 or fractional T1 lines to interconnect their branch offices or to access the Internet. Soon, however, its high cost created the need for a cheaper solution. The result was the Frame Relay (FR). FR is a high-speed packet public network offered by local and long distance telephone companies.

Companies that previously leased or owned costly private *dedicated* T1 lines of fixed capacity, could instead rent *circuits* on an FR network. Inexpensive access lines connect the customer premise equipment (CPE) with the FR network. Depending on the levels of desired service and cost, the FR circuits are either permanent virtual circuits (PVC) or switched virtual circuits (SVC). PVCs are logical predefined paths through the FR charged at a fixed rate, while SVCs are temporary circuits charged per use. In either case, the FR service offers a service level agreement (SLA) known as committed information rate (CIR), or the minimum guaranteed throughput. These rates can be guaranteed by the carrier given that they do not oversubscribe the capacity of the frame relay. Neither PVCs nor SVCs can offer absolute guarantees on throughput or Quality of Service (QoS).

FR was, and continues as, the preferred method for connecting branch offices, particularly where time critical data is not an issue. This preference is under challenge by virtual private network (VPN) solutions with similar connectivity at lower cost. VPN solutions may exploit multiple technologies and thereby obtain lower average delay for a fixed traffic class.

In contrast to frame relay service which excels in interconnecting LANs and carrying pure data traffic, network service providers now offer Asynchronous Transfer Mode (ATM) as a high-speed switching service capable of carrying mixtures of voice and video along with data traffic. ATM was developed by the telecom industry as a high-speed network technology specifically to carry isochronous streams (voice and video). Fundamentally, ATM is a connection-oriented data link that carries small fixed-sized cells of 53 bytes arranged as a 48-byte payload and a five byte header. Instead of routers, ATM networks establish virtual circuits (VC) and switch cells directly in hardware according to the header. Virtual paths multiplex aggregated VCs through virtual path connections (VPC) that define end points and QoS. The ATM standards define five QoS classes and a variety of admission control algorithms ensure consistent performance.

At this point we should compare data with the isochronous traffic of voice and video. From this discussion, it should become clear that some network services are better suited for data and others for voice. To the hosts and applications that deal specifically with one or more multimedia types, it may not matter exactly how the information moves or over what types of network the information flows. They communicate everything over IP. It is the underlying network fabric that has to contend with the different media requirements and here the differences are vast.

Consider real-time interactive voice and video applications [SEIF98]. These applications are

- Sensitive to absolute delay (i.e., real-time)
- Sensitive to delay variance (i.e., isochronous)
- Tolerant of information loss (i.e., receiver interpolation), and
- Assume *a priori* knowledge of the communications requirements

The design of real-time interactive services must consider the human aspects of perception, especially since the underlying technologies may have unexpected effects on the services. Human perception is extremely sensitive to short-term variations. This occurs, for example, through subtle variations in signal delay giving rise to the phenomena of jitter.

This human sensitivity to artifacts – even the infinitesimal variations in ambient noise – was crisply observed by an advanced student engaged in the programming of real-time experiments at the Human Perceptual Research Laboratory of Purdue University's Department of Audiology. Informed subjects, typically students, were trained in soundproof rooms to recognize minute, low-level signals produced by high-fidelity computer-controlled audio equipment. These subjects indicated what they heard by pressing the appropriate button on a console. Surprisingly, trained subjects demonstrated the ability to reliably detect the audio stimuli *even with the volume set to zero!* Upon investigation it was determined that background noise included artifacts of the computer-controlled switches. The subjects acquired a learned behavior that measured artifacts beneath the threshold of their direct observation. Their perception was better than the ambient noise. This lesson has not been lost on the communications community, driven as it is by customer perception.

The public telephone system conforms to ITU standards for the minimum requirements on voice quality to be acceptable; those standards stipulate the acceptable jitter, delays, and thresholds that for the majority of the people are below their threshold of perception. The standards recognize that a person's perception system can interpolate between drops in the signal and still be understood. That is why, for instance, we have moving pictures; a sequence of images presented rapidly at a fixed rate.

Compare this to the requirements for data. A data exchange may proceed unfettered with concern for small variations in the time scale, provided that content remains flawless and the protocol can adapt to the timing variations (as IP does). Such transfers are:

- Insensitive to absolute delay
- Insensitive to delay variance (only when the last packet arrives is the data whole)
- Intolerant of information loss (even one lost packet may make the whole content unusable), and
- Asymmetrical (data flows mostly in one direction, from the servers to the clients and vice-versa)

Thus compare data traffic with voice traffic. Data is very sensitive to packet loss but totally unaffected with delay and jitter, or the order of delivery. Voice traffic is, in every respect, the opposite. ATM was designed specifically to address the requirements of real-time interactive voice and video. Unlike data networks that tend to be connectionless, ATM is a connection-oriented network that guarantees performance characteristics of its virtual circuits and consequently is optimized for voice and collaborative video. Although ATM has been described by some as the ultimate solution for integrated broadband communications networks [DEPR93], others feel that this is true only in light of the limited bandwidth available today.

Throughout this book, we focus heavily and take advantage of the ubiquity of IP, but for this discussion, a technology that is equally ubiquitous is the Ethernet [GIGAET].

According to IDC, by 1997, more than 83 percent of all installed network connections were Ethernet. This represents over 120 million interconnected PCs, workstations and servers. The remaining network connections are a combination of Token Ring, Fiber Distributed Data Interface (FDDI), ATM and other protocols. Unlike the higher cost of the ATM and the higher complexity of mapping Ethernet frames to ATM cells, one contender to ATM that avoids these disadvantages is the Gigabit Ethernet.

Gigabit Ethernet is a data link and physical layer technology that support capacities in excess of 1Gb per second. It is an evolutionary technology from Ethernet that is similarly a connection-less, unacknowledged, variable-length packet delivery system. Currently, the Ethernet running at 10Mb/s and Fast Ethernet running at 100Mb/s dominate LANs; Gigabit Ethernet can offer seamless interconnection for the LANs in the backbone. This dramatically reduces the cost of equipment and operations over other heterogeneous solutions.

This brings us to the physical layer technologies in the WANs. A common signalling method across optical-fiber links is SONET. SONET is commonly used by the carriers to carry ATM, but it can also multiplex many different data link technologies simultaneously. What SONET offers is the simultaneous transport of ATM, DS-1, DS-3, connection-less packet over SONET (POS), as well as all the others. This creates opportunities to utilize the best-of-breed data-link technologies that are optimized for given applications, and combine them to run over a transport backbone. This can simplify the end point view of networks through support of the ubiquitous Ethernet LANs with end-to-end IP connectivity.

The best part of these new opportunities is the elimination of traffic bottlenecks, which become mere artifacts imposed by slow multiples-of-64Kb backbone connections. Today's fiber optics form the technology for moving vast amounts of information, and the routing and switching technology has quickly moved from megabit, to gigabit and now terabit capacities. A single switch that has a terabit capacity can move a lot of information. Consider what a terabit channel (actually composed of 1000 gigabit channels) can carry. One terabit capacity is equivalent to 300 years of daily newspapers sent in one second; the ability to stream 100 *thousand* television channels simultaneously, carry 12 *million* telephone conversations or support 10 *million* Internet users browsing the web. Although OC-192 is being deployed today, OC-758 and OC-3072 are already on the horizon.

2.3 Network Access and the Local Loop

To the majority of users such as consumers, small business owners and public organizations that access the Internet, the innovation in the backbone is of distant concern. Their online experience comes from the simple task of gaining access and maintaining an acceptable performance of their connections to the Internet through their ISPs or enterprise LAN connections. For most of them, the promise of rich user-experience with high-speed, 7 days by 24 hours (7×24) access using their LEC's local loop has lagged behind the state-of-the-art technology in the core networks. This has been due primarily to the need to avoid incurring the high cost of upgrading the "last mile" local loops from existing copper, twisted-pair wiring intended for analog signals. Yet, by late 1998, broadband-to-the-house services on wireless, DSL, and cable services began to be widely offered.

Up until about 1998, consumer access to the Internet was provided by ISPs mostly through dial-up modem access. A modem (short for MOdulator/DEModulator) converts a digital stream to an analog signal and vice-versa using the standard telephone lines in the local loop and the PSTN in the backbone. The first analog modems operated at only 110 baud (about ten characters per second), and the introduction of 300 baud modems (30 characters per second) was then viewed as a dramatic advance. Today the consumer-market modems operate at a peak performance of 56kbps, although their typical operational speed is slower due to the narrow effective band available for the analog signal.

Faster technologies use existing wiring in a digital mode instead of an analog mode. The first promising method was Basic Rate Interface (BRI) Integrated Services Digital Network (ISDN) that uses two standard "copper pairs" providing two 64kbs channel and one 16kbs signalling channel for a maximum throughput of 128kbs. This technology has not been widely accepted due to its difficulty to provision and install, as well as the typical pay-per-minute charges. ISDN, much like the basic modem traffic, travels through the telephone system and is an integral part of the circuit architecture. The only physical differences are the local loop and the equipment at the central office. Due to the digital signalling and aggregation of multiple copper pairs, the ISDN line supports a wider range of services, transfers more data over the same LEC and IXC facilities, and is subject to different FCC tariffs than the analog voice line.

A more attractive class of service, Digital Subscriber Line (DSL), has recently emerged. Unlike BRI ISDN, DSL's relation to the telephone system is only in the local loop, and it does not impose load upon the conventional circuits of the LEC or IXC transports. At the central office, a DSL Access Multiplexer (DSLAM) forwards all traffic to the appropriate ISP and bypasses the PSTN. DSL runs over standard Category 3 wiring, the basic telephone lines up to and inside the house.

DSL utilizes the untapped bandwidth available in the telephone wiring of the local loop. Audio voice traffic requires only a very narrow band (4k Hz) leaving ample frequency for data (typically 100k Hz). Thus POTS voice and the DSL data can move simultaneously over the same wires without interference. The frequencies are separated at both ends of the local loop with splitters or DSL modems, as shown in Figure 2-5.

There are several variations on the basic DSL service such as the Asymmetrical DSL (ADSL), ADSL Lite, High bit rate DSL (HDSL), Consumer DSL (CDSL), and Very high bit rate DSL (VDSL). These vary in basic service cost and speeds. DSL is very sensitive to the length of the wires connecting the Central Office DSLAM and the DSL modems at home. The actual rate obtained depends on the class of service and the distance. A typical rate is 1.5 Mbps downstream and 512Kbps upstream. For a full ADSL, speeds can be as high as 8 Mbps downstream and 1.5 Mbps upstream. Unlike cable which connects many users in the vicinity on a single shared segment of the cable, DSL provides dedicated access.

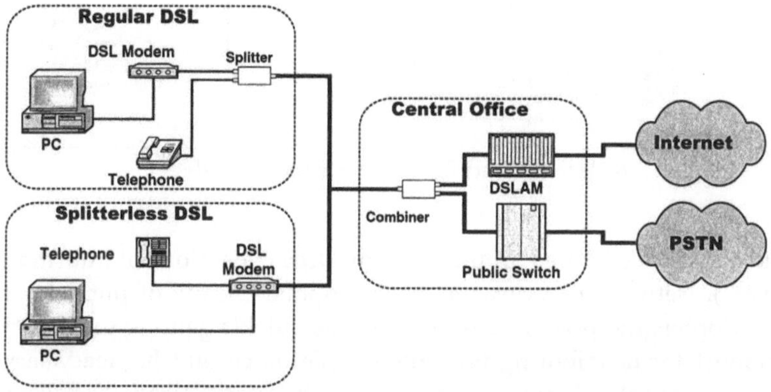

Figure 2-5: Internet and POTS with Digital Subscriber Loop

The same notion of piggy-backing data over a medium carrying a signal for another application is used with television coaxial cable. The main difference is that cable was designed as a simplex broadcast medium while telephones were designed as separate full-duplex circuits. With cable, the local-loop is one shared segment (basically a LAN) that services a small neighborhood (as shown in Figure 2-6). The cable segment is terminated at the SOHO end by a splitter and at the cable office with a combiner that merges the TV RF signal with the data signal from the Internet.

2.4 World-Wide Web

Before 1989, the non-commercial Internet that encompassed most universities and research labs was the clubhouse of "techies" and academics. It was a simple but elegant world of UNIX programming; information from other hosts was accessed through command-line networking; each user knew all the wire-protocols and commands needed to access the information on other machines using command shells for applications such as TELNET, FTP, network news, and email. Commercial networked systems were being deployed, but these were mostly large enterprise database solutions accessing large computer mainframes deployed outside the labs and campuses.

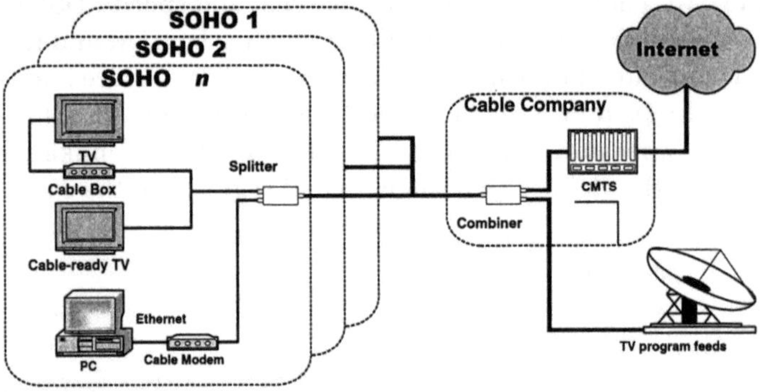

Figure 2-6: Internet and Television access over Cable

Even so, much activity centered around posting large collections of information online (see Figure 2-7). Network news was a highly popular means of publicly exchanging information; Gopher, the precursor to WWW was quickly gaining university and government support for distributing information; Veronica and Jughead, served as the Gopher search supports; Archie (derived from the word archive) was an effort to archive the content of FTP sites using several Archie servers; the Wide-Area Information Server (WAIS) offered detailed document indices allowing keyword searches through the archived documents. Gopher was a hierarchical menu-based system consisting of thousands of Gopher servers; it demonstrated the model for what the WWW would later generalize and improve upon. Archie was the model for how modern search engines and robots on the Web collect information, and WAIS and Veronica were the models for how they can be searched.

In the mid 1980's, a scientist in a wide range of disciplines began to collaborate over the Internet and to exchange information and access networked resources in geographically disparate locations. To a non-computer scientist or an engineer this was both an asset and a limitation. It was an asset because scientist in different continents could share information easily and quickly; a limitation because everyone needed to learn how to program and understand low-level networking.

As with most great innovations, the time was "right" to address this problem by combining several technologies: the Internet, the client-server model, hypertext authoring, multimedia mail specification, and scheme of universal resource addressing. Formerly intimidating technologies suddenly became simple and widely accessible. Tim Berners-Lee put these elements together in 1989 at the European laboratory for Particle Physics (CERN) creating the basic architecture we now call the World Wide Web (WWW). At that time, email was taking on additional media capabilities through the support of Multipurpose Internet Mail Extensions (MIME) for description of

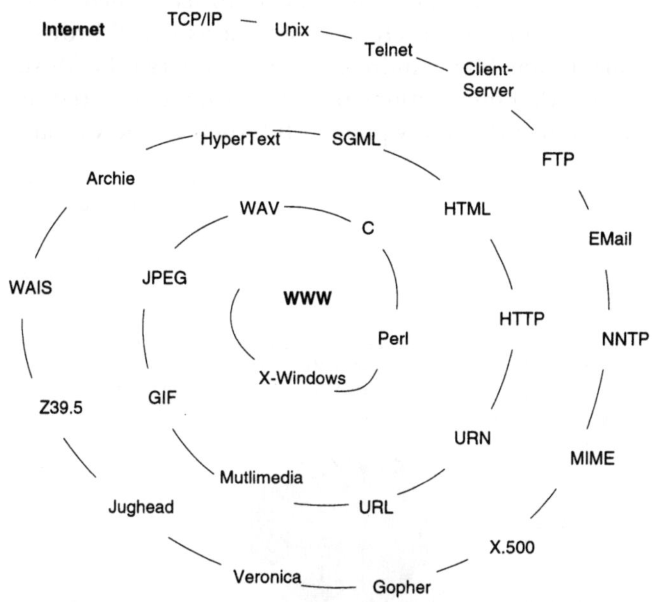

Figure 2-7: On the Road to the World-Wide Web

attributes of the content in SMTP, as well as encapsulation of multibody, multimedia content. At the same time, a hypertext technology was being standardized around SGML. Tim merged the two into a new protocol called the Hypertext Transfer Protocol (HTTP) that utilized MIME and a newly designed document type definition (DTD) of SGML called Hypertext Markup Language (HTML). These innovations were used to create the web as a collection of HTTP servers that individually formed portals into the local servers' information bases. Almost immediately, the physicists at CERN could offer their multimedia information without requiring the direct use of FTP or TELNET.

With the HTTP servers, the burden of the ease-of-access was shifted to the software clients accessing the web. Initially simple text-based clients were created to resolve the new Universal Resource Locators (URLs), retrieve the resource, and either store it locally or render it using a collection of existing applications. Almost immediately, the notion of a browser was formed. A browser was to be an GUI application that could render most of the standard multimedia formats: text, image, and sound. The browser would abstract even the higher level client-server details of the WWW from the user and offer a simple visual window based point-and-click interface to the information on the web.

Although Tim's WWW foundation was the single most important enabling factor for the industry, the catalyst that ignited the popularity of WWW happened at the

National Center for Supercomputing Applications (NCSA) at the University of Illinois. There, graduate students developed a graphical browser called Mosaic. Mosaic was a government sponsored project to create a standards-based browser for the WWW. One of those students was Mark Andreessen, who directed the Mosaic team and later co-founded Netscape Communications Inc. Mosaic demonstrated the potential of the WWW and helped launch the wildly popular Internet we know today.

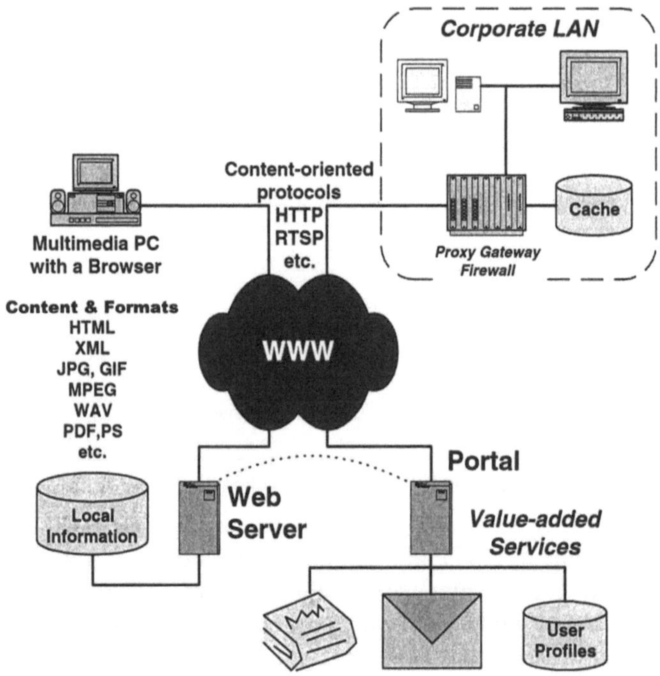

Figure 2-8: WWW Connectivity

Around that time, work resumed on extending the role of the servers, which then offered primarily static information stored on local disks. The first step was development of the Common-Gateway Interface (CGI) allowing HTTP requests to invoke external programs. These programs could deliver individualized content through interpretive shell scripts, Perl or TCL language programs. Currently, CGI programs are being replaced by Java servelets or server-side scripting languages such as Personal Home Page (PHP) and JavaScript. These are designed to dynamically generated pages. PHP is a particularly elegant solution in the form of a scripted language embedded in HTML and executed by the server as the HTML is relayed to the browser. PHP's strongest value is generation of database-enabled dynamic web pages, a role that it achieves easily and quickly through activates of diverse databases. This leverages vast information assets stored in dBase, FilePro, Informix, InterBase, mSQL, Oracle, Sybase, UNIX dbm and other repositories. It also supports interfaces to other services using protocols such as IMAP, SNMP, NNTP, POP3 and HTTP. In general, server-side scripting languages have changed the nature of the web; what used to be a domain of mostly static pages is now predominantly the domain of up-to-date, dynamic pages that integrate multiple sources and formats.

The original deployment of CGI led to the more general notion of generality and extensibility of the browsers themselves, leading to the notion of browser plug-ins. Third party developers crafted browser-oriented services delivering complex information through a collage of content-oriented formats including device independent Portable Document Format (PDF), macromedia, and Virtual Reality Markup Language (VRML). This soon transformed into a general notion of dynamically varying presentations through browser-resident programs, automatically downloaded through new scripting languages such as JavaScript. The unprecedented levels of dynamic interactions drove the browser from its stateless situation, and arrived at persistent browser-specific information.

To create scalable browsers with stable information and yet preserve subscriber privacy, the notion of cookies was developed. In computer jargon, a cookie encapsulates arbitrary name/value pairs. Servers can create cookies, and browsers selectively store such cookies locally upon receipt. The browsers return the right cookie on subsequent visits. This way a service offered via the server can store the state in the client (see Section 6.7.1).

Today, the notion of rendering HTML is being generalized to multiple translations performed by both the server and the browsers with HTML serving a very narrow function as the final presentation format. This involves information represented in the Extensible Markup Language (XML) suitably transformed to HTML according to rules described with eXtensible Style sheet Language (XSL). The browser presents the HTML through locally-stored presentation styles described by Cascading Style Sheets (CSS).

The proliferating WWW technologies hastened ongoing developments centered around security and privacy. Almost immediately, HTTP could be made to communicate authentication and access control attributes that the servers verified and implemented. This initiated a shift of the public WWW into subscription-based private subgroups with restriction of information to authorized users. To ensure information privacy, public-key encryption technology was incorporated into the client and servers thereby providing cryptographically-secured data streams, known as crypto-tunnels, between the servers and the browsers. Strong market-driven concerns for interoperability – the choice to use any browser or server – impelled the universal acceptance of Secure Socket Layer (SSL) technology which is a *de facto* standard of WWW privacy.

The web servers are no longer the sole sources of Web information. Proxies, which simply put, are HTTP relays with value-added functions, quickly became an integral part of the Web. Proxies supplement many server roles, while also adapting to many network configurations. One role is that of security for enterprises, whereby the proxies interoperate with corporate firewalls to enable data tunnels between internal machines that may safely contact external web servers. All browsers today allow traffic to be "proxied" through designation of the hostname and port that provide proxy services.

Proxies also provide scalability, the ability to support ever increasing loads. Caching proxies can retain content for subsequent replay. They also store content closer to the consumers. Such techniques are one remedy for the sluggishness typical in overloaded networks, and also seen in servers jammed with growing demands for content. The problem is a fundamental one; as we describe in Section 4.3 the classical client-server architecture creates "hot spots" and does not scale to large sizes; nor do the obvious variations on client-server. Reducing the amount of traffic that terminates at the servers is thus a key role of proxies. Specialized caching proxies retain copies of recently accessed information, in anticipation of further requests for the same content. Many large ISPs support their subscribers through a network of caching proxies, and this decreases request traffic going over the backbone networks. It also reduces bottlenecks at their peering routers caused by redundant web traffic. A client can obtain the benefits of caching proxies in several ways, for example by configuration of the web browser to send all requests to the caching proxy.

A more recent extension to the simple notion of WWW servers is the definition of portals. A portal is a WWW "super" site that offers a variety of online services including Web searching, news, weather, stock information, shopping, email, chat rooms and various directories such as white and yellow pages. The portal can provide a personalized user experience, one that reflects the usage patterns or explicit preferences of a specific browser. This happens without identification of the user, by merely tagging the browser with a unique but anonymous cookie[1]. Advertisements became the first, and for most the only, source of revenue on the Internet. This requires that users visit the site that supports the advertisement. The notion of proxies provides this point of contact, and the portal model supports this combination of the users' interest in personalized views, plus the providers' need to earn revenue through advertising. Some of the more prominent portals are Yahoo, AOL, Lycos, Infoseek, and Altavista.

1. The server-supplied and globally unique "tag" does not demand a description of the subscriber's personal identity. However, since the portal customizes the user experience by acquiring a description of the user actions, it is possible the description could also identify the specific user.

2.5 Java Language

The Java Language is without doubt one of the most important and one of the most successful programming languages used by network related applications and services. It combines a powerful yet simple object model, plus a Java Virtual Machine that allows "write once, run everywhere". Much of this success is related to its influence on the Internet. It is instrumental in our discussion of IP service Platforms to take a closer look at the history of the Java language.

2.5.1 Green Project

In 1990 Patrick Naughton, a Sun software engineer, wrote a memo to the CEO of Sun Microsystems detailing the problems their software division faced coming from the huge assortment of application programming interfaces (APIs) which Sun supported. As a response, Sun's management commissioned Bill Joy, Andy Bechtolsheim, Wayne Rosing, Mike Sheridan, James Gosling and Patrick Naughton to form a research group to explore opportunities in the consumer electronics market.

The team, codenamed Green, set for themselves the goal of creating a single operating environment with support for both processor and the software to run upon it. This environment was to be used by all consumer electronic devices, from computers and video game machines all the way down to remote controls and VCRs. Their vision was to enable interactivity between all such devices, as well as to speed up development and reduce the cost of implementing new features through the use of a single, small core operating environment.

In contrast to the workstation products, top priorities in the consumer marketplace are low-cost, bug-free and relatively simple, easy-to-use products. To compete in the consumer electronics market, companies treat underlying technologies, such as CPUs, as commodities that can be swapped for lower-cost alternatives. To accommodate the consumer market's demand for CPU flexibility, the Green team began extending the C++ compiler. Eventually, however, they realized that even with lots of extras, C++ would not suffice. After much research and testing, the result was a simple object-oriented programming language named Oak. The name came to Gosling when, while creating a directory for the new language, he glanced out his window, and spotted a tree - an oak - although other stories abound.

In a very short time, the Green project built an operating system (GreenOS), a language (Oak), a graphical toolkit, an interface, and a new hardware platform with three custom chips. By the fall of 1992 the Green project engineers developed a small hand-held device which featured an easy-to-use, graphic-intensive and appealing interface called "*7". The user's guide and helper for this device was an animated figure named Duke, who later became Java's official mascot.

The product was demonstrated around Sun and impressed important people like Scott McNealy and Bill Joy, but the next step was uncertain. The fledgling Oak had yet to develop the roots that now support substantial portions of the Internet.

2.5.2 First Person Inc.

In early 1993, Sun incorporated the Green project into First Person Inc., a fully owned subsidiary, and the company began searching for a market for its unique product. After learning about Time Warner's RFP for its interactive cable-TV trial in Orlando, Florida, First Person focused on the interactive television market, in particular on the set-top box operating-system market, and placed a bid with Time-Warner. Despite having the widely-perceived best technology, Sun did not win the bid.

First Person kept trying to pursue set-top boxes until early 1994, when it concluded that the market wasn't ready. After deals with companies such as 3DO and Time-Warner fell through in the interactive television area, the outlook for the fledgling company seemed bleak. Alternative First Person business plans centered around a CD-ROM/online multimedia platform based on Oak, and received very mixed reviews from Sun executives. Soon after that, First Person stopped pursuing the set-top box business and dissolved. Sun Interactive was created. Half of the FirstPerson's employees joined this venture with its focus on digital video data servers.

In summer 1994, a few people still pursuing the Oak technology joined the "LiveOak" team, established by Bill Joy to develop a *big* small operating system.

In the meantime, the National Center for Supercomputing Applications (NCSA) released Mosaic, an application which allowed users to easily and graphically access mostly text-based Internet. Within a year, this visually-based, readily accessible network of Internet sites known as the World Wide Web had grown from a mere research project into a revolutionary medium to transmit data. The number of web-sites accessible by a web-browser such as Mosaic was growing at a phenomenal rate.

2.5.3 HotJava and the "tumbling" Duke

By mid-1994, the World Wide Web was big. The LiteOak team realized that they could build, in their own words "a really cool browser", one that is architecturally neutral, real-time, reliable and secure. This resolved issues that were not "show stoppers" in the workstation world but were emerging as the essential challenges to an open Internet world. By early fall, Jonathon Payne and Naughton finished writing "WebRunner," a Mosaic-like browser later renamed "HotJava". At the same time Arthur Van Hoff implemented Java compiler *in* Java.

In September of 1994, the WebRunner browser was first demonstrated to SunLabs director Bert Sutherland and Eric Schmidt, Sun's chief technology officer (CTO). In an impressive demo, WebRunner showed off LiteOak language in a new light. In a most unusual move, the company decided to give the source for the Oak language away over the Internet.

Sun renamed the language to Java. Although Java could produce stand-alone applications, it was its ability to be transmitted chunks of Java code (applets) and run it over the Internet that brought it to the spotlight. Sun formally announced Java and HotJava at SunWorld '95.

The final piece to the puzzle was when Sun produced its HotJava Web browser and made license agreement with Netscape, which enabled the Netscape browser to execute these new Java applets as well.

2.5.4 JavaSoft

In January of 1996, Sun founded JavaSoft, the company that oversees development of the Java language. A few months later JavaSoft released the Java Development Kit (JDK) version 1.0. A number of companies followed with integration announcements that leverage this enabling technology:

- Oracle announced its WebSystem suite of WWW software which includes a Java-compatible browser
- Sun, Netscape and Silicon Graphics announce new software alliance to develop Internet interactivity tools based on the Java technologies
- Borland, Mitsubishi Electronics, Sybase and Symantec announced plans to license Java
- IBM and Adobe announced a licensing agreement with Sun for use of Java
- Lotus Development Corp., Intuit Inc., Borland International Inc., Macromedia Inc.,and Spyglass Inc. announced plans to license Java

On December 7, 1995 during announcement of suite of new Internet products, Microsoft announced plans to license the Java technologies.

The rest, as we say, is history...

2.6 IP Version 6

For several decades now, IP version 4 (IPv4) has been – and continues to be – the standard for the Internet. Over the last decade, however, key problems surfaced, stemming from limitations in the IPv4 protocol. Solutions to the problems presently come in the form of "workarounds". Thus, VPN technology and public key infrastructure resolve many challenges of security and privacy. The issues of a small IPv4 address space is resolved largely through network address translation (NAT). Tagged switching remedies many routing complexity issues.

Predicting these problems, in the late 1980's IETF started to consider the next generation IP (IPng) that would overcome IPv4's shortcomings and guarantee IP's usefulness in the future. From a number of proposals and much debate about the details, IPng was drafted and the IPng proposal was recommended by the IPng Area Directors of the Internet Engineering Task Force at a Toronto IETF meeting on July, 1994 in RFC 1752. The recommendation was approved by the Internet Engineering Steering Group and made a Proposed Standard in November of that year. The formal name of the IPng protocol is IP version 6 (IPv6). The core set of IPv6 protocols were made an IETF Proposed Standard a year later in September 1995.

In general, IPv6 addresses the Internet scaling problem, provides a flexible transition mechanism for the current Internet, and supports the needs of new markets such as those needed by nomadic personal computing devices, networked entertainment, and device control. IPv6 provides a platform for new Internet functionality including support for real-time flows, provider selection, host mobility, end-to-end security, autoconfiguration, and auto-reconfiguration.

IPv6 supports large hierarchical addresses that will allow the Internet to continue to grow and provide new routing capabilities not built into IPv4. It has *anycast* addresses, which can be used for policy route selection, and has *scoped multicast* addresses that provide improved scalability over IPv4 multicast. It also has local use address mechanisms that enable "plug and play" installation. The address structure of IPv6 can also carry the addresses of other Internet protocol suites. Space was allocated for IPX and NSAP addresses, and this facilitates migration of these Internet protocols to IPv6.

Most importantly, IPv6 does all this in an evolutionary way that builds on IPv4, instead of the complete redesign suggested by some of the early contributors. Ease of transition was an essential point in the design of IPv6, not a mere add-on. IPv6 is designed to interoperate with IPv4. Specific mechanisms (embedded IPv4 addresses, pseudo-checksum rules etc.) were built into IPv6 to support transition and compatibility with IPv4. Thus, IPv6 permits a gradual and step-by-step deployment with a minimum of dependencies. It can be installed as a normal software upgrade in Internet devices and is interoperable with the current IPv4. Its deployment strategy is designed to avoid "flag days" or other dependencies. IPv6 also runs efficiently on high performance networks such as Gigabit Ethernet, OC-12, and ATM. At the same time it is efficient for low bandwidth networks. Functions that work well in IPv4 were kept in IPv6, and the ineffective or unused functions have been removed. The changes from IPv4 to IPv6 fall primarily into the following categories:

Expanded Routing and Addressing Capabilities

IPv6 increases the IP address size from 32 bits to 128 bits, to support more levels of addressing hierarchy and a much greater number of addressable nodes, plus simpler auto-configuration of address spaces. The scalability of multicast routing is improved by adding a "scope" field to multicast addresses.

The longer IPv6 addresses identify interfaces; both as individual interfaces, and also as sets of interfaces. Addresses of all types are assigned to interfaces, not nodes. Since each interface belongs to a single node, any of that node's interfaces' unicast addresses may be used as an identifier for the node. A single interface may be assigned multiple IPv6 addresses of any type.

There are three types of IPv6 addresses: **unicast, anycast,** and **multicast.** Unicast addresses identify a single interface. Anycast addresses identify a set of interfaces such that a packet sent to a anycast address will be delivered to one member of the set. Multicast addresses identify a group of interfaces, such that a packet sent to a multicast address is delivered to all of the interfaces in the group. There are no broadcast addresses in IPv6, their function being superseded by multicast addresses.

Anycast Address

A new address type of is defined to identify sets of nodes. A packet sent to an anycast address is delivered to *one* of the nodes. The use of anycast addresses in the IPv6 source route allows nodes to control the path over which their traffic flows.

Header Format Simplification

Some IPv4 header fields have been dropped or made optional, to reduce the common-case processing cost of packet handling and to keep the bandwidth cost of the IPv6 header as low as possible despite the increased size of the addresses. Although the IPv6 addresses are four times longer than the IPv4 addresses, the IPv6 header is only twice the size of the IPv4 header.

Improved Support for Options

Changes in the way IP header options are encoded allow for more efficient forwarding, less stringent limits on the length of options, and greater flexibility for introducing new options in the future.

Quality-of-Service Capabilities

A new capability is added to enable the labeling of packets belonging to particular traffic "flows" for which the sender requests special handling, such as non-default quality of service or "real- time" service.

Authentication and Privacy Capabilities

IPv6 includes the definition of extensions which provide support for authentication, data integrity, and confidentiality. This is included as a basic element of IPv6 and will be included in all implementations.

The current Internet has a number of security problems and lacks effective privacy and authentication mechanisms below the application layer. IPv6 remedies these shortcomings by having two integrated options that provide security services. These two options may be used singly or together to provide differing levels of security to different users.

The first mechanism, called the **IPv6 Authentication Header**, is an extension header which provides authentication and integrity (without confidentiality) to IPv6 datagrams. While the extension is algorithm-independent and will support many different authentication techniques, the use of keyed MD_5 is proposed to help ensure interoperability within the worldwide Internet. This can be used to eliminate a significant class of network attacks, including host masquerading attacks. The use of the IPv6 Authentication Header is particularly important when source routing is used with IPv6 because of the known risks in IP source routing. Its placement at the Internet layer can help provide host origin authentication to those upper layer protocols and services that currently lack meaningful protections. This mechanism should be exportable by vendors in the United States and other countries with similar export restrictions because it only provides authentication and integrity, and specifically does not provide confidentiality. The exportable IPv6 Authentication Header encourages its widespread deployment and use.

The second security extension header provided with IPv6 is the IPv6 Encapsulating Security Header. This structure provides integrity and confidentiality to IPv6 datagrams. It is simpler than some similar security protocols (e.g., SP3D, ISO NLSP) but remains flexible and algorithm-independent. To achieve interoperability within the global Internet, the use of DES CBC is being used as the standard algorithm for use with the IPv6 Encapsulating Security Header. The IPv6 protocol consists of two parts, the basic IPv6 header and IPv6 extension headers.

In summary it is appropriate to discuss IPv6 in relation to the network middleware. IPv6 is addressing all the right technical issues and its early deployment would help solve the related problems plaguing the Internet and aid in the problems targeted by the IP service platforms. Unfortunately, the industry is as yet not pursuing a wide move to IPv6. This is mainly due to the large investment in IPv4 equipment and software, the continued economic benefits in supporting IPv4, and partly due to the ability to adopt IPv4. Somehow, IPv4 remains sufficient to function without requiring the move to IPv6. The move to IPv6 is, however, inevitable in the absence of new technologies that make it obsolete before its wide deployment.

2.7 IPSec: Internet Protocol Security

With IPv4's lack of security, and with the preparation for IPv6, the Internet Protocol Security (IPSec) has emerged as a standard for offering interoperable network encryption. IPSec is a set of guidelines developed by IETF as described in RFC2401 for enabling secure communication over insecure networks. The standard secures IP transport by offering service for data encryption, end point authentication, data integrity validation, and prevention against unauthorized retransmission. While IPSec is optional for use with IPv4, it will be required for IPv6. The source code is freely available and it is not subject to U.S. or any other nation's export restrictions.

IPSec enables secure communication-based activities on an insecure network. It provides a standard yet extensible "Security Architecture for IP" as described in RFC2401 and subsequent standards. Summarized briefly, the protocol secures IP transport through authentication, encapsulation and tunneling. The specific secure services are defined by Security Associations, or SAs. IPSec maintains a Security Policy Database (SPD) that defines protected traffic, protection methods, and sharing of these methods. The SPD may specify multiple levels of security as well as the granularity of traffic that receives a specific policy. Central features include key exchange (IKE, for example) and transport formats. The protocol allows both an authentication header (AH) and an encapsulated security payload (ESP).

IPSec operates between the internet layer (i.e., IP) and the transport layers (i.e., TCP or UDP) on a compliant host. IPSec works primarily in two ways. The first method is the transport mode (as shown in Figure 2-9) for communicating between two IPSec hosts. Here, the IPSec layer protects the application and TCP/UDP content.

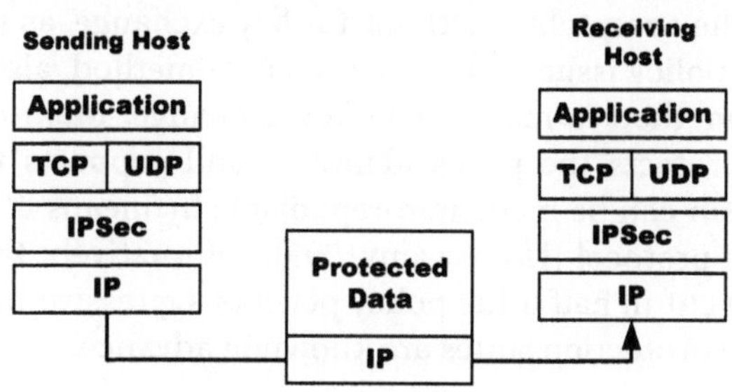

Figure 2-9: IPSec Transport Mode

The second method is the tunnel mode shown in Figure 2-10. This method is typical of corporate VPNs, over which all traffic outgoing from the corporate edge is encrypted and tunnelled to the destination (protected) network. The protection in applied by a security gateway that encapsulates the entire IP packet and forwards it over the public network to the destination security gateway, which strips away the protection before relaying the packet to the receiving host.

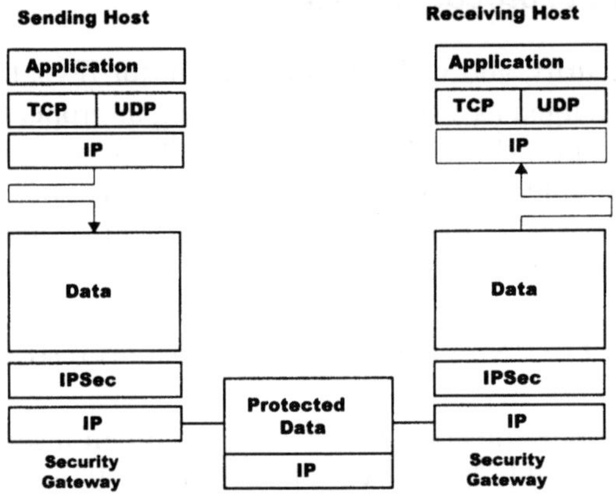

Figure 2-10: IPSec Tunnel Mode

To offer a complete security solution of IP, IPSec combines authentication with confidentiality. The protocol establishes the identity of hosts and gateways through multiple authentication mechanisms, including the Public Key Infrastructure (PKI) as defined by the standard X.509 v3. Automated key management, such as the Internet Key Exchange (IKE) may conveniently leverage the PKI. Once authenticated, the protocol negotiates appropriate security associations (SA) to ensure tamper-proof and confidential communication. The Security Associations define the specific secure services. IPSec also addresses the issue of non-standard security frameworks by permitting private encryption algorithms and consequently cliques within the private algorithm.

IPSec policies define the acceptable methods for key exchange, as well as subsequent security services. One policy issue is the key-exchange method, also know as Phase I. The most protective method is main-mode key exchange. Main-mode key uses six messages, and both protects the peer's identities and supports the negotiation of options. The negotiation can be made non-repudiable by means of public keys in the challenge-phase of the protocol [Doraswamy1999]. Alternatively, the number of message exchanges can be cut in half if the policy permits aggressive-mode key exchange. This is useful when the protection suites are known in advance.

The security services are defined in Phase II of an IPSec session setup. These determine the granularity, security attributes, and actions for each data flow. Both kinds of policy can be defined for every pair of entities. RFC2407 defines Domain of Interpretation (DOI), stating how the SAs are negotiated.

IPSec is *not* a panacea for security, despite its many potential advantages. Issues include the definition and management of the Security Policy Database (SPD), as well as transparency to other protocols. Faulty assumptions about key management can weaken the security. These key-management issues are important to the overall success of IPSec deployment. The cryptographic security described by an X.509 v3 certificate assumes that appropriate safeguards protect the private keys. Very serious security breaches could occur if private keys were improperly distributed. Compliance with correct usage policies is one way to retain the benefits of the underlying technology, and the networking middleware can help ensure this compliance. For example, the networking middleware can provide certified key-management services that a security-naive use may depend upon.

A second area of concern is interoperability with existing protocols. The IPSec protocol is only transparent on an end-to-end basis, and even then it introduces data latency, or delay. Standard network protocols may not work because of these changes. Three types of protocols may experience a "meltdown effect for end users" [Kaufman99]. These are *externally-bound protocols* (HTTP, SMTP), *internally-active protocols* (SNMP, RFC1537), and *latency-intolerant protocols* (VoIP). In general, a protocol that requires data "in the clear" may be adversely affected. An infrastructure platform should retain the functionality of the existing protocols, while including the security protections of IPSec.

To summarize IPSec, its advantages include:

- IP packet based authentication of source and destination as a simplex (unidirectional) flow
- Resistance to tampering, such as the insertion of extra packets into traffic, or modification of in-transit packets. This is detected and prevented on the IP layer. It impedes "cyberattacks" such as spoofing, flooding, or denial-of-service. For example, an attacker cannot insert a reset into the TCP stream by setting the TCP RST flag
- Connection-less IP packet integrity. Each packet is endorsed with an Integrity Check Value, thus authenticating the content as non-tampered
- Optional IP packet based confidentiality (encryption) when enabled packets are encrypted independently. This independence is important because the correctness of an IP connection is unaffected by out-of-sequence receipt at the end point. It also provides confidentiality for both connection oriented and connection-less protocols
- Protection against repays due partial sequence integrity
- Partial traffic flow confidentiality in tunnel mode. The address of the originator and final destination are hidden inside the inner encrypted IP header. The address of the security gateway is still exposed, as this value is needed by the IP routing network

Networking infrastructure can leverage certain advantages with particular strength, including:

- The Security Association (SA) is based upon user authentication at the IP level. The authenticated user is identified by the security provider index (SPI) inserted in the IP packet. This provides a significant advantage over the "traditional" use of the IP address and port as a client identifier

Consequently,

- It resists forgery
- It supports mobility, as one user may use multiple source IP addresses, and these can change dynamically

There are also disadvantages, including:

- To enforce access policy, IPSec authentication security option must be enabled
- There is a cost in bandwidth, as well as a computational cost in establishing the sessions

Much like IPv6, IPSec is quickly becoming the solution for the lack of privacy and data integrity of IP. Unlike IPv6, however, IPSec is already in general use on the Internet, and many vendors already have IPSec incorporated in their products.

2.8 Common Object Request Broker Architecture

Today's enterprise and carrier software system are complex, heterogeneous, distributed systems of communicating components. In many cases, these components do not interoperate effectively given that their integration consists of *ad hoc* or proprietary interfaces. This results in high maintenance costs and creates limited ability to evolve with new technology. It also results in redundant data, multiple conversions of data and *ad hoc* transfers, as well as redundant software functionality. Ultimately, this leads to an unnecessary increase in the overall system complexity.

It is for these reasons that an infrastructure called the Common Object Request Broker Architecture (CORBA) was developed for supporting systems integration. CORBA is an industry standard developed by the Object Management Group (OMG), the world's largest software consortium. It is also supported by X/Open, the Open Software Foundation (OSF), the Common Open Software Environment (COSE), CI Labs, and X/Consortium among some others.

CORBA provides a uniform layer encapsulating other forms of distributed computing and integration mechanisms. As a communication infrastructure, CORBA acts as an application layer interface that insulates the applications from the lower layer protocols, operating system issues, the server hardware, or language details.

CORBA is object oriented. Its encapsulation of system components presents all the components as objects that can be easily interconnected. This interconnection is facilitated by a wrapper around the component, so to speak, generated from the component's interface specification written in a common Interface Definition Language (IDL). The IDL specifications can be compiled into the language specific stubs to support components written in programming languages such as C, C++, or the Java environment.

The actual communication between the components (i.e., objects), is facilitated by the Object Request Broker (ORB). An ORB transparently relays the requests between the objects and handles the dynamic nature of object creation and event notification.

2.9 Virtual Private Networks

For some time, large companies that required networked connectivity for their employees operated their own LANs interconnected by private leased lines. This offered some benefits: control over their own equipment and operations, an argument similar to the use of PBX vs. Centrex; and guaranteed security given that the networks were isolated from public networks, or if connected, were well controlled by a few well-secured edge gateway systems. The commercialization of the Internet, which created a low-cost public-network for a large customer base, also highlighted some problems with VPNs: the cost of leasing external lines, lack of global customer reach, and the high cost of offering access to employees led to rethinking how to deploy and operate enterprise networks. The notion arose of deploying a secure and private network over a public network using virtual connections.

VPNs have arisen as the solution to address the cost and security needs of enterprise networks. It is estimated that by year 2002, VPN business will reach $10 billion. This comes from the estimate that over 73% of Fortune 1000 companies will move away from private networks and deploy VPNs. A company that switches from leasing lines to a VPN solution can reduce its operational cost by 60%. VPNs offer a one-time investment in systems that enable branch offices to interconnect over public networks, while their employees attain remote access via low-cost ISPs. Outsourcing remote access also leads to greater global visibility and the easier reach by customers. Of course, this all occurs while corporate privacy is maintained, local resources are hidden, and corporate networked data is protected.

Under a more detailed analysis, VPNs may provide a number of different features that collectively support the lower cost and high security requirements.

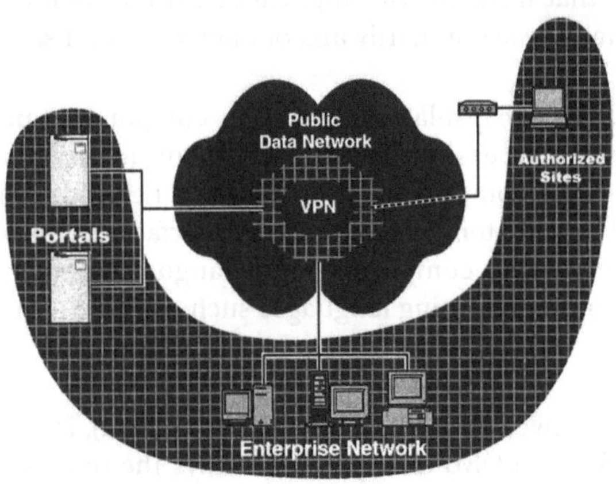

Figure 2-11: Enterprise VPN Combining Best Public and Private Networks

- *User authentication and authorization.* Remote users need to authenticate and attain access to only authorized information
- *IP addresses and hostname protection.* Local IP addresses and host names should be hidden and protected from inspection; NAT along with DHCP should be used to reduce the need for class A or B domains and a large number of dedicated IP addresses
- *Data privacy and integrity.* The flow of data between the branch office or to the employee should maintain privacy and integrity
- *Key and certificate management*: Session keys and certificates should be centrally managed
- *Multi-protocol support.* general packet tunnels should allow all IP traffic to move between the VPN users and remote sites
- *VPN management.* The system components should be easily managed and monitored as well as offering various levels of self-provisioning
- *QoS Control.* The VPN system should offer control over QoS parameters for managing performance for various levels of services
- *Combined data, voice, and video.* Besides data traffic, the VPN should also allow for secure voice and video collaborative and interactive communication as well
- *Intrusion detection and active monitoring.* The overall system should be aware of breaches in its security and offer alerts both for external intrusion as well as internal compromise from employees
- *Reliability, availability, and serviceability.* Above all, the systems should be reliable, highly available, and easily serviceable

VPNs are made up of varying collections of components and policies that collectively support the above features. They are usually composed of firewall, encryption, tunneling, proxy servers, authentication, access control, certificate authorities, monitoring, and management components. Figure 2-12 illustrates a typical VPN solution showing the relationship between these technologies:

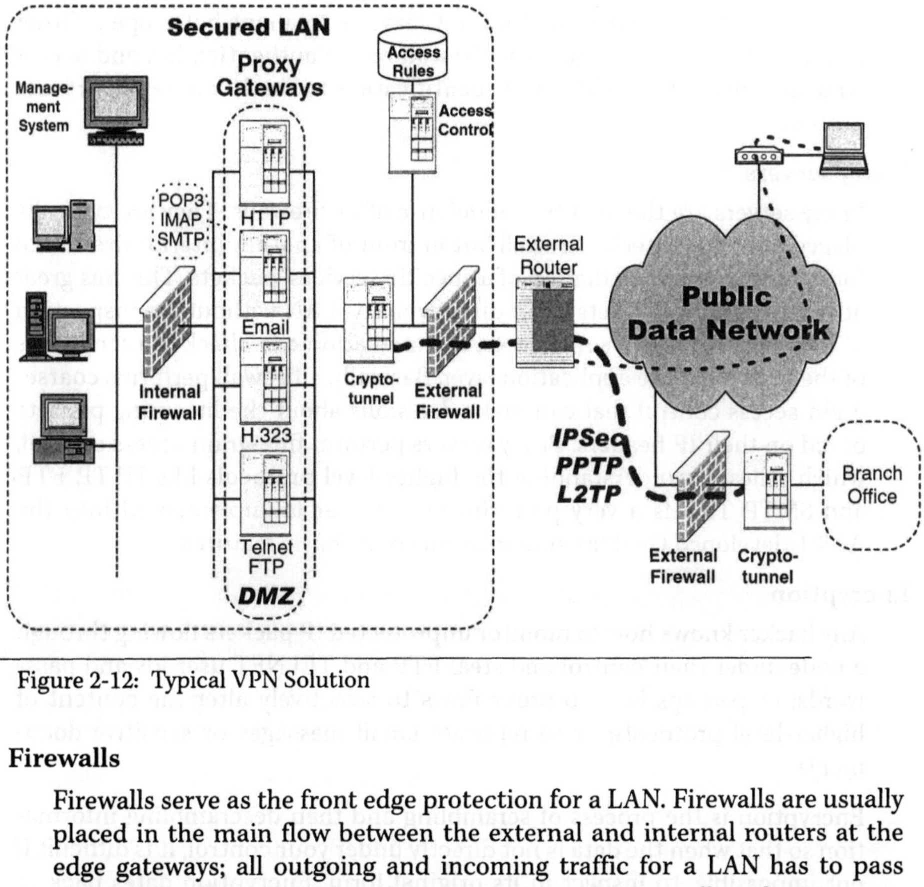

Figure 2-12: Typical VPN Solution

Firewalls

Firewalls serve as the front edge protection for a LAN. Firewalls are usually placed in the main flow between the external and internal routers at the edge gateways; all outgoing and incoming traffic for a LAN has to pass through the firewall. Although some perceive the firewall as the key component of a VPN, unless they are properly placed and combined with other VPN technologies and properly configured, they by themselves do not serve much use. Consider a firewall that protects a LAN with a mail server; if SMTP packets are allowed to enter and passed to an incorrectly configured or buggy sendmail server, the firewall does nothing to prevent the server from being abused as a SPAM relay by an external attacker. There are many examples of buffer overflow problems in daemons running under root ownership that allow an attacker to trivially enter through a firewall and take over all the functions of a system. Nevertheless, packet filter firewalls and filtering routes can be a powerful tool for controlling the inflow and outflow of packets. Firewalls are typically controlled by packet rules based on the source and destination IP addresses, ports, and protocols. The early firewalls were statically provisioned and an administrator had to manually tweak the rules to allow new services. New firewalls can be programmed dynamically through programmable interfaces based on the active state of services. For instance, some services such as FTP open multiple temporary TCP and UDP connections. These firewalls understand the semantics of the services and do not leave permanent holes open. Other recent features involve tying the firewall to the authentication and access control systems that add a user identification to the IP address, port and protocol.

Proxy servers

Proxy servers are the next line of defense after firewalls. They are typically placed after the exterior firewall but in front of another interior firewall to form a transparent mediation of a specific services' packets. This has great advantages as no packets enter directly in the LAN without the inspection of the proxy server. In some cases, the mediation can check the semantics of the packets at the application layer. Basically, a firewall performs coarse-grain access control that can make decisions about the incoming packets based on their IP headers. Proxy servers perform fine-grain access control, which relies on understanding the higher-level protocols like HTTP, FTP, and SMTP. This is a very powerful notion that is implemented into the AT&T-developed GeoPlex system as one of its basic features.

Encryption

Any hacker knows how to monitor unprotected IP packets flowing through a node under their control and steal FTP and TELNET user ids and passwords; or perhaps how to proxy flows to selectively alter the content of higher-level protocols; or to replicate email messages or sensitive documents.

Encryption is the process of scrambling and then descrambling information so that when the data is not directly under your control, it is difficult if not impossible, to inspect in its original form. Encryption dates back at least to ancient Egypt, and was used for military purposes by the Roman empire with the famous – though simplistic by today's standards – Ceasar cipher.

One problem with cryptography is that both the sending and the receiving parties have to share or posses some common secrets, or keys, that can used to lock and unlock the encryption process. Exactly what the keys are, how they are generated, exchanged, and used depends on the specific algorithm. The well-known algorithms are DES, 3DES, RSA, RC2 and RC4. Depending on where these are used systems like PGP, SSL, and IPSec utilize them to manage the encryption process. For instance, IPSec can be used to encrypt and tunnel all traffic over the public networks between the edges of the LANs. Many vendors such as Cisco, Cosine Communication, and Cylink offer IPSec for this purpose in their equipment.

Tunneling

Two or more LANs can be interconnected by tunnels to create private networks; these include Point-to-point Tunneling Protocol (PPTP), Layer 2 Tunneling Protocol (L2TP), and IPSec. Tunnels can be set up between two hosts or between two tunnel servers. With a tunnel, all packets entering the tunnel are encapsulated with a new IP destination of the terminating host and sent over a single connection. In VPNs, the tunnels are then bracketed by crypto relays that take the encapsulated packets of the tunnel and encrypt the payload.

Authentication and access control

Entry into a secured network through RAS or over a tunnel from a public network is usually proceeded by an authentication phase. Authentication verifies the user's identity, validates membership rights and supports the synchronization of session properties including encryption keys, data tunnels, and QoS characteristics. This phase also establishes the access rights and may enable access to services by reprogramming the external firewall. While user ID and password may seem sufficient to authenticate, this is the weakest and the least desirable form of authentication. Strong bilateral authentication is desired when the identity of both parties needs to be mutually verified; the user authenticates to the VPN and the VPN authenticates to the user. This is typically done by certificates and a secret that only the user holds locked away on his or her PC or on a smart card. There are also more sophisticated challenge-and-response systems by which a pseudo-random challenge is presented - different every time - that the user has to answer based on some algorithm under the user's control.

Certificate Authorities

The use of certificates presupposes the existence of a trusted authority that can be used to verify the authenticity and validity of a certificate. Without the use of well publicized public certificate authorities, individual certificates are only as good as the trust in the individual people or organizations that signed them. VPNs can utilize CAs to perform this service, especially where VPNs have to interoperate with partners and a large customer base.

Monitoring and management Systems

For large VPNs, the easiest way to operate a VPN is to locate all the VPN equipment in a single control root and hire administrators to manually provision and manage its operations. In most VPNs, it is more appropriate to allow self-administration by managers given a well defined hierarchical control structure. Combined with the ability to globally monitor the usage and the performance of the VPNs, VPN monitoring and management systems become an important integral component of the overall VPN.

The benefits of VPNs are clear and well received. Unfortunately, the need for VPNs is much like the need for QoS. In the case of QoS, it is the realities of limited bandwidth. Seifert's law of networking states that

No one needs a QoS guarantee when they have enough bandwidth.

Similarly, no one needs VPNs if the networks are secure and the hosts have operating systems that embed security features. This however, places the burden on the "dumb" networks and weak operations support systems (OSS) to address these issues by growing in intelligence and sophistication. As we discussed in the previous sections, IPv6 and IPSec are addressing parts of these issues, but that still leaves the need for more intelligence in the networks.

VPNs by themselves do not offer a complete solution and have their own set of problems. Without standards like IPSec and with national security export restrictions, deploying a proprietary security VPN solution in an international arena, as is the requirement for large multinational corporations, shows VPN in a greatly reduced effectiveness. Even if this is resolved, today's practice of frequent acquisition of companies and corporate mergers commands Interoperability between two incompatible VPN technologies. This frequently causes the less expensive VPN to fold and for the more expensive VPN to absorb the role of the other. On the management side, VPNs have a potentially major drawback that arises from the loss of control; some ISPs may offer unreliable connectivity and inconsistent throughputs due to factors such as over-subscribing their access networks.

2.10 Quality of Service

Perhaps the greatest growing pains for the Internet have centered around the issues of preferential service and resource allocation given limited bandwidth. The Internet predecessor, Arpanet, operated on a "best-effort" packet delivery mechanism that is for the most part the basis of today's Internet. Ironically, the operational and economic simplicity of this mechanism which has contributed to the Internet's success is now hindering the wide deployment and acceptance of new services.

Limited bandwidth and resources is a given. No matter how much the backbone is built out, it always seems to fill up. This causes congestion which results in delays and dropped datagrams. This becomes evident in very slow Web surfing; it is most evident in delay-sensitive applications such as IP telephony, video conferencing and multiplayer online gaming. These require isochronous delivery to obtain low-delay, low-jitter reception. The transport systems are called upon to support diverse application-centric traffic characteristics, and yet these characteristics vary without clear definition.

In general, quality-of-service (QoS) refers to the performance characteristics of a network. Packet traffic can be characterized at the routers and switches in terms of several attributes: transmission rates, error rates, variations in delay, average delay, priorities, data types, etc. The deployment of QoS systems can be defined as a way of measuring and affecting network traffic characteristics in order to allocate network resources (so packets can be delivered consistently and predictably).

One approach taken by large corporations is to utilize private data networks with ample bandwidth and resources to maintain low utilization. Low utilization offers ideal network performance for networked applications. This is called "over-engineering". This is of course an over simplification of the problem; nevertheless, over-engineering is a feasible solution if cost and global accessibility are not issues.

Most LANs are over engineered and do not employ any QoS support. Local hosts can communicate over a LAN with a very high level of QoS. Industry trends indicate that emerging higher capacity network components are being offered at continually lower costs and that will continue to make over engineering of LANs a viable solution for QoS over LANs. Within the public Internet, experience has shown that any bandwidth gets saturated quickly. There, over-engineering is a less successful practice; so employing QoS becomes a viable alternative.

The deployment of QoS deals with the management of bandwidth capacity and the available resources at the routers and switches. Deploying QoS systems cannot create more bandwidth or resources, but it can manage it intelligently. This requires a complete end-to-end support from one host, through all the network nodes, to the other host, that spans all the network layers up to the application layer. This requirement lies at the complete opposite of the original "best-effort", loosely coupled paradigm of the original Internet, and balances out the original notion of a dumb network with smart end-points. QoS techniques include traffic control policies such as bandwidth management through admission, shaping, and resource reservation. These complement the engineering of links and switch functionality, as well as capacity management.

Besides over-engineering, QoS architectures are evolving around the notions of reserving resources for specific flows and prioritizing traffic into classes, both supported by IETF.

Resource Reservation (IntServ)

Integrated Services (IntServ) refers to the extension of the Internet service model to handle packet switching protocols for transporting audio, video, and data traffic. Here, network resources are seen as a robust, integrated-service communications infrastructure in which applications can reserve resources at different levels of service for different users

IntServ requires that the network elements manage some state information for individual flows, communicate the flows' application requirements, and convey QoS management information. The communication is done with a signalling protocol for reserving resources called the Resource ReSerVation Protocol (RSVP). RSVP is a control protocol that conceptually establishes a path for the flow and sets up a communication circuit for the network elements to negotiate QoS resources. This requires the deployment of a complex mechanism that diverges from the simple "best-effort" model of IP networks and which requires major changes in the routers and switches; this also requires a fair amount of network middleware to support the policy management and state information

Traffic Prioritization (DiffServ)

Here, the notion is that applications can classify network traffic by labeling each packet (via the TOS octet of IPv4, or Traffic Class octet of IPv6) with a class of service tags; and network resources can be apportioned according to bandwidth policy managed by a given network. Thus the single, best-effort delivery service, is partitioned into differentiated classes of services. Unlike IntServ which micromanages the network resources for each flow and requires signalling to every hop, DiffServ is a reservation*less* method that instead macromanages the classes of services. This is similar to multi-lane freeways with slower moving traffic in the right lane, faster moving traffic in the left lane, and privileged traffic in the commuter lane

DiffServ pushes the policy management to the edge of the network where all policy decisions and packet tagging takes place. Policy decisions and their implementations are left to each individual network that the flows traverse. Each network core then handles only the problem of quickly forwarding the packets based solely on the tags inserted at the ingress and removed at the egress of the network

DiffServ and IntServ are complementary to each other. Each can be used independently, or they may combine to offer end-to-end QoS. While IntServ provisions network resources for each flow, DiffServ simply marks and prioritizes flows at the edges. Due to its increased complexity and fidelity, IntServ is more appropriate for LANs and corporate networks, where DiffServ, with its simplicity and ability to differentiate between flows of different classes, is better suited for the backbone.

Service providers negotiate QoS performances with their customers through Service Level Agreements (SLA). SLAs are contracts that define the service providers' responsibilities in terms of network levels and times of availability, methods of measurement, as well as consequences if the service levels are not met or the defined traffic levels are exceeded by the customer, and the costs.

In DiffServ architecture, service providers can offer each customer a range of network services that are differentiated on the basis of performance in addition to past pricing. These services are monitored for fairness and in meeting the SLAs. To do this, the edge routers implement traffic-conditioning functions that ensure the traffic entering a DiffServ network conforms to Traffic Conditioning Agreements (TCA). These functions perform metering, shaping, policing, and marking of the packets.

Metering

The metering function monitors traffic pattern of each flow and checks this against the traffic profile. Flows that fall outside the profile are either re-tagged or dropped

Marking

This function uses the performance level requested for a given packet as indicated by the DS field to classify and tag the packet for transmission over the DiffServ network

Policing

The traffic entering the DiffServ network is classified into aggregates that are policed according to the TCA. This function operates at the network ingress and polices the aggregates

Shaping

The relative forwarding rates of each aggregate can be adjusted so that the flows do not exceed the rates specified in the profiles. The shaping function ensures fairness between flows and guards against congestion

All of this depends on the ability of the networks to enforce, police, and administer consistent policy information among the managed network elements. This requires protocols for distributing the policy information such as LDAP, the Common Open Policy Service (COPS), SNMP or CLI over TELNET. It also requires policy repositories. One initiative for this purpose is the Directory Enabled Network (DEN). The DEN initiative is an effort to build intelligent networks and networked applications that can associate users and applications to services available from the network according to a consistent and rational set of policies.

With RSVP playing the role of resource reservation, the Real-time Transport Protocol (RTP) is the Internet-standard protocol for the transport of real-time data, audio, and video. RTP is a transport layer protocol riding on top of the User Data Protocol (UDP) which includes timestamp and synchronization information in the header. Although RTP is a transport layer protocol, unlike TCP, it does not offer any form of reliability or a protocol-defined flow/congestion control. RTP's control counterpart is the Real-Time Control Protocol (RTCP) which is used to exchange congestion information between network nodes and the hosts, and synchronization. In general, RTP is a stateless protocol and can be used over most packet networks; furthermore, most routers cannot distinguish RTP packets from other UDP packets. Note, that although it is called a real-time protocol, no end-to-end transport or application protocol can guarantee real-time delivery. That can be guaranteed only by the lower layers that are tightly integrated and in full control of the network hardware components.

What is driving the QoS development is the recognition of the need for bandwidth management and the tremendous business opportunities of turning the "best-effort" service into differentiated services. With QoS support in place, real-time services including audio and video, as well as data services will be offered over the same IP networks in support of new consumer and business services. However, enabling this QoS capability requires profound changes to the network fabric. Much of this fabric requires the a network middleware layer as an interface between higher-level services, and lower-level networks. Indeed, the middleware layer decouples the "what' of QoS from the "how" of QoS.

2.11 IP Telephony and Voice over IP

Interactive voice applications using IP networks have been around only since 1995. Yet already, this development has led to a broad range of IP telephony supporting communication between two PCs, between PCs and standard telephones, and between two telephones on the PSTN[1] bridged by an IP backbone. Carrying voice over pure data networks (unlike ATM), that use best-effort delivery under limited bandwidth and with little to no QoS control is very hard; unless of course the speakers do not mind what is called "the CB-radio to the moon" quality. Using digital packet backbone for telephony is not the issue here, as that is already the standard in the long-distance PSTN. The issue is the general voice application that can support all types of integrated services over IP networks. Probe Research estimated that by the year 2005, global voice/fax traffic over IP networks will amount to close to 90 billion minutes.

To leverage the lower costs of IP for long distance telephony, AT&T provides a service called the AT&T Global Clearinghouse. This is a financial settlement system that brokers the rates, billing and settlement to partners and call administration. For two ISPs to handle each other's IP telephony traffic, they have to have a bilateral agreement and then build connections between their POPs. Currently there are thousands of international LECs, and hundreds of IXCs, each offering different pricing. It is not possible for each LEC to form an agreement with all the IXCs and ISPs. The clearing house is a broker that establishes these relationships and then buys and sells the lowest-cost minutes to LECs. Thus, the call that leaves the LATA is dynamically routed through the global clearinghouse to the cheapest carrier. In many cases, the voice traffic originates and terminates in a LEC but may travel over private IP networks.

1. These are commonly referred to as the Class A, B or C telephony, where Class A is the PC to PC telephony.

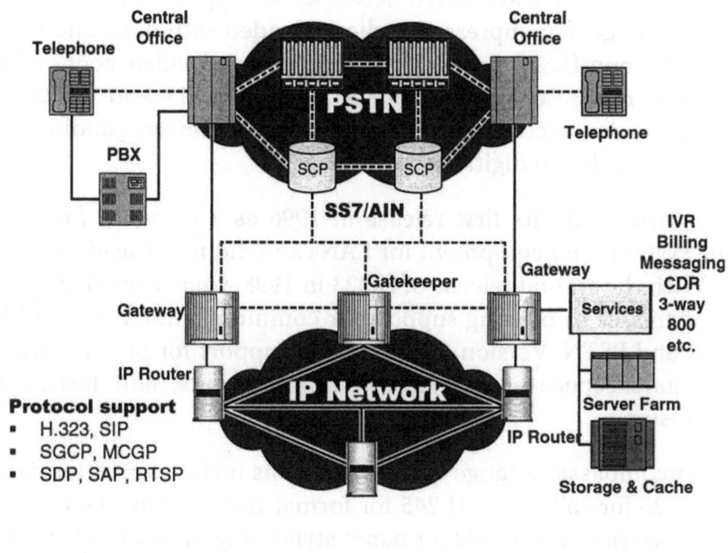

Figure 2-13: IP Telephony Components

ISPs and telephone companies which specifically support IP telephony and offer VoIP services are called Internet Telephony Service Provider (ITSP). ITSPs offer application software for PCs to place calls as well as access to the PSTN through specialized gateways that bridge the PSTN and the Internet. The current appeal of ITSPs to consumers is in the lower cost of placing long distance calls; this is due primarily to the ITSP's ability to bypass regulatory regimes and tariff structures, such as telephone access charges, imposed on carriers. The appeal for ITSP is that the declining margins for simple Internet access offered by ISPs can now be supplemented with profitable value-added services that leverage the best of the IN/AIN in the PSTN and the Internet.

There is already a move to offer smart phones and next-generation cell phones that offer IP-based PDA functionality. Through these, the telephony experience can be dramatically enhanced by changing the fundamental ways that users communicate over telephones. However, IP telephony already is having major impact on how existing communication-dependent systems operate; systems like call centers and customer support centers. Its use is paramount to applications such as multimedia conferencing, multicast, collaborative workgroup applications and unified messaging. Estimates for IP voice and fax services are close to 14 billion dollars by 2005. Figure 2-13 shows a simplified IP telephony arrangement that can be embedded on existing infrastructure.

IP Telephony revolves around two key, somewhat competing protocols, H.323 and SIP.

H.323

H.323 is an ITU standard for real-time multimedia communications (video conferencing) for packet-based networks. It supports call setup, the combined exchange of compressed audio and video with data, and interoperability with non-H.323 hosts. It specifies several video codecs including H.261 and H.263, and audio codecs such as G.711 and G.723. A codec (meaning coder/decoder) is a component that converts audio, speech, or video from analog to digital or vice-versa

H.323 started with its first release in 1996 as a standard for visual telephone systems and equipment for LANs and did not provide any QoS support. With the second release of H.323 in 1998, voice-over-IP requirements were addresses by offering support for communication between PC-based phones and PSTN. Version 3 will include support for fax-over-packet networks, gatekeeper-to-gatekeeper communications, and fast-connection mechanisms

H.323 encompasses a range of protocols; this includes RTP for data transport, H.225 for call setup, H.245 for format negotiation, H.450 for supplementary services and H.332 for panel-style conferences. H.323 itself is part of a H.32*x* family of recommendations specified by ITU-T which include specification for multimedia communication services over different networks. This includes:

- H.320 over ISDN
- H.321 and H.310 over Broadband ISDN (B-ISDN)
- H.322 over LANs with guaranteed QoS
- H.324 over PSTN

H.323 interoperates with these other networks through the use of gateways. These gateways perform any network or signalling translation required for interoperability

SIP

The Session Initiation Protocol (SIP) is a simple, light-weight, signalling protocol for creating, modifying, and terminating multimedia conferences, IP telephony, and multimedia distribution sessions between participants. It communicates with either a mesh of unicast connections or via multicast. It also support registration and the location of users, allowing for mobility and proxies

SIP is a text-based protocol based similar to HTTP that uses MIME in the messages. It is the result of an IETF working group that considered various proposals in 1996. The group's main objectives in developing SIP were to strive for simplicity, to rely on other existing IP protocols, and to integrate with other IP applications.

In summary, H.323 and SIP are competing standards that vary in many respects and do not necessarily address the same problem sets. Unlike H.323, SIP is highly extensible. H.323 is a stateful system that requires servers to keep call states for the duration of the call; SIP is stateless. H.323's architecture is very monolithic based on the H.323 family and related components; SIP is very modular. That is, while H.323 encompasses all aspects of the technology, SIP encompasses only a small basic set relying on other protocols for QoS, directory access, service discovery, and session content description. In general, while H.323 is highly inclusive, SIP is relatively simple, based loosely on HTTP, including URL addressing and relying on other IP protocols for support of the remaining functionality included in H.323. These differences came out of the philosophies of the two groups, the ITU and the IETF that support the two standards. While ITU pursues a sophisticated H.323, IETF strives for the simplicity with SIPs.

2.12 *Unified Messaging*

For most businesses and individuals, there are a few standard tools for distant communication. These center around the phone system, voice mail, email, and fax. The mid-1990s brought "store and forward" messaging services such as email and voice mail. More recently a new breed of real-time messaging services such as instant messaging and alerting/notification, became available. These solutions combined the common communication services in a single system, known as unified messaging.

Unified messaging creates a common repository for voice, email and fax messages, offers instant messaging, and provides a variety of access methods through phones, email clients, Web browsers and PDAs. This repository stores messages on behalf of users in private mailboxes that can be organized into folders and which can be further associated with various filters and rules. These mailboxes support the standard Internet messaging protocols such as Simple Mail Transfer Protocol (SMTP), Internet Messaging Access Protocol (IMAP), Post Office Protocol (POP), and Multipurpose Internet mail Extensions (MIME).

Some systems allow users to check voice mail, email and faxes by dialing a single number, including a personal 1-800 number, have email read to them over the phone, and finally administer their messages remotely. New types of systems, better known as personal assistants, also utilize speech recognition to offer a simple voice interface to the user's mailboxes. These system can also dial outgoing calls, announce callers, remember important numbers, and organize the messages through voice commands.

Instant messaging refers to the system's ability to notify users of messaging events through a number of end-user devices such as pagers, phones, email or PC-based notification clients. Users and system administrators can customize the system's triggering mechanisms by adding rules. These rules, personalized for each user, understand the source of the events and the delivery mechanisms. Messages can be delivered to text-based pagers or read to the user using text-to-speech support.

Unified messaging has a wide appeal to mobile users who spend a large part of their time away from their office. It also appeals to SOHO users that do not have the financial and technical means to deploy well supported multiple solution systems and phone-based solution. Instead these users can subscribe with unified-messaging service providers at a low cost.

2.13 Electronic Commerce

Even before the Internet was commercialized in 1995, Electronic Commerce (eCommerce) was a major driving force for conducting business online.

> *"In 1886, a telegraph operator was able to obtain a shipment of watches that was refused by the local jeweler. Using the telegraph, he sold all the watches to fellow operators and railroad employees. Within a few months, he made enough money to quit his job and start his own store. The young man's name was Richard Sears, and his company later became Sears, Roebuck."*[1]

Today, many may perceive electronic commerce as simply buying and selling products and services over the Internet. It is more. Electronic commerce spans the full spectrum of online business, from the handling of purchase transactions to transferring funds. It deals with both revenue generation and its support. This includes the means for generating demand for goods and services, offering sales support and customer service, or facilitating communications between business partners.

Early eCommerce facilitated transactions between large corporations, banks, and other financial institutions. It has been around for over two decades, in the form of Electronic data interchange (EDI) and email or FTP over value-added networks (VAN). VANs are private networks provisioned to support customized services such as Electronic Funds Transfer (EFT).

The focus today, is on moving eCommerce away from VANs and towards the Internet, resolving the obvious limiting problems or reliability, scalability, and security. The Internet brings eCommerce to the consumers. In this matter, eCommerce is changing business in much the same way that the Web changed publishing and the dissemination of information.

1. Obtained from the Tech Encyclopedia at http://www.techweb.com/encyclopedia.

The combination of the Web and the nature of the Internet is a strong motivator for eCommerce. Their use nicely supports the required business processes of sharing information with the customers, ordering goods and services, receiving payment, fulfilling the order and managing customer relationship through services and support. The Web has created an unprecedented medium for businesses to bring advertising and marketing information to consumers. The standard protocols and data formats, the rich multimedia presentation and the easy programmability of GUIs supported by Web browsers offer the ideal platform for presenting catalogs, information, FAQs, customer support, and technical support. The Web browser is the customer's electronic portal to the online business, while the server support through CGI, servelets, Email, and database backends offer businesses new opportunities to serve their customers.

This technology is removing certain physical constraints in doing business, in that online shops offer detailed, up-to-date catalogs and a 24 hours a day, 7 days a week business. This includes customer support and technical assistance. It is also bringing new ways of doing business. Companies such as Amazon.com act as a store front for publishers selling books online, although they have no physical stores. From the technology perspective three new eCommerce technologies offer the greatest changes. These include *micropayments*, *software agents*, and *smart cards*.

Micropayments are partial transactions that allow for very small charges to be incurred without having to fully reconcile the transactions. This can be used for instance to charge for content, place calls, or use premium channel services. This requires some form of usage tracking that accumulates the transactions and an integrated billing system as part of the system's middleware. Software agents are programs that can perform acts on behalf of the users such as searching multiple catalogs to locate the desired product at the lowest price. Finally, smart cards are credit-card size plastic cards that have an embedded microprocessor and some storage capacity. These can hold a variety of business related information such as digital cash, user profiles, certificates, and purchase history. They can be used for authenticating the user to end-devices such as ATMs, PCs or telephones, as is already done in Europe.

The discussion on eCommerce, much like the discussion on unified messaging, is intended to elucidate reflection on the enabling infrastructure or lack of it. eCommerce and unified messaging are new classes of services that can without doubt be built on top of very dumb networks. But at what cost and with what lasting value? Doing so goes back to our discussion of building vertical smoke stacks in the Introduction. Are there any benefits to eCommerce or messaging systems running over the public networks if the networks are made secure? Are there any benefits if many of the operational subsystems can interoperate and exchange information between competing service providers?

2.14 Summary

The last decade of the 20th century will be described as the closing of the 1st generation of telecommunication and the beginning of the age of global communication. The transition will be seen as the convergence of many different technologies for supporting the instantaneous and high-fidelity communication by anyone, anywhere, using many different types of devices. The telephone itself will remain the most frequently used, ubiquitous device, but not without undergoing major changes in its sophistication and the offered services. In some ways, IP telephony is the "killer application" that is driving the convergence between the data and the switched networks.

The technologies exists today to achieve the new age. All the pieces are in place to move to ultra-high speed data networks in the backbone and broadband to the homes; to offer a new generation of highly functional integrated devices; to offer all human knowledge and information online; to converge the various network services. What is missing is the intelligence in data networks to support this transition.

This chapter demonstrated the most pertinent technologies and the common thread of either offering or requiring a common service infrastructure. Consider again the issues of security, quality of service, and electronic commerce. In all three, common problems exist and similar solutions such as the need for accounting, billing, authentication, and management emerged. It is this commonality that drives the designers and architects of the IP service platform; to enable a common infrastructure in the network to support these requirements.

PART II

IP Service Platform Fundamentals

This part presents an introduction to GeoPlex – a set of requirements, a set of principles, and a set of capabilities used for the IP platform design and architecture presented in Part III. The requirements are the high-level problem specifications obtained from carriers, Internet Service Providers, universities, and business enterprise networks. The principles are the guiding axioms that were identified by the design teams in helping to create the system designs and the overall architecture. While there can be a competing set of different principles each satisfying a collection of requirements, designating a set of basic principles establishes a framework for the design and logically leads to the final architecture. With the design principles in place, a set of capabilities is presented that support the full range of the requirements.

CHAPTER 3

Network-enabled and Online Services

The telecommunication industry is navigating its way through a maze of technological crossroads that will ultimately determine what kind of networks the world will use in the 21st century. In this journey, the industry has already passed several essential hurdles.

One was the movement from pure voice over PSTN towards voice over data networks. It is now clear that voice and video are just another data type that can be transmitted through packet networks. While no one is proposing that the PSTN be retired, it is no longer a surprise to observe voice, video, and data running over the same high-speed data network. Another crossroad dealt with is the protocol above the network layer used at the network edge. Here, the TCP/IP protocol suite has emerged as a winner over other protocols to offer end-to-end convergence of communication and computing.

One challenge that still remains is the definition of the exact nature of the network middleware for the development and delivery of network-enabled and online services and its architecture. Service providers should be able to create a new service leveraging both their own resources and the features offered by the network middleware. Many basic service functions that have classically been built as a vertical solution in a stand-alone and non-interoperable product should be outsourced to the network. To this end, there are great benefits in standardizing some of these common service functions and building them into the network middleware.

To pass this juncture, the approach taken by network providers and service operators has been to:

1. Differentiate between the service functions that belong to the *applications*, the *network middleware*, and the *network infrastructure*

2. Deploy *mandatory and guaranteed network services,* such as active user and service directory as opposed to voluntary services offered by users or corporations, such as hosting that the network must guarantee, and
3. Develop a standard and open service supporting network middleware that implements the set of agreed upon capabilities and exports appropriate interfaces on which services can be developed, deployed, and managed

In this chapter we take a closer look at these three issues dealing with development and delivery of network-enabled and online services. We describe the problems, the opportunities for a new solution, and the benefits of the solution to the users, the corporations, the information content and service providers, and the network operators.

As we indicated in the Introduction, there is a broader issue here dealing with how and where such a solution should be deployed. Although the incentive comes from the Internet, the focus is not on the Internet itself. The Internet is driven by free market forces that do not react well to the imposition of new and untried standards. This is a self-regulating protection mechanism that partially led to its current success. The focus should rightfully be on the restructuring of privately owned and managed service network such as they exist in carrier networks, university campuses, enterprise networks, ISPs and ASPs. These network islands are the hot spots where most of the Internet activity originates or terminates. These are the places that can be reengineered or that can be constructed in a green-field environment to comply with service platform standards. They are also the places that can demonstrate to the rest of the Internet the successes or failures of deploying the proposed solution.

Before proceeding, we clarify some common terms used throughout this text. For instance, we speak of services and platforms which are heavily overloaded terms in the industry. Unless we precisely define these terms confusion may result in applying the terms outside their intended context. The most important terms are application, service, and offer:

Application

An application is any computer tool and its supporting resources, data, and interfaces employed by users. Here we are concerned mainly with network-enabled applications. These can be either client tools or servers. An email client, a web browser, or a document server are examples of network-enabled applications.

Service

This refers to application services as opposed to network fabric services such as QoS or VPNs. A service is any bundled collection of *applications* that comprises a specific policy and that can be accessed by a single IP address, port number, and protocol; a service is a registered server application(s). Some examples of services include chat services, web hosting services, and electronic commerce services.

Offer

An offer is a *service* provided by ISPs and carriers consisting of a complete set of business services. This includes the supporting customer care and billing services. Examples include hosting and IP telephony offers.

The following terms refer to the implementation of services and offer:

Interface

An interface is a connection and interaction between hardware, software and users. Different types of interfaces exist between different kinds of components comprising the user interface between users and computers, application programming interfaces (APIs) between various software layers but primarily between applications and the underlying system, and communication interfaces between distributed systems dictated by specific protocols.

Protocol

A protocol comprises the rules for inter-component communication. It includes a syntax to format data, a semantics on coordination and error handling, as well as timing for control of sequence and speeds. Protocols operate over many layers. For example, IP is a link-layer communication protocol. NNTP, SMTP, CIFS, and HTTP are application-layer protocols.

Component

A component is an *application* providing specific functionality to a larger *system* or an *offer*. We also equate this term with essential services of a *platform* such as an email component.

Environment

An environment is a specification configuration for a collection of software or hardware.

System

A system is a collection of *components* that perform a certain task operating within a specific *environment*. A system's value is in its *capabilities* offered to the compliant applications and in insulating the *applications* from the underlying hardware and network components.

Capability

A capability refers to a specific feature of a *system*. A component of a system implements various capabilities offered by that system.

Middleware

Middleware here refers to a network operating *system* that supports *applications*. Middleware is seen as both the supporting *system* and the application programming interfaces (APIs) that provide functionality to the applications.

Platform

A platform is a *system* in the form of *middleware* bundled with essential *offers* and providing a development *environment* for developing new and integrating existing *services* and *applications.*

Trust

Trust is a *technical* word, one that is subject to varying definitions in specific contexts. Attempts to rigidly define "trust' will instead establish standards for security, and provide methods to evaluate these standards. For example, the *Trusted Computer Security Evaluation Criteria* (known as the "Orange Book") defines many different levels of trusted computer systems.

In general, trust indicates that the systems' administrators are willing to allow some kind of access, for example the sharing or alteration of information. The establishment of trust typically includes administrative permissions and leverages cryptographically secure methods. These methods can establish identities, and provide various secure services.

Non-repudiation

Non-repudiation establishes the unique source or entity to which an action is attributable. There is a distinction between technical non-repudiation and legal non-repudiation. Technical non-repudiation assumes the algorithms and systems work correctly; for example, the private key has not been compromised in an asymmetric-key cryptosystem. Legal non-repudiation supports these assumptions; for example to establish that no one else had the private key; this is an issue for Laws and Courts that this text does not venture into.

3.1 The Market for Online Services

The market for network-enabled and online services is large and fast growing; the demand for these services by businesses and consumers is seemingly insatiable. As well, the associated media attention has spawned tremendous industry interest, financial investment, and business opportunity.

Forecasts predict fast growth in every sub sector of network-enabled and online services: access, hosting, electronic commerce, and intelligent communications. Businesses look to the "online" market as a mechanism to either provide better value or expanded business reach. They expect that network-enabled and online services will increase top line revenue growth and/or lower bottom line costs and expenses.

- Cheaper distribution channels and methods, access to broader, global markets, and expanded services are mechanisms to achieve more revenue (as shown in Figure 3-1).

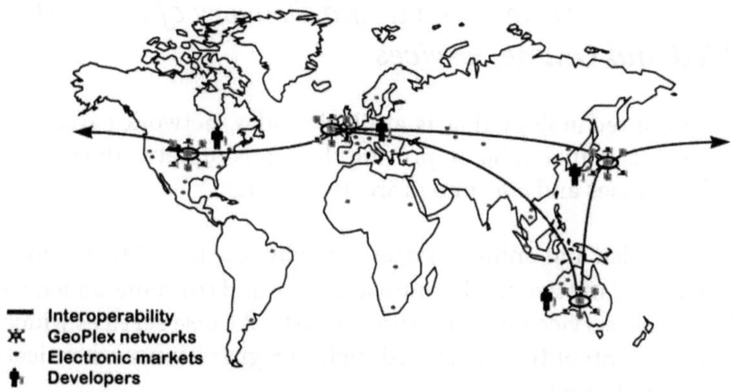

Figure 3-1: Building Global Markets

- Online product distribution, lower marketing costs and cheaper services are paths to better manage costs – both expenses as well as capital

Network-enabled and online services can be segmented into four sectors: access, hosting, electronic commerce, and intelligent communications.

- *Access* is defined as software, hardware, and services for the ability to connect to and then use any data space – typically the "Internet"
- *Hosting* is usually the capability to aggregate content and present it through a single venue. However, this content can be single, specialized services, or aggregated, broad consumer-oriented services such as America On Line (AOL) or Prodigy
- *Electronic Commerce* is defined as support of secure, transaction-oriented activities across networks such as electronic distribution, banking and finance capabilities; catalog sales, collaboration, software distribution, Cybercash, home-banking, electronic document interchange (EDI), electronic and fax mail, or work flow
- *Intelligent Communications* is the integrated (and intelligent) utilization of communications with and across other common information sources and devices (phone/voice, data, cellular, pagers, hand-helds, fax, etc.). From this base of PCs and telephony, the set-top "platform" becomes an easy extension. Examples include integrated multimedia phone, integrated wireless/cellular communications, personal digital assistants (PDA), pagers, conference linkages, translation services (language and data), and conversion services (voice-to-email, email-to-voice)

3.2 Issues with the Development and Delivery of Network-Enabled and Online Services

However, given the technology that is available today, network carriers and Content Providers are increasingly unable to provide the kinds of network-enabled and online services that businesses and consumers are demanding:

- Network-enabled and online services typically consist of (a) an underlying proprietary administrative service infrastructure and (b) value-added content. The administrative service infrastructure consists of those services which enable the value-added content to be delivered such as registration, authentication, customer care, or billing

  Currently, there is no available "off-the-shelf" administrative service infrastructure to run online services. This infrastructure has had to be developed– from scratch – for each new online service (as well as the existing content for the online service)

  Network carriers and Content Providers have found that the development of this administrative infrastructure dramatically increases the cost and significantly delays the delivery of the value-added content to businesses and consumers

  This approach, both incredibly expensive and time-consuming, may cause content providers to miss market windows (and lose any "first mover" advantages)

- Developed apart from telephone and digital video services provided by network carriers, most network-enabled and online services lack integration with the most fundamental network-enabled and online service – the consumer's telephone for voice and video services.

  Today's problems will become magnified as new data types such video, fax, expanded voice, and bandwidth-on-demand are added to the complexities of tomorrow

- Finally, even when developed, network-enabled and online services are typically not "carrier grade"; that is, designed for scaling to profitable volume. In most cases, this has proven to be very difficult as quality of service (predictable high performance with consistent reliability) deteriorates significantly when the number of consumers grows large

  Providing services to hundreds of thousands – even millions – of consumers around the world is a very complex and difficult task.

Today's solutions, given today's client-server technology architecture, is to over-provision. Often, addition of more machines requires more human resources as well. This cuts into operating profit and margins.

3.2.1 Implications of these Issues

These issues with the development and delivery of network-enabled and online services have had several implications for network carriers and consumers.

1. The result has been network-enabled and online services that, to date, have been unable to provide the value that businesses and consumers have wanted. Today's solutions are offered as individual, "point" solutions and have little "integration" capabilities such as the ability to technically interoperate or "semantically" link content with other solutions.

   From the Consumer's point of view, network-enabled and online services require additional telephone lines (when used extensively), have inconsistent performance, and lack satisfactory safety and security for electronic commerce. The services are sometimes difficult to install; for example, loading a new service may disrupt an existing service.

   With each having a separate, proprietary account registration process, the services are often difficult to learn. The services are standalone and non-interoperable; information from multiple services cannot be easily interconnected

2. Clearly, in spite of problems, these services are looked to by the market with great anticipation. Today, network carriers may already carry some portion of this content provider's network traffic. However, in many cases, this traffic fails to leverage the network carrier's primary assets – voice capabilities

   More importantly, these services are being conceived, delivered, and managed outside the partnership with the network carrier. This increasingly places the network carrier in the role of being a "tactical" provider of transport services and not as a strategic partner. Long term, network carriers could potentially lose their most valuable asset – their customer base

The resulting market is advancing at an uneven pace, sometimes racing faster than the technologies can follow, and other times proceeding unevenly, too slowly, and too expensively. Many problems still defy cost-effective solutions.

3.2.2 Network-Enabled and Online Services Architecture

To help solve these problems and enable network carriers and ASP's to become strategic providers, two areas must be reviewed: the current network architecture that is being used to deliver the network-enabled and online services as well as the future market requirements for these services.

Currently, the network architecture for delivering network-enabled and online services is client-server. Client-server features intelligent end points that communicate over a non-intelligent network (refer to Figure 3-2):

- The server endpoint provides the services with both the administrative service infrastructure as well the as service content. The infrastructure is the set of core

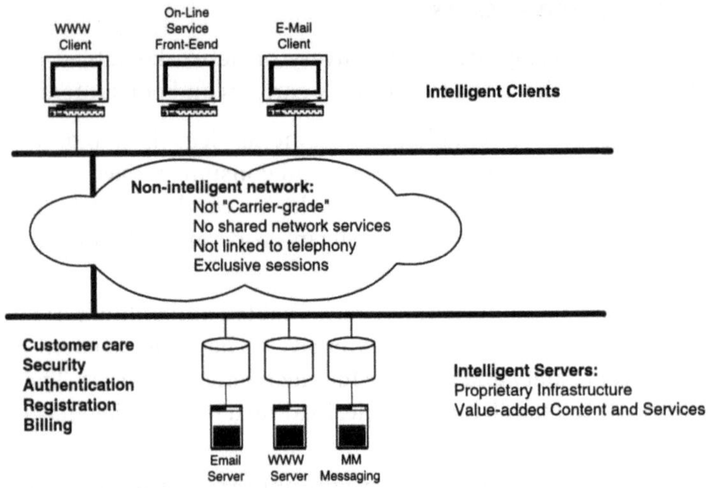

Figure 3-2: First Generation Architecture for Network-Enabled Services

administrative functions that enable the service content to be provided: registration, billing, security, authentication, tracking/reporting, customer care, network care, etc.

- Without the ability to leverage a commonly available, easily accessible, and reusable administrative service infrastructure, each content provider has had to develop its own proprietary set of core administrative functions. Content providers often reinvent their administrative infrastructure for each new application
- The client endpoint provides the user interface to access the service content; in most cases, the user interface is different from any other content provider's user interface
- The non-intelligent network simply transports messages to and from the servers and clients

Even if content providers could somehow overcome the above limitations, in the future these network-enabled and online content providers will face additional market requirements.

- First, the explosion in classes of services – data, video, fax, voice, bandwidth on demand, etc.– dramatically increases the technical complexity of reliably delivering network-enabled and online services to millions of consumers
- Second, the speed of market entry on a globally competitive basis will necessarily mean constant demands on lowering prices and increasing features
- Third, the growing base of experienced consumers will increase the sophistication of their expectations; consumers will be demanding capabilities that have not, as yet, been thought of

For content providers, the implications of these problems are also substantial. First, content providers who want to deliver new network-enabled and online services are finding that to build, install, and maintain a new service is expensive, time-consuming, and laborious:

- There is no available, off-the-shelf core infrastructure (registration, consolidated billing, security, authentication, tracking/reporting, customer care, network care, etc.) on which to build a new service and then make the service universally available
- These new services lack voice and data integration, worldwide availability, and integration with other services.

Second, with the number of subscribers growing quickly, "successful" new network-enabled and online services must quickly scale to increase coverage. Lacking the ability to scale automatically, the systems are manifest with technical problems such as: performance degradation, unpredictable response, and increased unreliability. Today's solution to scaling problems means adding more server machines: more people are needed to tend the machines. This erodes the profit margin.

3.2.3 The Opportunity for Network Carriers

For network carriers, against the economic backdrop of increased competition, deregulation, commoditized pricing, and the emergence of new forms of communications (packet-voice, satellite, cable, cellular), the implications of these problems are significant.

In many cases, network-enabled and online services are being delivered to consumers completely outside of the network carriers physical network. Increasing volumes of data traffic are residing outside the network carrier's domain; in the future, long-distance voice communication, through packet voice, will be achieved outside the network carrier as well.

When the network carrier's physical network is used, the client-server architecture reduces the network carrier to being a non value-added transport only. The network carrier's underlying physical network assets provide strategic advantage when integrating voice, data, and other sophisticated capabilities (as shown in Figure 3-3). This advantage should be leveraged to reduce the cost of Internetworking.

- First, since network carriers enjoy a "trusted service provider" relationship with businesses and consumers, network carriers are ideal partners for content providers
- Second, network carriers can provide voice, data, and other related sophisticated capabilities for content providers in a well understood, commonly accepted, standardized architecture

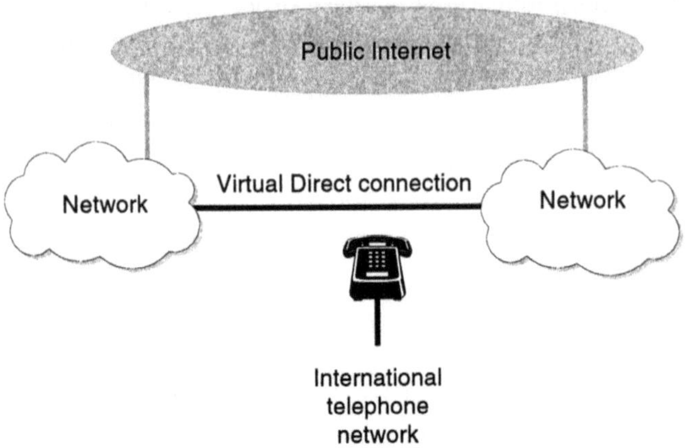

Figure 3-3: Merging the Internet and International Telephone Systems

- Third, network carriers have the capability to work with other global network carriers - around the world - to enable new services to be delivered globally. (This is analogous to network carriers originally pioneering integration and interoperability with other voice networks [such as US and Germany] through the development of the common signaling network)
- Lastly, network carriers have the engineering skill sets and talent pools, and understand the problems and complexities of global networking

3.3 A Solution: IP Service Platform

A solution we offer in this book is to take a complete approach of

Smart nodes coupled with smart networking.

The complete approach positions the network as performing necessary computational support for distributed and online applications. It should provide for multilateral security, scalable performance, and routine manageability. This requires a reengineered network that supports an IP service platform both in the network and at its edges (see Figure 3-4).

To distinguish existing networks that do not use this approach with those that are based on it, we will refer to networks with our approach as a *cloud*. From now on, when we refer to a cloud we are referring to

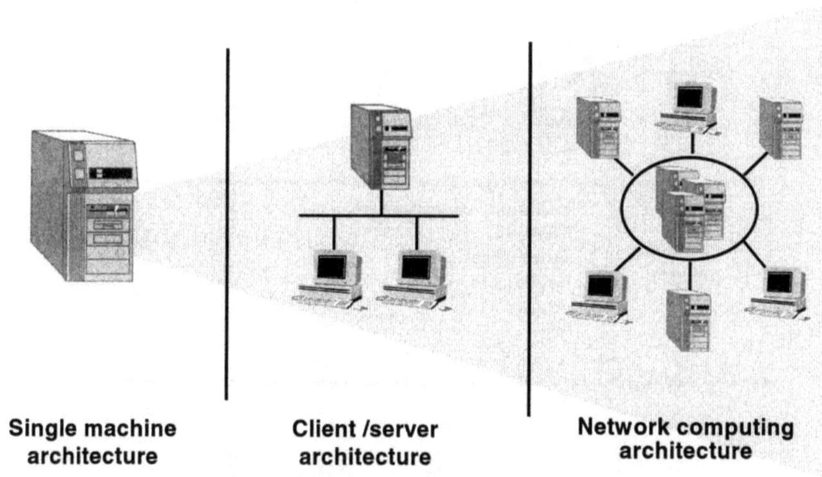

Figure 3-4: Reengineering of the Network-Computing Architecture

A network operating system and a network architecture that supports our proposed principles.

The next chapter outlines the requirements that the IP Service Platform must satisfy, and the principles we use for the design and implementation of our proposed architecture.

A cloud, as a concept, is the enabling software that provides a reusable, sharable intelligent "service" platform for network-enabled, online service applications. As software, its role is that of network middleware; it lives between the physical network topology and the associated online applications. In effect, it creates a "logical" network of services and capabilities living between the applications and the actual transport mechanisms (see Figure 3-5).

A cloud provides off-the-shelf, open components that make it is easy for a network carrier, as well as ISPs and ASPs, to build and operate a value-added digital network. The resulting network is based on standard protocols; is compatible with existing Internet application products; and is able to interoperate with other standard networks, including the International Telephone Network! Clouds can be linked together to handle any combination of network sizes and possible configurations, as we describe later.

Intelligent networks should offer a set of services which the online applications utilize as components. For example, a cloud should provide a commonly available, easily accessible, and reusable service infrastructure for all core administrative functions such as registration, consolidated billing, security, authentication, tracking/reporting,

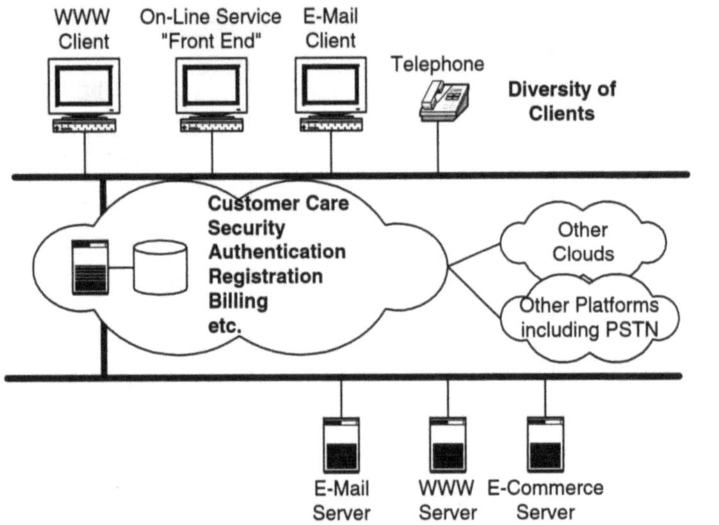

Figure 3-5: Distributed Online System

customer care, network care, and any other "services" which the service providers care to offer.

Instead of each content provider reinventing its own version of these services, the cloud offers the developer a set of consistent building blocks - reusable modules - that provide these services. Thus, the cloud speeds delivery of future applications to market.

The model of a smart network service platform - combined with the client-server model of smart end-nodes - provides the best solution for many of the complex problems facing online applications. These clouds can communicate with any other network - public (i.e., Internet) or private (companies) and share network information such as billing and other services.

Networking middleware is the foundation for true, global, online electronic commerce-based applications. Since a cloud can shield the applications from the physical aspects of the underlying networks, a cloud can begin to integrate different networks (topology and data types) and have them behave as a set of capabilities (as seen in Figure 3-6). In this way, intelligent communications with disparate devices can occur.

Obviously, off-the-shelf components make is easier for a network carrier to build and operate a value-added digital network. The resulting network is based on standard protocols; it is compatible with existing Internet application products; and its able to interoperate with other standard networks. A cloud can be bundled into product sets for a range of network sizes.

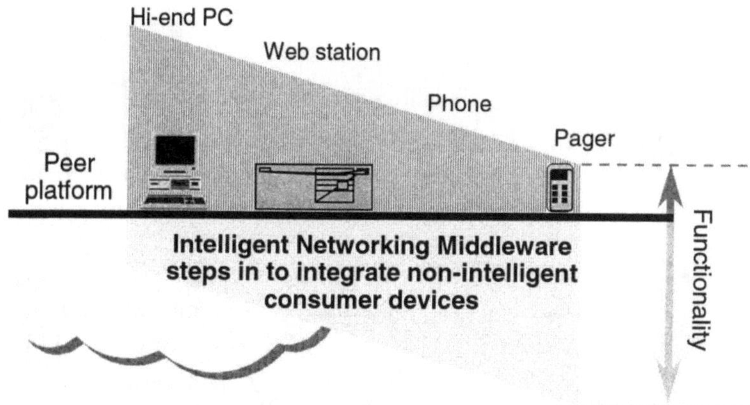

Figure 3-6: PCs to Phones – Middleware Networking Supports All Devices

Domains interconnect to form an economically viable global marketplace. Multiple network carriers can provide reconciliation, security, authentication, and billing information such that, to the consumer, there is seamless access across multiple domains.

End points

End points enable access, development, and deployment of network-enabled and online service applications on networks. Network end points are peers that connect content providers and consumers through clouds; and, provide a single point of access for all services (such as access, security, and billing) via a single dial-up or dedicated connection, giving consumers the ability to register, authenticate, and communicate in a secure fashion over these clouds.

Network Transport

The network transport components furnish the network and network-mediated services of a domain, and additionally provide the foundation for performance, security, scaling, management, and a range of value-added network features.

Network Services

Network services provide efficient, scalable services (e.g., directory, billing, customer-care, and naming services) and a host of network-provider and consumer visible services that create, maintain, or refer to information created and stored "in the network" (e.g., registration, directory, billing, parental control, and customer care).

To the consumer, this architecture pulls together – into a single account – all IP Service platform enabled-networks and online services (refer to Figure 3-7).

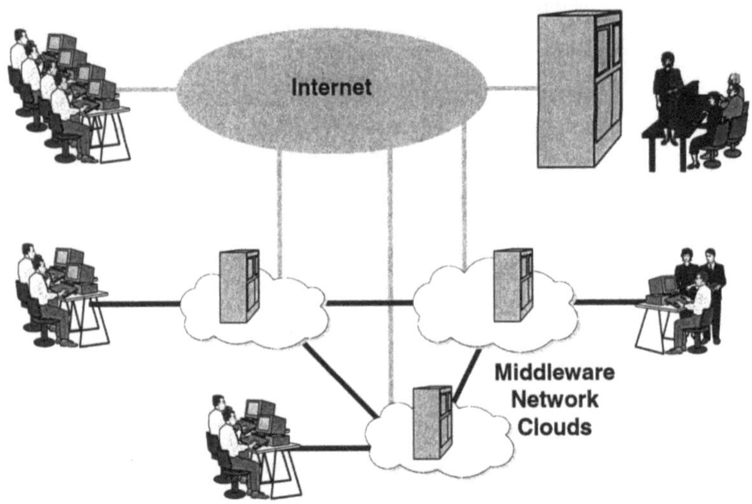

Figure 3-7: All Users Obtain Access to All Services

For example, if the following services were all supported by interconnected clouds, the consumer could log onto traditional content providers such as AOL, Prodigy, CompuServe, or Interchange; *and* onto Internet services such as personal banking, email, travel, or the local newspaper; *and onto* the office local-area network *all at the same time* – without the need to log into and out of each service individually. The reason: the consumer is actually logged onto the cloud itself, and the services are registered to the cloud(s).

Based on open platform and standards such as Microsoft Win32, UNIX, TCP/IP, Sockets, HTTP, or HTML, networking middleware leverages advanced technology that has already been developed by the market. Open architectures will be scalable yet inexpensive to own and operate.

For example, the architecture isolates and protects applications and networks, allowing each to evolve independently. With this evolutionary approach, existing applications run "as is." This can provide better support for wireless mobile models. Different networks can be aggregated: voice, data, video, wireless, "commerce," future(s).

For network carriers, this reusable, open standards-based intelligent service platform leverages not only existing assets in physical networks, but also engineering skills and corporate credibility. Network carriers will be able to rapidly solidify their market leadership position for existing and new content providers, because enabling middleware will dramatically expand network traffic over existing network assets. This concept provides the pathway to offering new services, generating new revenues, participating in the new networking world, and leveraging the value of global assets.

A cloud should be a one-stop shop for a complete engineering solution. For that reason it needs to be evolutionary – it should provide additional value for the network carriers' existing physical network. It should provide the network server and customer care functionality that enables new services to be easily developed, introduced, and managed on the network.

Instead of content providers developing their own network infrastructure to deliver their content, network carriers and application service providers (ASPs) will enable these content providers to provide their online services much more quickly, to many more customers, at much lower cost. In this way, network carriers will enable content providers to focus on content and user interface innovation, and differentiation, and then to extend their access to much larger markets.

3.3.1 Benefits of Networking Middleware

With an IP Service Platform as the solution, it is possible to describe the benefits to four communities consisting of *end users*, *corporations*, *information content and service provides*, and *network operators*.

End Users

For end users, the solution provides a platform accessing online services in a controlled and secure manner, and for automating and integrating internal information systems in a comprehensive, multimedia fashion. The solution provides the ubiquity and standard structure of the Internet with the convenience and security of a commercial online service. The solution networks support a single point of contact for registration, billing, and customer care, and a standard navigation and location mechanism and encryption for all data. The solution networks provide end users with a range of services such as caching, security, predictable performance, parental control over content, simultaneous voice and data, that make using the network safer, easier to use and more convenient.

Corporations

For corporations, the solution provides an Intranet platform which supports a comprehensive set of features, while still leveraging Internet and online services technology. With the solution, a corporation can deploy an internal information system which integrates corporate e-mail, voice mail, telephony, document management, secure communications, and collaboration.

Information Content and Service Providers

For information content and service providers, the solution provides a set of services to build electronic commerce and communications applications. The solution networks factor out common functions such as authentication, billing, and access control, move them from the individual servers into the network and provide them for all content services in a simple, standard manner. The content provider can concentrate on the organization and presentation of their content, using standard tools for content management, while letting the solution network provide the commercial infrastructure and security. Non-programmers can create services easily through the server capability of a peer, and a simple programming interface based on industry standards and languages. With the solution, technically proficient content providers can build next-generation telephone/ Internet/commerce applications more quickly than from scratch.

This solution adds to the arsenal of tools available for service development. An information content provider can attack a global multimedia-commerce enabled market, innovate more quickly, and retool existing applications while using the latest technology.

Network Operators

For network operators, the solution provides a way to keep telephony and video conferencing traffic running on existing network assets. This multimedia traffic is integrated with Internet applications, but travels on network operators' existing networks. This strategy delivers better quality to the end user, enabling increased usage through new generation network applications.

A complete solution provides everything needed to build an online service. The network server and customer care become reusable functions. This eases the creation of new services developed, introduced, and managed on the network's application server farms, including directory management software, security, network management, and billing systems, which collect and handle the alerts and events generated by the service-consuming and service providing systems (peers) attached to the network. The infrastructure provided by the solution makes it easier to support end users and service providers on their network.

For network operators, the solution provides the pathway to offer new services, generate new revenue, participate in the new Internetworking world, and leverage the value of assets.

3.4 Service Provisioning Scenario

A middleware-enabled network changes the way services are developed and deployed, and the way users access these services. Here we delve a little deeper on the changes that are required and then present several scenarios illustrating the interactions with the network.

The Internet Protocol (IP) is defined as a stateless and best-effort protocol. Data between two end points can follow multiple paths and even arrive out of order. This affords considerable advantages in scalability and performance, but presents unique challenges for secure services. Network-based systems must be secured against potential security attacks. A secure network "substrate" allows development of secure services within the network, further improving performance as well capabilities and security. A cloud can develop precisely such a substrate by forcing all packets through a security gateway. The gateway monitors packets and ensures a consistent security policy with service support.

The design principles make this explicit – see Chapter 4, "Platform Requirements and Principles". The secure cloud framework never reveals protected resources. Complete insulation is guaranteed by the cloud's security gateway. Traffic is allowed only between authorized components. Communication with elements on insecure networks (such as the Internet) employs mandatory encryption. In all cases, the traffic must pass through the security gateway. This suggests that the routing cannot be arbitrary, which violates the "stateless" nature of IP.

The solution lies within the domain. Domains may be viewed as slices of the IP address space. All services are hosted within the domain, and hence must pass into a domain gateway. This domain is protected by the security framework. When a service portal is within the domain, there it receives full support of all applicable APIs. Elements inside the domain are "trusted" and accorded appropriate rights and privileges. Elements outside the domain must obtain a "trusted" status. These external elements may then operate as proxy services, with appropriate network support.

3.4.1 How a Service is Deployed

Network middleware, as a general technique to simplify application development, resolves many troubling design issues that have plagued the architects of client-server applications. The network middleware assumes responsibility for all aspects of the information that passes through its borders, including its accuracy and distribution. Issues such as device capabilities and format conversions are engineered by the network rather than customers. The network insulates both users and providers from the intricacies of components and architecture. Reusable components now move into the network, where they can actually be reused in a coordinated manner through standard network APIs. As an architectural issue, this simplifies many design issues; for example, information management and scalability. The providers and users now concentrate on their particular areas of expertise. This approach is entirely consistent with the layered architecture approach that simplifies many engineering designs.

The differences in system design are profound. Formerly, a provider began with the specification and design of every resource. Consider the challenge of designing a database as part of a larger service offering. The contents must be defined, secured, monitored, and maintained. Formidable networking challenges include high availability with low delay to a geographically dispersed user community. Such designs typically cannot be achieved at low cost by an end user, and even large service organizations must use precious resources for design, deployment and operation. Such expertise is marketed as *hosting services*, the electronic equivalent of department stores and malls. They reduce costs of simple sites, but constrain the development of innovative and compelling services.

When a service is deployed, however, there are substantial vulnerabilities. These vulnerabilities are seen commonly in the security violations and limited routing controls of the Internet, as well as management of bandwidth and delay. From a security perspective, data packets can be forged, copied, replayed, and mangled in various ways. The routing limitations complicate efforts to prevent unauthorized capture of a data stream, and the consequent security problems. The very definition of IP is a "best-effort" protocol, which makes it difficult to predict, let alone guarantee bandwidth and delay characteristics.

The new network eliminates these cumbersome steps. The previously restrictive deployment issues give way to flexible location of servers. Formerly nightmarish security challenges are replaced by authenticated and managed traffic. Gone are the difficult management problems that often straddled divergent interfaces at several layers of applications and networking. The enterprise can now concentrate upon its primary goal of developing compelling new services for both end-user clients as well as other providers.

> *Let's consider our prototypical service – Jane the Dandelion Wine Merchant. She knows everything about dandelions and making fine wine from them, but she is rather naive about the Internet. She buys a web server, has some friends over for wine, and together they put up a simple web site. They do not go through the long system engineering process because they trust their computers. Together, she and her clients and suppliers start to build an electronic business. Their network looks something like the one in Figure 3-8, below.*
>
> *It is not long before Jane's site is "hacked" by the infamous "Coalition Against Dandelion Wine". Her connoisseur client received spearmint tea instead; the dandelion supplier shipped fresh flowers to a competitor; and Jane's merchant bank account was cancelled. There should be a better way – and there is. That is why you are reading this book.*

Let's make this concrete by taking an existing server and placing it onto the new network. The network will grant service only to components (clients) that can prove their identity and maintain an authenticated connection. This is achieved with a standards-based authentication module which supports the open APIs of the network. The simplest solution provides this by installing a program component that allows the server

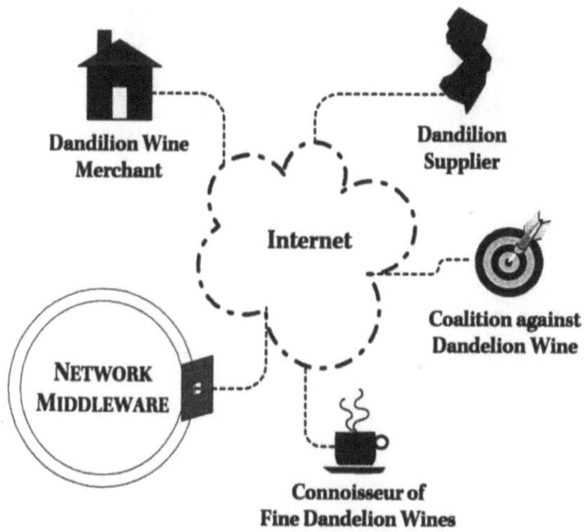

Figure 3-8: Jane the Dandelion Wine Merchant's Unmanaged Internet

to securely identify himself to the network, as well as continually validating the authenticated status. The module can be either a Java class or a pre-packaged "peer" program that supports self-provisioning and management with a Graphical User Interface (GUI). These tools counteract the Internet's notorious vulnerability to "cyberattacks" – exploitation of weaknesses through specialized mangling and forgery, as well as more sophisticated traffic hijackings.

Jane has heard about the new middleware network, especially how easy it is to implement. So, she takes the plunge, installs a certified peer, and connects her system with the middleware network. Things seem much better. Jane settles down for a cup of dandelion tea (the new wine is not ready yet). Her system now looks like the illustration in Figure 3-9.

While sipping her tea, Jane leafs through the catalog of services available to the middleware users. Value-added services include billing, credit transactions, and even suppliers of fermentation equipment. Each user belongs to the polite society of the middleware network. Simple graphical interfaces let her publish her subscriptions to services. Jane reads about a special kind of user, called an authenticated user, who is specially protected with a secure user identity. Nobody can change his identity without authenticating again.

But then she wonders about her arch nemesis, the Coalition Against Dandelion Wine. What if they *become members of the middleware network? Stirring her tea, she decides they may buy her wine as long as they pay for it. Since the Coalition cannot forge someone else's identity (or even repudiate their own), they can be held strictly accountable for all orders they place. The middleware net-*

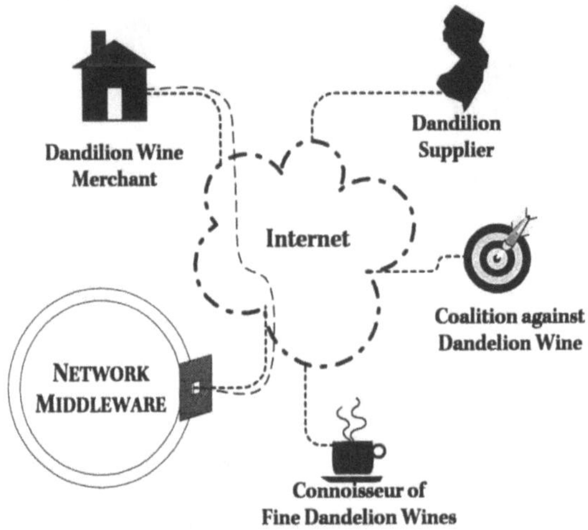

Figure 3-9: Jane's Partially Managed Internet

work enforces uniform authentication and access control. If their behavior becomes too obnoxious, their access can be abridged or revoked.

Being something of a flower child, Jane the Dandelion Wine Merchant feels that it's unfair to exclude people who have not yet joined the middleware network. She also realizes that presence on the public Internet will remain an important aspect of her sales. What can she do about this? At first, it seems nearly enough to send her back to risky, unmanaged world of the public Internet.

Jane now understands why there are three kinds of services supported by the middleware: full-public, cloud-public, and private. By providing limited access as a full-public service, she can reach unregistered users. Her cloud-public view will reach registered users. Jane's accountant will be given private (subscription-only) access to both billables and receivables, whereas her receiving department does not need access to the billables. Well, finally her wine is ready to taste. Between the wine and the middleware she is again optimistic.

The full use of network APIs is reserved for managed users. These users have an identity on the network, and therefore are trusted to interact with their piece of the network. This server becomes a trusted member of the network by authenticating itself to the network and continually validating its authenticated status.

An authenticated user obtains many benefits, as we will discuss in the following chapters. One of these benefits is the event mechanism. This provide reliable delivery to multiple subscribers by use of intuitive publisher/publish and subscriber/subscription relationships.

Example: *Jane wants her air-freight shipper to be notified automatically every time she receives an order for wine. So, she registers an event with the middleware, and her server generates an event notification every time an order is received. The events are reliably delivered to the shipper of her choice. Jane also receives event notification from her suppliers. Whether the cost of dandelions decreases in the spring or increases during the winter, she can subscribe to the pricing information and obtain the best pricing.*

The server now authenticates *with* the network. This is a two-way authentication (technically, we call this bilateral-authentication) where the network and server prove their identities to each other. They also compute a secret symmetric key for the secure exchange of data. Every securely transmitted packet is encrypted before entering the Internet, and decrypted upon exit. Cyberattacks cannot extract or modify any information, but instead they generate improperly keyed packets. These packets appear as garbled data, forcing retransmission, and potentially triggering countermeasures. An attacker can still disrupt the client, but cannot alter any encrypted stream. We have protected the data between the network and the server machine, but this is only part of the solution. Traffic that bypasses the new network is not protected.

The server receives two sources of data. Some of it passes through the new network, and is secured on Jane's behalf. This traffic is a mixture of management information and traffic that the network has secured on Jane's behalf. Other traffic, however, did not pass through the new network, and is not secured. Since the server is sitting on the web it is still subject to a number of attacks on the unsecured data. The traffic mixture occurs because IP does not require any specific kind of routing. Jane receives reliable services from the network middleware, but the traffic is still vulnerable.

Jane's membership does not completely shield her from non-middleware traffic, and she continues to receive threatening digital packages from the Coalition. Jane's site is on the Internet, the Coalition is on the Internet, and Jane has not learned how to control routing to her machine. Fortunately, she can exclude them from her services, but still feels uncomfortable when those Coalition packages arrive.

The components have a trusted session with the network middleware. Some traffic between them does not have to go through the middleware. It may route through the untrusted connection that rides on the Internet. This bypasses the security, and it also bypasses all other functions of the new network middleware.

Jane now understands why all traffic must pass through the middleware network in order receive the full benefits of the middleware. She wonders if its necessary to move her server (right now it supports several flowerpots of dandelions, so she's not eager to move it). She thinks of an inexpensive private line into the middleware, but would prefer a software solution that doesn't increase her costs. She also wonders why the middleware network keeps talking about protocol mediation as a service enhancement. She adds a touch of organic sugar to the newest batch of wine, and ponders the choices. Fortunately, none of her software will have to change. She seals the new batch of wine and hopes for a vintage year.

One example is protocol mediation, where the middleware enhances the data traffic, for example by providing a service to the data stream. Jane and her cohorts immediately purchase a secure IPSec "tunnel router" on their systems, and their traffic goes directly into the middleware network. We have ruggedized the sites with a protected data tunnel, and provided a standards-based authentication module. This ruggedized connection provides a safe passage to the gateway, as shown in Figure 3-10.

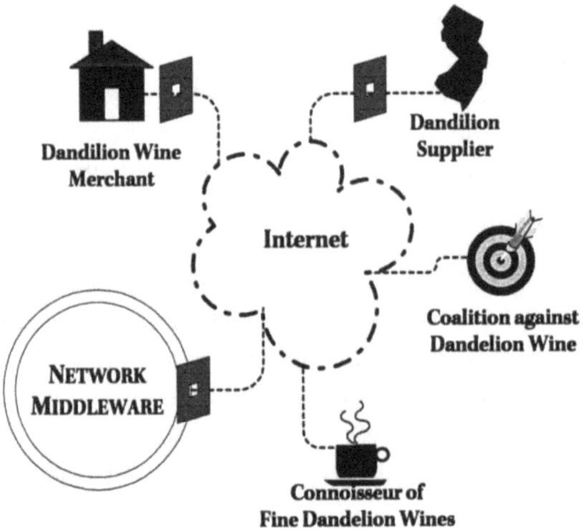

Figure 3-10: Peered Tunnels

Explicit tunnels provide a networking solution, but the server is still physically connected to the Internet. Full-public traffic continues over the basic Internet Protocol (IP), and cannot be compelled to route through the middleware network. Their traffic does not enter the middleware network, and cannot take advantage of it.

The safest solution places the server in a physically protected location, with routing on a private network. This network could be physically protected for maximum benefit, or it can be a virtual private network when the networking connectivity affords sufficient reliability. A second, simpler, solution is redirection, where the service is known by an address within the middleware network. Data to this address is forwarded by a proxy to the Internet-located address. All traffic must route into the middleware network. The network assumes the role of a security gateway and forwards traffic to the server as appropriate. Developments in the Internet Engineering Task Force (IETF) recently concluded the design of Internet security capabilities known as IPSec. This protocol is making its way into the mainstream of networking software.

3.4.2 Where do Services Run?

We have thus far discussed services that run on a server machine, and presented a progression from unmanaged, to authenticated, and then to routed. Authenticated traffic uses software, either standard APIs running in a protected Java Virtual Machine, or certified peer. This can interact with software tunnels to protect traffic between the server and the middleware network. The routed traffic can also be directed by physical routing. The choice affects the clients that benefit from the route.

Some services run on servers, and others run on the network itself. The latter are gate-based services. Users do not generally write gate services, although we anticipate that active networks[1] will open this capability to a wider user community.

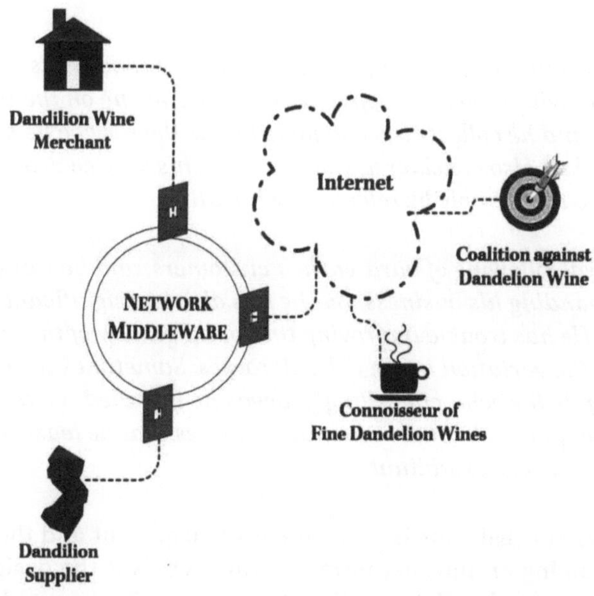

Figure 3-11: Services as Stores on the Middleware Network

A general server can run either on the Internet (as a server) or on the middleware network (as a store-based service, as shown in Figure 3-11). Clients on the Internet authenticate to the network, and their traffic passes through the Internet. The store-based services have a physically protected network connection and hardware-based routing through the middleware network. Server-based services use the Internet as the

1. The field of *active networks* understands the profound advantages this can provide. See references.

network connection. Server-based services need to use encryption as the minimum method to ensure data authenticity. A server-based service also needs some way to make the traffic route through the cloud from the client. This is done either by a software tunnel or by Internet extensions.

Consider a service. The middleware network has special "service hosting" gates. Client traffic cannot pass directly into the cloud because the gates maintain a security perimeter. They are not on the public Internet; there is no problem with security of the traffic hitting the machines.

3.4.3 Network Integration Services

Let consider Victor, the Entrepreneur of Internet Telephone Services.

> *Victor knows three things: He was the first. he was the best, and he will never sell out.*
>
> *Victor has a problem. His company has been selling phone cards and recently became involved with Internet Telephone services. Anyone on the Internet can use his service, and he collects a reasonable fee for the service he has put together. Victor has also considered ways to make his service available as a general web resource, simply by referencing his URL.*
>
> *Victor has a loyal following of hard-earned customers, and he wants to keep them while expanding his business. But he has also lost significant revenue through fraud. He has trouble improving the sound quality of the calls, as he cannot control the variation in the calls' IP routes. Sometimes the call echo is intolerable despite the echo-cancelling gateway he installed. Victor considered buying more equipment, but his accountant advises that he lease it, and the lease arrangements are exorbitant.*

What business is Victor really in? Is it customer management and the crafting of service offers? Is it running an Internet infrastructure? Or, is it the design and development of telephony standards? Victor realizes that revenue is generated through service to the end-user customer, not the design of a new network. Hence, it makes sense that Victor should outsource his technology needs to a network provider.

3.4.4 How Authentication Tokens Can Protect Network Web Content

As simply one example, consider the web servers that provide the common delivery of content including valuable media such as entertainment, news, financial information, as well as personal data. Secure requests and delivery of this content must be assured, and a single-sign-on (SSO) capability enhances the usability. In the past, there was no scalable and industrial-strength solution to this requirement. A user had to maintain multiple passwords and use the more expensive HTTPS (SSL protected) protocol of the Internet.

A user of the enhanced network finds a far simpler world. He can log into the cloud and work from a standard browser, and then receive security services that protect his connection. The network provides special authentication tokens that are encrypted by the cloud. The encryption key changes frequently, and a secure channel provides the browser with the authenticated user's currently valid tokens. The tokens must be presented to domain-based web servers as a condition to receive content, and only authorized clients possess these tokens. Of course, it is possible that a determined hacker will steal an authentication token. However, the tokens are only valid for a short time, and will be recognized only for the browser they were intended for. A stolen token is likely to be of little use to a hacker.

Let's see how this works. First, the user Bob opens a session by authenticating to the cloud. On his browser he enters the URL of the cloud login site. His browser verifies the cloud's X.509v3 certificate, so he can be certain the site is an authorized provider. He then provides his user name and authentication information. This can be either a password or a digital certificate previously issued by the cloud certificate authority (CA). The certificate resides either on his machine, or on a removable device or smart-card. Once Bob logs in, he will be recorded as an active user within the cloud's list of active users. The system now provides his browser with authentication tokens over a secure channel.

If Bob logs out, or his connection is broken, he will be removed from the list of active users. The system maintains a control channel with his browser, and violation of the channel's protocol will terminate his session.

Now Bob attempts access to any cloud-protected web site. The site can be a standard HTTP site which does not include an encrypted SSL channel, or it can be a protected HTTP channel using the SSL protocol. Many services are not SSL protected, but nevertheless they benefit from greater security. For example, this prevents theft of information even when the information is of only modest value. The encrypted authentication token lets the cloud validate his privilege to receive content.

Bob's browser sends a request which includes site-specific information. This includes his encrypted authentication token. This token is validated by the cloud, which also recognizes that Bob is still logged in. The cloud has verified that Bob is allowed to have the content, so it establishes a proxy connection to the web server. The cloud then delivers requests and content as required.

Bob accesses several sites in this manner, and never has to provide a password to any of them. The sites can verify that Bob is an authenticated user. The cloud can validate his privilege to access the site, since all users' access rights are stored in the membership database. Thus, both user and service provider are protected. Bob can also benefit from other features of the network, for example, a managed cache or licensed content.

Suppose Tom, Bob's nefarious neighbor, has managed to steal one of these authentication tokens. It will do him little good. First, expiration makes the token invalid for retrieval of information (although use of expired tokens could trigger a security alert to disable Tom's connection). Second, Tom's browser is not authenticated to use Bob's token, so he will fail for a second reason. Third, Tom is likely not an authenticated user because use of invalid tokens could disable his authenticated session.

3.4.5 Multiple Networks and Accounts

Suppose a network user wants to access a non-HTTP content-service that gives privileged materials; for example, games, or printers. These resources are protected by their owners, and such protection schemes often limit a client to only one membership. A user must request an account from each content provider, and may pay usage fees. Since there are many content providers, each may have membership requirements that are somewhat different. For example, changing from one provider's name (or domain) might "shut off" the other providers. The content providers, for their part, each must collect usage fees. They too would benefit from a single system due to subscriber management. Windows NTLM is one such protection mechanism, and its content includes executable programs such as games, video content, and the like.

Single-Sign-On (SSO) simplifies access to participating systems. The user does not have to establish an account with each content service. The cloud receives the client's request and only permits access when the client has previously subscribed to the content-provider's site. The cloud contacts the content-service with valid credentials, and proxies between the client request and the server's information. Depending on the service, the cloud can either provide its own credentials, or per-user credentials. Subscription and access events are generated by the cloud and can update network resources such as naming services and credential services.

Consider the client who requests protected content. The cloud receives the request from an authenticated and subscribed user. Correct security credentials are electronically inserted into the client request. The content provider gladly provides content for with these credentials. The credentials are not stored on the client machine, and this protects the provider from misuse. The client access to all services is controlled from a single point, allowing prompt refunds as well as disconnects. The client can even access content from different providers at the same time. This was not possible before networking middleware, and is now achieved simply for both clients and content providers.

Technically, this is achieved because a cloud maintains a trust relationship with each content provider. This authorizes the cloud to provide authentication information as required. It can be achieved in several ways: running a peer on an authorized account maintenance machine is one such method. Shared trust takes other forms as well, as will be discussed subsequently.

3.5 Summary

Conceptually, networking middleware requires a global standard and compliance. Compliant and certified applications will enable these network operators to achieve better account control and increased network traffic. In summary, with a cloud, network carriers can reduce costs, increase traffic over existing networks, retain valuable customer relationships, ease the entry into new markets, and be the vehicle for key partnerships with software vendors, content providers, and other businesses.

CHAPTER 4 Platform Requirements and Principles

Network solutions range from the very broad to the very specific. Typically, the lower down the level of abstraction a solution falls, the broader and the more general it has to be. This also holds for its requirements. The lower down one attempts to solve a problem, the requirements one encounters deal with broad issues dealing more with the nature of the problem instead of the specific details and features found at the higher levels. In this chapter we describe the requirements used in designing extant examples of networking middleware, and we state principles that lay the foundation for the subsequent design and implementation. As we described earlier, any problem can be solved in a number of different ways; one way to choose a solution is to collect requirements that drive the solution. The fulfillment of these requirements serves as a litmus test for judging its success.

4.1 Requirements

The requirements presented here are basic, general requirements taken in the context of future data services. They form a generalization of what is certainly a wide range of requirements and consequently may be too general in some areas and too specific in others. What we are attempting here is to state a set of requirements that address the shift from the first-generation Internet to a service-aware network infrastructure. Regardless of one's perspective as an end user or a carrier, the requirements provide a common understanding of what a network should achieve.

Our requirements focus on the network's infrastructure and middleware capabilities to support online services and applications. We offer 13 requirements.

Security in the Network

We tend to think of public networks as no-man's-land thus putting all security solutions on the hosts. Our requirement is to balance out the responsibility for security between the end point hosts and the network.

Scalability of Services

Here the issue is not the scalability of the network infrastructure but the scalability of online services. It is always relatively easy to deploy a new service for a few customers. Overseeing the expansion of the service to thousands or millions of customers is a complex, costly, and difficult undertaking. Our requirement is to offer a support in the network for scalability without the complexity, cost, or difficulty.

Extensibility of the Platform

Any initial solution in this space creates an immediate opportunity for improvements. The only certainty is the constancy of change. The design for change is the third requirement. However, this has to be done in a way that allows the network middleware to be upgraded without requiring necessary changes in the end point devices and vice-versa.

Cloud Manageability

Powerful network management has always been a key requirement for carriers and ISPs. Network administrators should be able to monitor and manage all aspects of the network elements and key system components. Customer-controlled services deployed on top of the network providers systems require a different management approach; that of self-management and provisioning. Here, service providers need to monitor and manage their systems in addition to what the network providers can already provide.

Interoperability between Clouds

Interoperability is the ability to seamlessly utilize products from different vendors through insulating layers of abstraction that hide the products' details and differences. The network middleware should aid the network and service providers in interoperating by again offering appropriate abstraction layers that provide suitable information hiding.

Implementation Efficiency

Adding protocol mediating and translating proxies, additional information systems, and management frameworks must be done in a way that does not adversely affect the performance of raw network switches' capacity. Although the transition from dumb to smart networks is without some penalty, it is a balancing act that achieves the combined requirements without unduly sacrificing efficiency.

Device Ubiquity

In addition to the standard personal computers (PCs) and workstations, the network must support diverse end point devices such as telephones, personal digital assistants (PDA), network computers (NC), pagers, and cellular phones. For some devices, such as the NCs and PCs, providing the devices with supporting software should permit direct communication with the network that can be easily programmed.

Internationalization and Localization

The network middleware must be capable of handling different human-readable languages. Internationalization can be thought of in terms of the data flows through the system. Due to the many different flows passing through such systems and the variety of platforms and operating systems, internalization poses a large design and implementation problem. Only a system that stores, manipulates and displays international character sets and changes from one set to another without recompilation of the entire system can be considered truly internationalized.

Commercial Viability

The network middleware needs to create a framework within which everyone can benefit financially and which pays for itself. It has to be commercially viable. Much like the internationalization requirement the network middleware must be aware of value added services, who controls them, and who uses them, and in the end must offer accounting to appropriate billing systems for reconciling usage and online transactions.

Easy Provisioning

It must be easy to create, provision, advertise, control, manage, outsource, and bundle services through the platform either through integrated methods using service-side APIs, or through remote administration tools.

Mobility

Mobility supports changes in viewpoint, resource availability, auditing, as well as location independence. Users and their end point devices are becoming much more mobile as new technology allows them to connect to the network in various places. This leads to the need to manage and track resources as dynamic entities and not static one.

Openness

To facilitate the platform's extensibility and interoperability, the platform must support global and open standard specifications. It must be an IP-based platform built on top of standard sockets and provide easy migration from IPv4 to IPv6, while easily integrating standard protocols such as HTTP, LDAP, SMTP, POP3, H.323, NNTP, and LDAP.

Usability

The platform must be designed for minimal disruption and ease-of-use. Users should not have to deal with network configuration and management tasks such as specifying DNS addresses, masks, domain names, phone numbers or proxy settings. Users should see little difference from their previous system, yet observe the network's value through their ability to access new services easily and with added values. Once installed on the users' clients or servers, the enabling-software should be transparent and nonintrusive during network sessions.

In the remaining sections of this chapter, we take a closer look at some of the key requirements; security, scalability, and extensibility. The other requirements are addressed in other parts of the book.

4.2 Security

In targeting security, the overall emphasis should be on developing a framework for the implementation and deployment of the next generation of Internet, telephone, and global electronic commerce networks. It should combine, in a single seamless whole, the best characteristics of digital packet and circuit-switched services and provides to its subscribers a degree of convenience and assurance comparable to that enjoyed by the users of today's modern telephone networks.

As a comparison, people who use modern voice-grade landline telephones do not worry about the security or integrity of their calls. For most, eavesdropping is a remote possibility; the telephones are used daily to discuss and exchange with friends and colleagues an astonishing variety of sensitive and personal information. Nor do we often doubt the integrity of the telephone network in the sense of one telephone instrument (telephone number) masquerading as another, or the transparent substitution of one speaker for another.

However, the same degree of confidence and trust is not shared with respect to digital data networks. Here the issues of security, integrity and authentication arise repeatedly, since the ease with which digital information can be manipulated makes such networks susceptible to a wide variety of attacks. A viable security architecture needs to be explicitly designed to address such concerns, and set for its end users, be they consumers or vendors. This must provide a standard of confidence and trust comparable to that enjoyed by the switched telephone network.

The reader should understand that security and trust pervade networks. We previously defined "trust" on page 78. The current chapter describes the main concepts. We will later detail the theory and practice of security in Chapter 6, "Interoperable and Scalable Security".

4.2.1 Adequate Security for Acceptable Cost

An architecture should be based on the principle of *adequate security for acceptable cost.* Many systems, particularly those designed for military or government use, mandate complete security at any cost, an approach characterized by high overhead, burdensome procedures, and draconian enforcement. The commercial world, in contrast, evaluates the benefits, risks, and expenses (money, time, overhead, infrastructure and such) of security in the context of a strategic business plan. These industries approach security pragmatically and balance the potential damage of a security breach against the costs of protecting themselves against such losses.

For example, credit card companies take precautions against credit card theft and fraud, balancing probable losses against consumer convenience. These vendors tolerate modest loss due to fraud as the cost of doing business; that is, the cost of the malicious misuse of a credit card is a small (and acceptable) percentage of the total revenue. In other words, security is a *business* decision made in the context of business goals, common practices, tolerable losses, and ease of use.

The numerous and varied trust relationships that exist among businesses is another important element of commercial security. For example, it is in the mutual interest of telephone carriers to establish intercarrier exchange agreements that permit the "purchase" of telephone service across carrier (geographical) boundaries. These agreements are enforced by procedural, social, economic, and legal mechanisms with technical security as only one element in a complex web of overlapping safeguards. Consider how two carriers, *A* and *B*, might reconcile, for billing purposes, their use of one another's network:

- *A*, relying on its own usage records, determines both its use of *B*'s network and *B*'s use of *A*'s facilities; *B* does likewise with respect to *A*. These two reconciliations are compared and any discrepancies are resolved using procedures detailed in the intercarrier agreement
- *A* and *B* present their billing records to a neutral third party who performs the reconciliation. The reconciliations are checked, at regular intervals, by each carrier using standard accounting techniques
- *A* accepts the reconciliation determined by carrier *B* and, as a safeguard against error, double-checks *B*'s accounting periodically

In the first case, neither party relies on the other for reconciliation, but each trusts the other to apply mutually accepted procedures for the resolution of differences including the mechanisms of contract law. In the second case, the parties rely upon a trusted, independent intermediary. This is a common business practice that has been institutionalized in a variety of forms including escrow agents, banks, underwriters, and notary publics. In the third case, the trust relationship is direct and unmediated. *B* may be a substantially larger carrier than *A* and it is simply not in *B*'s best interests to violate *A*'s trust, since the consequences (loss of face, legal costs, increased regulatory interference) would be far more severe than the value of a deception (say, skimming a few percentage points off the reconciliation in *B*'s favor).

4.2.2 Technical Security Differs from Organizational Trust

The point is simple, but worth repeating for emphasis — technical security is but one element of many in a trust relationship. Society has developed numerous mechanisms for mutually suspicious parties to transact business, such as social relationships, legal contracts, bonding and insurance, mediation, regulatory agencies, and courts. The consequences for duplicity are as varied as the mechanisms themselves and include social stigma, loss of livelihood, fines, imprisonment, loss of business, destruction or confiscation of property, and personal loss. These mechanisms and others, developed over thousands of years of commerce, are time-tested and effective.

There are many examples of security architectures that promise to replace these rich mechanisms and their long history of successful application with "superior" technical solutions. Frankly, such solutions, if possible at all, will be a long time in coming and at this point we have neither the expertise nor the experience to put them into daily practice.

The technical mechanisms of a security architecture should not be designed to replace the elaborate trust relationships and safeguards that already exist in the world of telecommunications and commerce. Instead, the security architecture should supply a necessary technical basis for these older business procedures, allowing them to be transplanted, largely unchanged, to the new world of digital networking and electronic commerce. Not only should the architecture carry the old world forward into the new – it should be also designed to take advantage of advances in technical mechanisms and business practices.

The security architecture can evolve as carriers, vendors, and consumers gain experience. To a large extent this evolution is transparent, since the architecture is not just a specific implementation. Rather, it is a framework in which methods may be transparently upgraded or replaced with improved subsystems. Thus, all parties in using this architecture have the added assurance that their investment (be it hardware, software, content, training, or experience of use) will not be wiped out overnight by unexpected advances in digital security, code breaking, or network-based business models. The ability of an architecture to be both stable and adaptable will encourage content suppliers and third-party manufacturers to produce compliant products, since their investment will retain value over a long period of time.

4.2.3 Security Goals

Security needs to be a fundamental, ever-present theme of the architecture. Unlike many early systems, security has not been added after the fact or designed as an extension grafted onto an earlier architecture. The security architecture should be fully integrated into the architecture as a whole; consequently, all actions are mediated by the underlying security mechanisms. To this end, the security architecture has four goals:

- *Maintain information secrecy*; that is, prevent sensitive information from being revealed to unauthorized parties
- *Ensure information integrity*; that is, prevent the undetected alteration or adulteration of information
- *Guarantee accountability*; that is, prevent one user or service from either undetectable assuming the identify of another or denying, at some later date, their participation in a transaction
- *Ensure availability*; that is, prevent a malicious subscriber or external agent from denying service to others

The security mechanisms should be designed so that they:

- Cannot be circumvented accidentally
- Cannot be circumvented deliberately without a high probability of detection and a significant level of effort by an adversary
- Do not present an unreasonable burden to either the system operators or the end users

To prevent accidental circumvention, the various security mechanisms are introduced at the lowest appropriate level of the system and the system structure prevents a higher level service from bypassing any lower level. To prevent deliberate circumvention, the architecture should employ cryptographic checks. The cryptography, based on widely adopted and rigorously inspected industry standards, will frustrate a determined adversary by requiring effort well in excess of the likely value of the information.

Finally, almost all of the security measures should be automatic and occur transparently without end user or operator intervention. By making every effort to minimize the burden on users and operators, the architecture ensures that the security mechanisms will not be ignored or set aside by frustrated users or harried system operators.

To summarize, no accident may lead to loss of secrecy (disclosure), loss of integrity (undetected modification), or loss of accountability (repudiation of identity). Furthermore, any effort to deliberately disclose information, modify information, or substitute one identity for another is so likely to be detected or require such a large expenditure of effort (time, money, equipment, or personnel) that it is unwise or unprofitable. The security mechanisms themselves are either simple enough, or sufficiently transparent, that they do not intrude upon users or prevent the system operator from administering the system with reasonable ease and efficiency.

4.2.3.1 Information Secrecy

Information secrecy and information integrity are related, but independent, properties. Secrecy refers to the prevention of the unwanted disclosure of information. When *A* and *B* communicate, each wants to ensure that no third party *X* is eavesdropping and extracting information. Integrity refers to the veracity of the communication; that is, both *A* and *B* want to ensure that no system fault or a malicious action by *X* has led to the deletion, insertion, or alteration of information.

4.2.4 Information Integrity

Encryption in the network middleware platform serves double duty: the protection of information from disclosure (privacy), and protection from alteration (which supports that integrity). Encryption is a necessary, but not sufficient, underpinning for information integrity. To understand this we prevent a case analysis of a malicious intruder *X* who, frustrated by his failed attempts to break the code, is attempting to destroy the integrity of the information passing between *A* and *B*. *X* has three avenues of assault.

- *Altering ciphertext bytes.* When the receiver decrypts an altered byte it will likely be gibberish – particularly in the context of the plaintext immediately preceding and following the substitution
- *Deleting one or more ciphertext bytes.* All ciphertext bytes from the point of deletion on will be incorrectly decrypted by the receiver since it will be using the wrong keytext to decrypt the ciphertext byte. In other words, from the point of deletion on, the stream will probably decrypt into garbage since the ciphertext stream is out of phase with the key stream by an amount equal to the length of the deletion
- *Inserting bytes into the ciphertext stream.* An argument similar to the case above applies since the introduction of additional bytes will throw the ciphertext stream out of phase with the key stream by an amount equal to the length of the insertion

Since any change made by *X* to the ciphertext stream must be some combination of alterations, deletions, or insertions, the best that *X* can hope to achieve is a lucky shot in the dark that will lead to the undetected loss or alteration of vital information. Nonetheless, if the end points *A* and *B* fail to take defensive measures, then *X* can potentially do serious damage, particularly if *X* has detailed knowledge of the application-specific protocol that *A* and *B* have layered atop the stream connecting them.

Imagine that *A* and *B* are client and server, respectively, using a data stream passing through one of our clouds to conduct a business transaction. Any competent and responsible client/server implementation requires extensive error checking at the application layer to protect both sides against transmission errors, lower level protocol failures, program bugs, and so on. Failure to do so leaves *A* and *B* open to a wide variety of ploys. In other words, the stream encryption supports, but does not supplant, application-specific integrity checks.

If the applications at either end of the connection are reasonably robust, then at worst they will recognize that an error has occurred and gracefully close the connection. In this case, *X* has achieved a denial of service but there is no loss of information integrity. Well-constructed applications might try to recover by flushing a portion of the stream and coordinating a retransmission; or, assuming sufficient redundancy in the stream, might be able to reconstruct the correct plaintext. Thus, the stream encryption of a managed cloud can transparently supply an additional layer of protection over and above application-specific deterrents. The combination of stream encryption and application self-checking ensures that even moderately sophisticated attempts to alter information or steal service will be frustrated.

4.2.4.1 Accountability

To guarantee accountability, the architecture should enforce bilateral authentication; that is, not only must all users and services identify themselves to the network in a manner that, for all practical purposes, denies impostors access, the network in turn must identify itself to its users and services in an equally strong manner. Consequently, when a connection between cloud and peer or cloud and user is established, both parties to the connection are assured that the opposite end point is legitimate and valid. In addition, this process of bilateral authentication establishes, for the lifetime of the given connection, a *billable entity* that is responsible for all charges and transactions generated, either directly or indirectly, over the connection. A billable entity can take many forms, ranging from a private individual to the procurement arm of a large corporate or government organization. The architecture guarantees that each and every transaction will be associated with exactly one known (to the cloud) billable entity.

This strong association has direct practical implicates. It alleviates a critical concern of administrators or service providers, namely, reliable billing. The introduction of the security architecture prevents users (and providers alike) from ever denying their participation in a transaction. Since the architecture ensures that every transaction generates a billing record(s) and that every billing record is tied to a known billable entity, all parties to a transaction are assured of comprehensive and accurate accounting.

In an effort to reduce the burden on a user or service, authentication should occur only once for any given session[1]. Consequently, unless a service provider requires additional service-specific authentication, a user, once connected, can freely tour and exploit all of the services offered by the network without additional effort. As we shall see, the same authentication may transparently give the user access to services in other net-

1. For our purposes, a session and a connection are synonymous.

works in keeping with the trust relationships that exist between the user's home network and other foreign networks.

4.2.4.2 Availability

The high service standards set by telephone service providers lead us to expect, as a matter of course, the continual availability of the switched telephone network. We assume, without question, the presence of dial tone and sufficient circuit capacity to complete the call. The network architecture should strive to offer comparable guarantees of *availability* for its digital network services. However, in the case here the challenge is greater since the switched telephone network is, by its nature, more resistant to denial of service attacks. Consequently, the platform should incorporate into its base architecture a variety of mechanisms to protect itself and its end users from attacks initiated either by other legitimate users or by forces outside the sphere of influence. Examples of such attacks include, but are not limited to:

- Packet flooding, insertion, and sniffing
- E-mail bombing
- Packet hijacking

In addition to corruption of service, the architecture must prevent service attacks that seek to either monopolize resources or deny access outright. Such attacks may be accidental or deliberate; for example, a service peer may, as a consequence of a previously undetected bug, run amok, flooding the network with superfluous accounting records. On the other hand, a malicious user may attempt denial of service to others by sending to the gate boundless amounts of traffic in the hopes of exhausting cloud resources. A managed architecture should provide several mechanisms to both localize such attacks, and to reduce the effect of such circumstances on "innocent bystanders".

One approach leverages the unique capabilities of packet filters/firewalls. A firewall is able to monitor the throughput of individual TCP/IP sessions as well as the combined throughput of sessions associated with particular peers or particular IP addresses. It is possible to define firewall actions to use this information to control traffic by dropping packets after thresholds are crossed. Since these actions can be customized to each user or service, the platform could tailor such thresholds for different users or services, or classes of users or services. Thus, the platform should be able to localize and limit potential performance "damage" caused by a malicious or misbehaving user.

In addition, since much service is enhanced by active gate "mediation" or proxying, the platform should support another level of control through monitoring and throttling of service requests in each "mediation agent". For example, the stored profiles of users and services may associate network parameters with specific services. For example, electronic mail could use a high bandwidth but low priority connectivity, whereas certificate validation can use a lower bandwidth but high priority connectivity.

Finally, the nature of the architecture should tend to localize most traffic. The interposition of a gate element could mean that if the previously described mechanisms fail to control an overload condition, many will cause overload circumstances to become evident only to users of the affected gate. Users and services served by other gates will tend to be unaffected. Each gate provides redundancy to the attached users.

4.2.5 Security Summary

The requirements and principles given in this chapter are one way to reduce complexity through middleware. This simplifies the mechanics of network access and service, and improves the capacity to grow and evolve. Service providers can be assured that their investment in this platform will continue to have value and that their procedures, practices, and goals will be supported long into the future. This groundwork defines fundamentals that allow providers and companies to establish and maintain the policies best suited to their business needs. The platform does not dictate solutions; it provides freedom of choice amid a wealth of mechanism.

4.3 Scalability

The typical architecture of an information system (shown in Figure 4-1) consists of clients that make requests in order to retrieve data from the servers. Clients and servers are connected through points-of-presence (POPs) to the interconnection network. The interconnection network could be for example the Internet, a private network connected to the Internet, or just a private network.

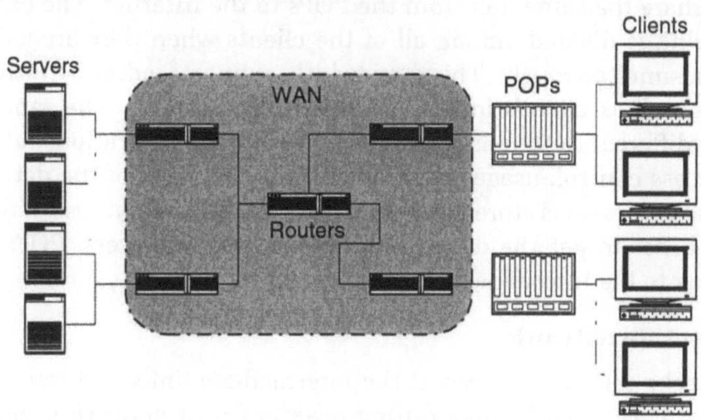

Figure 4-1: Typical Architecture of the Internet

Typical connections from clients to the POPs are telephone dial-up connections, ISDN dial-up, LAN, etc. POPs enable not only physical connection to the interconnection network, but they also provide some other functionality; e.g., authentication, routing and connection termination for dial-up connections. POPs provide links to interconnection network such as T1, data dial-up (POTS or ISDN), etc.

An interconnection network consists of the intermediate links that provide point-to-point connections between POPs and servers.

This architecture imposes many hotspots that could become bottlenecks if the amount of the traffic increases. These hotspots can be categorized according to their location:

Servers

At the server side, there are two hotspots that can become bottlenecks: the number of connections that can be handled by the server simultaneously and the bandwidth of the link by which the server is connected to the Internet. For most applications there is a limit to the number of connections that can be handled by the server simultaneously. Once this limit is reached, no new connection can be established without additional ones being terminated. On the other hand, the bandwidth of the link that connects the server to the Internet is divided among many clients. If the number of the requests increases, then the response time to the clients is much higher than what users can tolerate.

POP

At the POPs side, a similar problem occurs. There are two types of bottlenecks: the number of connections provided for the clients and the bandwidth of the link that connects POP with Internet. A large number of clients share the same link from the POPs to the Internet. The bandwidth of this link is divided among all of the clients when they are using it to transfer simultaneously. This bandwidth supports administrative functions as well as client's interactions with the Internet. The same link is used by different functions provided by the POPs: registration, authentication, access control, usage recording, billing etc. Most of the data needed for these processes is stored by one of the special server across of the Internet. In order to get the data from remote special servers, POPs use the same link to the Internet as the clients are using.

Interconnection network

Bottlenecks can happen also at the intermediate links and routers of the Internet. This could happen during peak hours of network usage during which many connections between servers and clients exist. Since many connections can be handled by the same intermediate links and routers, these links and routers can become bottlenecks.

There are many attempts to resolve each of these bottlenecks, but there were no suggestions for the integrated solutions that could resolve most of these hotspots.

4.3.1 Current or Known Solutions

The current and known solutions are presented through the short history of architectures applied thusfar to the Internet; they range from the classical client/server architecture to the communicating proxy architecture. Multiple machines are introduced in order to run very popular services, and more and more POPs are distributed all over the country to enable connections for the clients.

4.3.1.1 Client-Server Architecture

The client-server architecture (as shown in Figure 4-2) was the first architecture of Internet-hosted information systems. In this architecture, each client sends requests for Internet objects directly to the server, and the server responds to all requests. This simple architecture was efficient for small systems. However, scalability problems occur with moderate increases in the number of clients, the number of requests, and the size of the Internet objects. Internet information systems continue their dramatic global climb, as measured by the number of clients, number of requests, number of servers, and also the amount of available information. It is possible that forthcoming services will escalate this growth. For example, multimedia significantly increases the size of the objects through sound, pictures, and video. Such services may even support interactions between multiple video entities (consider, for example, personal videoconferencing).

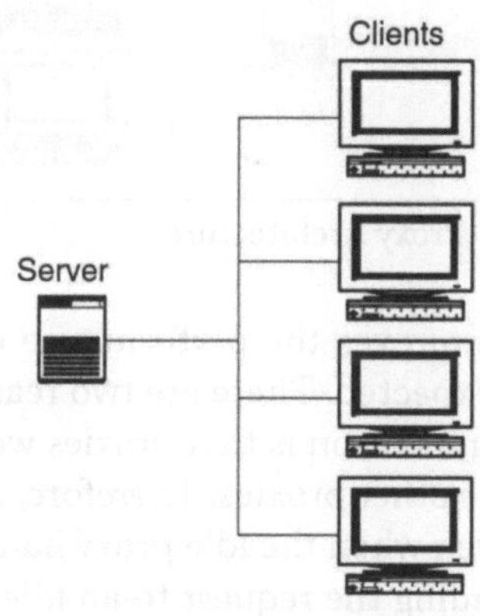

Figure 4-2: "Classical" Client-Server Architecture

Advanced applications, if left unmanaged, can significantly increase the traffic over the Internet, as well as increase the load on servers and POPs. At some point, the network, servers and POPs become bottlenecks. In addition, many other functions are implemented on servers: registration, authentication, access control, usage recording, billing, etc. These further increase server load; combined, they may increase network load beyond the capacity of the client-server architecture.

4.3.1.2 Client-Server Architecture Extended with Proxy Machines

In order to decrease traffic through network and reduce load on servers, the proxy machines are introduced. Requests from the clients are not longer sent directly to the servers. They are sent to the proxies located nearby the clients (see Figure 4-3). Proxy machines act on behalf of both servers and clients. By caching objects, the proxies are able to directly respond to the clients without sending any request to servers. This reduces traffic over the network and decreases server load. These improvements can significantly reduce latency. Since proxies communicate with servers on behalf of clients, the communication between proxies and servers can also be optimized. For example, if multiple clients request the same object, only one request will be sent to the server instead of multiple requests from all requesting clients. The replication technique can also allow local "proxy-based" services such as registration, authentication, access control, usage recording, billing, etc. This further improves system performance.

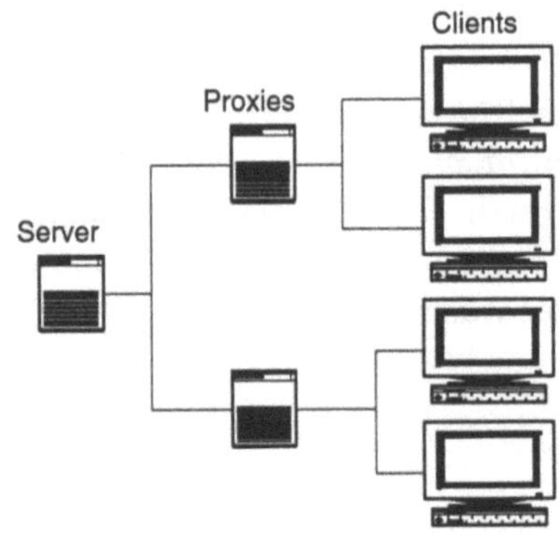

Figure 4-3: Proxy Architecture

While the proxy architecture improves the performance of the Internet information system, the gain was less than expected. There are two reasons. First, the proxies soon became the hot spots. The second reason is that proxies were isolated; they lacked any knowledge or connections to the other proxies. Therefore, they were not able to benefit from some nearby idle proxy, even when the idle proxy had the necessary functionality and information. Instead of sending the request to an idle proxy, the request was sent directly to the server. To make matters worse, nothing ensured the proxies would have the necessary information to satisfy the requests. Servers could be still become easily overloaded.

4.3.1.3 Architecture Based on Communicating Proxy Machines

To gain from nearby proxies, proxy servers, such as the Harvest cache, enabled communication between the cache proxies (see Figure 4-4). The communication scheme can be organized in many different ways, mostly in hierarchical communication structures. Hierarchical structure enables several levels of request-filtering before the request arrives at the server. It also checks whether neighbor proxies can handle the request more efficiently than the server.

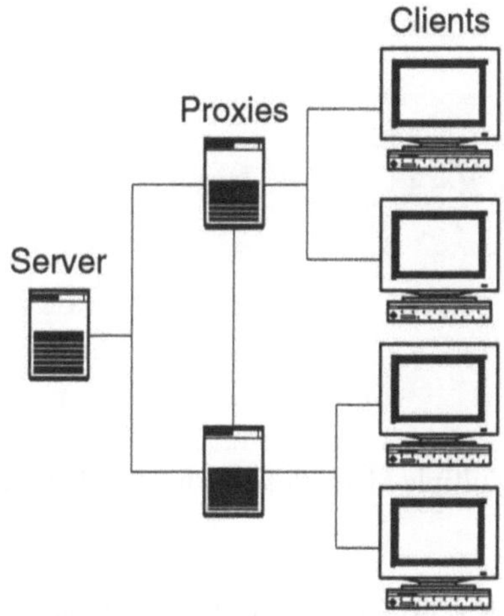

Figure 4-4: Communicating Proxies Architecture

This approach additionally reduces server load and traffic, but it could increase latency by a significant amount. Inappropriate and *ad hoc* communication schemes, as well as too many hierarchical levels, can push data requests through many stages. This significantly increases latency and traffic. Therefore, there is a need to organize the proxies into structures that can control the communication in an efficient way. In addition, without organized proxies in more firm structures it is not possible to efficiently implement all other functions such as registration, authentication, access control, usage recording, billing, etc.

4.3.1.4 Multiple Servers and POPs

In order to reduce the load on servers and POPs, multiple machines can be introduced. While this solution reduces the number of the connections and/or clients per machine, the link that connects these machines to the Internet could be overloaded. The solution with multiple machines and a single link to the Internet is presented in Figure 4-5, below.

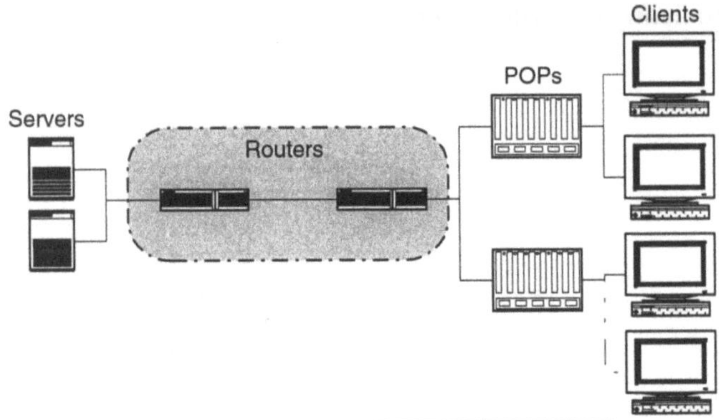

Figure 4-5: Multiple Machines Sharing Single Link

Each of the machines, which replicate the function of the server of POP, could have its own link to the Internet. This solution is presented in Figure 4-6. In this solution, both machines and links are no longer hotspots of the Internet information system. However, the interconnection network remains bottlenecked.

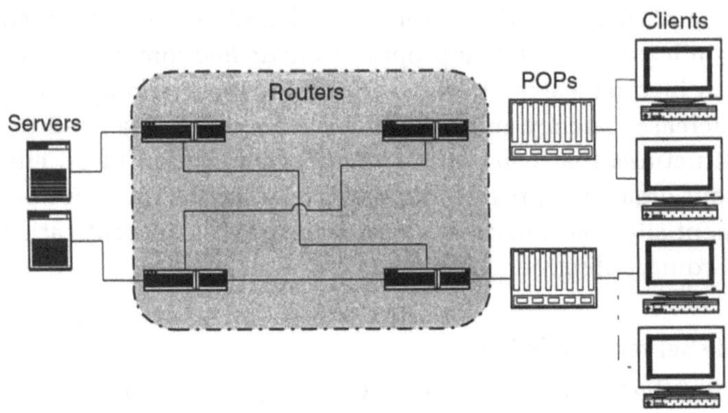

Figure 4-6: Multiple Machines Sharing Multiple Links

4.4 *Extensibility*

The network must be highly extensible to permit the adoption of new services. Deploying new services that take advantage of the enhanced network support must be relatively simple and cost effective. This extensibility must be possible for a wide spectrum of providers and their capabilities. The network should support large, well-supported and designed services such as AT&T Worldnet, as well as one-person operations hosted in their homes or small businesses.

This would be possible only if there are well defined and standardized sets of interfaces that insulate the services from any particular network's implementation. Conceptually, this requires an analog of the telephone dial tone and the RJ-11 modular plug in one's wall. The interfaces must provide the following:

- The interfaces must be provided as APIs that target standard and widely used programming languages. For example, the network core functionality is typically written in C and C++, while client software may be written in the Java language
- Different interfaces must target different subsystems and their use. It is neither practical nor desirable to create a single universal interface with the obligatory major overhead in marshaling data for various subsystems. Multiple access control issues only frustrates extensibility more. Instead, multiple interfaces – each addressing different subsystems and features – should be created. This assumes modularity of the underlying system

Interfaces insulate the two sides from each other. They simplify extensibility through the addition of new services or systems, and they also enable the transparent improvement of existing services.

4.5 Design Principles

The requirements, such as security, scalability, and extensibility, are technical and economic requirements which the final design and architecture have to satisfy. They offer a guideline for what has to be done but not how they should be achieved. Any given requirement can be achieved in a number of ways; independently or collectively; elegantly or add-hoc, etc.

To guide the process of designing an IP Service Platform, we further define a set of design principles. These principles collectively form the basis of the design process. Their definition comes from the efforts of a core group of architects. Once the set of design principles is established, much of the specification of the design and architecture becomes an exercise in execution. Furthermore, understanding the principles is of key importance in attempting to understand the final system, its components, and the relationships between the components.

In our definitions, we use the term *cloud* to refer to an IP-based network implementing the policies of the network operators, offering the service logic, and managing its users, services, and resources.

These seven principles are partially ordered to reflect their interdependence; the later principles depending on the adaptation of the earlier ones. The principles state the cloud's role in routing, membership, authentication, activity, mediation, access, and tracking.

4.5.1 Routing Principle

Hosts associated with a cloud direct all traffic between users, services, and other networks to flow unconditionally through its edge gateways.

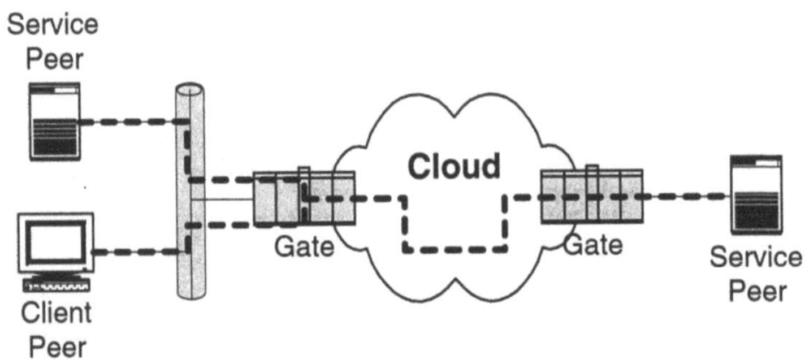

Figure 4-7: Routing Principle: Peer-Gate-Peer Communication.

For a given cloud, the edge gateways need to be under the cloud's control and they need to mediate all packets between its hosts and other networks (clouds) even if it means only relaying packets from one host to another. Here, an edge gateway can be perceived as a next-generation router or switch that has computational capability and can be dynamically controlled from the cloud's service logic. If hosts are interconnected over LANs or extranets that do not regulate the host-to-cloud flows, then mediation of the edge gateways requires explicit routing. This can use tunnels between the hosts and the edge gateways thereby directing traffic to the cloud (see Figure 4-7).

This is a very strong and somewhat controversial principle. It states that for any two hosts to communicate, their packets flow unconditionally through a mediating edge gateway. It is relatively easy to configure a host's routing table to forward all packets to a gateway. Doing so however, does not deter someone from bypassing the policies and required services of its home cloud by simply reprogramming the host. The only way to protect against this is to either dedicate a private line to the edge gateway, or tunnel all packets. In the case that this is subverted, the benefits and services offered by the cloud become inaccessible.

A weaker and somewhat more pragmatic form of this principle states that the connectivity to the cloud is optional and established only for specific networked applications. While this offers the enabled applications the benefits of the clouds, overall security cannot be guaranteed and other nonenabled applications do not benefit.

4.5.2 Membership Principle

All users, services, and other networks that establish a relationship with a cloud must register with the cloud.

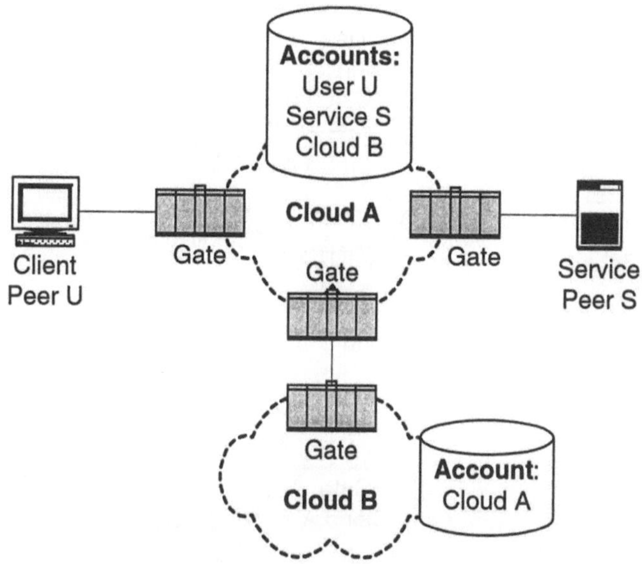

Figure 4-8: Membership Principle – One-time Initial Registration

A cloud must know the identity and profiles of its users, hosted services and other clouds with which it has working relationships (as shown in Figure 4-8). This identity is known either explicitly through prior registration or indirectly via a third party representative. Anonymous users may use a registered service as an access proxy to support a class of services on behalf of the user. Anonymous users, services, and clouds can form shared identities that yield a restricted access to otherwise registered services. To support this, a cloud needs a core directory service.

This principle states that for any traffic to pass through the cloud, the identity of the user (or other services) and the service accessed by the user be known and managed. This enables the cloud to manage the network resources and access rights for the users, services, and other clouds assuming the next principle.

4.5.3 Authentication Principle

All traffic passing through the cloud must be authenticated.

Given the Membership Principle, all traffic through the cloud needs to be authenticated by a strong bilateral authentication process (see Figure 4-9). All flows need to be associated with registered users and services. These need not belong to the cloud in question, but can be obtained by agreement from their respective clouds.

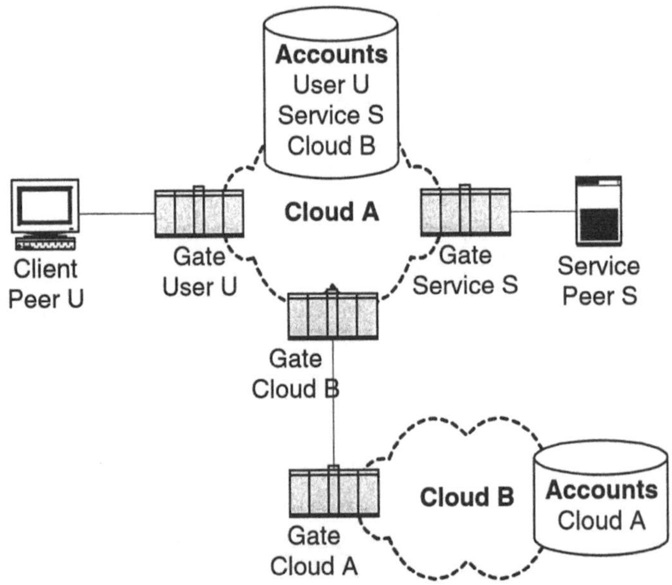

Figure 4-9: Authentication Principle – Gates Identify Access to Cloud

A strong bilateral authentication can be done either per flow or per session. This strong form of authentication allows the support of services needing strong identification such as VPNs and E-Commerce applications; it also nicely supports services needing only a weak form of authentication such as DiffServ and IntServ for which the identity of the application is sufficient, or no authentication at all, such as public and anonymous web access. Given this principle, the identities are used and offered to services based on the specific policies of the cloud and agreements with the users and service providers.

4.5.4 Activity Principle

The cloud tracks all active users and services.

The act of authenticating and the subsequent connectivity activity by a user or a service are tracked, as shown in Figure 4-10. The awareness of active participation is needed for the proper management of resources and nicely supports services requiring that information. Active directories automatically keep track of users' sessions and their locations. This function combines nicely with the Authentication Principle that can trigger log-in and log-out events to automatically update the active directories.

Given the Routing Principle, the knowledge of the activity is guaranteed for all flows through the cloud, independent of the applications. That is, the responsibility to keep track of the users' activity - at appropriate flow or session levels - falls on the cloud and not the applications.

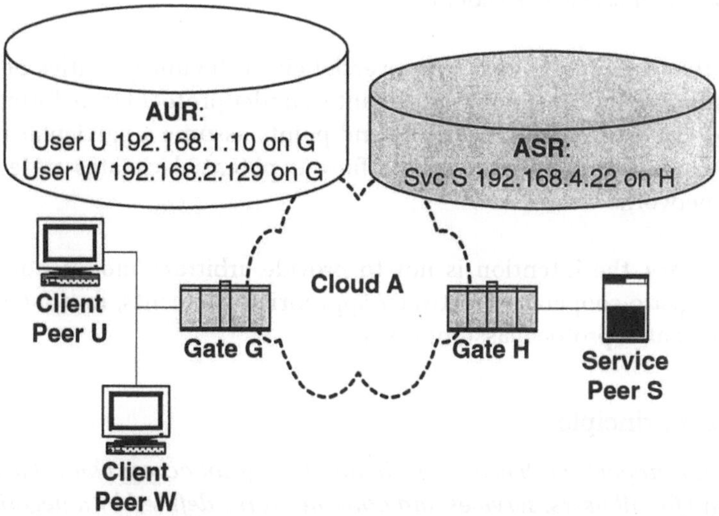

Figure 4-10: Activity Principles - Gates Monitor Authentication

4.5.5 Mediation Principle

The cloud must have the ability to mediate and translate flows through the cloud without compromising the data privacy and integrity.

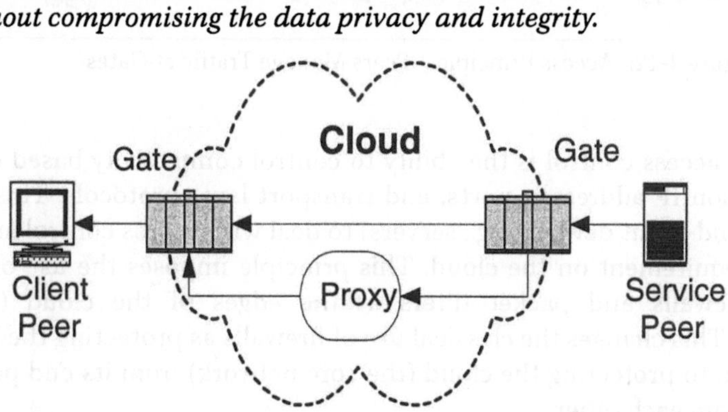

Figure 4-11: Mediation Principle - Clouds Redirect to Service Proxies.

Application-layer protocol (e.g., FTP, HTTP, or TELNET) mediation and translation can be supported via protocol-specific transparent proxies managed by the cloud (see

Figure 4-11). The cloud can redirect certain control protocols at the edge gateways to network-side proxies driven by the service subscription mechanisms. This mediation can be used to enforce service policies, implement network-level resource management and services such as fine-grain access control or usage tracking, or provide value-added services for service providers.

The mediation principal is also controversial given the uncertainties of nonintrusive correctness preservation of network semantics under protocol transformation. Changing the flow can be problematic. If the end points assume a particular network state and one changes characteristics of the flow, it potential violates state assumptions within the network.

On the contrary, the intention is not to provide arbitrary modification, but rather enable synergistic cooperation between appropriate elements, in a manner that preserves the essential protocol assumptions.

4.5.6 Access Principle

The cloud supports both coarse-grain and fine-grain access control at the edge gateways for all users, services and other networks defined by a negotiated policy.

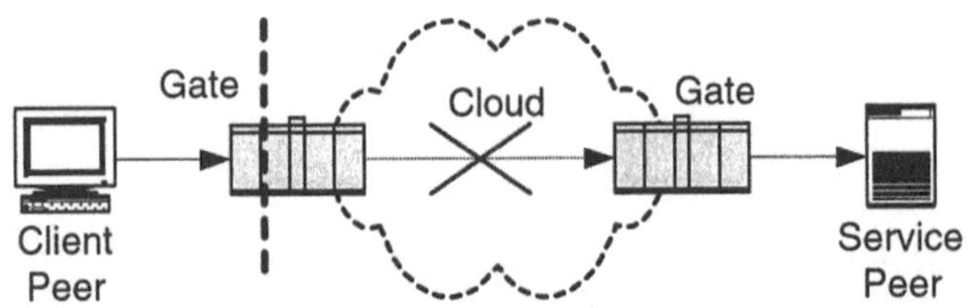

Figure 4-12: Access Principle – Peers Manage Traffic at Gates

Coarse-grain access control is the ability to control connectivity based on the source and destination IP addresses, ports, and transport layer protocols. This removes the need of the end-point devices (e.g., servers) to deal with access control and policy, and places the requirement on the cloud. This principle imposes the use of dynamically managed firewalls and packet filters at the edges of the cloud (as shown in Figure 4-12). This changes the classical use of firewalls as protecting the LAN from the outside world to protecting the cloud (the core network) from its end points, and the end points from each other.

It is instructive to reconsider the Routing Principle in view of the Access Principle just described. Fine-grain access control is the tightly coupled support of transparent proxies performing application protocol mediation redirected at the edge gateways. Fine-grain access control is the ability to control access by understanding the specific protocol and the data content of the messages. For example, simple HTTP coarse-grain access mechanisms can easily be bypassed by placing an HTTP relay (i.e., a proxy) outside the gate since the destination URL is encapsulated in the HTTP header, which firewalls and packet filters do not analyze. This can be easily controlled by analyzing the header by an HTTP access control proxy or similar forms of content inspection. Such access-control proxies can be collocated with the edge gateway; they may also refer the credentials and request to a legacy application that contains the access-control logic.

The access control at the edge gateways depends on both the Authentication and Activity Principles for managing state information about individual sessions or flows, and on the Mediation Principle for fine-grain access control.

4.5.7 Tracking Principle

The cloud generates usage and audit records for traffic generated by subscribed services and users.

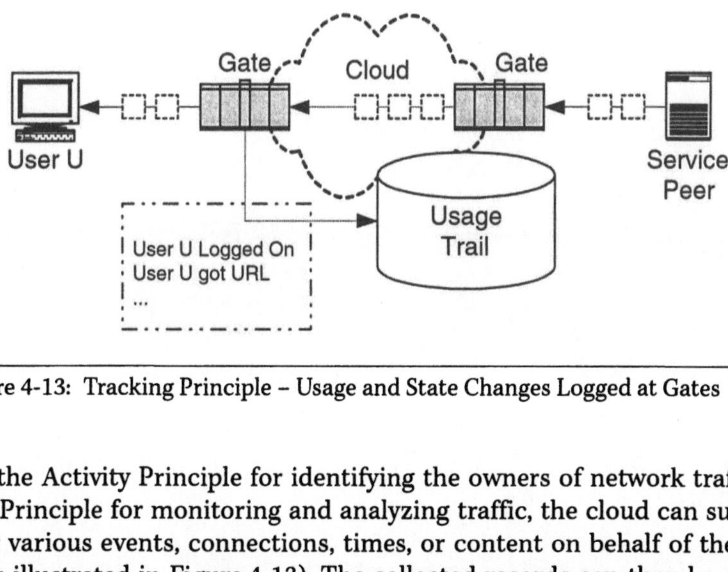

Figure 4-13: Tracking Principle – Usage and State Changes Logged at Gates

Assuming the Activity Principle for identifying the owners of network traffic and the Mediation Principle for monitoring and analyzing traffic, the cloud can submit usage records for various events, connections, times, or content on behalf of the registered services (as illustrated in Figure 4-13). The collected records can then be accessed by authorized users and services. This principle enables the cloud to support accountability, microbiology, and self-administration. The Routing Principle along with the Authentication Principles guarantee that all usage is accounted for.

4.6 Summary

The design principles presented form a basis from which the design and architecture of a IP service platform can be built, on which existing and new services can be deployed, and on which network and hardware vendors can design their components. Their choice is distilled primarily from the collective consideration of the requirements and the changing nature of the Internet as it relates to large service providers. In most cases, however, the adoption of such principles becomes the decision of the corporation undertaking the design of the IP Service Platform.

CHAPTER 5

Cloud Architecture and Interconnections

In order to realize the vision of moving some applications into the network, where they can provide better service at lower cost, we need to reengineer the network slightly. This chapter describes how to evolve the network through service-oriented clouds, and to interconnect these to create a flexible network fabric. This builds upon legacy networks, commercially available IP networking products and standards-driven protocols. Such tools are one element in the design of appropriate redundancy, specific interconnections and the trade-offs between centralization or distribution. The resulting networking middleware readily satisfies the complex and changing operational requirements for capacity, throughput and reliability. This achieves low cost through use of "off the shelf" general-purpose computers.

As part of the network reengineering, clouds will tend to rely upon optional distributed network elements (DNE). These unify a wide range of network elements through a single virtual network connection and APIs, as presented later in Section 5.5. Consider the example of VPN services superimposed upon lower-level capabilities through platform-based software. This leverages the underlying network capabilities, while drawing upon higher-level VPN techniques of tunneling and secure routing. This could secure IP routes through L2TP or IPSec for one user, MPLS for another, and custom encryption for yet another.

Network elements should exhibit a predictable and stable behavior that is largely immune to changes in configurations or components. Middleware achieves this through a uniform set of open APIs that satisfy detailed functional requirements irrespective of specific configuration. This is fundamental, particularly given the recognition that networks – and the Internet in particular – are fluid, "moving targets" that defy any purportedly "optimal" configuration. The middleware itself caters to a business-oriented service model supporting flexible provider roles. This service model accommodates the changing definitions of providers and infrastructure.

This entire section presents a concrete discussion of hardware and software that accomplish these goals. The current chapter begins with the architectural description of general architecture comprising an internal backbone network with externally facing SNodes (service nodes). The SNodes provide services near the network edge, where computing engines can serve the locally attached networks, thus attenuating the increased backbone traffic. Scalability relies on nearly stateless protocols and intelligent network interactions.

The chapter proceeds through a sequence of increasingly powerful systems - starting with a small cloud built from three computers, which supports the full middleware capabilities and the APIs. This configuration adeptly supports community-scale SNodes, and is also suitable for service development. The small cloud can evolve to support a wider range of services by joining a larger network comprised of multidomain clouds (Section 5.6). Cloud capacity and reliability can be increased by adding processing power - either through more engines, or faster multiprocessors. These larger clouds leverage the "elastic capacity" designed into the middleware though techniques such as caching and load balancing. These techniques support smooth evolution into a substantially larger cloud by adding gates, disks and internal networking. This evolutionary path eventually leverages hundreds of computers, fault-tolerant components, optimized router networks and long-distance backbones. It supports nationally deployed services. These retain the same software and data stores as the smaller systems.

Such capabilities enable fully reliable eCommerce and other essential services. These services are reliably exported to other clouds *without modification.* This model combines multiple autonomous clouds and draws upon middleware capabilities of internationalization. Each cloud supports a domain composed hierarchically of accounts, users and services. Intercloud trust relationships extend privileges to specific accounts or users from other clouds. Multiple fully autonomous clouds thereby interoperate and provide mobility of services and users.

The chapter also discusses a novel distributed cloud utilizing the public Internet for the cloud interconnections. We conclude with a discussion of Internet routing as it affects middleware.

5.1 Cloud Architecture

All clouds share the prototypical architecture of an edge gateway enforcing a security perimeter, thereby protecting core services and network-switched traffic. The gateway supports intelligent services through service-hosting and network intelligence such as routing and protocol mediation. The core services include databases that contain both dynamic and persistent object-oriented information. The gateway and core are *logical* entities that may be deployed in multiple components or distributed configurations as required.

5.1.1 Applications, Kernels and Switches

A cloud functionally consists of three major layers: application layer, kernel layer and switch layer. Each layer controls traffic according to the authentication and encryption policy. The traffic is either encrypted/decrypted and passed through a given layer, or it is redirected to a higher layer.

Application Layer

The application layer supports registration, authentication, encryption/decryption, etc. This layer replicates the data and functions in order to efficiently control traffic on all three layers. The application layer also provides fine-grain access control mechanisms. Communication through the security perimeter is regulated at multiple granularities.

Kernel Layer

The kernel layer is mainly responsible for the routing and coarse-grain access control through the support of firewalls, such as packet filters.

Switch Layer

The switch layer supports physical transport and encryption/decryption functions are performed by specially designed hardware devices, such as ATM switches. The application layer provides all needed data for the switch layer and prepares the switch layer to work at high speed. The main task of the switch layer is to support high-speed communication and real-time applications that need high bandwidth, such as telephony, video conferencing, and the like.

5.1.2 Points of Presence (POPs) and System Operation Centers (SOCs)

The physical architecture of a cloud is structured to concentrate most of the service logic as a distributed environment at the edges of the managed network. At the edges, physical Points-of-Presence (POPs) aggregate traffic from hosts and other networks, and send it into the cloud through a Service POP (SPOP), as shown in Figure 5-1.

POP

POPs are the physical points of presence that aggregate traffic from a variety of hosts and networks into the cloud. This consists of IP traffic ingress from LANs and WANs; terminating PPP connections from modems over PSTN; or terminating voice and FAX traffic from a POTS line. All traffic becomes IP based once it passes into the physical POP.

SPOP

SPOPs are the Service POPs that implement middleware layer service logic. In addition to other functionalities, SPOPs act as gateways to the backbone

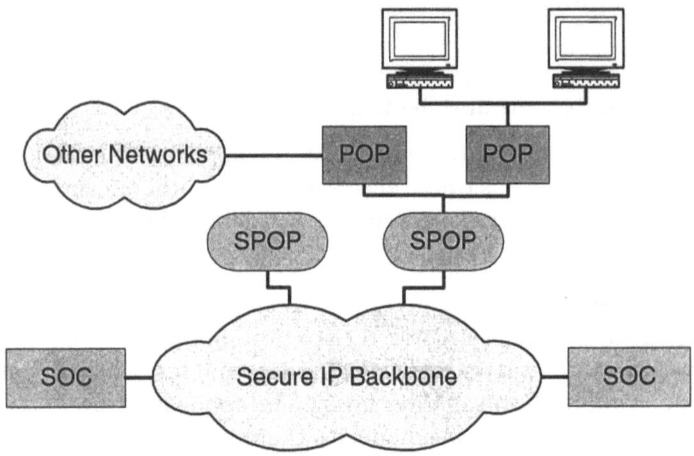

Figure 5-1: Points of Presence and Operating Centers Located at Network Edge

of high bandwidth/low latency IP transport to other SPOPs and POPs, as shown in Figure 5-1.

SOC

System Operating Centers (SOCs) are SPOPs dedicated to the system monitoring and management purposes of the cloud. SOCs may, or may not, have POPs connected directly to them as traffic to the SOCs must flow exclusively through the backbone.

An SPOP can be provisioned in a number of different ways depending on the capacity and throughput of its connections. For small to medium throughputs and a limited number of users accessing the cloud through this SPOP, the platform's service logic systems can be placed on a single (possibly a multiprocessor) machine. Here, the edge gateway implements functions such as routing and firewall as well as the service functions such as usage recording and access control. A single SPOP constructed with current technology can provide all service logic and network functions for several thousand users.

For a much larger workload and a greater number of active users and services, the SPOP can be provisioned as a group of distributed network elements in which high-speed smart switches support the network functions. The service functions utilize a cluster of edge gateways that offload the router/switch functions to a distributed network element (DNE, see Section 5.5.2). These two configurations are shown in Figure 5-2, where SPOP #1 supports large user bases through replicated processing and a distributed network element (DNE), and SPOP #2 is a single node.

The SPOPs actively support the conventional end points – users and servers – thereby enabling their active participation in the cloud's service logic and networking. These end points must support IP-based communication and an active control channel to an edge gateway in an SPOP. The channel enables and controls the managed interactions between the peer and the cloud. A peer may, for example, ensure nonrepudiation of action as well as interact with active directories.

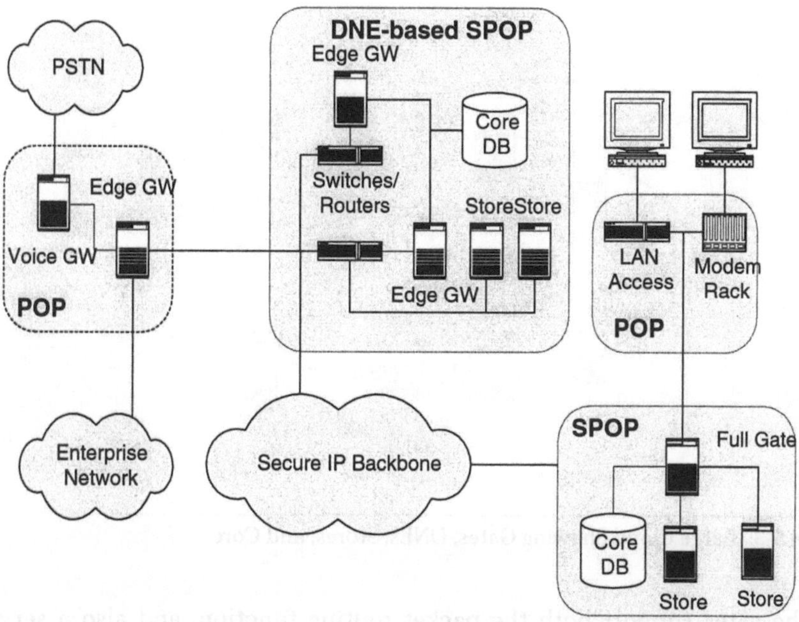

Figure 5-2: Interconnected SPOPs Using DNE and Full Gates (non-DNE).

Peers interact securely with other peers through the SPOPs of their cloud, as well as with other clouds with established peering agreements. Mandatory encryption protects the authentication and control functions, and optional encryption protects other interactions when deemed necessary. For example, a user who desires Internet access, would first establish an authenticated connection to the cloud through an SPOP. The user could then access other SPOPs, including the Internet-connected POPs.

5.1.3 Gates, Cores, and Stores

The overall networking middleware architecture is organized upon three types of the logical function: gates, cores, and stores. These form the basic elements of the distributed system, and can be combined into points of presence, or POPs, as shown in Figure 5-3.

Gates

The gateway is composed of one or more gates. These form a security perimeter protecting the system and its users from intrusion or improper use of resources. The perimeter builds upon a dynamic rules-based firewall that blocks unauthorized traffic, removes fraudulent packets, and identifies legitimate traffic. All authenticated data transmissions traverse the firewall and become subject to the security infrastructure.

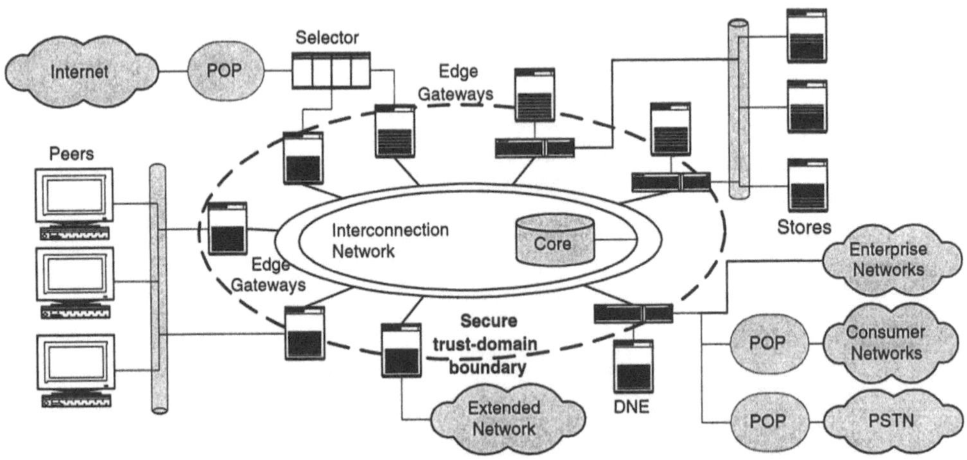

Figure 5-3: Large Cloud Showing Gates, DNEs, Stores, and Core

The gates support both the packet routing function, and also a service logic function. The gates enforce authentication, advanced security services, access control, resource usage tracking, caching, and internationalization. Gates provide protocol mediation and service as needed.

The routing functions enable connections by external networks, thereby supporting communications with the core servers and other external networks. These networks connect clients, servers, stores and POPs residing outside of the firewall, as well as noncompliant legacy and enterprise networks. The gateways are constructed from one or more gate machines.

Section 5.5.2 "Distributed Network Element Integrates Gate with Network Elements" describes the architecture that distinguishes these to roles.

Core

The Core maintains distributed information, thus supporting highly responsive and reliable operations. Distributed algorithms are used to maintain a consistent system state, thereby providing a degree of "locational independence". The core server maintains dynamic service-specific and connection-specific information on both authenticated and nonauthenticated entities. It manages local caches, providing minimal latency delay. Global correctness is preserved through locking and hashing algorithms. Dedicated hardware supports this repository of global information, which can be deployed on one or several machines, either at a single location or distributed through networking.

The Core contains both dynamic data and persistent information. Dynamic data is rapidly changing as it reflects the state of all cloud-supported connections. It includes substantial authentication data necessary for strong authentication of user sessions. Maintaining global correctness for all of this data exceeds the capabilities of commercially available LDAP servers, yet is nevertheless essential for active directories and closely tied access control and usage recording. Resolving the problem through highly optimized code, the system caches the relevant state upon establishment of a secure session, and the state is maintained for the duration of the user's connection to the network.

The Core also maintains persistent information about accounts (users and services), recent usage records, and stored cryptographic credentials:

- *Registration database.* This associates a uniquely numbered billable entity with each individual account, user or service. Data for the billable entity includes the user's name, address, point of contact, and other pertinent account information
- *Usage Database.* Operating as a nonrepudiation service, the usage database retains the details of an account's resource usage
- *Authentication base.* Secure services and transport utilize cryptographic keys, X.509 certificates, passwords and associated information. These are retained in a structured authentication base and are protected by the security perimeter

Store

A store implements services dealing with maintenance, provisioning, and daily use of the system. This includes white and yellow pages directory functions, customer care, billing, e-mail, voice mail, and paging messaging. It also covers such related databases as customer contact and tracking, archival usage records, billing histories, and historical network logs.

5.1.4 POP Based Authentication and Aggregation

The combination of gates, cores and stores forms the POP, which provides an access point and service point, as shown previously in Figure 5-3. This provides multiple granularities of network connectivity and authentication services. The finest granularity is an individual subscriber. The individual subscriber registers an identity with the cloud and then authenticates directly to the cloud for access to both subscriber-hosted services and cloud-supported services.

At a coarser grain, the POP supports externally hosted aggregation services typically operated by an aggregation provider. The provider is a corporate entity, whereas the services are the "electronic commodity" available through the provider. The aggregation service combines the traffic of many subscribers. Aggregation services are configurable through the aggregation provider, an entity that operates a pool of modems or LAN connections and provides value-added services to its subscribers. The provider registers subscribers, accepts responsibility for their activities, and supports an authentication method. Standard authentication support includes RADIUS, NAT-based Web-browser access, and Microsoft internetworking. The aggregation server passes the composite traffic to the POP, where the users receive services in accordance with access permissions of the aggregation provider.

Aggregation by Internet Service Providers (ISPs) supports public use of cloud services, for example through bulk sale of services. The SPOP allows administration as well as "branding" of an ISP's service. A corporate enterprise, by way of contrast, receives specialized and private aggregation. The enterprise augments existing corporate services through cloud-managed services available to authorized employees. Attractive elements of these models include the preservation and extension of existing logon identities and their associated business relationships.

In summary, the POP interacts closely with cloud security structure. Consider the example of a dial-up service building upon the RADIUS authentication server common to corporate and public networks. These servers may authenticate their users with the RADIUS server and proxy software of the cloud, thereby leveraging the provider's existing infrastructure. This specifically includes RADIUS as an authentication mechanism to obtain cloud access, and also RADIUS authentication as a supported cloud service provided to other authentication platforms. Both of these leverage the existing infrastructure to support rapid construction of scalable and reliable services.

5.2 Small Cloud: Development and Providers

A small cloud (see Figure 5-4) supports the complete functionality of a smart network, including routing, authentication, access control and proxies. When such a cloud is connected to the backbone network, we call it a service node (SNode). SNode users may obtain membership in supported services, security protection, and other essential services. The architecture is suitable for small-scale (entry-level) providers of either networks or consumer services, and it provides a scalable approach for services development.

Within this small SNode, all secure information resides on a single core server (labelled `coredb` in the figure). Essential cloud services run on the `store1` machine and provide web server, mail and key applications. This cloud shows one external gate (`gate2.vanecek.com`) connecting the "insecure" internet with the cloud and services. The gate supports all standard services, including authentication, access control, and submission or retrieval of usage information. The gate supports Internet standards including routing and DNS.

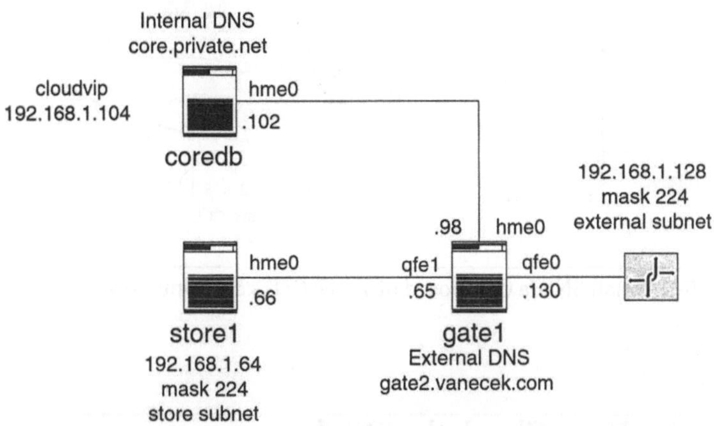

Figure 5-4: Single-Gate Cloud with Centralized Store

The reader will notice special "virtual IP address" named `cloudvip`. This protects the internal cloud address, insulates the users from the internal network dependencies and variabilities of a distributed network, and also provides a means by which the cloud can provide subscriber-specific services. The `cloudvip` name is advertised by the domain name service (DNS) running on the gate. The gates determine the services that will be provided to all internally-bound connections. The gate may route the connection to a cloud component, and may also proxy the connection when appropriate.

Protection of the cloud's internal addresses is not inappropriate. A user should never directly address core services. The core is only addressable from inside the cloud, where it provides service to cloud components and systems management. This mechanism not only protects the core, but permits resolution of `cloudvip` to different addresses in a multiple-gate environment, and is one means of load balancing.

The small cloud of Figure 5-4 can grow by adding more gates, stores, or network adapters. Figure 5-5 shows an SNode with three edge connections. This leads incrementally to the construction of larger service nodes.

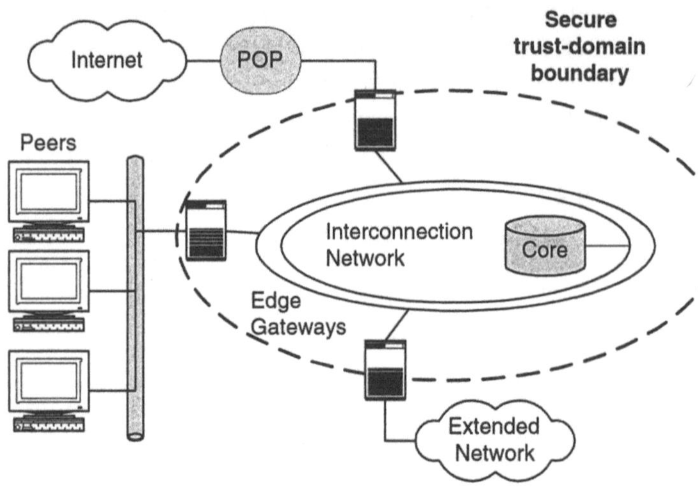

Figure 5-5: Small SNode Composed of Three Gates and One Core

5.3 Large Service Node Cloud, the SNode

The SNode architecture scales to very large sizes and reuses the value-added services that were developed on smaller SNodes. A very large configuration combines fault-tolerant processing with a high capacity self-healing transport network. This class of system delivers coordinated services through the aggregation of many multiprocessors, having a value of many millions of dollars. The system load is reduced by caches at the gates, and all components (gates, core and store) run in a failover mode. The disk arrays, for example, include multiported disks with failover software. Internal switching uses fast network switches supporting various routing protocols. Management functions leverage the additional fault-tolerant routers, disk arrays, and failstop processors. The configuration supports continuous "24 x 7" operation.

Due to the large size, we partition the large SNode into three major subsystems. The *mediation subsystem* dynamically mediates protocols, supports authentication, and provides access control. It can interact with the transport subsystem to ensure satisfactory network performance by dynamic adjustment of switches and routers.

A distinct *Hosting Subsystem* provides peer-enabled server machines. Many of the hosting machines support network-enhanced proprietary applications. Others are dedicated to operations support such as customer information, billing and manual interactions. The third major subsystem, the *transport subsystem*, is composed of hops that provide the dial-based as well as IP-based connectivity to other SNodes.

While the specific management algorithms require capacity-based "tuning" for optimal performance, the basic middleware runs unaltered on clouds of different sizes. Software-based services retain the same API interfaces. The platform middleware supports these APIs through large-scale versions of the underlying components, as well as through platform-managed extensions. These extensions augment and combine components through middleware techniques described in Chapter 9.

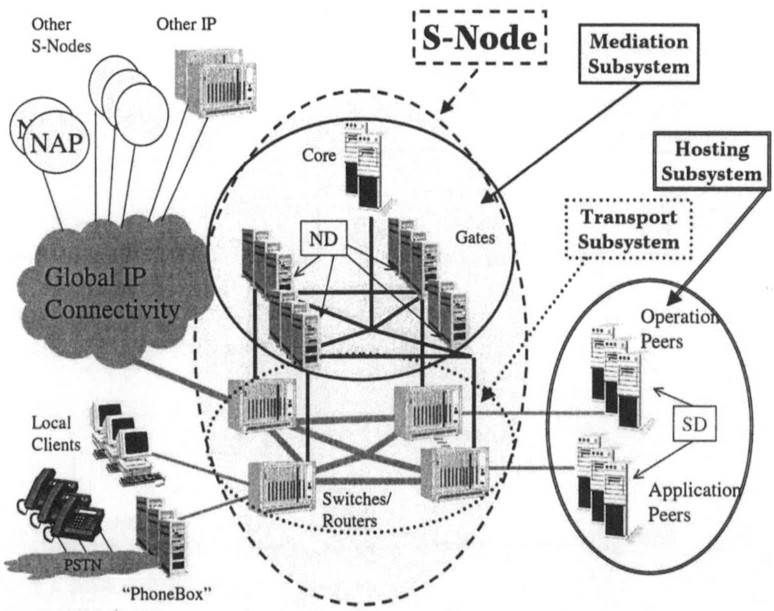

Figure 5-6: Logical View of a Large Middleware Service Node

5.4 *Distributed Network Cloud (GuNet)*

The networking middleware also runs on a rather surprising configuration utilizing the public Internet as the connection between the gate and core components. Known as GuNet, the gates are geographically distributed at University campuses. Instead of secure routers with spare capacity, the IP traffic follows the often-congested public network that is subject to long delays, outages, and security attacks. Security attacks are a virtual certainty because the Internet is not secure in any sense. Connectivity by Virtual Private Networks (VPN) is mandatory for the core interconnect in such cases. This can be provided with hardware devices (such as Cylink's Secure Domain Units (SDU) encryption engines), or through software methods, although this increases CPU load.

A diagram of a GuNet cloud is shown in Figure 5-7. This shows multiple SPOPS, represented by gates such as uoregon-gate, cmu-gate, and drexel-gate. These SPOPS maintain private core information; for example, cached information about the users and services that the SPOPs communicate with. The SPOPs also share a central core on the cloudvip subnetwork of the sj-gate. Access to the core uses the VPNs that link the gates through the Internet.

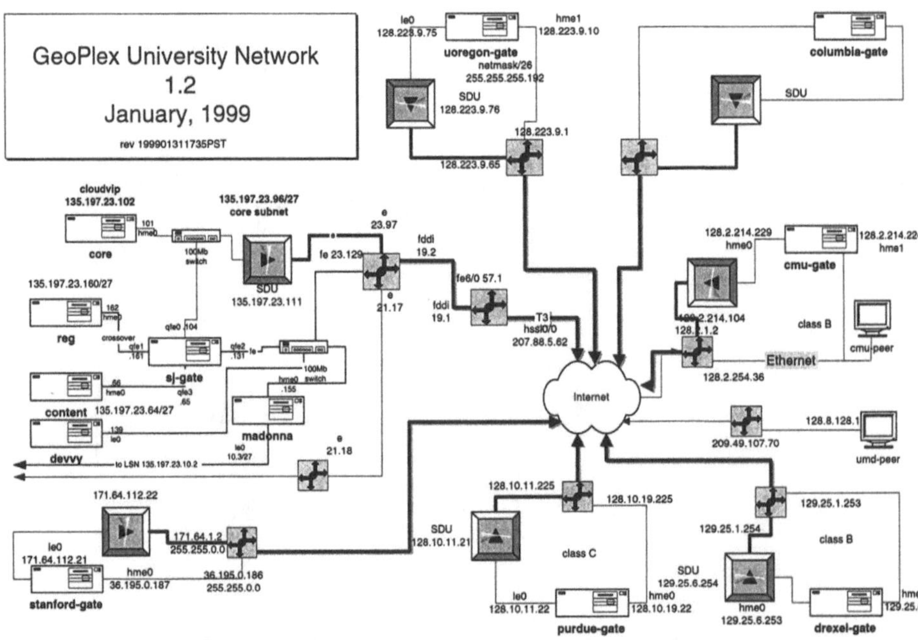

Figure 5-7: Distributed GUNet Cloud Via Cylink's VPN Solution Over Internet

The unreliable and unmanaged public Internet interconnections can be viewed as a well-nourished "petri dish" of network pathologies. This is quite important in the design and development of reliable systems. The relatively large error rate and the unpredictable error model guarantee an effective "stress test" of the network middleware. The actual test environment presents fault scenarios not found in simulated testing. Although network engineers frequently use fault simulators (such as the TAS®) to understand system behavior under erred conditions, such simulations are constrained to specific fault models. The simulation of "real world" error scenarios is frequently elusive. The distributed GuNet cloud leverages the changing error profile of the Internet, thereby providing a test bed for interesting network problems.

The fact that GuNet has been "running live" in this environment for several years is a convincing demonstration that the software is perspicuous and adaptable. It is refreshingly free of timing dependencies, link-delay assumptions, and their ilk. This validates our design assumptions, particularly that of a single software definition that supports many configurations.

5.5 Gates as Distributed Network Elements (DNE)

Service functionality is concentrated at the network edge where the SNodes provide intelligent network-based services. The cost-effective realization of these services requires careful resource management. Unfortunately, data networks today do not contain much integrated intelligence; they transport data packets between hosts by routing and switching the packets. In relation to the network topology, the path taken by a data packet varies from moment to moment. The hosts typically have only an indirect influence on the routes, bandwidth or delay. These routing algorithms are designed for reliability and good aggregate behavior, but their typical behavior does not necessarily satisfy the specific resource requirements of diverse applications. The performance of the edge gateways, not surprisingly, presents several technical challenges in the areas of network management, including routing and resource allocation within the network elements.

5.5.1 Routing Protocols and the Inherent Difficulty of Resource Allocation

Routing is inherently difficult due to the large number of routers under multiple autonomous systems (AS), dynamically changing loads, and variation in topology. Routes between ASs rely on external gateway protocols (EGPs), thereby achieving independence from the routing within the AS. EGPs consider coarse-grain constraints imposed by independent ASs, which may belong to different network providers. Border Gateway Protocol (BGP, RFC-1771) is the best known EGP.

Routing within an AS considers different constraints through an internal gateway protocol (IGP). These include the Routing Information Protocol (RIP, RFC-2453) and the substantially more powerful Open Shortest Path First (OSPF, RFC-2676). OSPF is a dynamic routing protocol in the sense that it detects topology changes and adjusts routes accordingly. It is the most powerful of the current link-state routing algorithms.

OSPF describes route characteristics through the type of service (TOS) feature and corresponding DS header of the IP packets. TOS describes route characteristics such as monetary cost, reliability, throughput and delay. However, routers are not required to support all TOS values; nor can the routers ensure suitable routes for each service type. In practice it is quite difficult for a host application to control either the specific path or the characteristics of the path. It is very difficult in standard IP to make the association between data flows and the application to which they belong.

This gives rise to one of the most difficult aspects of implementing an end-to-end resource allocation policy in a network environment. To run properly, a multimedia application needs a variety of resources. Host behavior is sensitive to allocations of CPU time, memory allocation and I/O cycles. Network behavior such as bandwidth and delay are sensitive to the specific routes between network elements, as well as the low-level allocations in the switches or routers, for example queue space and I/O ports. These allocations are difficult to assign.

Two models describe different forms of network resource allocation. IntServ (RFC-1633, RFC-2210) strives for "guaranteed and predictive service". Thus we have protocols – such as RSVP (RFC-2205) – which provide a method, rather than guaranteed and scalable service. The differentiated services (DiffServ, RFC-2475) model for QoS is satisfied with more modest goals that do not require substantial saved state, and hence DiffServ is scalable.

Under DiffServ an application can suggest bandwidth allocation. The network element can either satisfy or reject the request; the element does not provide remedial actions for rejected requests. This model cannot provide direct support for resource allocations, simply because the network elements do not possess sufficient information about the availability of resources throughout the network. The DiffServ model nevertheless provides guidelines for the management of network resources, and identifies the problem as the responsibility of the administrative domain such as the network operator. As stated in the RFC:

> The configuration of and interaction between traffic conditioners and interior nodes should be managed by the administrative control of the domain and may require operational control through protocols and a control entity. There is a wide range of possible control models. *The precise nature and implementation of the interaction between these components is outside the scope of this architecture.* However, scalability requires that the control of the domain does not require micromanagement of the network resources. [DiffServ, RFC-2475, page 20]

Even without the combinatorial explosion that micromanagement would bring, the control models, protocols and entities still impose a performance penalty and generate extra traffic in the network.

The DiffServ model recognizes that substantial performance improvements can be obtained simply by providing several classes of traffic. In the simplest form this distinguishes low bandwidth traffic from the high bandwidth isochronous traffic. The primary origin of low bandwidth traffic is control messages. These are typically generated by value-added services and receive gate mediation. Control messages must receive rigorously enforced security services. On the other hand, high bandwidth isochronous traffic carries mostly raw data such as video and audio. The transport is the exclusive domain of specialized switches and routers. Control of the high-speed transport may use either a low-speed link or specially coded control words embedded in the high-speed stream.

Refinements of the SNode architecture can ameliorate the major bottlenecks on high-speed transport. The bottlenecks occur due to the conventional hosts and IP transport delays. Regardless of CPU power, the transfer of data from an input network interface (NI) to an output NI limits the sustained throughput of the gateway, and may also imposes substantial overhead on the CPU. The distributed control of the TCP/IP protocol is another bottleneck. For example, the sliding-window methods of congestion avoidance (such as "slow start" as well as "fast retransmit") impose limits that may best be resolved through supplementary signalling.

The central concept is the avoidance of NI-based hosts in the path between the originating host and network. The data must travel, as much as possible, on network elements exclusively. Shifting traffic from the slow network nodes to the fast network elements is desirable because the network elements provide better switching than any host can provide.

5.5.2 Distributed Network Element Integrates Gate with Network Elements

To address these challenges, we devised an edge gateway architecture that is based on a Distributed Network Element (DNE), as shown in Figure 5-8. A DNE is a new generation of network gateway that provides the services offered by our clouds without compromising the performance of the network.

A DNE is a network element which has its main functionality implemented on a system formed by at least one transport element (an ATM switch or a router) and one service element (a gate in the SNode). The DNE provides APIs and hardware that combines multiple forms of transport with the varying service requirements of the service elements.

5.5.2.1 DNE Specialization of Gate Functionalities

The DNE behaves like a single virtual network device supporting the gate functionality. This functionality can be split into two parts, one dealing with the handling of packets and one dealing with the handling of services. The transport related functions are controlled by the DNE network element, while the service related functions are placed on the service node (which we'll continue to refer to as a gate). The gate is then seen as a higher-level controller for the associated network switch or switches. This is shown in Figure 5-8.

The high-speed transport utilizes any of the new generation switches or routers that can be dynamically controlled via either a custom protocol, or a standard protocol. The DNE adapts to standard switch protocols including Virtual Switch Interface (VSI) and

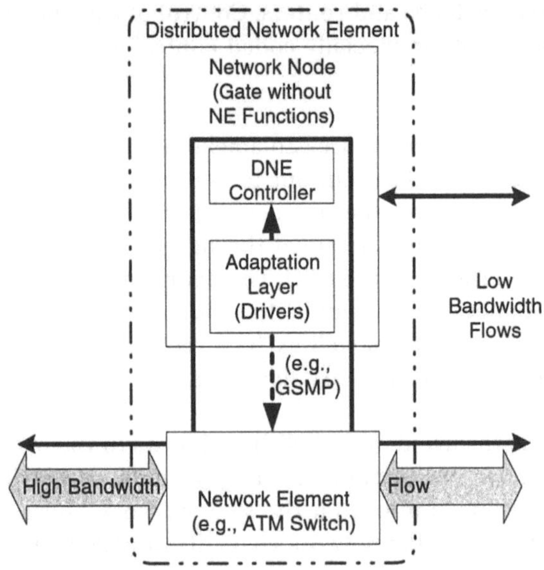

Figure 5-8: Distributed Network Element (DNE)

General Switch Management Protocol (GSMP, RFC-2297). It interacts, for example, with Cabletron's Smart Switched Routers controlled through SNMP; Cisco's BPX ATM switches controlled through Virtual Switch Interface (VSI); or Cisco's IP routers (IOS 12.05X) controlled through their proprietary Application Service Architecture (CASA) protocol. The DNE provides a clear separation between the intricacies of these protocols, on one hand, and the function areas required by the gates, on the other.

5.5.2.2 DNE Functional Areas

The network element can itself be a single unit or a tightly coupled set of units that collectively support low-level packet functions related to quality of service, packet filtering, firewall, authentication, resource allocation, stream encryption and decryption, tunnelling, routing tables, and data flows. More specifically, consider the following:

Filtering

Coarse-grain access control by rejecting or forwarding packets based on the source and/or destination IP addresses, ports and protocols. Traffic can be allowed or disallowed at the network elements. The network may implement partial access control, as well as software-defined routing, as shown in Figure 5-9.

Routing, Switching and Load Balancing

Redirection of a stream to a new destination IP address/port based on the source and/or destination IP addresses, ports and protocol to balance the load of the network or satisfy QoS SLAs. Network elements can receive specific traffic routes, as shown in Figure 5-9.

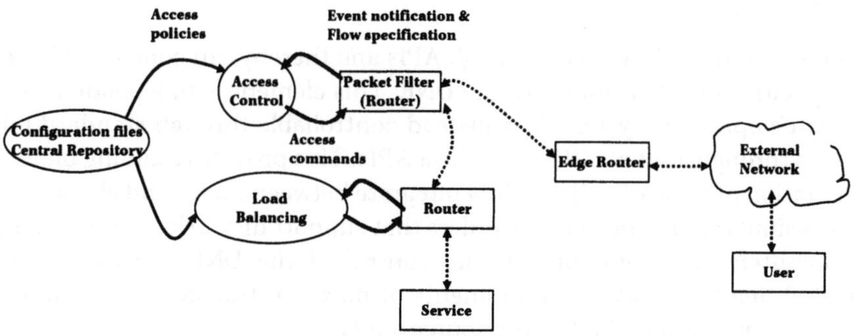

Figure 5-9: Network-Based Access Control

Control and Management

Distribution and dynamic control/management of network elements though VSI or GSMP. We present a management interface for relatively static management and monitoring of the DNE in Chapter 9.

Resource Allocation and Monitoring

Collection and monitoring of traffic statistics, utilization and performance data. As service-based network systems become more complex and distributed it becomes critical that a network management system employ real-time expert management tools. These tools dynamically monitor and allocate system resources, while also adjusting the parameters of the network control algorithms. Operating as the natural extension of a firewall, traffic management can be deployed within networking elements such as routers and switches.

QoS

Allocation and assignment of traffic classes and switch resources. The DNE provides an API and formal protocol to control supported QoS by access control devices, network elements and applications. These define "service spaces" that map QoS policies to traffic flow attributes. This allows layer 2 to layer 4 switching/routing. The industry trend is to access network elements and nodes in a unified way using directory services and protocols such as Lightweight Directory Access Protocol (LDAP, RFC-1777).

Network Development APIs support increased integration of the software-defined gate architecture as it interacts with the DNE hardware and switch infrastructure. We refer to this as the DNEAPI; this software is provided in C++, CORBA and Java, as discussed in Chapter 9.

Transport

Integration of IP Multicast and tunneling protocols with the cloud middleware functions. This improves scalability and supports virtual private network functions with efficient network-level technologies.

5.5.2.3 DNE Behavior

The SNodes obtain DNE services through APIs and thereby can control and exploit the streaming-data capability built into the DNE. This element is independent of its controlling gate's operating system. It is instead controllable through standard interfaces with access through a set of C/C++ and Java APIs. This provides building blocks for the next generation of networks that tightly integrate between nodes and elements. In concept this is similar to the device controllers that support disk drives or printers on personal computers, although the internal control of the DNE is considerably more complicated due to stringent requirements of maximal transfer rate, minimal delay, and zero lost data despite fluctuating source loads.

To illustrate a scenario, suppose that a client wants to connect to a video-streaming server. The client traffic needed for the "negotiation phase" (e.g., authentication and access control) requires high security due to the authentication and billing content. The DNE forwards this to the network node via a secured connection. The node verifies the client identity, access permissions and service requests.

When a service requires high bandwidth with QoS support, the DNE commands the network element to open a direct connection between the client and the server. This traffic does not need to be encrypted by the distributed network element, since it will bypass the network node and therefore it cannot endanger the secure domain. Of course, the traffic can still be encrypted at the application level. The node thus implements the user, provider and service policies and maps them onto the network elements. During the client-server communication, the gate can monitor the connection, monitor the end point identities and resource usage, and also redirect the traffic at the start or end of a connection. This supports the mediation design principle while also satisfying the performance requirements of transport services.

To summarize, the DNE is a concept for a new generation of network gateways. This architecture is highly scalable and avoids a significant bottleneck for high bandwidth traffic – the network node – while allowing the network nodes to act as general-purpose computers that add intelligence to the network. In this, it should be clear that our design principles and the proposed cloud architecture make up but one model of this system. In any case, this dual system behaves like a single virtual and intelligent network element with its functionality implemented in a distributed manner. It promotes a new concept: by using open and dynamic APIs and standard protocols, the network elements and nodes constitute a tightly coupled dual system.

5.6 Scaling with Multiple Clouds

DNEs allow scaling at edges of a given cloud. Scaling can also be achieved in a number of other ways. We previously described a single high-capacity cloud (scaling of the processing power) and a single geographically distributed cloud (scaling of location). The cloud architecture can support multiple account hierarchies (called domains, as will be discussed later). The domain structure may also vary in accordance with the administrative concerns that are relevant to the domain.

Independent domains can be hosted on fully autonomous clouds. Each cloud is separately administered. Each cloud hosts a unique domain, providing a convenient partitioning of the users while also bounding the necessary cloud size. New domains can then be added without affecting the other clouds, and the complexities of increasingly larger clouds can by managed through several smaller domains.

A cloud may establish trust relationships with other clouds, and subsequently request authentication of "visiting" users or services. The trust relationship supports the selective sharing of domain objects. The reader may view multidomain as similar to post office routing – each user has a unique address. These addresses can be used to obtain any necessary information about the user and provide appropriate services of the user's "neighborhood".

There are a number of important considerations in multidomain deployments. These include the problem of unique names, as well as maintaining the trust relationships between each of the domains. Consider Figure 5-10. This views each cloud as a unique administrative domain. These administrative domains may be composed of multiple domains. Domains trust each other on a bilateral basis, but not on a transitive basis. Thus, $cloud_A$ and $cloud_B$ trust each other, and $cloud_B$ may share mutual trust with $cloud_C$. This does not require that $cloud_A$ trust $cloud_C$. In this example, trusting domains are willing to accept the authentication services of other domains, and will then provide access control to the authenticated user. The clouds enforce the trust policies with mechanisms of nonrepudiation, usage recording, and domain information.

Trust is administered at the level of accounts and services, not at the cloud. Each user or service in an account can be granted a subscription to other elements of any trusted domain's structure. In keeping with the hierarchical trust model, the account path from service to the client must permit service access, and in addition the client must be subscribed to the service. This information is contained in active registries; the content and programming of these registries is given in Section 8.2.

5.7 Summary

This chapter presented the cloud architecture and examples. The functional architecture consists of distinct layers designated as switch, kernel and application. These operate at physical Points of Presence, called POPs. The POP provides aggregation from ingress networks. A Service POP (SPOP) extends the POP through a gateway

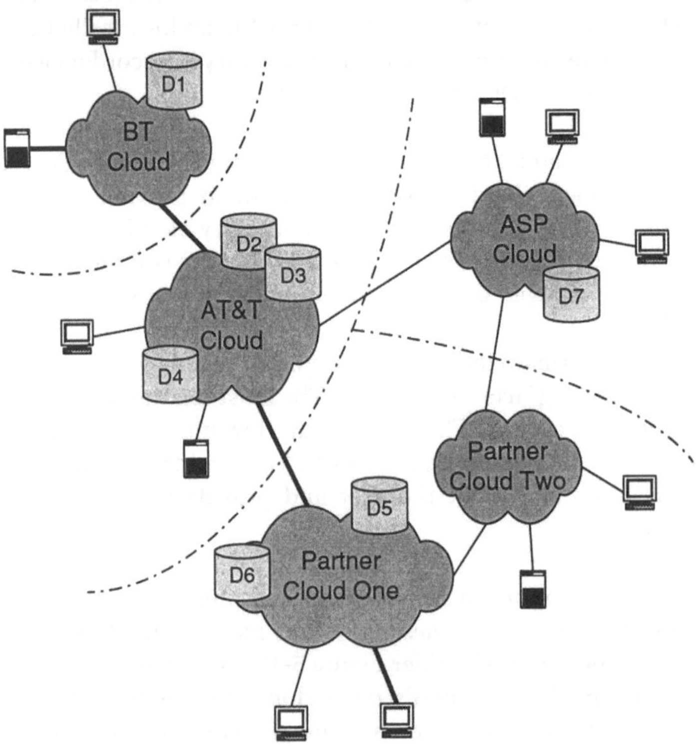

Figure 5-10: Networks Scale with Multiple Autonomous Domains

function to the backbone network, as well as middleware layer service logic. The SPOP gateway includes routers and switches; highly efficient SPOPs utilize a distributed network element (DNE) providing an extended interface to the switch layer. Dedicated SPOPs provide monitoring and management as Systems Operation Centers (SOCs). A localized configuration of POPs, SPOPs and SOCs is called a service node (SNode).

The logical SNode organization consists of gate, core and store. The logical gate operates at the switch, kernel and application layers. At the lowest layer the gate forms a security perimeter through a dynamic rules-based firewall, authentication mechanisms and the optional DNE. The gate provides access-controlled routing at the kernel layer. At the application layer, the gate executes middleware service logic. Global system information resides within the security perimeter, through the logical core. This including dynamic tables and persistent databases; in particular the domain database. Stores support the servers and applications for the consumer-oriented applications as well as archival information pertaining to cloud operations.

A common set of open APIs supports application development, as will be discussed beginning in Chapter 7. The APIs are architecture independent and configuration indpendent. They are designed for simple scalability and reuse on a wide range of physical deployments. The APIs receive support through middleware mechanisms as discussed in subsequent chapters. A service that is developed on one configuration can migrate unchanged to another configuration, either through soft configuration (such as load balancing) or by reinstallation of the service on a new cloud. This scalability allows designers to deploy services that previously were too expensive, cumbersome or risky.

These principles are validated on a variety of clouds - from a single gate SNode up through large SNodes composed of many dozens of multiprocessor gates, stores and switching fabric. A variety of interconnections support communication within the SNode, as well as between them. Multiple autonomous clouds can interconnect to form larger aggregate networks through multiple domains with shared trust. Services are share the same APIs and the same IP infrastructure. Thus, the services leverage the most recent IP advances including IP switching.

We will now turn to an in-depth description of the software environments for development of such systems.

PART III

Building the IP Service Platform

The first two parts of this book describe the history and technology background, motivate the need for moving intelligence into the data networks, and define requirements and design principles. Part III shows how to achieve the requirements within a network infrastructure characterized by security, extensibility, manageability, and programmability. The focus here is on specific solutions that support the premise that certain components belong with the network, rather than with clients and servers. We begin with discussion of the system security. We proceed in subsequent chapters to describe the software, and elaborate on the architecture, APIs, and support for systems that are scalable, interoperable and secure.

Global connectivity provides an amazing selection of resources. Some, such as databases, newspapers, or motion-picture archives, focus upon data. Others focus upon actions – for example, authentication, purchasing, and problem-solving. Examples of advanced action services include rule-based diagnostics, machine translation, and text-to-speech generation. The composition of such services can quickly create compelling new services. Such composition leads to the view of individual services as "service modules", underscoring the need for an intelligent, extensible platform into which to plug the modules.

We base much of this part on the GeoPlex architecture and APIs, as described in the preface to this book.

CHAPTER 6 Interoperable and Scalable Security

Networking middleware challenges a basic dilemma of system security: security *constrains* privileges, whereas interoperability and scalability *extend* privileges. Secure systems ensure information privacy and integrity. They resist noxious interactions that could arise from component failure, malicious elements, or simple error. System security may achieve these goals through precise definition of the systems' objects, and enforcement of the permissible relationships between them. This approach relaxes the many restrictions found in closed systems, such as their dependence on the specific hardware, software, interconnects and physical access – such restrictions are incompatible with open systems. Specifically, scalability increases the number and locations of the secured entities, and typically, these locations are not controlled. Interoperability facilitates the seamless integration of diverse products and networks. Rather than restrict the permissible components, we resolve the dilemma by integrating multiple technologies within a secure fundamental structure, and making them accessible through common APIs. We call this an "extensible framework".

Security is a fundamental, ever-present theme of the architecture. Unlike many other systems, security has not been added after the fact or designed as an extension grafted onto an earlier architecture. The security architecture is fully integrated into the architecture as a whole; consequently, all actions are mediated by the underlying mechanisms. These enforce the object relationships. To this end, the security architecture has four goals:

- Maintain information secrecy; that is, prevent sensitive information from being revealed to unauthorized parties
- Ensure information integrity; that is, prevent the undetected alteration or adulteration of information

- Guarantee accountability; that is, prevent one user or service from either undetectable assuming the identify of another or denying, at some later date, their participation in a transaction
- Ensure availability; that is, prevent a malicious subscriber or external agent from denying service to others

The security mechanisms are designed so that they:

- Cannot be circumvented accidentally
- Cannot be circumvented deliberately without a high probability of detection and a significant level of effort by an adversary
- Do not present a unreasonable burden to either system operators or end users

To prevent accidental circumvention, the various security mechanisms are introduced at the lowest appropriate level in the system. The system structure prevents a higher-level service from bypassing any lower level. To prevent deliberate circumvention, the middleware networking employs cryptographic checks, as well as administratively secured networks where appropriate and verifiable. The cryptography, based on widely adopted and rigorously inspected industry standards, will frustrate a determined adversary by requiring effort well in excess of the likely value of the information.

Finally, almost all of the security measures are automatic and occur transparently without end user or operator intervention. By making every effort to minimize the burden on users and operators, the middleware network ensures that security mechanisms will not be ignored or set aside by frustrated users or harried system operators.

Networked security services support a flexible service model through the integration of multiple security mechanisms. These include access control, management of cryptographic credentials, and the integration of disparate security domains. A subscriber authenticates to the platform exactly once, at the beginning of a session. This initial authentication provides a proof of identity by secure methods such as challenge-response or authentication certificates. Access to services is granted in accordance with the user and service profiles. A data path is established only for the permissible requests.

6.1 Secure System Structure

Security services for the cloud are provided by appropriate functionalities built into a managed platform. One cannot assume that encryption, for example, resolves all security issues. Indiscriminate use of security mechanisms would be expensive, yet provide few guarantees. On the other hand, structured and managed use of the platform enables large-scale interoperability within reasonable cost. Managed security strives to provide the appropriate security features within specified resource limits. Instead of globally imposing security restrictions, we provide an open platform that manages security at multiple granularities. This provisions the security mechanisms that are best suited for particular applications. Thereby, managed security enforces well defined safeguards, while also controlling the cost of information protection. For example, cloud-managed key lengths and key redistribution are two security management services.

The elements of our middleware security framework, shown in Figure 6-1, include:

- Platform authentication, access control, and transport security. These are based upon custom- and standards-defined protocols
- Secure protocols, algorithms, syntax and devices. These include standards-based methods and a suite of private methods
- Secure subsystems. These are composed from the protocols, algorithms, syntax and devices
- Management of the secure subsystems. This enforces policies such as permissible usage, strength of protection, and the granularity of information that is affected by a security association. For example, are all resources of one end point under the same security association – or is each resource protected independently? Similarly, multiple locations might share a security association (SA). Managed subsystems validate the correct operation of the systems
- Credential formation, account creation and credential enrollment. This constructs an association between a resource and a secure subsystem. This may also describe permissible use and interactions between resources
- Authentication procedures. These establish object identity through the defined subsystems
- Authorization procedures. These define the permissible object interactions, and are mediated by the platform when interactions utilize multiple subsystems
- Enforcement procedures. These guarantee that approved interactions occur as defined

Platform authenticators support multiple authentication methods. In addition to the platform's own native methods, other well known schemes supported include X.509 certificates, Transport Layer Security (TLS - RFC 2246), IPSec, and validation of Microsoft Windows NT accounts by means Windows NT 4.0 server, for example.

The platform security framework ensures that only authorized components and users gain access to the cloud, thanks to strong authentication and access control mechanisms. One benefit of this is a single-sign-on (SSO) capability. SSO addresses many

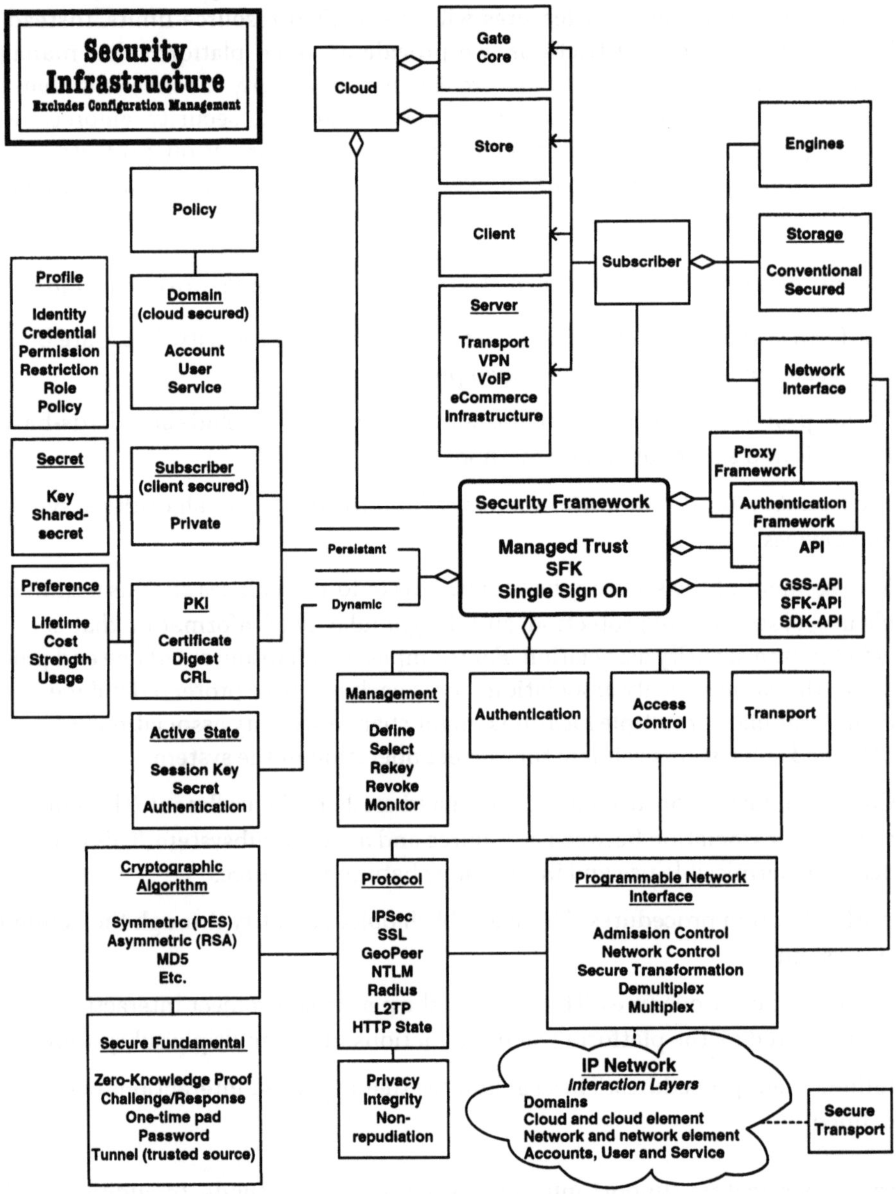

Figure 6-1: Architecture of Middleware System Security

common security concerns, ranging from such practical issues as user convenience to evaluation of security threats:

- Practical concerns include the difficulty of providing diverse clients with suitable authentication software and credentials, while maintaining reasonable user friendliness
- Policy concerns include the decision to reveal client identities to additional cloud services
- Threats include possible exposure to crypto attack whenever a credential is allowed outside of a secure domain

The platform approach provides an easily administrated method for supporting SSO. Specific accounts may be assigned administrative authorization required by specific types of credentials. For example, specific services will accept the Microsoft NTLM (or other) credentials for particular users. The middleware network then provides access to the network-protected applications, while not restricting the account's access to NTLM file/print services.

SSO leverages the platform's trusted status through service logon and network setup. The cloud obtains access credentials and uses them on a client's behalf. This form of platform mediation provides benefit to both third-party service provider and the client. Consider network-brokered access that dynamically augments a client's request through appropriate login credentials. These credentials are not disclosed to the client, thereby avoiding improper disclosure or usage of the credentials. Cloud-held credentials also shield the client's identity while retaining nonrepudiation. We discuss SSO in Section 6.7.

6.2 Cryptographic Fundamentals of Secure Systems

Open networked systems protect information by appropriate cryptographic methods. These include the *cryptographic hash* (or simply, hash) and *cryptographic encryption* (simply, encryption). An ideal hash function computes an irreversible result that does not disclose information about the input. Computation of an appropriate hash value, given a shared random "challenge", demonstrates knowledge of the information. Encryption, on the other hand, is easily reversible given the proper key. Encryption produces a coded sequence that does not disclose the content of the original information. Decryption recovers the original information, also called *cleartext.* Encryption functions are either *symmetric* or *asymmetric.*

Symmetric encryption uses one key for both encryption and decryption. Parties that have the key can securely communicate, in the sense that no party without the key will be able to impersonate or eavesdrop on the communication. However, it is not possible to directly determine the actual source of any information. The parties are in many ways indistinguishable. One common symmetric encryption algorithm is the Data Encryption Standard (DES).

Asymmetric encryption is a recent technology based on pairs of specially related keys. Data encrypted with one key can be decrypted *only* with the other key. Given only one key, recovery of the other is computationally intractable despite the encryption/decryption relationship between them! This enables secure and nonrepudiable communication between parties. For example, in public/private key systems, each party obtains a key pair, holds one key privately, and distributes the other. Information encrypted with the private key can be recovered through the appropriate public key, in a computation that uniquely identifies the sender. This capability, however, comes at a cost: asymmetric encryption is computationally more expensive than - by several orders of magnitude - symmetric encryption.

Cryptographic methods have specific characteristics affecting the suitability for a given purpose. These characteristics include cost, the layer where encryption occurs, susceptibility to attack, as well as the disclosure of side-effect information. For example, asymmetric encryption is expensive. This cost applies to the key generation, as well as actual encryption and decryption with the given key. It may therefore be desirable to distribute the less costly symmetric key through a secure distribution that is established with asymmetric encryption. Similar principles affect the keys; for example, the cost of large and highly secure keys can be offset by periodic updates that use smaller keys. Lower security keys, valid for a specific transaction or session, can be distributed by means of the higher security keys. Correctly used, these methods constrain cost while effectively providing privacy and integrity. Nevertheless, it is essential to recognize the different properties of these encryption methods, and specifically the absence of a nonrepudiation property to standard symmetric encryption.

6.2.1 Symmetric Cryptography

In the world of digital communications, secrecy and encryption are synonymous; encryption is the technical means by which networks can ensure privacy. Networks also can use well-provisioned switching systems to ensure privacy, though we do not consider this approach in the current text. Stream encryption converts a plaintext byte stream $b_0, b_1, b_2, \dots b_n$ into a ciphertext byte stream $c_0, c_1, c_2, \dots c_n$ where each ciphertext byte c_i is the encrypted form of plaintext b_i. The sender produces the ciphertext by generating a pseudorandom sequence of keytext bytes $k_0, k_1, k_2, \dots k_n$ and then for each plaintext byte b_i transmits c_i where

$$c_i = b_i \oplus k_i \quad \text{(EQ 1)}$$

that is, c_i is the result of exclusive-or'ing plaintext byte b_i with its respective keytext byte k_i. We will describe several algorithms through the notation of Table 1.

TABLE 1: Cryptographic Elements

X	A random number
$x \oplus y$	The bitwise exclusive-or of x and y
$x \cdot y$	The concatenation of bit strings x and y
I_e	The unique identifier of entity e
a	Public half of public/private key pair
b	Private half of public/private key pair
$E_k(x)$	Encryption of x using key k
$D_k(x)$	Decryption of x using key k
$[x]^n$	The n high order bits of x
$[x]_n$	The n low order bits of x
h	A hash function
MD_5	The hash function MD5

The sender and the receiver share a secret that provides the receiver with sufficient information to generate, on its own, the identical pseudorandom keytext sequence k_0, k_1, k_2, ... For example, the xor operation (designated ⊕) has many useful properties. It is transitive and reversible, as in:

$$c_i \oplus k_i = (b_i \oplus k_i) \oplus k_i = b_i \oplus (k_i \oplus k_i) = b_i \oplus 0 = b_i \quad \textbf{(EQ 2)}$$

The receiver can trivially recover the plaintext. This process is illustrated in Figure 6-2 with the sender producing ciphertext on the left and the receiver recovering the original plaintext on the right.

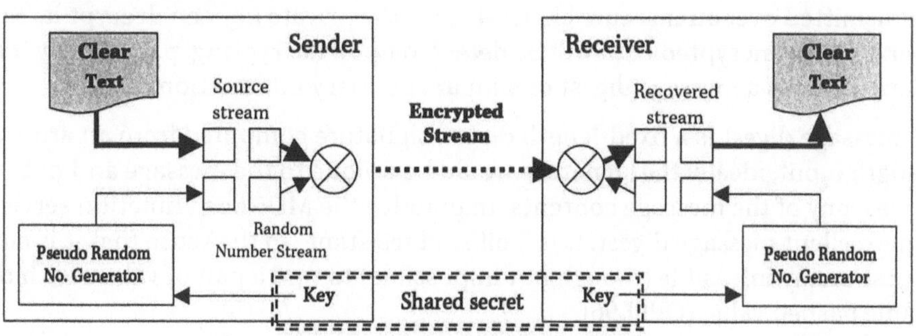

Figure 6-2: Encryption and Decryption with Shared-Secret Key

From the perspective of eavesdropper *X*, the ciphertext stream $c_0, c_1, c_2, \ldots$ looks like a sequence of random bytes from which it is impossible to extract any useful information. Exclusively, the intended receiver, armed with the knowledge required to generate the corresponding keytext sequence, can decode the ciphertext stream. Since the keytext stream itself never passes over the communications link, *X* faces a formidable challenge when eavesdropping on *A* and *B*.

For our purposes, "breaking the code" means obtaining sufficient information to reproduce the keytext sequence used by *A* and *B*. An *attack* on an encryption scheme is a systematic computational procedure that *X* follows to break the code. The *strength* of an encryption scheme is a measure of the difficulty *X* will have in pursuing an attack and is expressed in terms of the average amount of computation *X* must perform to achieve that end. Strong schemes require so much computation that even with the fastest computers now available *X* could require tens, hundreds, or even thousands of years to break the code. A general discussion of the comparative strengths of various encryption methods and their known attacks is well beyond the scope of this text; interested readers are encouraged to consult [Schneier].

6.2.2 Asymmetric-Key Encryption

Asymmetric-key encryption generates a pair of keys that can mutually encrypt and decrypt information. Data is transformed into encrypted information by either key. The data is recovered through the other key of the pair. No distinction is made between the secure properties of either key: they each support equally strong encryption. In a *public-key* structure, one key is publicly distributed, and the other is held privately. There are referred to as the public and the private keys. The key pairs support several important security services:

- *Confidentiality*: Confidential data is encrypted with the public key, and then transmitted over an insecure channel. Only the private key can decrypt it. Tampering with encrypted data will be detected upon decrypting, particularly if the data includes a message digest or similar summary information

  A message digest is a fixed-length digital signature computed from an arbitrary-length input; ideally the signature would be unique to the message and not reveal any of the message contents. In practice the MD5 hash function serves as an excellent message digest. It is "collision resistant" in the sense that it is computationally infeasible (though not impossible) to find a pair of values with the same hashed value [OPPL96]

- *Authentication*: Information is encrypted with the private key, and then transmitted over an insecure channel. Anyone with the sender's public key can decrypt the message. The result is an authentic message, provided it was not tampered with in-transit. A message digest, encrypted with the private key, allows tamper detection. This is often called a signature. The message can be validated by decrypting the signature with the signer's public key, and then comparing the recovered digest to the computed digest

More formally, given a public/private key pair α/β, the encryption function $y = E_\alpha(x)$ transforms an m-bit string x, using public key α, into an m-bit string y, the ciphertext of x. Using private key β, $D_\beta(y) = x$ performs the inverse transformation and returns the original cleartext x.

The distinguishing characteristic of public/private key encryption schemes is that the roles of keys α and β may be interchanged, in other words:

$$D_\beta(E_\alpha(x)) = x = D_\alpha(E_\beta(x)) \quad \text{(EQ 3)}$$

If party A holds the private half of the public/private key pair and party B holds the public half, then A and B can securely communicate, since each can decrypt the messages encrypted with the other's key.

Furthermore, if B can decrypt a message using the public key, then it has a high degree of assurance that the message was sent by A since, if the message had been encrypted with any other private key, if would have decoded into gibberish. Thus, public/private key encryption not only secures communication but also proves identity.

Additional secure services can build upon the asymmetric encryption. For example, a two-message protocol allows a peer to prove that it holds a private key. One peer starts the challenge by forming a message (called a "challenge") and encrypting it with the public key. The challenged peer decrypts it with the private key, modifies the message in a predetermined manner (this is called "response"), and securely returns it to the inquiring party. This "challenge-response" algorithm allows a peer to identify itself as the possessor of a private key.

6.2.3 Digital Signatures – Cryptographic Seals

Information integrity ensures that data cannot be undetectably modified, either during transmission or during storage. Seals, also known as signatures, have historically been tools in the service of integrity. Cryptographic tools provide similar functionality in a digital world. A cryptographic algorithm identifies its input data without disclosure of the data contents. The seal and data form a composite message that can be stored or transmitted. The seal can later be recomputed from the data. Comparison of the original and recomputed seals will detect modification to the message. Modification renders the message invalid.

The design of cryptographic hash functions is a very difficult problem. An excellent and widely used function is $\text{MD}_5(x)$, described in RFC-1132. This method accepts an arbitrary bit string x (of any length) as input and produces a 128-bit string y as output.

The $MD_5(x)$ method is a widely accepted standard for the generation of cryptographic seals.

Cryptographic seals provide data integrity in the following manner. Let m be an arbitrary message (bit string). Consider a communication between A and B, which are two arbitrary devices with a connection between them. A can send m to B and supply B with a means for determining that the message B receives is exactly m and nothing else. To do so, A transmits $m \cdot s$ to B where s is a cryptographic seal augmenting m, such that:

- In general, $s = h(m)$ for a *hash* function h known to A and B. Hash functions map a bit string of arbitrary length into a fixed-size (typically smaller) bit string
- It is computationally infeasible to invert s. That is, given s and h, it is effectively impossible for any outside party X to compute any m such that $s = h(m)$. h is said to be a *one-way* or *noninvertible* function
- If h returns a bit string s of length n bits for any input string, then there are 2^n possible values for s. On the average, a single bit change in the input alters half of the output bits. This makes it very difficult to recover a message from its hash, assuming an effective hash such as MD_5.

  Given a specific message m' and the hashed result $s_{m'}$, the average number of trials required to find an input m'' with a specific hash value $s_{m'}$ is 2^{n-1}. If n is sufficiently large, say $n = 128$, then at the rate of one trial per nanosecond it would take well over a billion times longer than the scientifically estimated total lifetime of the universe to arrive at some input m'' for which $s = h(m'')$. Moreover, this does not even prove that $m' = m''$ since the domain from which m is drawn typically is larger than the n bits of s, and there can be multiple messages with the same hashed value. Consequently, additional mechanisms might be necessary to determine whether the discovered m'' is the transmitted message m', in particular if the message content is "shuffled" before hashing.

The cryptographic seal may be used as follows. Let E and D be any encryption and corresponding decryption function, respectively. and let f represent an appropriate hash function. A transmits

$$u \cdot s \text{ where } u = E(m),\ s = f(m) \qquad \textbf{(EQ 4)}$$

to B, who upon receipt extracts $m = D(E(m))$ and computes $f(m)$ for himself. If the seal validates the message through equality $s = f(m)$, then B has a high degree of assurance that the transmission has not been tampered with in any way.

The hash and encryption must resist various attacks intended to modify or disrupt the message. Consider X, a malicious third party unable to break encryption scheme E, and who chooses instead to undetectably alter *m* so that *B* receives a message different from what *A* intended (if *X* has broken *E*, then *X* can freely substitute fake messages, suitably encrypted with E, the specific algorithm and key). Given the transmission $u \cdot s$, an attack by X will typically fail to recover *m* from $u \cdot s$, since *X* does not know *E*.

Since *X* cannot discover *m*, *X* may instead try to alter *m* through substitution of replacement bits for a portion of the message. This modifies either *u*, *s* or both. For an arbitrary substitution and an *n*-bit message, *X* has only one chance in 2^n that the modified message and seal will agree. Given an *f* with a large *n*, *B* is almost certain to detect any tampering by *X*. To make things even more difficult for *X*, it is common practice to encrypt both message and seal for transmission as

$$u \cdot v \text{ where } u = E(m),\ v = E(f(m)) \qquad \textbf{(EQ 5)}$$

thereby denying *X* knowledge of even the value of the one-way hash calculation.

The attacker *X*, who by now recognizes the futility of either generating a new message or modifying an existing one, may resort to simple replay of a previously captured message. Such a replayed message contains the correct seal *s* corresponding to the given content *u*. The capture and replay of an important message (such as "yes," "buy," "sell" or "delete") could, if left unchecked, inflict major damage. Replay of an arbitrary message, though less forceful, might disrupt communications.

Fortunately, these replay attacks are foiled through sequence-sensitive encryption of message contents. Rather than encode each byte independently from others (ECB mode, shown in Equation 1), one can use cipherblock chaining mode (CBC, shown here in Equation 6) in which each byte is encrypted by the key combined with a previous byte of the stream; when replayed out of sequence it will be incorrectly decrypted by the receiver.

$$c_i = k_i \oplus (b_i \oplus c_{i-1}) \qquad \textbf{(EQ 6)}$$

An attacker would have to inject the replayed message into the traffic stream so that it is received immediately after the identical c_{i-1}; it would also need to be 'in phase" with the other elements of the cipher chain. Failure to satisfy such stringent requirements will result in incorrect decryption of the replayed message. The receiver instead decrypts the message into some kind of gibberish. An alternative to chain encoding is a shared-secret counter that augments the encrypted data and thereby detects duplicate or deliberately mis-sequenced messages. Recent results [Wong99] extend these ideas to efficient multicast communication.

6.3 Peer Credential and Key Management

A cloud-aware system provides the option of a custom security method that offers low cost and high security. This is utilized in so-called "peer-based" methods, in contrast to more recent work that uses SSL and PKI-based methods. The peer-based methods are customizable to limit the computational cost of encryption, as well as ensure compliance with Federal export regulations or the restrictions imposed by certain foreign governments upon encryption. These peer-based methods nevertheless provide enhanced security within the regulations. Such methods support three distinct phases specific to data communications: forming credentials, authentication of end points, and session behavior. Internally, the methods manage encryption keys, thereby enhancing security within the constraints or costs.

The credential-formation layer is invoked at enrollment time – when a peer client first subscribes to the cloud. This layer utilizes a public/private layer cryptosystem based upon asymmetric encryption. During registration, a peer computes a public/private key pair. Each key can be 300 or more decimal digits long, so typically they have to be stored on stable storage. The client's *public* key is shared with the cloud, which stores it in the client's user profile. The client's *private* key should never leave the peer. To protect it within the peer, it is encrypted with a passkey known only to the user of the peer, and stored on the user's peer device. It can also be stored on a smart card to support removable credentials. Conversely, the cloud supplies the peer with the public key half of one of its own public/private key pairs. Although the smart card provides removability, it is not yet a reliable method to provide mobility.

The authentication layer is invoked at connection time, when a peer and a cloud mutually identify (authenticate) themselves to one another. The session layer is invoked at session establishment (immediately following authentication) to provide encryption for the communication session that the peer and cloud are conducting over their connection.

These three times – credential-formation, authentication, and session – have direct analogies in the world of commerce. Imagine a consumer applying for a credit card online. An applicant asserts an identity to the credit card company. The company validates this identity, and establishes policy for use of the credit privileges. Authentication occurs whenever a consumer presents a credit card to a merchant for a transaction. This can take many forms, such as physical inspection of the card, a demand for additional corroborating identification such as a driver's license, or a query to the credit card provider to confirm the validity of the card. Finally, swiping the card through a reader corresponds to a session in this sequence of events. Note that barring loss or replacement of the credit card, the credentials are formed only once, while authentication precedes with each session.

The credential-formation phase typically occurs during registration, and consists of two phases:

- In the first phase, the peer and the cloud cooperatively generate a set of cryptographic keys that will be used for authentication and session security including the secure exchange of registration data. This may use Diffie-Hellman key exchange [DIFF76] or other methods to establish a secure session between anonymous clients
- During the second phase, the peer supplies the cloud with sufficient information to establish a billable entity for the peer. This includes the given name and surname of the peer user, a postal address, and payment information such as a credit card number and a billing address

Both phases are described in detail below. We assume, for the purposes of this discussion, that the peer is a personal computer or a server and not a narrowly specialized device like a pager or a cellular telephone. In this scenario, the peer obtains the registration software by downloading it from a public web site maintained by the service provider, or by ordering the software by post or telephone. The software package contains cryptographic checks to ensure that it has not been tampered with.

The outcome of the registration process is twofold:

- An X.509 *digital certificate* that encapsulates the client identity and public key. A certificate authority (CA) places a tamper-proof cryptographic seal onto the certificate. This process should also provide secure storage of both the certificate and the private key in the client's record
- Secure generation of a shared-secret *authentication key,* known to the peer and the cloud. This key is used in the subsequent login sessions for mutual authentication of the peer and the cloud

The key generation phase produces a 56-bit DES authentication key that is a shared secret between the registering peer and the cloud. The key is computed through an inherently distributed computation. The end points reach agreement on the authentication key, yet never reveal the specific values utilized in the key generation. Instead, each end point computes random values, exchanges a portion of these values, and conceals the full information internally. Each end point accumulates the other's partial information through a series of data exchanges. At this juncture, both end points possess sufficient information to compute the identical value of the shared symmetric key. However, an outside observer lacks the concealed data that each end point retained privately, and cannot obtain the key. The steps in the key generation process are:

1. The cloud calculates a system-wide unique identifier for the peer, I_p, thereby providing a global identifier
2. The peer p generates:

- A public/private key pair α_p/β_p, and
- A 184-bit random number X_p

3. Simultaneously, the cloud c generates:
   - Its own 184-bit random number X_c. Recall that at installation time the cloud was assigned its own unique identifier I_c
4. The peer transmits its public key α_p to cloud c, thereby enabling c to encrypt transmissions to peer p with $E_{\alpha p}$. Since only the peer knows β_p, it alone can decrypt messages to which $E_{\alpha p}$ has been applied. The computation is structured to deny benefit to an eavesdropper that obtains α_p
5. The cloud, in response, delivers two messages to the peer:
   - A digital certificate C_c containing the public key half α_c of one of the cloud's many public/private key pairs α_c/β_c. The peer extracts α_c from C_c for future use. Since this is a public key, it is also available to the eavesdropper
   - An encrypted message

   $$E_{\alpha p}(E_{\beta c}(t \cdot MD_5(t))) \text{ where } t = I_c \cdot I_p \cdot X_c \qquad \text{(EQ 7)}$$

   This message is encrypted with the peer private key, and hence protects its contents. These contents are further protected by the $MD_5(t)$ cryptographic seal for t. This permits the peer to detect tampering or a transmission error. Using α_c, the peer extracts I_c, I_p and X_c from the message
6. The peer transmits an analogous message back to the cloud of the form

   $$E_{\alpha c}(E_{\beta p}(u \cdot MD_5(u))) \text{ where } u = I_c \cdot I_p \cdot X_p \qquad \text{(EQ 8)}$$

   Since the cloud obtained α_p from the peer in Step 2 above, it can decrypt the message to obtain X_p. At this point, both peer and cloud possess X_c and X_p, and given the cryptographically secure exchange, it is unlikely that any party eavesdropping on this "conversation" can discover X_c or X_p.

   At this point the peer and cloud uniquely possess the quantities t and u. These contain the randomly selected 184-bit values hidden in the end points, prefixed by unique cloud and peer identifiers
7. Both peer and cloud can now independently generate a shared authentication key, k_A, and a shared session key, k_S, where

   $$k_A = \lfloor h(X_c, X_p) \rfloor_{56} \text{ and } k_S = \lceil h(X_c, X_p) \rceil_{128} \qquad \text{(EQ 9)}$$

   The authentication key is a 56-bit DES key and the session key is a 128-bit RC4 key. The session key will be used in the second phase of the registration process to encrypt all further registration information passing between peer and cloud. The modulus, floor and ceiling functions truncate the sequence without loss of randomness

At this point, the peer and cloud establish a secure control connection (channel) that is encrypted with the newly generated session key. The final act of the registration process is the transmission of the peer's digital certificate, C_p, from cloud to peer over the secure control channel. C_p defines the lifetime of the peer's public/private key pair (hence the rekeying frequency of this key pair) and may be used by the peer as proof of identity in a variety of transactions. This method augments the relatively small key by frequent rekeying, which can resist "session hijacking".

6.3.1 Authentication and Session Layers

The purpose of the authentication process is to mutually identify the peer and the cloud to one another. Authentication involves the secure mutual exchange of random information in a manner that makes it difficult for an adversary to impersonate a peer to a cloud or a cloud to a peer. The outcome of authentication is twofold: the secure mutual identification of both parties one to the other, and the generation of a shared session key that will be used to encrypt all further communication for the current session. This so-called "stream encryption" has the least cost, and operates at the bottom layer in a hierarchy of encryption mechanisms safeguarding peer/cloud communications. The hierarchy is organized with stronger (more resistant to attack) methods at the top of the hierarchy and weaker methods at the bottom, as shown in Figure 6-5. Each layer is identified by its time of use.

The session key is used by the session layer to ensure the security and integrity of two communication channels. The first is a secure control channel utilized by both peer and cloud for out-of-band signaling and control. This channel provides a cloud with a secure "toehold" on a peer client. The peer and the cloud exchange heartbeats and a variety of configuration, security and control information. Since the control channel is implementation specific, it can employ a wide variety of strong mechanisms – cryptographic and otherwise – to ensure the secrecy and integrity of its traffic.

The second channel, the data or bearer channel, is the pathway for all data communications between peer and cloud and, at the option of the peer, is stream encrypted. The encryption, if enabled, uses the session key generated following authentication as the starting point for the generation of the keytext stream discussed above. It is important to note that stream encryption is transparent to the peer applications since the peer software is responsible for session management, including the encryption and decryption of session streams. The communication paths between peers and cloud are illustrated below in Figure 6-3.

This securely produces a 128-bit RC4 session key, k_S, that will be used to encrypt the peer/cloud control channel and optionally the peer/cloud data channel. The protocol

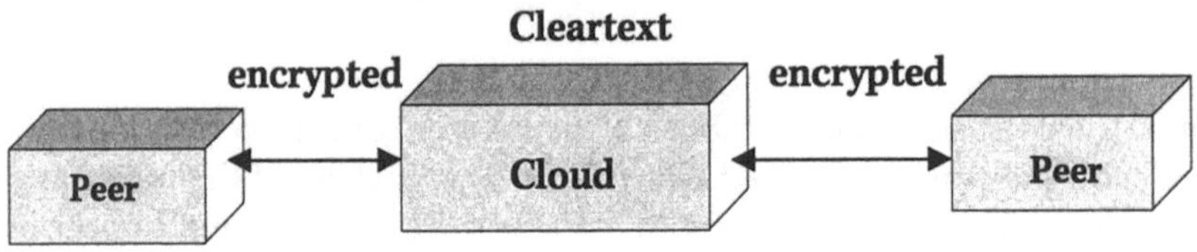

Figure 6-3: Encrypted Links between Peers and Cloud

is based on DES and relies on the shared secret 56-bit DES authentication key, k_A, produced by the registration protocol described above. Here, E_{kA} and D_{kA} denote the DES encryption and decryption functions, respectively, based on the authentication key. The steps in the protocol are:

1. The peer and cloud generate 128-bit random numbers X_p and X_c, respectively
2. The peer sends

$$I_c \cdot I_p \cdot E_{kA}(X_p \cdot I_c \cdot I_p) \quad \textbf{(EQ 10)}$$

   to the cloud. The cloud uses I_p as a database key to retrieve the secret authentication key, k_A, shared by the peer and the cloud and applies D_{kA} to decrypt $X_p \cdot I_c \cdot I_p$. Comparison of the cleartext and decrypted versions of I_c and I_p serves as a message integrity check and proves to the cloud that the peer possesses k_A and is I_p as claimed
3. The cloud replies to the peer with the message

$$m = E_{kA}(X_c \cdot X_p) \quad \textbf{(EQ 11)}$$

   Successful decryption of m confirms for the peer that the cloud received X_p and I_p. If the cloud received another peer identifier, $I_{p'}$, then

$$m = E_{kA}(X_c \cdot X_p) \quad \textbf{(EQ 12)}$$

$$D_{kA}(m) = D_{kA}(E_{kA}(X_c \cdot X_p)) = u \cdot v \quad \textbf{(EQ 13)}$$

   would have yielded garbage where $v \neq X_p$
4. The peer sends $E_{kA}(X_c)$ back to the cloud as proof that it received the random number generated by the cloud
5. Both peer and cloud generate a new session key

$$k_S = h(X_c \cdot X_p) \quad \textbf{(EQ 14)}$$

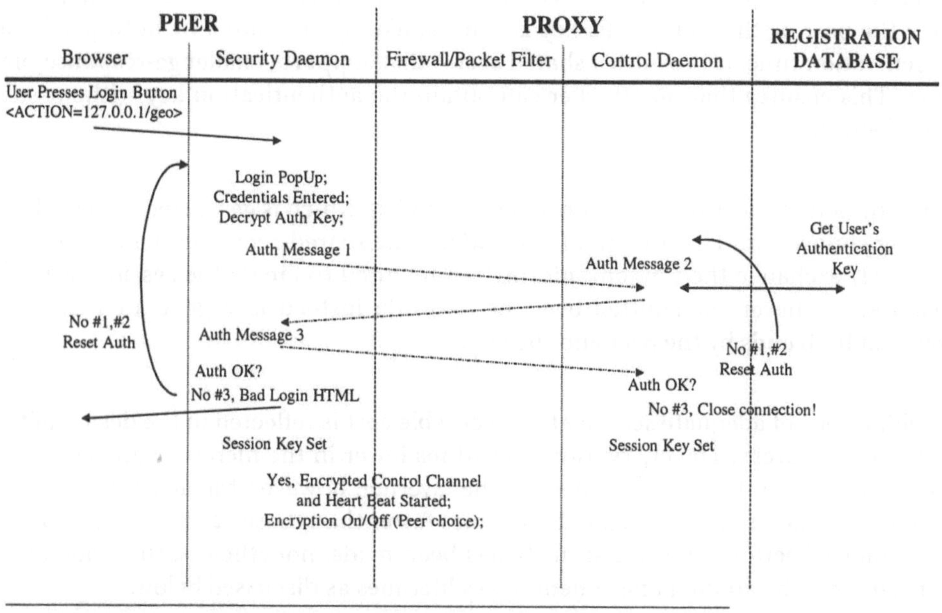

Figure 6-4: Authentication Protocol

6.3.2 Key Hierarchy

The registration, authentication, and session keys form an unbroken chain of protection in which each key in the chain secures and protects the key immediately below it in the encryption hierarchy. This chain is illustrated in Figure 6-5.

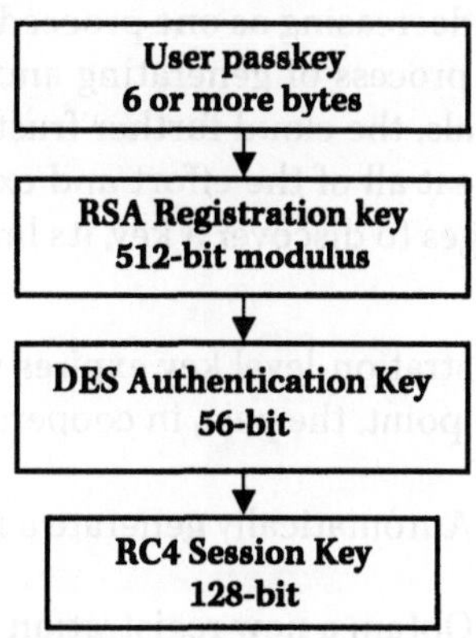

Figure 6-5: Key Hierarchy

At the top of this chain is the user passkey. The passkey encrypts the private half of the registration public/private key pair. The private key is *never* shared, in any form, with any element. It is *never* sent out of the peer. Even removable storage media – either a "smart card" or a disk copy – contains only a passkey-encrypted form of the private key. The passkey itself is known only to the peer user/owner and is never stored on the peer itself. Protection of this key is the responsibility of the user alone, who must take all typical precautions, including defenses against password cracking such as dictionary attacks, and maintenance of physical security. The passkey is typically an alphanumeric string selected by the user.

The passkey also encrypts the shared authentication key. The authentication key never leaves the peer or the cloud. This key is simultaneously computed by both parties at key generation time. It provides a shared secret that supports challenge-response protocols. This ensures that no attacker can obtain the authentication key without substantial effort.

Finally, the authentication key secures the session key, which is generated anew at least once per connection. The peer and the cloud use the shared-secret authentication key to securely exchange the random information required to create the session key. The session key is never transmitted over the network; instead it is generated simultaneously at both ends by the peer and the cloud.

Our philosophy of adequate security for acceptable cost is reflected in the design of the encryption hierarchy. The encryption algorithms lower in the hierarchy are less resistant to attack than those above them in the layering; however, the algorithms at the bottom of the hierarchy are roughly 1,000 times faster than those at the top. Here a reasoned trade of performance for security has been made; nonetheless, the trade-off is balanced through careful management of key lifetimes as discussed below.

6.3.3 Key Lifetimes

Key lifetime is a function of the key's position in the encryption hierarchy, with key lifetimes decreasing as one proceeds from the top to the bottom of the hierarchy. *Rekeying* is the process of generating and substituting new keys for old. By rekeying at regular intervals, the cloud further frustrates attackers, since each new key forces an attacker to repeat all of the effort and expense of discovering the key and, even if the attacker manages to discover a key, its limited lifetime further reduces its value.

A registration-level key expires when the associated registration certificate expires, at which point, the peer, in cooperation with the cloud, will:

- Automatically generate a new public/private key pair
- Obtain a new registration certificate for the public/private key pair
- Generate a new authentication key

Cloud-issued certificates have a lifetime of one to two years, well under the estimated time that a non-government entity would likely require to crack a given key. Once the certificate expires, the private key may no longer be used, and the cloud would not allow authentication with this key. The peer must regenerate the registration keys at least this frequently.

The lifetime of an authentication key is on the order of weeks to months and is determined, as a matter of policy, by the cloud administrators. Session keys are the most ephemeral of the three, with a new session key generated for every peer/cloud session. Additionally, in order to increase resistance to penetration attacks, the cloud administrators can require than an ongoing session be rekeyed at frequent, regular intervals; hence a session key will have a lifetime measure in minutes to hours. In all cases and at all levels (registration, authentication, and session), rekeying is automatic and transparent to the peer user. Table 2 summarizes the key lifetimes at each level.

TABLE 2: Crypto Key Lifetimes

Encryption Level	Key Lifetime
Registration	One to two years
Authentication	Weeks to months
Session	Minutes to hours

The various levels of key lifetime support manageable security policies that provide the best available security pursuant to resource availability as well as the regulations of multiple governments.

6.3.4 Rekeying

There are three forms of rekeying, each corresponding to a different key in the key hierarchy. The peer's public α_p, supplied by the peer to the cloud at registration time, has a lifetime of approximately one year. The period of validity of α_p is defined by a digital certificate issued by the cloud to the peer at registration time. When the certificate expires, the peer and cloud rerun the registration protocol enumerated in Section 6.3 and establish a new peer public key, authentication key, and session key; α_p, k_A, and k_S, respectively.

6.3.4.1 Authentication Rekeying

A new authentication key, k_A, is generated on the order of every few weeks. The protocol resembles the registration protocol and proceeds as follows:

1. The peer and the cloud each generate a 184-bit random number X_p and X_c, respectively
2. The peer sends the cloud the message

$$E_{\alpha c}(X_p) \quad \textbf{(EQ 15)}$$

   Note that the peer uses the public key of the cloud to ensure secrecy
3. The cloud replies with the message

$$E_{\alpha p}(X_c \cdot \mathrm{MD}_5(X_p)) \quad \textbf{(EQ 16)}$$

   Note that the cloud uses the public key of the peer to ensure secrecy and includes a cryptographic seal of the peer's random number, X_p. By comparing the cloud's seal with its own value for $\text{MD}_5(X_p)$, the peer can determine with a high degree of assurance that the random number received at the cloud is indeed the random number generated by the peer

4. The peer's response is the message

$$E_{\alpha c}(\text{MD}_5(X_c)) \quad \text{(EQ 17)}$$

which enables the cloud to determine that the random number received at the peer is truly the random number generated by the cloud

5. The peer and the cloud now both possess X_p and X_c, permitting each to compute

$$k_A = \lfloor h(X_c \cdot X_p) \rfloor_{56} \text{ and } k_S = \lceil h(X_c \cdot X_p) \rceil_{128} \quad \text{(EQ 18)}$$

6.3.4.2 Session Rekeying

Finally, session rekeying occurs every few minutes to hour, and is invoked periodically during a session. This generates a new RC4 key through a sequence of DES-protected transfers that protect the values the new key is generated from. The protocol resembles a stripped-down version of the reauthentication protocol just given. More precisely:

1. The peer and the cloud each generate a 128-bit random number X_p and X_c, respectively
2. The peer transmits $E_{kA}(X_p)$ to the cloud
3. The cloud responds with $E_{kA}(X_c \cdot X_p)$
4. The peer confirms its receipt of X_c by replying with the message $E_{kA}(X_c)$
5. At this point, both parties have confirmed the receipt of the other's random number and each independently computes a new $k_S = h(X_c \cdot X_p)$

6.3.5 Peer-Based Credential Usage

Once a peer is authenticated to the cloud and a session is established, additional security mechanisms come into play. Section 6.3.4 described how stream encryption and regular, frequent rekeying protect the secrecy and integrity of information passing between cloud and peer. Section 6.3.1 presented the protocols employed by the cloud and its peers to create new encryption keys at scheduled intervals. However, these precautions alone cannot ensure 100% resistance against malicious intrusion, damage, or deliberate misuse. The cloud must:

- Ensure that the peer has access to just those services – and no more – for which the peer's billable entity has agreed to pay
- Guarantee that no information passing between peer and cloud will lead to denial of service to other peers

- Prevent the delivery of inappropriate or unwanted information within the context of a legitimate service
- Establish a *user-cloud trust relationship*, as determined the user's form of authentication, account privileges and cloud policy. Access to services may be based on this trust relationship
- Ensure the privacy and authenticity of information exchanged between the client and the cloud. Privacy uses cryptographic services, for example, the platform-wide encryptor module. This establishes a key for encryption during authentication (we call this the session key). The deployment uses different elements for each operating system, and can use hardware-based encryption when available.

  On the Solaris operation system, transport level encryption is handled by a streams module. Encryption is handled through the WinSock2 Layered Service Provider on the Win32 platform, but comes standard on Windows 98, NT and Windows 2000

To summarize the cryptographic discussion of the earlier section, secure registration must precede authentication. This requires that the Peer and Cloud exchange public certificates to establish a trust relationship, and then a 512-bit RSA public/private (asymmetric) key-pair is established during registration. This key is used to protect the registration data and the authentication key. The private key is stored encrypted in the peer's `user.properties` file. Only the peer knows this key. The public key is stored unencrypted in the peer's `user.properties` file, and unencrypted on the cloud – it is meant to be publicly available. During registration, a shared-secret key is also established for future authentication. This 56-bit DES shared-secret key will be used for subsequent authentication. This key protects the authentication data and the session keys. This key is stored encrypted in the peer's `user.properties` file, and in the cloud. Only the peer and cloud know this key.

To authenticate, both cloud and peer must possess the same shared-secret key. This key is established during registration. Only the peer and cloud know this key. They exchange random messages encrypted with the shared key, and reach agreement which allows them to mutually authenticate. Authentication succeeds when both parties return an encrypted combination of the messages.

As part of the authentication process, a shared-secret streaming session key is established. This key is used by both the cloud access gate and the peer for symmetric encryption and decryption of subsequent connections through the cloud. This key is the 128-bit RC4 key established during authentication and used for subsequent streaming encryption on socket sessions[1].

Ongoing data security requires selective encryption. The platform encryption module contains a table of rules to consult when initiating a socket connection. The rules determine whether to apply streaming encryption to the connection. Because the encryption is symmetric, encryption and decryption have the same effect.

6.3.5.1 Selective Encryption

The decision whether or not to encrypt new connections is made using a two-step process:

- The first step checks an encryption setting that applies to all new connections. If this global setting is false, then new connections will not be encrypted
- If this setting is true, then an ordered list of rules will be consulted to determine whether the new connection should be encrypted

Each rule in the list of ordered rules consists of a base address, a netmask, a port, and a boolean indicating whether connections matching the rule should be encrypted:

1. To determine if a connection matches a rule, the destination IP address of the connection is logically AND-ed with the netmask of the rule
2. The result of that operation is then compared to the result of logically AND-ing the base address of the rule and the netmask
3. If the two results are the same, and the destination port of the connection matches the port for the rule, then the rule applies for that connection

As an example, consider a netmask of 255.255.255.0, a base address of 198.155.70.0:80 and an encryption flag of true. A connection to 198.155.70.2:80 will receive encryption. The result of step 1 ($198.155.70.2 \times 255.255.255.0$) equals the result of step 2 ($198.155.70.0 \times 255.255.255.0$). The ports are also equal, and hence the rule applies; since the rule specifies the flag as true this connection will be established with encryption.

6.3.6 Cloud Security

This section describes in some detail the security mechanisms at work within a single cloud. These mechanisms form the basis for all aspects of information security within a cloud as a whole and generalize gracefully to support intercloud information security.

Given this architecture, there should be three crucial relationships: peer-peer, cloud-peer, and cloud-cloud. *Intra*cloud security is devoted to the secrecy, integrity, accountability, and availability of peer-peer and peer-cloud interactions while *inter*cloud secu-

1. The actual key size is configurable, for example for a 40-bit key where required by export regulations, and a 128-bit key domestically.

rity focuses on cloud-cloud services. However, the notion of identity for both peers and clouds is fundamental to all three of these relationships:

Peer identity

Every peer receives a cloud-unique identity. Permits clouds to support peer-specific secrecy and integrity. The peer ID also provides the basis for caller ID, a service by which one peer can securely and unambiguously determine the identify of an end point in a peer-peer connection (called ID in this context has nothing to do with the POTS system, using instead IP-based transport).

The peer identity also provides the foundation of resource allocation, as well as complete and detailed accounting of all peer-peer transactions, The cloud provide quality of service (resource availability) guarantees for peers based on their membership (a form of identify) in one or more service classes corresponding to the Differential Service (DiffServ) model, for example, basic, extended, or premier service. The cloud accounts for activities by collecting non-repudiable usage records.

Cloud Identity

Since all transactions could be made traceable to some billable entity, the cloud must supply the identities of all parties to the transaction: the consumer, the vendor, and the cloud itself. The authentication mechanisms described earlier implement the mutual identification of peer to cloud and vice versa. Since both consumers and vendors are cloud peers, this establishes two of the three elements required for billing; namely, the identities of the two end points, consumer and vendor, respectively. The missing third element, the cloud identity, is examined here. A cloud identity is composed of at least three elements: a cloud name, a set of cloud-specific public/private key pairs, and a certificate.

Cloud Names

Unlike other networks, a cloud supporting this architecture is not an anonymous bitway. Each cloud should have a unique name that identifies the cloud to its peers and to other clouds worldwide. Cloud names are managed by some central authority, which acts as the issuing authority for cloud names in much the same fashion that the IEEE is the issuing authority for Ethernet addresses (a unique 48-bit integer assigned to individual Ethernet devices). A cloud name could be a 16-byte unsigned integer that is guaranteed to be unique among compliant clouds worldwide.

Cloud Keys

Each cloud also holds one or more public/private key pairs. These keys are generated by the cloud itself at installation time, or may be assigned to the cloud by an outside agent. The public keys are shared with the cloud's peers and fellow clouds. The private halves of each key pair are secret and are never revealed outside of the security perimeter of the cloud.

Cloud Certificates

Finally, each cloud possesses *digital certificates* that attest to the binding of the identity of the cloud with a public key. The certificate is analogous to a driver's license or a passport; it is a credential containing information that establishes the bearer's identity. A digital certificate is a non-forgeable, tamper-proof electronic document that binds an entity's identity to its public key. Since a digital certificate is nothing but a (long) binary string, it must rely on cryptographic features to foil attempts at forgery or alteration. Information contained within the certificate is verified and sealed with the digital signature of a trusted third party, known as a *Certificate Authority.* The digital signature relies on strong cryptographic methods that are judged by experts to be exceptionally resistant to attack. The cloud has a separate certificate for each of its public/private key pairs.

The digital certificates comprise an essential element of the Public Key Infrastructure (PKI) incorporated into the network middleware. We discuss this at length Section 6.5.

6.3.6.1 Gates and Peers

To guard a cloud's information security perimeter, the cloud needs to be bordered by edge gateways, simply referred to as gates. Within that perimeter lies critical and sensitive network information such as registration, usage, billing, and customer care databases that must be protected from unwanted intrusion and modification. Beyond that perimeter lies a world of untrusted service and client peers whose access to, and use of, the cloud must be governed and regulated peer by peer. A gate is a peer's sole point of contact with a cloud and the relationship between gate and peer proceeds through three main phases from the beginning of the relationship to its end:

- *Credential establishment.* The peer or an agent acting on behalf of the peer defines an identity and securely provisions the fundamental parameters and its future relationship with the cloud. Barring unusual circumstances, the establishment of credentials occurs exactly once
- *Authentication and connection.* The gate (representing a service node called the SNode) and the peer mutually identify themselves to one another (authentication) and establish a bidirectional communications path (connection) from one to the other. Typically, over a lifetime of the relationship a gate and peer will authenticate and connect with one another many times
- *Use and access.* Following authentication and connection, in which the gate and peer cooperate in the exchange of information and service until the connection is broken by either side

The information and security relationships between a peer and a cloud gate are initiated at registration time and continue unbroken until termination time.

6.3.6.2 Corporate Intranets

One significant use of large-scale Internets should be the provisioning of Corporations, including the essential services of such organizations' networks. Geographically dispersed offices can operate local clouds but share a company-wide base of information services by interconnecting the local office clouds into a single corporate virtual cloud. Company employees would enjoy uniformity of service irrespective of location and could freely move from one office to another. Furthermore, the framework would encourage companies to implement and field information services tailored to their business needs and customer base.

The security mechanisms would encourage the implementation of partitioned and compartmentalized clouds where, even though a community of users (say, both employees and customers) access the same cloud, different classes of users see vastly different services and features. For example, customers access automated order placing and tracking services, but the corporate engineering databases are inaccessible to anyone but company engineers. Similarly, the online personnel files can be accessed and edited by only those employees (managers and administrators) with a need to know. The same approach can be extended to offices which specialize in serving a given geographical region or a particular line of business.

6.3.7 Intercloud Security

A cloud should treat another cloud as it would any peer; all of the relationships that exist between peers and clouds are replicated in the dealings between two clouds. If *A* and *B* are two independent clouds, then *A* must register with *B* prior to *A* using *B*'s services, just as a peer must register with a cloud before taking advantage of its service offerings. Consequently, *A* obtains from *B* a "peer identity," a digital certificate signed by *B* that attests to *A*'s identity, and an authentication key, shared by *A* and *B*, that permits session establishment by *A* to *B* and the generation of per-session encryption keys.

Each cloud makes available to its peers a detailed description of its service offerings. This description can, for example, be based on a directory or service identification protocol. We will, for the present, describe it in the context of PICS (Platform for Internet Content Selection), a language originally developed for describing both content rating services and their individual ratings for specific Internet content such as web pages. The language is quite general and can be used with equal ease to describe the services of digital vendors such as mail, video-on-demand, various forms of electronic commerce, or Internet telephony. Using the PICS language a cloud specifies the basic services that it supports, such as white and yellow pages directory lookup, customer care, and electronic mail as well as cloud-specific optional services such as digital paging, access to financial transaction networks, or dedicated high-bandwidth data services.

In addition to a cloud's description of its offerings, all of the service peers connected to a cloud also provide descriptions to their particular services. Once a peer is connected to a cloud it can, using standard mechanisms in the peer software, access all of a cloud's service descriptions irrespective of their source, be it the cloud itself or service peer.

Not only was PICS designed to describe network content and services, it was also designed to support filtering. Using cloud-aware peer software, a peer can tailor, restrict, or block altogether the services it receives either from the cloud directly or via the cloud's service peers. For each peer, the cloud maintains a set of peer-specific content and service restrictions that, based on the PICS specifications of content and services provided by vendors and rating agents, specify in precise detail the access rights and service privileges of the peer. This mechanism allows:

- Parents to restrict a child's access to content or services that may be unsuitable or inappropriate, such as violent network games or electronic brokerages
- A cloud provider to create and maintain differentiated service pools for classes of users; a premier service pool may include quality of service guarantees and service offerings (say, digital paging) that are not available to the members of a basic service pool
- Business subscribers to restrict their employees' access to content and services that are not relevant to their line of business

In addition, the filtering specifications can be arranged hierarchically, allowing an organization to mandate a generic set of filters for its members overall with various subgroups appending group-specific restrictions. For example, a business that owns a cloud for its internal intranet can prevent the members of the engineering department from accessing the personnel database and at the same time grant the engineers exclusive access to high-performance computing resources attached to the cloud as specialized service peers.

The cloud gates provide a logical location for the enforcement of a peer's filtering specifications; a natural filtering point since all peer/cloud interactions are gate-mediated. Service providers' self-monitoring can be validated and enforced. Thus, the gate guarantees that the peer receives just the content and services for which it is permitted.

Let *A* and *B* be two independent clouds. Like the intercarrier agreements that exist now between phone providers, it may be advantageous for the two clouds to establish either a unilateral or a bilateral service agreement. In the former case, *B* may wish to be a service peer with respect to *A*'s cloud. All of the mechanisms described above apply here, since from *A*'s perspective *B* is just another (large) service peer. All of the services that *B* makes available to the other peers of *A* are described in PICS as would the offerings of any other service peer. Furthermore, access to *B*'s offerings are governed by the same PICS-based filtering mechanisms that are already part of the cloud infrastructure of A (just as identical mechanisms are also present on B).

In a bilateral service agreement, A and B each agree to act as a service peer to the other. All of the specification and filtering mechanisms apply now to both sides; for example, the two may agree to support high-quality Internet telephony between the two clouds, and the filter specifications will guarantee that no peer of B ever uses cloud A as a bit-way for an Internet telephone call to some other foreign cloud C. Each can also restrict service access at times of high processing load to prevent, say, A's peers from degrading a service for which B ensures preferential access to its own customer base.

6.3.8 Roaming

One common form of intercloud relationship should be the support for "roaming;" that is, a peer using the network connectivity of a foreign cloud to contact the peer's home cloud. Roaming allows users to reach their home clouds from remote locations where their cloud may not have a direct presence. It is essential for mobile users, whether they utilize a laptop computer or any other networked device. Cloud carriers will, like their telephony counterparts, arrange intercarrier agreements so that cloud "point of presence" patches a roaming peer through to its home cloud. This arrangement is strongly analogous to the support offered by cellular telephone providers whereby roaming cellular users are automatically registered for temporary service with the local provider so that distant incoming calls are transferred to the roaming cellular telephone and outgoing calls are routed via the cellular and landline network to the destinations.

Let S and T be two independent clouds with an agreement that cloud S will provide connectivity for the roamers of cloud T. In describing the mechanics of roaming, the following notation will be used. Let p be the roaming peer of T; g_S be the gate of S to which p connects; $g_{S \to T}$ be the gate of S connected to cloud T; and $g_{T \to S}$ be the gate of T connected to cloud S.

As part of the implementation of the roaming agreement, a gate of S, $g_{S \to T}$, maintains a continuous connection to $g_{T \to S}$ of T. This is the logical equivalent of two separate telephone carriers sharing a landline that is the principal connection between the switches of both carriers. With this assumption in place, the roaming protocol is as follows:

1. Peer p sends its usual authenticate message

   $m = I_T \cdot I_p \cdot E_{kA} (X_p \cdot I_c \cdot I_p)$

   to foreign cloud S via gate g_S
2. Cloud S, noting that the authenticate message it just received is prefaced by a cloud identity, $I_T \neq I_S$ consults its database of service descriptions to determine if it supports the roamers of cloud T. After determining that roamers from T are allowed to

connect through, S forwards the message m to T via gates $g_{S \to T}$ and $g_{T \to S}$ along with an addendum indicating that p is roaming

3. Cloud T, using the same database mechanisms employed by S, consults its peer service descriptions to determine if p has roaming privileges. If p is not allowed to roam, then S is informed as such, and subsequently the connection between gate g_S and p is broken by S.

   Otherwise, T acknowledges the presence of roamer p to S and dynamically alters the firewall rules of its gates $g_{T \to S}$ to allow the network packets carrying p's authentication protocol messages to pass through

4. S, upon receiving T's acknowledgment, dynamically alters the firewall rules of gates g_S and $g_{S \to T}$ in a like manner to allow the network packet carrying p's authentication protocol messages to pass on to T

5. At this point, the authentication protocol proceeds as if p were directly connected to its home cloud T. The role of cloud A throughout this phase is to transparently forward network packets back and forth between p and T

6. Upon successful completion of the authentication protocol, cloud T sends a p-specific set of roaming firewall rules for addition to the p-specific firewall stacks that exist on $g_{S \to T}$ and g_S. In addition, the p-specific firewalls are adjusted to permit all network packets to pass transparently through S on their way between p and $g_{T \to S}$.

   Once these firewall amendments are in place and acknowledged, p can proceed from this point as if it were directly connected to home cloud T

The implementation of roaming depends, in a critical way, on many of the novel features of this architecture, including:

- Worldwide unique cloud identities
- A powerful and cryptographically secure authentication protocol
- The use of high-level machine-interpreted service descriptions for both cloud/cloud and peer/cloud relationships
- Peer-specific and dynamically adjustable firewalls

The combination of these features can allows a cloud to provide a degree of convenience and functionality that, in many respects, is comparable to that found in the switched telephone network. These same features can be applied in other interesting ways, such as favored treatment of roamers of T by S in contrast to the roamers of another cloud U, time-limited connections, or the incremental improvement of quality of service based on total cumulative roaming connections, thereby favoring frequent roamers over infrequent ones.

One obvious generalization is the use of intermediate clouds to allow interconnection between two clouds that do not have a direct intercarrier relationship. Let the notation

$A \Leftrightarrow B$ denote that clouds A and B have a direct intercarrier agreement. If A, B, and C are independent clouds where $A \Leftrightarrow B$ and $B \Leftrightarrow C$ but *no* direct intercarrier agreement exists between A and C, then the mechanisms outlined above, with appropriate elaboration, are capable of supporting B as an intermediary in a connection chain $A \Leftrightarrow B \Leftrightarrow C$.

6.3.9 Security Applications and Benefits

The primary goal of the security architecture is to provide adequate security at reasonable cost. That goal can be achieved by using sophisticated, but widely accepted cryptographic techniques, embedded in a framework specifically designed to adapt and grow in response to advances in security techniques, modern business practices, and the burgeoning field of electronic commerce. Furthermore, it seeks to unify disparate services such as authentication, billing, and service provisioning into a single seamless whole.

The combination of cloud and peer identity, secure authentication and communication, the automated adjustment and filtering of service offering based on a machine-readable service description language, and transparent interconnect from one cloud to another allows a cloud to control the appearance, quality, content, and timeliness of both intracloud and intercloud service offerings.

Directory Services

Extensive white (user directory) and yellow (service directory) pages are a natural focal point for intercloud cooperation. Clouds may offer yellow pages and specialize them by concentrating on a particular geographic region or selected industries. A query may be transparently passed on to another cloud allowing clouds to offer white pages and yellow pages well in excess of their own individual holdings.

Secure Communications

Secure communications are essential for sensitive or personal information. Vendors and clients alike enjoy secure, encrypted communication that is transparent to both end points. Applications should be made compliant with a minimum of alteration and yet enjoy immediate benefits. The secure protocols need to be upgradable without disturbing any application (however, the underlying peer software may change); users will be assured that their transactions are protected by the most modern and secure cryptography commercially available.

Specialty Markets

Over time, general and special-purpose clouds will emerge to serve horizontal and vertical markets, respectively. The architecture should serve both equally well. It is, first and foremost, a broad spectrum solution for Internet provisioning and contains all of the requisite component for the administration, management, and servicing of a large digital network.

However, the platform should also be a framework for hosting custom services that address the needs of a specific, homogeneous clientele.

Since the trust[1] and security mechanisms, along with the ability to establish and maintain intercloud relationships founded on enforceable business contracts, allow cloud operators to profitably share service offerings, cloud operators can now specialize without fear that their users will turn elsewhere for an important service. Nor are they condemned to offer service over an extensive arena in which they cannot hope to effectively compete. Instead, using the mechanisms discussed previously, operators can cooperatively agree, in a manner that is enforceable by the platform itself, to exchange connections, sessions, information and services to the mutual profit of all parties.

In short, intercloud cooperation permits more service offerings than any one single provider can supply and simultaneously supports familiar business models and practices, their continued evolution, and the implementation of entirely new models and practices crafted solely for digital electronic commerce.

6.4 Trust Boundaries: Firewalls and Protocols

We have thus far presented cryptographic algorithms and standards for the verification of identity and protection of data. We now turn to network-based mechanisms that harness these techniques. These place the system security directly into the network, thereby frustrating attackers. The first method we discuss is firewall technology, with the example of a managed firewall. We then turn to the Public Key Infrastructure (PKI) and, following, the IETF IPSec standard that defines IP security in a general and open manner.

6.4.1 Managed Firewalls

The GeoPlex system developed at AT&T Labs is one example of firewall technology. This uses multiple packet filters on each data stream. These validate all traffic that enters the cloud, whether from a client-peer or a service-peer. These define the destination of packets. The filters further can be active on the egress gate as well, and this is appropriate for highly-secure traffic. Since the data content is also encrypted, fraudulent packets are easily detected, and the firewall discards incorrectly encrypted traffic.

Since a peer's sole point of contact with a cloud is a gate, all information passing between a peer and cloud must transit a gate in the form of network packets. Each of

1. The reader may review the definition of trust page 78.

the packet headers will be inspected by the gate *firewall*, a low-level software filter, executed by the gate, that is interposed between the hardware network interfaces of the gate and the higher-level network applications. If the packet is incoming (from peer to gate), the firewall either allows the packet to pass on or destroys (drops) it, thereby preventing the packet from ever reaching its destination (application). If the packet is outgoing (from gate to peer), the firewall either transmits the packet to the peer or destroys (drops) it, thereby preventing the peer from ever seeing the packet. The firewall may modify the destination of the packet as well, as we will discuss.

Understanding the details of firewall construction requires knowledge of the structure and contents of an IP (Internet Protocol) packet. IP packets are the fundamental "coin of the realm" for information exchange within the Internet. Internet hosts intercommunicate by converting all information transfers into an ordered sequence of IP packets that are routed to their destination by the network. When the packets arrive at their destination, the destination host is responsible for reassembling the packet sequence into a meaningful unit of information such as an electronic mail message, a web page, a few seconds of audio, or a frame of a digital movie.

Each Internet host has a unique IP address (a 32-bit quantity) that identifies the location of the host within the Internet. An end point of an Internet connection (session) from host to host is denoted by a: p where a is an IP address and p is a *port*, a small positive integer in the range (0, 2^{16} - 1]. A connection between IP hosts A and B is fully specified by naming its end points $a_A : p_A$ and $a_B : p_B$ and a protocol. Port numbers in the range (0, 1023] are assigned by the Internet Engineering Task Force and represent the connection points for well known Internet services such as file transfer, mail delivery, network time, web servers, and the like. Port numbers above 1023 are used by network applications for their own purpose.

The packet filter applies one of four actions to every packet, as shown in Table 3. Firewalls are driven by *rules* that specify just which packets may pass and which must be dropped. A firewall rule has the form $t \Rightarrow a$ where t is a conjunction of zero or more conditions $c_1 \wedge c_2 \wedge \dots \wedge c_n$, $n \geq 0$, and a is any of the permissible actions: PASS, DROP, LOCAL or MAP. The individual conditions c_i are simple true/false tests on the elements of the IP packet and include but are not limited to:

- Comparison tests ($=, \neq, >, <, \geq, \leq$) on addresses and ports
- Comparison tests ($=, \neq$) defined over protocols
- Range tests on addresses or ports

A test $t = c_1 \wedge c_2 \wedge \dots \wedge c_n$ of a rule $t \Rightarrow a$ is true with respect to a packet p if and only if each condition c_i is true with respect to p, otherwise the test is false. The action a is taken with regard to packet p only if the test evaluates to true, otherwise the action is

TABLE 3: Firewall Actions

Rule	Action
PASS	Allow traffic to its destination unmodified
DROP	Stop traffic from passing. Can optionally redirect the connection to an error-handler
LOCAL	Process the packet locally
MAP	Redirect the *connection.* This supports proxy connections, where the traffic is redirected to the proxy framework. This permits manipulation of the traffic, as well as implementation of a server directly by the network. The framework will be discussed in detail subsequently

ignored. A rule with an empty test (no conditions c_i at all) is denoted $\Rightarrow a$; always evaluates to true irrespective of the packet contents.

Multiple rules are organized into ordered sets of rules, $R_i = \{r_{i,1}, r_{i,2} \ldots, r_{i,j} \ldots, r_{i,m}\}$. We use the notation $r_{i,j}$ to indicate the jth rule of the ith ruleset, $t_{i,j}$ is the conjunctive test and $a_{i,j}$ is the action. When a packet p enters a firewall, the packet is evaluated with respect to each rule $r_{i,1}, r_{i,2}, \ldots$ of the applicable rule set R_i starting with $r_{i,1}$. If the test $t_{i,j}$ of rule $r_{i,j} = (t_{i,j} \Rightarrow a_{i,j})$ evaluates to true, then action $a_{i,j}$ is taken; otherwise the firewall turns to the next rule $r_{i,j+1}$ in the rule set, and begins evaluation of the conditions. Optimizations of the evaluation order are permissible provided the results are indistinguishable.

If action $a_{i,j}$ is PASS, then packet p is passed to its destination application. If action $a_{i,j}$ is DROP, then packet p is destroyed and is never seen by its destination application. Such traffic can, of course, be analyzed as part of proactive security measures, for example intrusion detection. If action $a_{i,j}$ is LOCAL, then packet p is "proxied" or routed to a listening application on the local host. Finally, if action $a_{i,j}$ is MAP, the filter substitutes the new destination into the packet p. The firewall records the LOCAL and MAP modifications thereby allowing the downstream redirection of the traffic to the original destination.

Once a packet is passed, dropped, blocked or remapped, the firewall immediately turns its attention to the next arriving or outgoing packet. Furthermore, a rule set $r_1, \ldots, r_m$

must be arranged such that for any packet p there exists a rule in the set $r_i = (t_i \Rightarrow a_i)$ for which t_i is true with respect to p. This ordering rule ensures some action for all arriving packets. In practice, the rules provide a "local" action that directs unrecognized packets to a cloud access-control component for creation of an appropriate rule.

6.4.2 Discussion of Rules-Based FIrewall

The packet-filter rules define the action or routing for IP packets of a given protocol, source (IP/port) and destination (IP/port). Rules are organized into rule sets representing peers or services. The active rules are cached for runtime efficiency, and cache lifetime is configurable. The firewall architecture is novel in several further respects:

- Each packet is evaluated with respect to multiple *independent* rule sets $R_1..., R_k$. Complete rule sets R_l may be added to, or removed from, the collection at any time
- The contents of the individual rule sets R_i consulted by the firewall may change *dynamically* as well, enabling the cloud to fine tune its packet ingress and egress policies on the fly in response to changing conditions
- The LOCAL action allows the firewall to locally process matched packets by means of a "proxy" active on the firewall device. This mediation capability allows the gate to mediate traffic and provide enhanced service that deploy mechanisms unavailable to the firewall
- The MAP action creates an efficient mechanism allowing the firewall to alter the headers of the matched packets. The firewall can redirect traffic destined for one host to a different one, or to redirect traffic from a particular port to another

The evaluation of multiple rule sets $R_1, ..., R_k$ is a generalization of the evaluation of individual rule sets. A packet p is permitted to pass if and only if it passes each individual rule set R_i; p is immediately dropped if any matching rule specifies the drop action. The rule sets are evaluated in the order given, starting with R_1.

Like other firewalls, the GeoPlex firewall is organized into two parts, an incoming filter and an outgoing filter as shown in Figure 6-6. The incoming side inspects packets traveling from peers to the gate, while the outgoing side filters packets traveling from the gate out to peers.

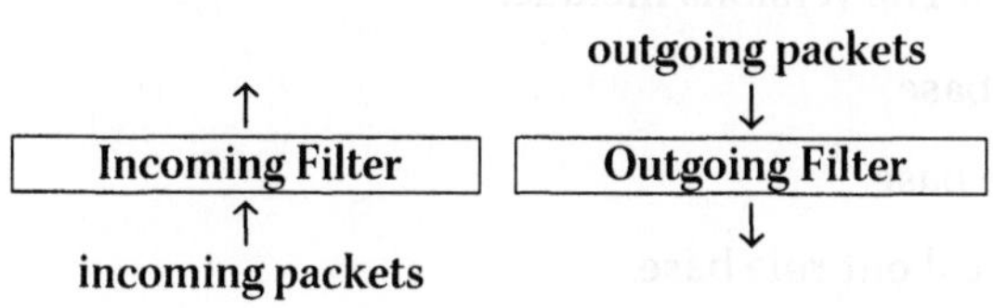

Figure 6-6: Incoming and Outgoing Filters

These two distinct and independent processing paths are illustrated in Figure 6-7. Stage one forms a distinctive *session cache* of frequently used information, including recently-used rules, as well as connections that should be immediately dropped due to invalid-access attempts or other intrusion-detection software. The stage-two rules are consulted when the packet does not match any cached rule. The stage-two rules describe global behavior and the user-specific behavior specified through service subscriptions.

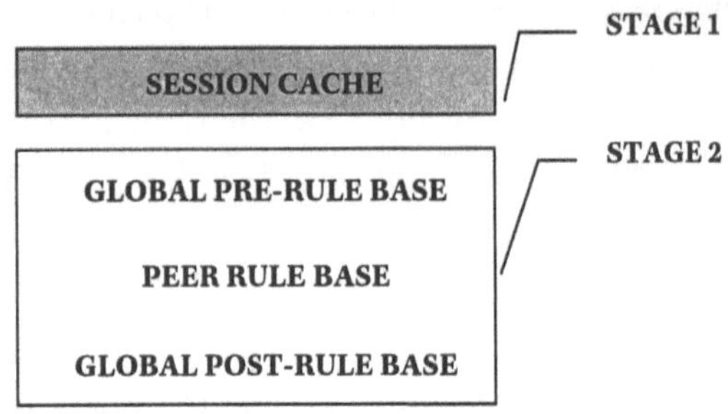

Arriving packet proceeds first through STAGE1 for match to cached rules. If unsuccessful, it proceeds to STAGE 2 for match to pre, peer and post rules.

Figure 6-7: Rule Sets Enforce Session Level Policy

Logically speaking, each peer connection to a gate is assigned its own firewall, as shown in Figure 6-8. Each half, incoming and outgoing, of this firewall is further subdivided into a stack of three independent rule sets: a cloud-specific prologue, a peer-specific rule set, and a cloud-specific epilogue. Irrespective of whether the packet is incoming or outgoing, the order of rule set evaluation is identical: cloud prologue, peer, and finally cloud epilogue. All six rule sets (three on each side) may be completely different and each may be changed over the lifetime of the session.

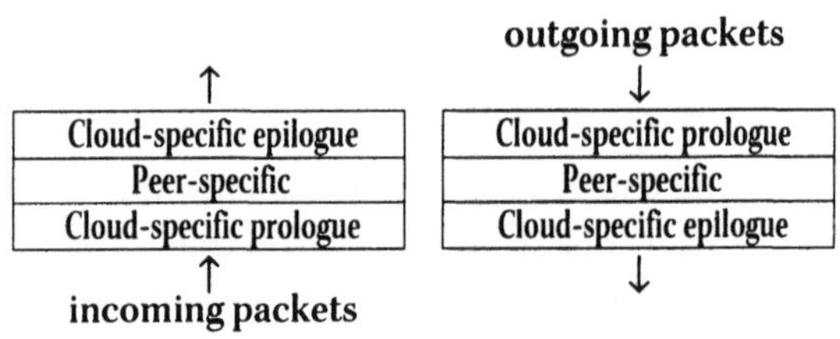

Figure 6-8: Packet-Filter Rule Stacks

Whenever an entry is added to the session cache, a maximum of four version numbers are stored in the entry. There are up to four versions that need to be saved: the version of global pre-rule base, the version of the global post-rule base, the version of the source peer's local out rule base, and the version of the destination peer's local rule base. The session cache assigns monotonically increasing version numbers to each cache entity. These are updated upon modifications to the rule base. Whenever an entry is added to the session cache, a maximum of four version numbers can be stored and saved in the entry. The versions include:

- global pre rule base
- global post rule base
- source peer's local out rule base
- destination peer's local in rule base

One or more of these rule bases are used to derive a particular entry. Only the versions of those rule bases that are used to derive a cache entry are stored in the entry. A flag in the entry is set to denote rule bases that need to be checked once a packet arrives.

When a packet matches a entry of the session cache, the entry must be checked to verify consistency with the rule bases that it was derived from. A matching entry that is inconsistent with the rule base is immediately marked as invalid and will be removed from the session cache. Processing proceeds to the next stage:

- At the start of the next stage of processing, a packet exists for which there is no valid matching session in the session cache
- The global pre-rule base is checked for a rule which matches the packet. If a match is found in the global pre-rule base, an entry is added to the session cache. The rule's action is performed and the processing of this packet ends
- If a matching rule is not found in the global pre-rule base, then a search is made for one or more applicable local (peer's) rule bases. A hash function is applied to the IP source address of the packet, and the "peer out rule base" hash table is searched for a match
- If a matching rule base is found, then it will be referred to as the "source rule base." Similarly, a hash function is applied to the IP destination address of the packet, and the "peer in hash table" is searched for a match. If a matching rule base is found it will be referred to as the "destination rule base"
- If a source rule base is found, it is searched for a rule that matches the packet. If a matching rule is found in the source rule base, then the matching rule's action will be referred to as the "source action". If a destination rule base is found, it is searched for a rule that matches the packet. If a matching rule is found in the destination rule base, the matching rule's action will be referred to as the "destination action"
- If a source action is found, and it is a DROP action, then an entry is added to the session cache, the DROP action is performed, and the processing of this packet ends. Similar steps are performed if a destination action is found
- If a source action and a destination action are both found, and they are both PASS actions, then an entry is added to the session cache, the PASS action is performed, and the processing of this packet ends
- If a source action is found, it is a PASS action, and no destination rule base is found, then an entry is added to the session cache, the PASS action is performed, and the processing of this packet ends. If a destination action is found, it is a PASS action, and no source rule base is found, then an entry is added to the session cache, the PASS action is performed, and the processing of this packet ends
- If there are no matches, the post-rule base is checked for a rule which matches the packet. If a match is found in the post-rule base, an entry is added to the ses-

sion cache, the rule's action is performed, and the processing of this packet ends. Since the global post-rule base must contain a default rule whose condition matches all packets, not finding a match at this point is considered an error condition

- The LOCAL and CHECK actions are similar to the PASS, except they modify the packet and maintain the tables of local and remote mapping

These techniques support extremely fast firewall behavior. The benefits of the firewall architecture include:

- Each peer/cloud connection is protected by a peer-specific firewall that can be tuned to the needs and service demands of that peer alone without affecting the service relationship of any other peer

- Feedback from monitoring tools and instrumentation can be used to prevent or limit the damage of denial of service attacks by restricting or severing particular packet flows

- Rule sets can evolve with the addition of new network services and experimental services can be offered to privileged or trusted peers without fear that the rest of the cloud or untrusted peers will be affected

- Network services can be switched on or off based upon the time of day. To ensure a high quality of service, the firewalls can be dynamically adjusted to temporarily deny or limit access to services that are regularly in high demand during known time periods

- More generally, network services can be throttled based on server and network load. Automatic limit switches (analogous to circuit breakers) can use the firewalls to shed load in order to prevent network congestion

- Network operators can easily move a peer from one service pool to another (say from basic to premium) by adjusting the peer-specific firewall rule sets

- Rule sets can be equipped with time locks thereby allowing network operators to offer limited "trial periods" for services

Firewall technology provides a simple and reliable method that controls the IP packets that may enter or exit a network. In conjunction with software that defines the packet filters (or firewall rules), this provides a powerful mechanism capable of providing specialized processing for any connection. This technique can support multiple policies for authentication and access control. A specific managed firewall has been presented as a specialized example that shows the utility of this technique.

6.5 Public Key Infrastructure - PKI

Most people have heard something about "electronic signatures" or "public keys", and yet it is difficult to estimate the impact these technologies may have upon our daily lives. Consider for a moment a view of the February 4, 1997 State of the Union address by the President of the United States, William J. Clinton, as cited and discussed by eminent physicians and scientists of the National Academy of Sciences:

> *In his 1997 state of the Union address, President Clinton noted that "we should connect every hospital to the Internet, so that doctors can instantly share data about their patients with the best specialists in the field." The security and confidentiality implications of web-connecting the nation's clinical data are a major impediment to realizing this noble goal.* [HALA97]

One resolution of the "impediment" is the public key infrastructure (PKI). Indeed, the underlying asymmetric cryptography and public-key cryptosystems constitute the axioms of distributed security. By structuring cryptographic methods through well-defined syntax and algorithms, the Public Key Infrastructure (PKI) formulates the authoritative basis of open yet secure systems. As an accepted standard with global deployment, this enables applications including eCommerce, encrypted file systems, secure email, as well as the configuration and security of system software. A network middleware structure integrates these applications through a common structure that supports multiple PKI components.

The areas of middleware and PKI are receiving substantial attention within the Academic and Government sectors as well as the Private sector. The University Corporation for Advanced Internet Development (UCAID) considers the PKI within the context of "glueworks" middleware; see http://www.internet2.edu/middleware. At the Federal level, the National Institute of Standards (NIST) hosts the PKI technical working group (PKI-TWG); see http://csrc.nist.gov/pki/.

PKI builds upon asymmetric encryption, in which key pairs are generated by a trusted source. As described in Section 6.2.2, information that is encrypted with either key can only be decrypted with the other key of the pair. One key is distributed publicly, and the other is held privately. The security of PKI requires the private key is securely held by the certificate owner[1]; unless otherwise stated we always assume private keys are securely held. This secures many activities. For example, a message that is decrypted with a public key must have been encrypted by the owner of the corresponding private key, and hence we know who provided the message. Conversely, any entity that encrypts a message with the public key may be fully confident that only the intended

1. A wide range of biometric technologies are emerging as products to enforce the assumption of securely held private keys, even in the consumer market.

recipient can decrypt it. We refer to this property as non-repudiation, as defined on page 78. Indeed, the IETF definition of PKI states in RFC-2459:

> *A certificate user should review the certificate policy generated by the certification authority (CA) before relying on the authentication or non-repudiation services associated with the public key in a particular certificate. To this end, this standard does not prescribe* legally *binding rules or duties.*

Central to the PKI is the digitally signed certificate for storage and transmission of public keys. The ITU X.509 v3 standards specify syntax and semantic for certificates. The standard includes cryptographic seals that detect any alteration to a certificate. The seal is typically computed as an MD_5 message digest[1] and then encrypted with the private key of the issuing Certificate Authority (CA). The encryption protects the digest from modification, as it cannot be rewritten without the CA's private key. The CA publishes its public key, and hence the digest can be recovered. Alterations are detected by comparison of the certificate with the recovered digest.

6.5.1 PKI and the X.509 v3 Certificate Authority

Asymmetric encryption, as a pure mathematical algorithm, does not directly support secure operations on a public infrastructure. Various standards organizations, including the International Telecommunication Union (ITU) and the Internet Engineering Task Force (IETF) address these issues in standard X.509 and associated documents. These standards define a *digital certificate* consisting of the public key, a subject (or identity), as well as additional information including a serial number, validity dates, information on the issuer as well as an identification of the signing algorithm and key-extension fields.

The Public Key Infrastructure (PKI) standardizes the format for representing the keys. In particular, the public key is encapsulated in a structured form called a *certificate*. The X.509 v3 certificate is currently a standard with wide acceptance[2]. This defines the algorithms for key pair computation, as well as a framework for certificate policies and procedures concerned with methods to establish the initial identity of the principal

1. The digital signature is a tamper-proof digital fingerprint. The fingerprint is typically formed with the MD5 function, a one-way function producing a 128-bit result that is sensitive to any change in the source. Tamper resistance is provided by encryption, typically RSA algorithm using the signer's private key. The signature is verified by recomputation of the message digest, and comparison to the digest stored in the digital signature. Everyone with the signer's public key can obtain the correct message digest.
2. The reader is referred to the Internet Engineering Task Force (IETF) at `http://www.ietf.org/html.charters/pkix-charter.html` and to the RSA Corporation at `http://www.rsa.com` to reference the standards information.

who requests a key, and recommended formats that facilitate interoperable storage and communication of the certificates (see RFC-2527 and IETF pkix drafts).

Central to the idea of public key infrastructure (PKI) is the certificate authority (CA), an organization whose importance cannot be underestimated with the current tchnolgoies. As stated in testimony to Congress:

> *While digital signatures can be used to support sender authentication, non-repudiation, and information integrity, it is necessary to establish a hierarchy of trust that will provide the ability for users to verify that the public key used to verify a signature is actually the key of the individual or organization that signed the electronic message or transaction. The term* certificate *is used to describe the technique used to establish confidence in the legitimacy of a public key. A certificate is a digital document which attests to the binding of a public key to an individual or other object. An entity, usually referred to as a* Certificate Authority, *serves as the trusted third party to provide independent authentication of a public key with a specific user. This is accomplished through the issuance of certificates. Commercial Certificate Authorities are now being created to meet the growing need for the authentication in an electronic environment.* [BIDZ97]

The CA issues the certificate by placing the necessary information into the standard format and then signing with a digital signature (see Table 4). Analogs of Certificate Authorities are commonplace in the non-digital world. Each document, like a driver's license or a passport, has an issuing authority, an individual or organization that is recognized, through social, political, or legal means as legitimately possessing sufficient authority to grant such documents. Passports are issued by national governments while drivers' licenses are issued by state bureaucracies. All such certificates bear physical features that make them difficult to forge or alter, such as watermarks, seals, stamps, signatures, distinctive colors, and materials.

A Certificate Authority, like its non-digital counterparts, must:

- Issue certificates to those parties that meet its issuance criteria
- Verify its certificates on demand to third parties who wish to check the validity of a certificate
- Revoke certificates that have expired or been compromised in some respect

These rights and responsibilities are similar to those of a national government when it issues, verifies and confiscates passports.

Digital certificate authorities are organized into hierarchies resembling our legal and social structures. The United States, assuming powers granted by international law and common agreements among nations, supplies passports to its citizens while granting the individual states the authority to issue a wide variety of certificates. The state of California, in turn, then empowers various agencies and licensing bodies within its jurisdiction to grant licenses (certificates) ranging from drivers' licenses (Department of Motor Vehicles) to physicians' licenses (Board of Medical Examiners). Further down in the hierarchy, city governments supply business licenses and building permits to individuals and commercial entities. Indeed, a complex web of certificate authorities predates the Internet. These authorities already influence much of our daily lives.

6.5.2 Certificates Characteristics and Syntax

A digital certificate is tamper resistant by virtue of the digital signature included in the certificate. The signature provides *data integrity* through a cryptographic message digest that must be decrypted with the public key. Its properties include:

- *Unforgeable, hence authentic.* There can be no doubt that it was deliberately issued
- *Not reusable.* The digital signature cannot be moved to a different document
- *Unalterable.* The document cannot be changed undetectably
- *Not susceptible to repudiation.* A signatory's plea of forgery is void of technical merit, since the signer retains exclusive possession of the private key. Furthermore, the certificate identifies the client's identity as verified by a Certificate Authority

The PKI relies on X.509, an international standard for the structure and interpretation of digital certificates. An X.509 certificate includes the fields shown in Table 4, where:

TABLE 4: Certificate Fields

Version
Serial Number
Algorithm Identifier
Issuer
Period of Validity
Subject
Subject Public Key
Signature

- *Version* specifies which generation of the X.509 certificate structure is employed by the issuer
- *Serial number* is a unique integer assigned by the issuer who guarantees that no two certificates it creates have the same serial number
- *Algorithm identifier* specifies the encryption algorithm employed by the issuer to create the digital signature that seals this certificate. The signature is appended to the certificate (see item *Signature* below). The algorithm field also presents the relevant algorithm parameters
- *Issuer* is a representation of the identity of the party that issued the certificate, such as a cloud identifier

- *Period of validity* defines the time interval over which the certificate is valid
- *Subject* is a representation of the identity of the party to whom the certificate was issued. This is also known as the *distinguished name* (DN). A trustworthy CA must validate the subject information prior to issuing a certificate
- *Subject public key* contains the public key of the subject named above, as well identification of the algorithm used for this key. The algorithm identified here is independent of the algorithm affiliated with the digital signature placed on the certificate signature
- *Signature* is a cryptographic seal, computed by application of the algorithm identified by the *Algorithm identifier* field to the contents of the certificate, and then appended to the certificate. This signature embodies the attributes enumerated above and is generated using the algorithm and parameters specified in the algorithm identifier field
- Additional fields may be included in the certificate with suitable encoding, for example the `signingTime`, `counterSignature`, `challengePassword` or `extendedCertificateAttributes`. These are defined in PKCS#9 and other standards

The encoding of the certificate fields uses DER, the Distinguished Encoding Rules for Abstract Syntax Notation (ASN.1) as defined in X.509. Certificate fields are identified with registered Object Identifiers (OIDs). For example, a private key may be identified as PKCS #1 `rsaEncryption` having the OID `{1 2 840 113549 1 1 1}`.

6.5.3 Certificate Validation

Certificates validation should precede certificate usage, as a means to ensure the certificate is authentic; that is, no modification has occurred. Cryptographic integrity attests to authenticity by recomputation of the signature and comparison to the certificate's signature. Dissimilar signatures refute virtually any tampering or forgery. The correctness of this method assumes authenticity of the certificate that holds the signer's public key. The validation problem is simplified when the certificates are signed by a well-known and trusted authority.

The certificates of trusted authorities can be indelibly written into software or hardware during manufacturing, and indeed the major web browsers include the certificates for AT&T, VeriSign, and others. These certificates serve as the trusted roots for sequences of certificates. Given a new certificate *C* issued by an unknown issuer Issuer_{C_1}, a client can validate the certificate by retrieving a series of issuing certificates: $\mathrm{Issuer}_{C_1}, \mathrm{Issuer}_{\mathrm{Issuer}_{C_1}}, \mathrm{Issuer}_{\mathrm{Issuer}_{\mathrm{Issuer}_{C_1}}}, \ldots \mathrm{CA}_{\mathrm{Trusted}}$. Validation requires that the chain eventually reach $\mathrm{CA}_{\mathrm{Trusted}}$. The peer already trusts $\mathrm{CA}_{\mathrm{Trusted}}$ as an authority, and holds a correct copy of its certificate. The peer unwinds the chain of signatures by verifying each issuing certificate, and then verifies the new certificate.

Signature verification is a purely mathematical process that proves the information was not tampered with subsequent to issuance of the certificate. It asserts (without proof) that the CA correctly verified the information before writing the certificate. A CA should enforce policies that validate information on certificates. They may, for example, require that applicants sign a legally binding document, or post a cash bond.

The cryptographic properties of typical certificates are static, and cannot be reversed. Certificate authorities also provide a list of revoked signatures that are no longer acceptable. Revocation services provide a means to check for certificates that should not be trusted, much as an invalid credit card can be listed on a registry of revoked cards.

Certificates of specific CAs are *legally binding* signatures in many States within the U.S. as well as Europe, although the standards and procedures vary both domestically and internationally; we previously discussed the difference between legal non-repudiation and technical non-repudiation. On November 9, 1999 the U.S. House of Representatives passed, by a vote of 356-66, HR 1714 "A bill to establish a single, nationwide legal standard for electronic signatures and records. The bill does not mandate a particular type of authentication or technology." The bill also states that "... nothing ... shall be construed to limit or otherwise affect the rights of any person to assert that an electronic signature is a forgery, is used without authority, or is otherwise invalid for reasons that would invalidate a signature in written form."

6.5.4 Middleware Networks and the Public Key Infrastructure

An open PKI is one component of networking middleware. This leverages the CAs' current role of providing verification of subject identities, as well as signing the certificates that serve as non-repudiable credentials. Under an open PKI the users can freely select whatever CA they prefer, much as the Telco customers may select the carrier of their choice. The middleware enables this through certificate-aware and vendor-neutral components providing services from IP connectivity to service access. Trusted network middleware also ensures that users do not need to become security experts.

One means in which service-oriented middleware achieves this is the integration of multiple CAs by means of a flexible CA interface. The resulting interoperability combines multiple independent CAs into a single interoperable PKI intrinsic to the network. These CAs may operate either independently or as a network service. As a network service, the CA receives pre-screened certificate requests that conform to a particular user community's business requirements. Such CAs retain complete responsibility for the issuance of new certificates, maintaining revocation lists of compromised certificates, and supporting the validation of existing certificates.

As an instrument of credential management, middleware defines policies for the issuance, enrollment and use of the certificates. Enrollment takes an existing certificate and validates it for use by the system. No modification is made to the certificate; rather, the enrollee presents the certificate with proof of ownership (i.e., an authentication through private-key signing). The platform subsequently recognizes enrolled certificates for authentication or enhanced services. This autonomous enrollment and usage ensures that the PKI remains open, nonintrusive and reliable. Certificate enrollment does not curtail the revenue growth of reputable CAs, since it enhances the user's freedom to select the best CA for his needs. Indeed, both the CA and the network provider can offer advance time-of-use services as described in Section 6.5.4.3.

6.5.4.1 Five Principles of an Open PKI

Based on the above discussion, we offer the following categories and five general principles in support of the open PKI:

Vendor neutrality

The infrastructure permits all legal actions of internally hosted or externally accessed certificate authorities. This ensures a "level playing field" in which any entity may establish a certificate authority, as well as create services that require certificates. The subscribers and providers of middleware services may, at their own discretion, utilize all certificates and CAs without platform constraints.

Select trusted CAs

The trusted CAs define the acceptable sources of certificates that are eligible for enrollment; eligibility is defined through administrative controls over accounts and subaccounts. There is no *a priori* restriction on the CAs that can be trusted.

Select issuing CAs and certificate content

Middleware-mediated issuance of certificates constrains the mandatory or forbidden content of requested certificates, as well as the authorities that may issue certificates on the behalf of the network. This enables standardized services that leverage multiple CAs through uniform content.

Undiminished Trust

The platform may use any certificate of a platform-trusted or a platform-issuing CA without change to the trust relationship between the certificate owner and the issuing CA. Section 6.5.5 discusses the Certificate Practice Statement (CPS), a CA-issued document that includes required usage procedures for certificates of their issue. Trust management and the mathematics of trust are tools that ensure this principle; see [GOLL99] or [FEGH99].

Enhanced Usage

The middleware or service may grant any privilege to certificate holders.

The granting and exercise of privileges are under the control of the platform or account administrator.

These broad principles provide advantages to *all* parties in the PKI structure, as discussed in the next section.

6.5.4.2 Advantages of PKI Principles

The above five principles offer a number of practical benefits, which we discuss here.

Mobility

Mobility between PKI providers – regardless of the certificate interface or protocol issues – with continued use of existing X.509 certificates. Vendor independence prevents "legacy lock-in" with concomitant substandard service or excessive price. Lock-in occurs when a customer is compelled to keep using a provider simply due to the costs of changing to a new provider.

Management

Certificate management ensures that all users have ample notification of any potential problems with their certificates. This includes notification of impending expiration or revocation of a client's certificates. These management services are essential to ensure uninterrupted availability despite dependence on external authorities.

Issuance Policies

Certificate issuance is controlled by policies that define the permitted providers, as well as the content of X.509 certificates. The PKI is integrated with the customer information profile thereby providing uniform policy definition and enforcement.

Policy Content

Certificate contents are determined by the administrator through definition of preferred policies. For example, the customer rather than the CA vendor defines the naming structure.

Preferences

Administrator-defined preferences for the maximum permissible and minimum acceptable security of certificates, as well as service-specific extensions.

Innovation

A PKI provider may deploy improved software or hardware without requiring any customer changes. The certificate infrastructure accommodates the "front end" changes.

Compliance

A platform-issuing CA is assured of a well-defined community of pre-screened applicants. Middleware-mediated requests are guaranteed to be "in compliance" with the policies and procedures of the user's community or organization.

Protection

Services may subscribe to network certificate protection. Prospective users of a service first register the credential through the network. The network only allows access by clients who possess a registered and valid certificate. This can be augmented through network-based *intrusion detection* thereby detecting attacks on security, for example by identification of inappropriate usage patterns. Since invalid attempts are eliminated, this reduces the operational costs incurred by service providers.

Services Unconstrained

Third-party services remain free to accept certificates that have not been registered with the network. Such services must perform independent validation of the certificate. Services may define their preferred certificate-validation methods.

Simplicity

Platform use is simplified by allowing users to authenticate with their current credentials. The authentication maps the DN to a specific account within the platform's hierarchy of accounts and users. Subsequent access-control decisions rely upon the account hierarchy. This form of authentication may amplify or attenuate the user's rights.

Platform-Bundled Services

PKI-based services can be bundled with platform-managed services supporting access and communication. For example, IPSec components may choose to use IPSec for specific traffic, and rely on firewall-based access control when this is an acceptable lower-cost alternative. Non-IPSec components continue to use either firewall-based access control or open-Internet routes as appropriate to the application.

The PKI also allows extended associations between certificates and users.

Multiple Associations:

Certificates are more general than a conventional computer login. We distinguish between a *user identity* and a *user object* (the present discussion avoids the term *account*, as this will later be associated with a collection of objects). The user identity may be defined through a certificate.

The user object is represented by a unique element in a tree of users and accounts. Associated with the object are privileges including access rights. The user object may also contain credentials that allow the object to perform additional actions; we do not discuss the signing procedures necessary to ensure accountability for use of a stored credential.

Various registration processes may form associations between a user identity and a user object. Multiple user identities can be associated with a single user object, and conversely a single user identity can be associated with multiple user objects. Instead of the prior 1:1 relationship between users and privileges, we have the general N:M relationship.

This may be viewed through two distinct scenarios:

- *Multiple user identities with one user object*

  Multiple user identities are enrolled for a single user object. Each user identity may subsequently acquire the privileges of the one user object.

  1. Define the administrator or owner of the user object, by designation of one identity as the unique "primary owner"
  2. Enroll additional certificates as valid for the same user object
  3. An enrolled entity presents a valid credential and name of the target user object. The privileges of the user object are assigned to the user identity for the duration of the authentication. Application of these privileges (i.e., "doing something") is recorded in the system usage files. Nonrepudiation through transparent usage structures may employ multiple signatures including the user identity and a unique identification of the user object

- *One user identity with multiple user objects*

  One user identity enrolls for multiple user objects. The one user identity may subsequently acquire the privileges of any of these user objects. For example:

  1. When authenticated to the user object named "operator" the subject's privileges include placing a call on a customer's behalf. Actions are non-repudiable and are attributable to the user identity that performed the activity
  2. When authenticated instead a different user object, or one that is uniquely associated with the user identity (i.e., the "home" id), the privileges include placing calls but not on a customer's behalf

6.5.4.3 Additional Value-Added Services

Based upon fee-for-service, many value-added services leverage the fundamental security properties of PKI. The services can be provided within the middleware thus increasing the value for diverse services, ranging from eCommerce though pocket-size communication services. These service can also be offered by CAs.

Certificate usage monitoring and accounting

A *non-repudiation service* preserves detailed chronology of certificate usage, including the time, service name and duration. A middleware-based deployment leverages existing usage systems by placing a signed message into the secure usage objects. The IETF is currently considering drafts on similar non-revocation services.

Bonded certificate validation

Transaction semantics allow atomic commit, which is contingent upon validation of the certificate chain, certificate revocation list (CRL) and permissible usage. Under atomic transactions either *all* the actions complete successfully, or *none* of the actions make any modification to stable storage. A transaction aborts without effect when the usage criterion cannot be validated within a fixed duration. Bonded validation can provide monetary incentives to use the service, since the transaction semantics forbid improper usage.

Certificate suites

A suite of certificates is protected by the platform and unlocked on-demand by the client. The required certificate is provided to the appropriate service. This supports, for example, software leasing through a distributed and sharable certificate structure.

6.5.5 Conformance and Compliance with External CA

Whereas the certificates' cryptographic properties are mathematically provable, the decision to trust a certificate is frequently not subject to formal proof. Instead, a formal Certificate Practice Statement (CPS) provides a basis to voluntarily trust the certificates of a CA that complies with the CPS. The CPS is a legal document, not one that automatically affects computer deployments. The statement describes:

- Policies a CA utilizes in the handling of certificates
- Legally binding liabilities
- Permissible certificate usage

Violation of the CPS may invalidate the contractual liability assumed by the CA as a guarantee of their service. Non-permissible use may, in some cases, have a tangible effect upon the assumptions that support the trust of a certificate. For example, it would be inappropriate to use a Commercial Bank's eCommerce certificate to send a private SMIME-encoded message: this might imply an endorsement of the Bank! This would, at the very least, suggest improper protection of the certificate, and might indicate compromise of the credential.

The CPS may be surprisingly detailed in its requirements. These details are concerned with auditable processes, rather than the cryptographic validity of the identity on the certificate. Consider, for example, the "VeriSign Certification Practice Statement Version 1.2"[1], a lengthy document carrying the names of 18 lawyers, 11 experts in Engineering & Technology, eight Management & Consulting experts, and ten experts in Audit and Business Controls. They require eight distinct steps, including:

- Establish certificate chain
- Ensure the chain is the "most suitable"
- Check for revocation of or suspension of certificates in the chain
- Confirm the certificates in the chain (step one merely established it, but did not confirm it). Thus, each party in the chain must be validated at time of use, which may demand reevaluation of the assumptions that permitted any policy decisions to trust the certificate
- Ensure that all certificates in the chain authorize the usage as a private key
- Delimit between signed data, and other data carried on the certificate
- Indicate the digital signature time and date
- Establish the assurance intended by the signer

Middleware services can encourage compliance with the CA policies. For example, the platform can maintain a network-wide certificate revocation list (CRL) in part through Online Certificate Status Protocol (OCSP, RFC-2560) as described briefly in Section 9.2.5.4 on page 303. Revocation services can be queried to verify the validity of a certificate. The logging of such queries an element of the operational procedures that may be required to prove compliance with the CPS.

6.6 *IPSec*

Complementary to firewalls – which define permitted traffic at the IP layer of a specific host – is IPSec. IPSec is an IETF standard for secure IP. This standard defines policy enforcement mechanisms for peer authentication and secure transport, including data integrity, data privacy, as well as tunneling and security policies. It operates in either tunnel mode or transport mode. We previously introduced this protocol in "IPSec: Internet Protocol Security" on page 53.

Platform synergies occur when IPSec combines with the networking middleware. For example, the peer-authentication can provide a satisfactory proof of client identity. This requires suitable policies in the Security Policy Database (SPD), as well as appropriate storage of security associations. The middleware can, in addition, extend IPSec-secured services to platform-authenticated entities, even when they are non-IPSec

1. VeriSign ™ CPS VeriSign Certification Practice Statement, Version 1.2,© 1996, 1997 VeriSign, Inc. ISBN 0-9653555-2-7.

hosts or networks. Deployment of IPSec within an infrastructure can also reduce the interoperability problems with certain protocols. This utilizes the networking middleware as a trusted partner, thereby leveraging the SNode as a security gateway.

Consider the question of IPSec-enabled peers and network-cached content. Caching typically assumes the content is recognizable to the cache-server. The content can also be reused unless the "do not cache" header is set. The header merely describes correctness, and should not be relied upon for security purposes. IPSec clients cannot directly interact with this cached content, due to potentially different security associations (SAs) of the cache and the client. One resolution is a specialized Security Association (SA) for cached content. Given suitable authorization, the networking middleware can obtain cached content from the cachable security association (SA), and provide it to clients.

IPSec-enabled components may also connect *to* the middleware and subsequently use middleware-hosted services. The network's trusted status eliminates the need for uniform encryption of traffic within the security perimeter. This allows continued operation of all protocols on the internal network, as well as protocol mediation. The client and service benefit from the tunnelling to the cloud, and standard protocols continue to work transparently.

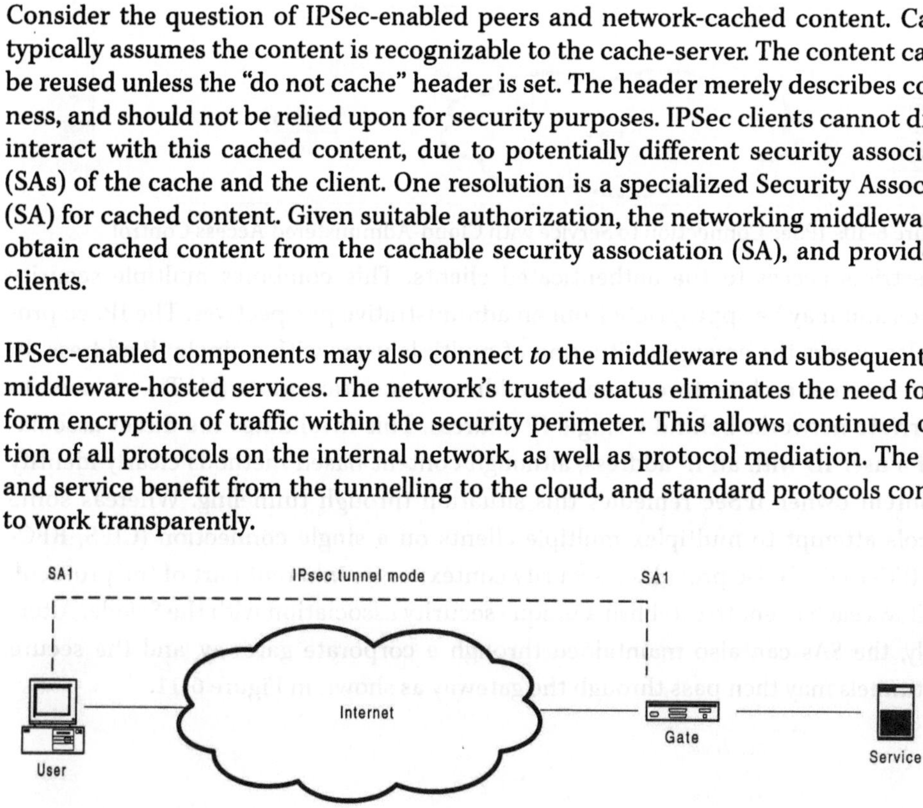

Figure 6-9: IPSec Tunnel Between User and Gateway

This case is shown in Figure 6-9. IPSec provides a secure tunnel from the client to the SNode. A Security Association (SA) is established between a user and the SNode security gateway. This gateway restricts service access to authenticated users. It enforces subscription-based access control and proxy functions. IPsec provides data origin authentication for each packet on IP layer, and provides data payload encryption and detection on application layer. It also provides connectionless integrity, anti-replay protection, and optional data and traffic flow confidentiality.

On the other hand, connections that tunnel *through* the network may also maintain an association with the SNode and middleware, thereby obtaining network managed services. This uses two security associations: one to the cloud, and one to the service, as shown in Figure 6-10. The security association between the user and the SNode can provide access control; for example, by controlling access through a firewall. The fire-

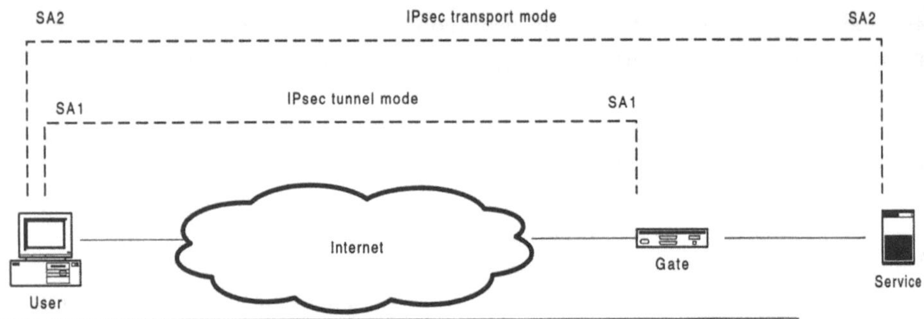

Figure 6-10: IPSec Connection to Service with Cloud-Administered Access Control

wall restricts access to the authenticated clients. This combines multiple security methods and may be appropriate from an administrative perspectives. The IPSec protocol also covers the emerging situation of multiple users with a single IP address. In modern internet architectures, network address translation units (NATs) are used to hide private networks behind a single IP address. This invalidates the direct association of a user ID with an IP address, although content-based methods clearly identify the content owner. IPSec remedies this situation through tunneling. Whereas some protocols attempt to multiplex multiple clients on a single connection (CIFS, RFC-1002, RFC-1002), IPSec provides a security context as an inherent part of the protocol. This allows each client to establish a unique security association with the SNode. Alternatively, the SAs can also maintained through a corporate gateway, and the secure IPSec tunnels may then pass through the gateway as shown in Figure 6-11.

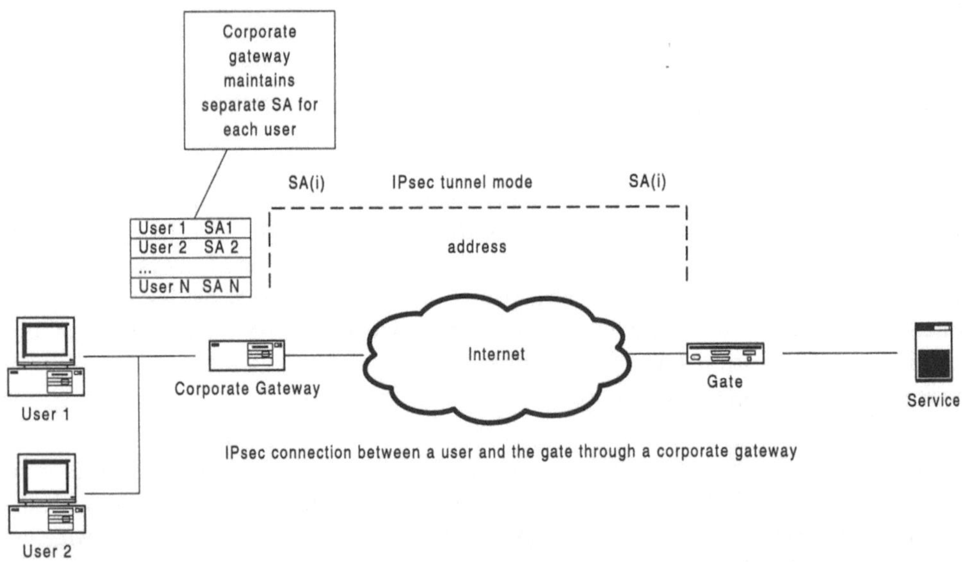

Figure 6-11: Security Associations with SNode and Service – IPSec Through Gate

6.7 Authentication, Secure Single-Sign-On and Service-Access

The security mechanisms discussed thusfar are deployed through an extensible middleware structure that supports common security components. The critical characteristic of the authentication structure is the ease with which it supports the secure mechanisms described in this chapter. The following shows the usage of these methods to support single-sign-on (SSO) and other capabilities

We previously discussed single-credential login through X.509 certificates that are acceptable to multiple domains. We now turn to single signon through multiple credentials. The middleware obtains valid credentials through mechanisms such as shared LDAP servers or service-specific agents programs. The cloud uses these credentials to assist the client in obtaining service. The assist can take several forms:

- Obtain service through a proxy to the service, and return the answer to the client (see Section 6.7.1)
- Splice the credentials into the network traffic (see Section 6.7.2)

One embodiment of SSO runs a security agent that runs on a third-party system. This agents authenticates twice: once to the middleware network, and once to the third party. It is now trusted by both parties, and mediates between them. To make this even more specific, consider a security agent that provides access to Microsoft-hosted domains, for instance using NTLM authentication. An authorized administrator installs an agent as a privileged program on the login server, specifically the Primary Domain Controller (PDC). The agent authenticates to the middleware network, and also to the NTLM domain. The agent henceforth performs as a trusted member of both networks. The module's control logic creates and modifies user accounts on the PDC, and the middleware translate the satisfies the client's requests by a proxy login to the newly created account.

While in many cases the platform can negotiate a single-sign-on (SSO) on the client's behalf, there also are situations where the client's platform must be directly involved; for example, to digitally sign a document with the client's private key.

As the current chapter focuses on security, we defer detailed discussion of these mechanisms until Section 8.2.4.1 ("Validation of Identity - Peer and HTTP CallerID" on page 253). Summarizing briefly, the section describes an authentication mechanisms using a proxy called AuthProxy.

> *The AuthProxy is the only component that is permitted to establish the cloud-authentication status between a client outside of the cloud and the cloud itself.*

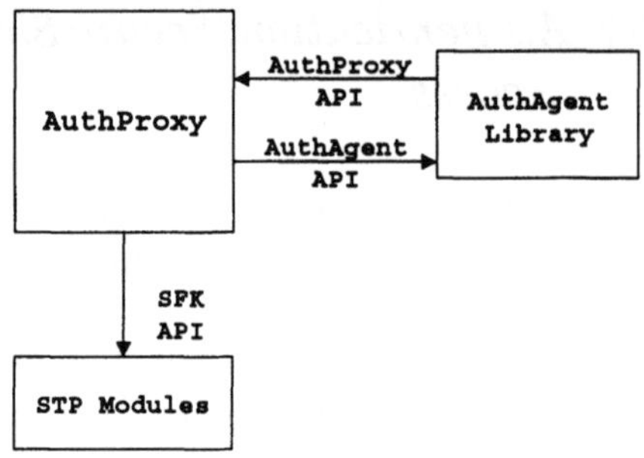

A separate authentication agent, or AuthAgent, must be developed for each type of supported authentication mechanism. These AuthAgents communicate with the clients to negotiate the form and content of keys or other credentials. The AuthProxy communicates with the AuthAgents through a bidirectional protocol, and based upon the protocol content the AuthProxy selectively decides whether to allow the authentication. The AuthProxy and AuthAgent APIs also leverage the industry-standard General Security Services GSS-API and defines security provider interfaces (SPI) to security transport providers (STP). These operate within protected security contexts as identified by private storage describing particular security architectures.

6.7.1 Web Browser Security – Peerless Web *Login* and Service Access

The HTTP and HTTPS protocols support several authentication techniques, although they do not directly provide actual "login" to the remote server.

The primary authentication methods are:

1. *Authentication Request/Response.* The web server presents an authentication method and requests the credential type. The browser suggests a known method, such as clear text or a generic challenge/response protocol. The Microsoft Internet Explorer also supports the NTLM protocol
2. *SSL-Based.* Using the secure session layer protocol (SSL) the client and server authenticate with various credentials. The most common are X.509v3 certificates and passwords. Certificates support mutual authentication through the public keys that validate each end point's identity. Passwords are more portable since they do not require storage of one's private key. These can be combined through middleware to reference a security state stored in a secure network. Password information is safely transmitted through the HTTPS protocol

Repeated authentication on a per-request basis is not a substitute for login. Authentication is relatively costly due to the multiple message exchanges. The client might also have to reenter the credential for each request, as a means to protect the information and also demonstrate permission to use the credential. Fortunately, web browsers support "cookies" that can, in a reasonably secure manner, carry a secured payload that identifies the authenticated session.

Persistent session state can be preserved through HTTP cookies. Such cookies may tag a client's session and allow the serving end to provide client-specific service. This also avoids the need to frequently reauthenticate.

6.7.1.1 Saved State in RFC-2109 "Cookies"

HTTP cookies (see RFC-2109 "HTTP State Management") provide a format and access-control that augment HTTP requests with browser-specific information. The browser and server may pass information between them in the form of the cookie, and the browser may store cookies that are specific to a given server. Such cookies are automatically replayed to the server upon request. Using the `Set-Cookie` and `Cookie` headers, the server and client may negotiate the update and authorized replay of information.

Cookies are subject to a coarse-grain access control known as *domain matching*. This compares the host domain with the domain contained in the cookie or header. Only the domain-matching cookies can be accepted or transmitted. Identical domain names (or addresses) match. A maximal-length suffix also matches a dot-prefixed domain containing an embedded dot. The usefulness of domain matching assumes knowledge of the end point domains. For this and other reasons, the end points may encrypt the cookies thereby protecting against a variety of attacks including a domain impersonation.

Cookies support a pseudo-login as follows. The client provides proof an initial proof of identity. Once established, this identity can be stored in a server-provided cookie and securely set into the client browser through HTTPS under control of the authenticating host. Browser software then provides this cookie to domain-matching requests. This "tags" the client's HTTP requests. The server recognizes these tags in subsequent traffic, and associates the appropriate server-side state with the requests.

A client contacts a web site within the network, and is redirected to a secure (SSL) site. Identities are exchanged and proven through either certificates or passwords. Once the authentication is complete, the SNode provides the client with an encrypted authentication token – stored in the form of an RFC-2109 cookie. This cookie is encrypted, and will be honored for only a short time. A secure control channel refreshes the cookie on a continuous basis.

The identity, now untethered from a particular IP address, is subject to access control lists (ACLs) at the SPOP, host, or service levels. This is essential when the IP address may change, cannot be relied upon as unique, or is shared amongst multiple identities. The cookie-based identity allows validity checks to ensure the client is authenticated, and supports various service models including subscription or private services. All domain-matching hosts receive the cookie, and should enforce access control by reference to a common directory or shared ACL. The underlying IP network can also detect the cookie contents – given suitable firewalls, switches and routers – and may provide appropriate behaviors.

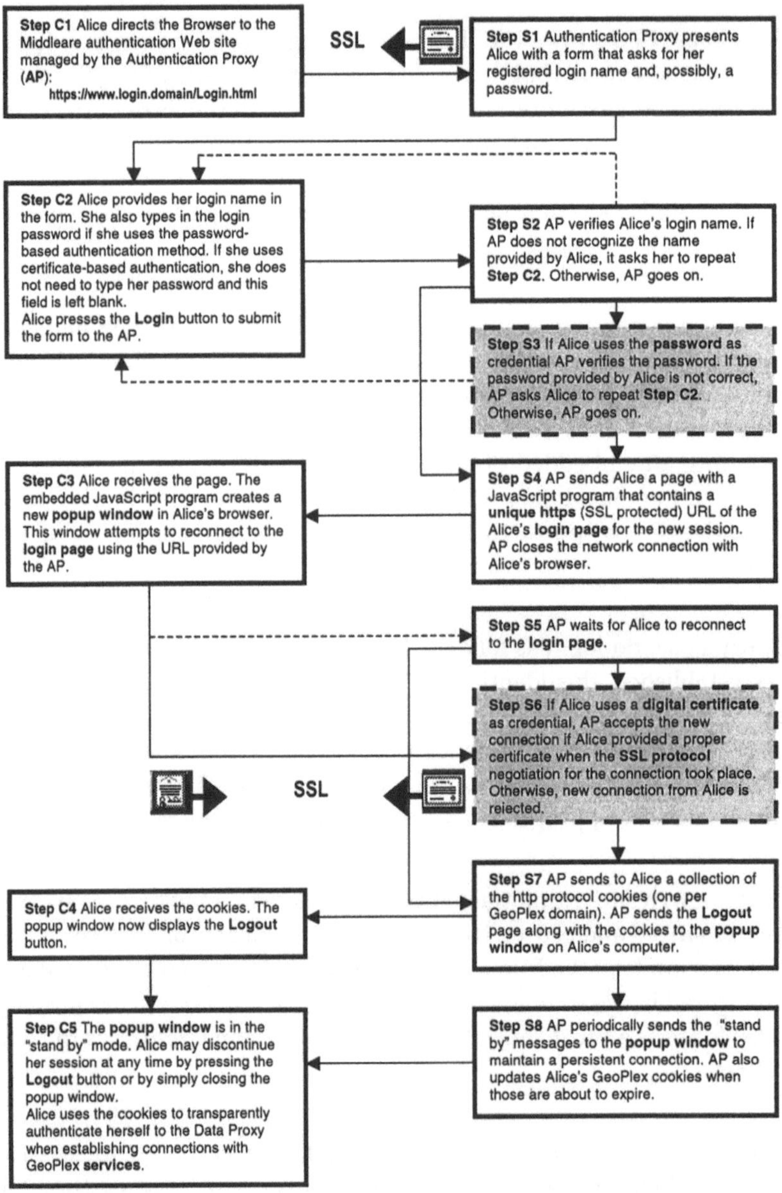

Figure 6-12: Web-Based Authentication

6.7.1.2 Encrypted Cookies from Authentication to Termination

The detailed information flow is shown in Figure 6-12 on page 204. A user first authenticates through a standard browser such as Netscape Navigator or Microsoft Internet Explorer. Authentication is carried out on the cloud side by the Authentication Proxy (AP). AP negotiates a protocol identically to a WWW server, and indeed appears as a server to the web-based clients.

Consider the example of a user named Alice. She begins the authentication procedure by directing her browser to the login HTML page located in the cloud and managed by the AP. Alice uses the HTTPS schema to reach the login page. In response, AP presents her with a form in which Alice types her name and her password; alternatively, she leaves the password field blank and uses a browser-resident X.509 certificate as the credential. Then Alice presses the "Login" button to submit her request.

The AP receives Alice's message and attempts to verify her credential. Assuming it is valid, the AP sends Alice a new page containing a small JavaScript security monitor, and closes the connection to Alice's browser. The script creates a new SSL browser window and reconnects with the AP at a uniquely named page. This page is subsequently managed by the AP. For the duration of the login session, this connection serves as a control channel between the AP and the Agent running on Alice's machine. This control channel supports, at lower cost than general SSL mechanisms, the download of encrypted cookies, as well as invalidation of the user upon logout.

The AP maintains this connection with the client, and manages the client's authentication tokens through it. New cookies are sent to the client browsers prior to expiration of the current cookies; timing is defined by the periodic regeneration of the master secret key by the AP. The AP places a unique identifier of the key in each authentication token encrypted by the key, and later the AP removes a key from the ACT when it generates a new key.

DP uses the unique identifier value in the authentication token to locate a correct decryption key in the ACT. Key removal immediately invalidates all authentication tokens having the identity of the key. If that key is not found in ACT, the authentication token is not valid, and access is denied.

The authentication tokens are stored as cookies. These must be protected against interception or replay. Interception can only occur during access to non-secure services, as these operate over a clear channel. Client-initiated replay can occur on either a clear of encrypted channel.

Limited lifetime encrypted cookies are the primary protective mechanism against replay or modification. This host-supported encryption layer shields against undetectable modification, while rekeying prevents replay or stale or stolen cookies. These cookies contain an encrypted authentication token that is valid only for a short duration.AP sends each authenticated user a new set of tokens prior to expiration of the current ones.

When Alice wishes to terminate her session, she presses the "Logout" button displayed in the Agent browser window. This removes her from the ACT and invalidates the authentication tokens. This measure allows invalidating transient client credentials almost instantly when the client disconnects. The methods foil well-known attacks including capture/replay on the network, as well as "core peeking" by a program through access to the browser memory. These protective techniques are in common use, although they are not currently standardized.

6.7.2 Microsoft NTLM and Browser Authentication

We now discuss integration with users of popular Microsoft networks. Clients that belong to a Microsoft domain can use their existing authentication as a method for gaining access to networking middleware. These credentials are verifiable by reference to the hosting Microsoft domain. This leverages the security mechanisms of Microsoft NT and its clients, as these are widely accepted by the industry. We take the view of reusing *without modification* these native client's capabilities wherever possible. This principle of non-modification preserves the intrinsic security model. Furthermore, there is *zero per-client cost* for development, operation, or maintenance.

Security extensions for SSO are obtained primarily by adding functionality at the SNode. This also uses an AT&T Security Agent for NT (ASNT); the security module is active on the primary domain controller of the Microsoft domain. Its purpose is verification of authentication information. The middleware maintains a secure channel communicating this authentication information between the cloud and ASNT active on the NT-hosted Primary Domain Controller (PDC).

6.7.2.1 Microsoft Security Architecture

The enterprise logon authenticates a Windows computer directly to a domain, typically over a LAN or direct dialup. This combines secure logon to a domain, with per-connection authentication for clients not logged into the domain. A non-enterprise user authenticates each connection by use of a challenge/response protocol such as NTLM. Under secure logon:

1. Clients identify themselves, for example, by a Graphical Identification and Authentication (GINA). This requires a domain, an account name, and a proof of identity; passwords or X.509 certificates are the most common methods to "prove" identity
2. The server authenticates a client by means of the Local Security Authority and Sub Systems (LSA and LSASS). LSASS invokes a replaceable authentication library such as MSV1_0 for NTLM under NT 4.0, or Kerberos v5 under Windows 2000
3. Client obtains an access token referencing the required resource. The Windows operating system provides access control by comparison between a token and an object's security descriptor. The amplification or attenuation of access rights occurs at the thread-level by a technique known as impersonation, or the temporary use of a different access token

Under the NTLM challenge/response for file access:

1. Client initiates a session setup
2. Server responds with a challenge, which is a random byte value called a *nonce*
3. Client irreversibly transforms the password and computes a hash of the challenge using the transformed password; this response goes back to the server
4. Server repeats the calculation. It grants access if the client response is appropriate for the challenge transmitted in step two

6.7.2.2 Single-Sign-On to Middleware Services through NTLM

The authentication provided by a trusted NT domain can be acceptable, given appropriate administrative controls. Specifically, the challenge-response of the native browser method is captured and then verified by a component running on the PDC. This validation includes checking the domain controller to validate the credential and prevent a replay attack. This protocol mediation does not modify the data stream, but rather performs auxiliary actions to "network-enable" the client's access. The client's trusted status within its enterprise server provides sufficient proof of identity. This agent receives the browser-generated security credentials and validates them. The validation of the credentials ensures they belong to the same active session that provided them to the network.

Consider the data flow of Figure 6-13, below. When the browser accesses a URL (1), the browser is redirected to the authentication proxy for login (2), and requests login credentials *over a secure SSL connection* (3). A Microsoft IE browser returns the NTLM authentication information (4), whereas other browsers return an encrypted cookie containing the account name and password[1]. The NTLM authentication is passed to the security agent on NT (4) running the AT&T Authentication Server for NT (ASNT), which uses the Microsoft Security Support Provider Interface (SSPI) to validate the token. Since the ASNT is privileged it can obtain this information and relay the status back to the AP (6), thereby preventing replay attacks from unauthenticated clients. Upon successful authentication, the authentication connection table (ACT) is updated and the browser is directed to the content (7).

Windows 2000 can optionally replace NTLM with Kerberos v5 as the primary authentication method thereby supporting mutual authentication and transitive trust, even in a noxious environment of traffic spoofing and modification. Kerberos is a basic authentication scheme exploiting a trusted Key Distribution Center (KDC) as a "third-party" authenticator providing security for clients. Clients are known by their Principal Names and receive a pair of tamper-proof credentials in the form of a ticket-granting

1. The password is provided under SSL by the user upon initial connection (repeated only when the password changes), and is securely stored in encrypted form on the client's machine as a cookie.

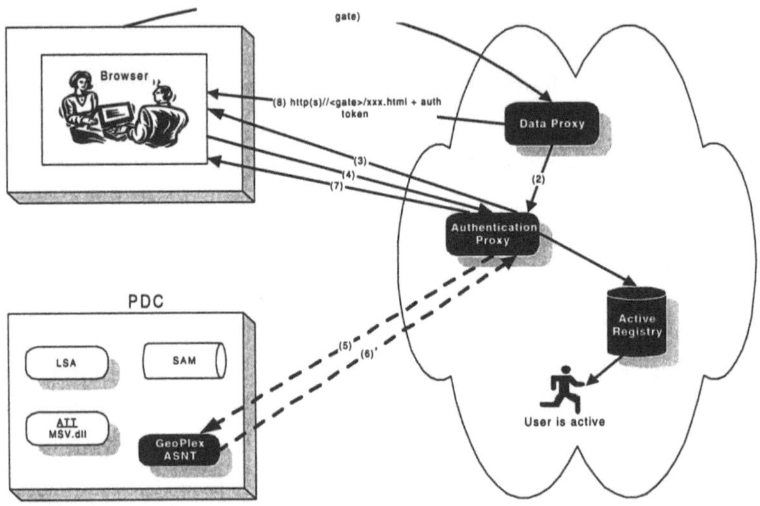

Figure 6-13: Data Flow Validating Access via NTLM Credentials

ticket and ticket session key. The credentials must be presented to the KDC in order to access a service.

Kerberos interoperability relies upon administrative domains, called realms. Each realm supports a Kerberos database. The feature of cross realm operation supports operation across organizational boundaries (Kerberos V5, RFC-1510, RFC-1964 RFC-2623) by means of inter-realm keys and suitable registration APIs. The realms are typically arranged hierarchically. This mechanism permits, for example, one service provider's realm to share trust with another provider's realm.

The Kerberos tickets may include authorization data that refines a ticket's rights. Specifically, Microsoft encodes access control information by means of Microsoft security identifiers (SIDs). Although stored in RFC-1510 compliant format, the data and format have little value to non-Microsoft entities. Consequently, they may require a Microsoft-aware component running on an edge vehicle. This component can be integrated by running a peer on the Microsoft-aware component. A related question is the assignment of permissions to a principal name within an X.509 certificate instead of through a Kerberos ticket. The server may map the principal name to an SID and file access. Alternatively, each principal name can have a corresponding Windows directory. See [Tung99] for more information about MIT Kerberos and Windows 2000.

6.7.2.3 Single-Sign-On to Microsoft Services through Middleware

Platform usability is simplified by allowing users to authenticate in the simplest way possible. Not only does this leverage NTLM from browsers, as described above, but it also provides login credentials by means of a proxy. The NTLM authentication provides the users' identity, and maps it to a specific user within the platform's hierarchy of accounts and users.

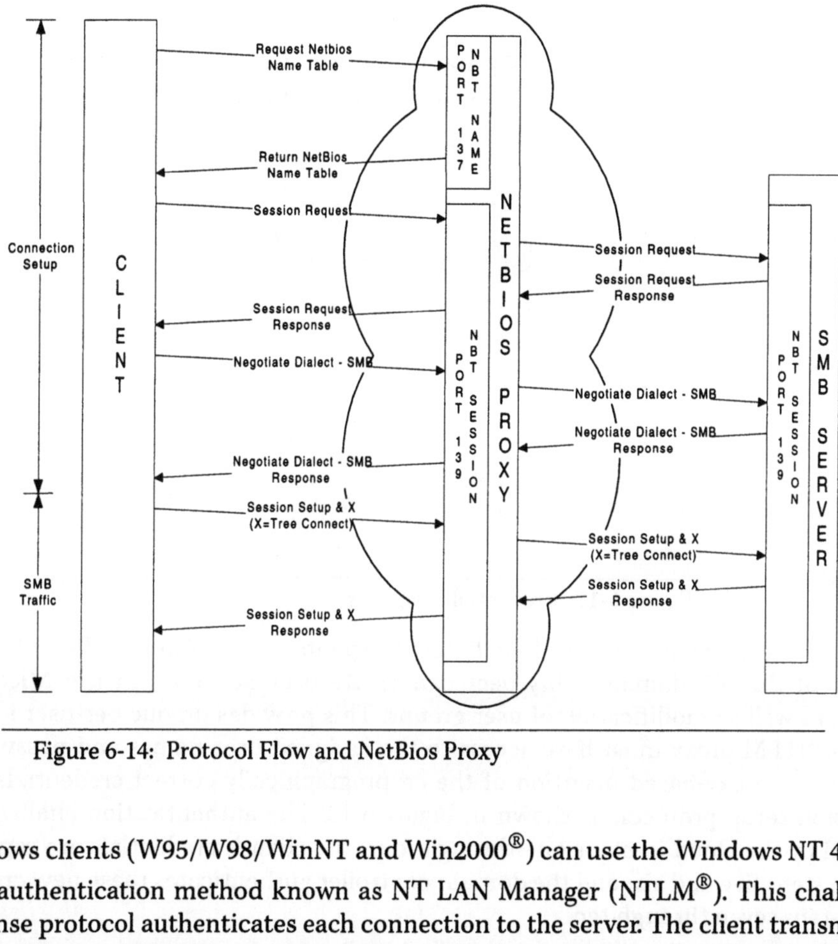

Figure 6-14: Protocol Flow and NetBios Proxy

Windows clients (W95/W98/WinNT and Win2000®) can use the Windows NT 4.0 network-authentication method known as NT LAN Manager (NTLM®). This challenge/response protocol authenticates each connection to the server. The client transmits an irreversible cryptographic transformation of the logon password. Although the password cannot be recovered, the NTLM protocol can be manipulated by 'on-the-wire' protocol mediation to *change* user credentials, specifically the domain, user name and password. This protects the NTLM HTTP authentication method from the man-in-the-middle (MITM) attack by doing it over an SSL-protected connection.

The cloud can capture the server's challenge as the traffic passes through the network. As shown in Figure 6-15, the network then replaces the account name and login password as they return to the server[1]. This allows replacement of the client's password

1. This technique will not work with NTLM v2, which prevents the "man in the middle" attack. Either the NTLM v2 extended security can be negotiated "off", or the Kerberos security can be used with appropriate realms and proxiable (forwardable) tickets.

with some other password maintained by the middleware. In this manner, the protocol mediation grants privileges by changing the user's identity. GeoCIFS provides SSO in this manner.

The replacement of the user's identity grants the user access according to pre-stored permissions of the new identity. Technically, this technique exploits the privileged

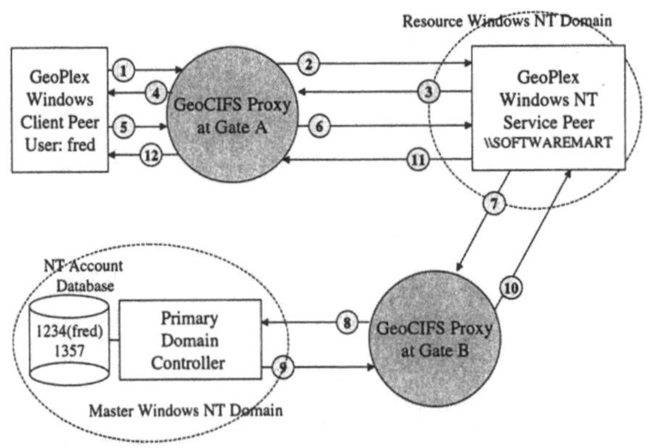

Figure 6-15: Credential Swapping

position of the cloud as a protocol mediator. It exploits a peer configured as a trusted member of the NT domain. This peer can create user accounts in the Microsoft domain, as well as modification of user groups. This provides unique per-user identities. The NTLM proxy must have access to the assigned user names and passwords. This permits proxy-based insertion of the cryptographically correct credentials into the session setup protocol, as shown in Figure 6-15. The authentication challenge is captured by the cloud in steps one through four; the client's credentials are replaced between steps five and six; and the domain controller authenticates these new credentials in steps seven through ten.

The resulting credentials are indistinguishable from native NT credentials, because they are computed with the same algorithm. The NTLM proxy provides access to NT services that would otherwise be unavailable to the client.

6.7.2.4 LDAP Credentials with Microsoft Commercial Internet System

The Microsoft Commercial Internet System (MCIS) is an integrated offer of Microsoft components including a web-based SSO supported by multiple applications. It does not require X.509 certificates or Kerberos-compliant applications. Instead, MCIS embraces standards such as LDAP as a protocol for the storage and access of authentication information. For example, authentication information (groups, users, memberships, passwords) are provisioned through LDAP v3. They information is stored as a SQL or other database. The database entries propagate to other compliant databases depending on the configuration. Access validation functions – typically provided by the Security Access Monitor (SAM) – are replaced by the MCIS monitor. This validates access requests through impersonation accounts and private validation checks. The fact this operates "outside" the NT kernel is sometimes considered irrelevant to the Internet users' experience, and we do not argue the merits of "in kernel/out kernel" security. Suffice it to say that Windows 2000 corrects the issue.

Possible security vulnerabilities of the MCIS architecture are resolvable through firewall-integrated SSO. The network enforces coarse-grain access control through appropriate firewall rules. These rules are added selectively for specific users, and are subject to access permissions. These rules forbid access unless an authenticated and authorized component allows the access.

In a heterogeneous SSO environment (i.e., not pure Microsoft), the MCIS administrator grants administrative access to a trusted third party such as the network operator of a network cloud. The authorized party may then runs software that registers its clients into the LDAP directory containing accounts, groups and users. These clients' subsequent access control is subject to the identical constraints as native MCIS clients.

Upon user registration to the network cloud, a small piece of custom code is notified of the event. This updates the MCIS account structures via LDAP. At some later time the client authenticates to the networking middleware. The middleware opens the firewall and allows connection to MCIS service. Since the client's authentication credentials are valid, the user can access the services according to the MCIS group permissions.

This LDAP compatibility uses Microsoft APIs and SQL server and IIS to ensure full compatibility. In principle the MCIS system can also be configured to a third party LDAP server. In either case, both MCIS and the authentication daemon should possess appropriate authentication credentials in order to update the LDAP directory. This model also supports the update of existing credentials as new services are added, or when clients select them.

6.8 Summary

This chapter provided an overview of the fundamental methods and the specific applications of system security. This presented the core cryptographic methods and applications of these methods. The reader is cautioned not to assume this discussion is comprehensive (for example, DES is no longer certified by the National Institute of Standards), though this chapter does provide a firm core.

CHAPTER 7

APIs and Managed Infrastructure

Network middleware enriches the communications infrastructure, infuses the network with managed resources and imparts uniform interfaces to diverse technologies. As a cohesive large-scale system, this network integrates technology with policy as depicted in Figure 7-1. The topmost plane provides APIs for declaration of external characteristics, as well as requests for internal activities. Managed objects carry out these requests through interactions in the horizontal supporting planes. The vertical planes ensure consistent network-wide behavior, ranging from security policies to open interoperability over multiple networks.

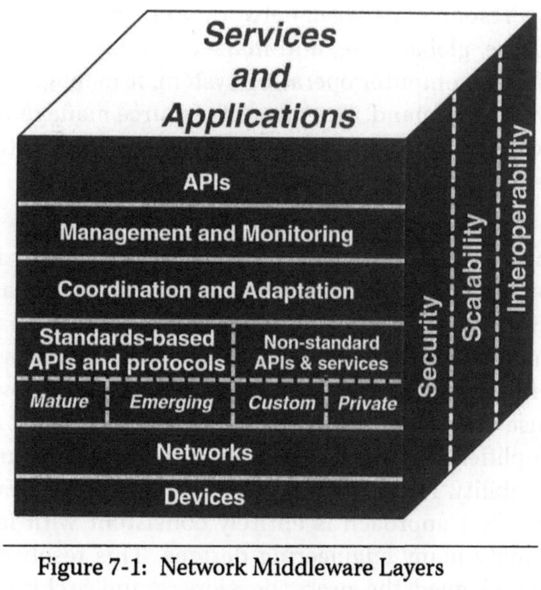

Figure 7-1: Network Middleware Layers

This layered approach supports the rapid construction of reusable and integrated services, by means of the open APIs. The network infrastructure selectively accepts, refines and fulfills the API requests, subject to subscriber profiles, access rights and network resources. Execution draws upon appropriate computational processes and communication protocols.

7.1 Viewpoints on Middleware

Building upon the principle of common APIs, middleware consolidates vendor-specific APIs and features. This simplifies interoperability, and eases the introduction of new technologies. Consider the example of integrating multiple vendors' HTTP caches. The caches were not designed to interoperate, and this constrains design of interoperable systems. Each vendor provides a different feature set and distinct API. We can restore the freedom of "vendor independence" by use of a single API empowered with platform-supplied mediation between feature sets. This is not simply a question of syntactic transformation. The feature sets are substantially different. For example, Netscape's NSAPI initializes cache size and defines selective memory mapping. Apache permits explicit handlers with memory pools, per-directory configuration and fine grain controls. Other cache systems require identification of the specific pages eligible for cache-residence, and automatically refresh the cache. Middleware can mediate between these distinct frameworks.

As a resource manager, network middleware provides fundamental support for secure storage, global state, and managed datapaths between cooperating processes. Like a modern computer operating system, it manages resources to provide requisite service levels on demand. The value of resource management applies to networking resources, access to a service, maintaining the target hit-ratio on a content cache, or guaranteed system security.

Network middleware assumes responsibility for information that passes through its borders, including the authenticity of its source and distribution. Issues ranging from device capabilities through billing and security can leverage network-provided intelligence. The network insulates both users and providers from the intricacies of components and architecture. Reusable components now move into the network, where their reuse is coordinated through standard network APIs. As an architectural issue, this simplifies many end point design issues; for example, information management and scalability. The providers and users now concentrate on their particular areas of expertise. This approach is entirely consistent with layered architecture approaches that simplify many engineering designs. This resolves many troubling design issues that have plagued the users, developers and architects of network applications. Myriad details are abstracted into the platform layer. The platform provides a reliable means to fulfill the API calls by its clients.

This service framework provides a powerful means to build systems that resolve these issues. The framework combines open APIs, data protocols, and system resources in a holistic view. That is, the APIs interact with the whole system, rather than simply demanding a standard procedure invocation by the platform. This view integrates the APIs for diverse areas including network control, end point interaction, and manipulation of hierarchical account structure of users and services.

7.1.1 Middleware as Integrator of Standards

Standards specify required behavior within precisely circumscribed domains of applicability. This provides an essential link between the myriad components of multiple vendors. Although written by industry experts, standards nonetheless cannot address every question or interaction. Important items fall outside the scope of ratified standards. Proprietary designs and diverse technical perspectives occasionally forestall standardization. Variant interpretations, incomplete conformance, or non-enforcement may diminish a standard's utility. Is there little wonder at incompatible products purporting compliance to the same standard? Standardization improves quality but does not resolve all issues of design or function.

Middleware resolves many of these challenges. It unites components despite variations in abstraction, standards or artifacts of implementation. Horizontal middleware layers select suitable elements, and vertical layers ensure proper overall behavior. Middleware-based systems, as compared with their non-middleware counterparts, can more easily prevail over the complexities of global networking. This empowers the human-chain – from architects and developers to the customer. They are freed from concern for artifacts, version dependencies, or multilayer interactions. This profoundly affects the information industry, which is increasingly reliant upon programmable devices at every layer above physical transport. These devices can interact more easily and at lower cost. Compelling examples even show these devices sharing the same object-orientation through the Java language. There is little wonder that Sun Microsystems has stated "The Network is the Computer", that Cisco routers run a sophisticated operating system, and that Microsoft is extending its products toward the network layers.

The effectiveness of advanced services – from Unified Messaging (UM) through Voice Over IP (VOIP) and interactive multimedia – hinges upon rapid deployment with faultless behavior. Reliability, performance, and simplicity must rival the traditional "black phone" despite the vastly greater complexity. This leverages the adaptable networking middleware. The areas of networking middleware services includes authentication and access control, remote access, interoperability, fault-tolerance, security services including encryption acceleration and digital certificates, policy-based management, and QOS/bandwidth management. For example, flexible software systems can craft a consumer service in a manner suitable for a particular client or market. The success of such activities is dependent on the infrastructure's guarantees of reliability and performance. Middleware solutions provide an element of success.

The platform uses standards when available, yet there are many cases where the public standards do not address critical platform requirements. We briefly consider three examples, including one where currently available standards are now integrated into the networking middleware:

- *Firewall packet-filter.* The current standards do not describe packet filters with the generality or functionality necessary for a multi-domain network middleware. Consequently, we depend on our own APIs and implementation for firewall control. Since the firewall is a fundamental of system security it is entirely appropriate to go outside of the standards to obtain required functionality

- *Platform storage.* Because the data storage has many unique characteristics, we provide our own API and storage known as the domain API. This builds upon the best-in-class engines in object-oriented databases. This provides network middleware with the necessary flexibility, and harnesses third-party technology for their expertise in areas such as replication, caching and fault-tolerance. Standards for Directory Enabled Networks (DEN) can be combined with the platform's APIs when required
- *Authentication and transport security.* These are widely available in the standard SSL/TLS protocol. The middleware leverages this in support of browsers, as well as other secure data transport. However, prior to widespread availability of SSL, the middleware developed a powerful encrypted control protocol supporting authentication, callerID, a heartbeat to monitor the connection, and tight integration with the server-side functionality. This peer continues to be used for applications that require close integration with the middleware

7.1.2 Middleware as Extender of Standards

Middleware uses *transport* protocols and *application* protocols. Standards-based transport protocols enable the exchange of information, whereas application protocols are specialized to a particular kind of information or interaction. Protocols are the essential means to communicate between networked components. There are advantages to the use of standards based protocols. They improve interoperability. They also improve correctness through public scrutiny, since no proprietary wall hides a detail or flaw. A wide range of vendors can provide standards-compliant components thereby driving the software (and hardware) markets towards innovation and quality.

Networking middleware manages and leverages these protocols. Bandwidth management is a prime example where advanced features enhance IP transport performance while retaining compliance with industry standards. The underlying principle is well understood:

> *Standards do not constrain an implementation from extensions – such as optimizations or features – provided that such extensions do not contradict any of the relevant standards.*

For example, multiple classes of service can be enforced at servers through management of local resources. This may take the form of directing a particular client's packets to a specific network interface with "premium" characteristics (say, a T3 line instead of a highly congested T1 line). Middleware components also influence the routing, albeit indirectly, through appropriate advertisement of type of service (TOS) metrics they are willing to provide, using for example OSPF (RFC-2328, RFC-2676) messages. Management of local computational resources (CPU priority, buffer space) also has measurable upon TCP performance.

In particular, the "best effort" requirement of IP has never been defined as "identical results". Systems manage their internal computational and network resources according to policies that prefer some activities over others. This is typically done in keeping with underlying principles of "fairness", as this improves overall system function. Fairness prevents the indefinite postponement of pending activities, and in a more technical sense, bounded fairness tries to limit the degree of postponement [FRAN86]. As it is in processors (buy the fastest you can afford) so it is in software (contract the resource you need).

This is not to say that end points cannot directly control traffic through standard protocols. A number of tunneling protocols such as L2TP and IPSec support end-to-end characteristics as virtual private networks (VPNs) with specific security properties. Through potentially provides better service for the applications riding on the IP network. However, direct control of bandwidth and delay remains difficult through standard protocol, due in part to the diverse networks. These limitations are currently being resolved through specialized network elements as well as the IETF standards for IntServ (RFC-1633 and subsequent) and DiffServ (RFC-2430 and subsequent).

For standards-based *application* protocols the situation is somewhat different. Networking middleware infuses the application protocols with enhancements for better performance and improved functionality. The underlying protocol remains unmodified, and the protocol behavior becomes integrated into the network. The processing of application protocols may occur either at the connection end points, or directly on the data path. Section 9.4.3.1 gives an example of end point-based enhancements to DNS. Datapath enhancement elevates the transport mechanism from a mere replicator of bits, into an active element that adds significant value to services. Section 9.4.3.2 of presents data path-enhancement for hypertext (HTTP), followed by enhancements for the Common Internet File Systems (CIFS) in Section 9.4.3.3.

7.1.3 Characteristics of Network Middleware APIs

The middleware APIs give control over the network, end points and domains. Features include authentication, routing, and protocol mediation. A user on a service-oriented platform can announce the services that his network provides, define the clients that may subscribe for the service, and later retrieve the usage records that account for these clients' use of the service. The APIs operate on a managed network thereby avoiding the myriad problems that emerge on an unmanaged network. The platform supports the APIs by direct execution of processes, as well as control of protocol flows between distributed components. Since the APIs are *open*, users can potentially develop self-hosted services that utilize the API elements. The system elements prohibit actions that might compromise system security or information privacy.

All interaction is by common application program interfaces (APIs) that are common to all systems. This facilitates the essential and powerful ubiquity principle:

Any component on any network can obtain authorized services by use of the standard APIs

APIs declare behavior. The framework then addresses the steps necessary to achieve the API-defined behavior. This can use object inheritance, reference to user-profiles, or other framework features.

Although the APIs are open, the network is not. API functionality can be restricted. Consider the roles of network operator, an individual user, and a corporate user. Network operators can establish acceptable usage policies for groups of users. These operators can use all administrative APIs. However, the users function within the constraints of the applicable policies. These restrict a user's permissible actions. This leaves several subtle questions unresolved. For example, in regards to reusable resources, how should a system share cached information? A customer who pays for a large web cache might balk at sharing this cache even when the content is publicly available.

7.1.3.1 Object Oriented and Extensible

The design of the middleware APIs adheres to object-oriented techniques of composition and inheritance. The APIs are polymorphic, both in the sense of supporting multiple signatures, as well as adapting their function through the platform layers. The APIs combine multiple components that can be inherited through an underlying object-oriented model. They deliberately do not establish a new object framework, but instead are designed to work with existing frameworks. Thus, we prefer to use these APIs from a framework such as Enterprise JavaBeans (EJB) rather than define yet another framework.

Specific APIs also provide a standard means to extend system functionality. Authorized peers can define services that reside outside the firewall yet communicate securely to components inside the firewall. Other APIs allow the definition of services that may run inside the firewall, for example to define new protocols. This can be done with a proxy development framework, as well as through the standard GSS-API.

7.1.3.2 Abstraction

Given the complexity of these domains, the APIs depend upon abstraction to achieve simplicity without compromising completeness. This supports the design of the salient aspects of the middleware network, and frees the developer from handling many irrelevant details. For example, network components are described with nearly independent concepts such as flows, filters, domains, events, and sessions. At a different abstraction the security APIs describe the authentication and authorization between components such as peers and networks. Interaction is expressed through inheritance and composition, for example definition of a firewall filter that enforces authentication. Ease-of-use is achieved because the APIs' abstractions shield the developer from non-essential detail.

The APIs operate at several levels of abstraction. Consider routing. *Packet filter* APIs describe routes at the layer of IP connections, and provide fine granularity controls including timers and composite filters. The *access control* APIs describe permissible routes from the perspective of the *domains* that organize hierarchies of accounts, users and services. A *Virtual Private Network* (VPN) naturally abstracts both packet filter, access control, and also route control. The creation of a VPN defines routes with broad parameters such as membership, bandwidth and delay. This extends even to the control of edge routers in the network.

As a second example, from the perspective of an eCommerce service, the APIs allow definition, announcement and management of the service. Service definition describes operating parameters, as well as the access controls on specific users and accounts. Announcement can define the location of the service. Management functions include resource monitoring and the control of specific service features. Each uses an appropriate API that operates within the context of the service.

7.1.3.3 Complete Coverage

The APIs achieve *complete coverage* by partitioning the networking middleware into functionally distinct areas. All necessary functions are defined in each of these areas. Interactions are controlled in two ways. One is the object model's inheritance structure. The second is composition of multiple items as executable code. These codes utilize a functionally complete suite of interfaces that interact with the edge gateway, the internal cloud components, and the external client components.

Middleware components support API calls from outside the cloud via authenticated channels, and from inside the cloud by means of internally-issued calls. The APIs generally use the same syntax for the internal calls and external calls, but can provide different functionality. The user's capabilities define the valid API calls and imposes limits upon them. The cloud can enforce these limits and protect resources, since it maintains information about all accounts, users, and services as well as active sessions. Firewall filters and gate mediation eliminate service providers' concerns about invalid access to resources.

For example, the internal components are not required to authenticate when accessing most other internal components. Communications from outside the gate, on the other hand, require authentication in order to access a cloud-public service. An additional access control check occurs when the service is cloud-private. The internal systems also enforce domain-specific rules; for example only an authorized account administrator can define the subscription rights of users.

7.1.3.4 Comparison with Remote Procedure Call (RPC)

Networking middleware provides abstraction, complexity management and scalability through fundamental design principles. Network middleware is aware of the operational requirements as well as the "data semantics", and can therefore apply intelligence in the network. The deployment is "network aware" and integrates at multiple levels of infrastructure. For example, the middleware is integrated with usage systems, common open authentication, and network switches and routers. Remote Procedure Call (RPC), on the other hand, combines mechanisms for marshalling/unmarshalling parameters, and data transfer between the processes at two end points., While embracing the client-server paradigm, it does not directly support managed services. Because RPC is not network-managed, each routine must independently activate the required network services. These can include security, network bandwidth, and management services. Indeed, there are hybrid RPCs with aggregate objects. Some of them are highly advanced with XML interfaces, and these would be better classified as middleware than RPC.

7.2 Managed Networks

The text now discusses various ways to manage networks. It covers several challenges in network routing and presents the concept of a service model that rides on the network. This raise the issue of managing state information.

7.2.1 Substrate: Middleware-Defined Networks

The edge gateway defines two distinct views of the cloud, shown in Figure 7-2. From the *outside,* the cloud appears as an address-space that imposes end-to-end requirements upon information exchange. Components outside the cloud may request functionality, but may not instruct the cloud how to provide it. *Edge components* mediate between the internal and external interfaces to specify behavior. The edge components complement the external interfaces when necessary, for example to provide encryption when the interface is not verifiably secure.

From the *inside,* the cloud as a middleware layer provides APIs, protocols, algorithms, databases and common infrastructure. Platform-internal functions may either directly enforce the behavior or defer to other middleware components. For example, security operates at network, middleware and application layers, and end-to-end guarantees are essential. The middleware layer applies *correctness-preserving transformations* for data, as a kind of adapter between the client's request and the platform's overall requirements for correct behavior. These enhance the user experience by providing appropriate network behavior. Support of HTTP cache and Single Sign On are examples.

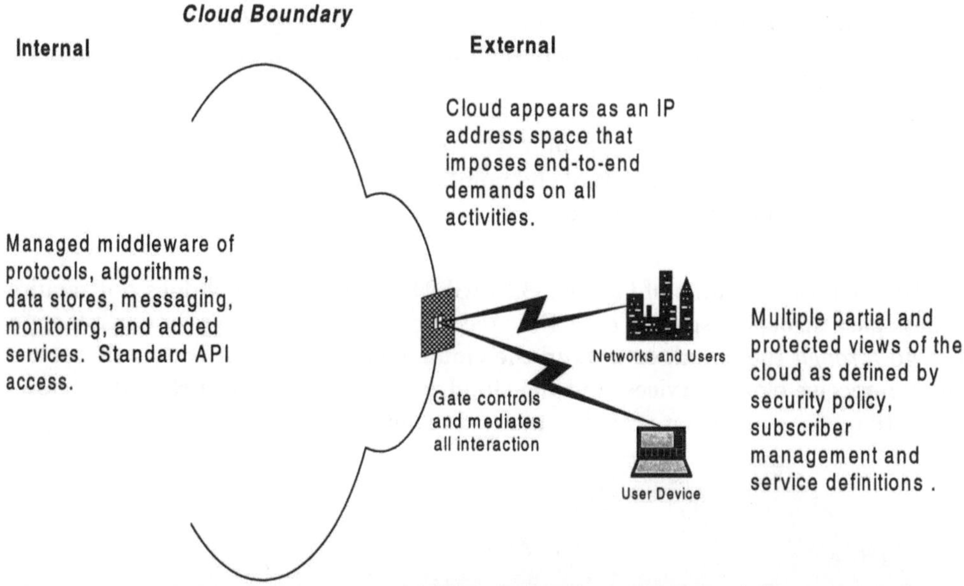

Figure 7-2: Internal and External Views of the Cloud

Consider a user who requests a service, say downloading a movie to a consumer. The cloud is willing to provide this information to the authenticated and authorized user. The service is a private and secure "premium" service, and the data should be delivered quickly and accurately. The edge gateway should negotiate an appropriate connection to the client. This must consider the verifiable properties of the external network. The gateway may detect and adjust the network's delay and bandwidth through selection of network interface, by labelling a traffic flow, or through allocation of buffers and schedulers at the switch level. Other controllable network characteristics may include security; secure links can be used when they are available, and the gateway must otherwise interact with the client to establish encryption keys. We discuss this network integration in depth in Section 9.5.3 ("Distributed Network Element - DNE").

An essential part of middleware-defined networks is th routing that determines the path and policies of data-transport. The path is the sequence through switches and routers. The policies may describe packet loss, bandwidth, delay, as well as privacy. The pure IP protocol neither requires nor forbids adjustment of the path or allocating of resources along the path. The potential for such adjustments depends in part upon the administrative domains a path intersects:

- *Internal route.* Internal routes are under a single administrative domain. The traffic can be directed to services as needed. The domain defines and enforces policies as necessary

- *Route Between Independent Networks.* These networks are connected exclusively through the cloud. Each gate maintains an unique security association of every authenticated peer. The gate also provides services as required. Service-level guarantees may be negotiated between the cloud operator and the external network provider

- *External-with-External:* Traffic only receives cloud services when it routes through the cloud. The external end points require *partial route control* that directs the traffic into the cloud

Consider the possible paths of Figure 7-3 [REGL99]. The IP protocol does not require that data pass through a specific gate. Data passing between the two peer consoles can either go *through* the cloud, or *around* the cloud. Only traffic that routes through a cloud can receive cloud services, and the cloud must load-balance such traffic. However, the IP protocol does not provide a method to define specific routing.

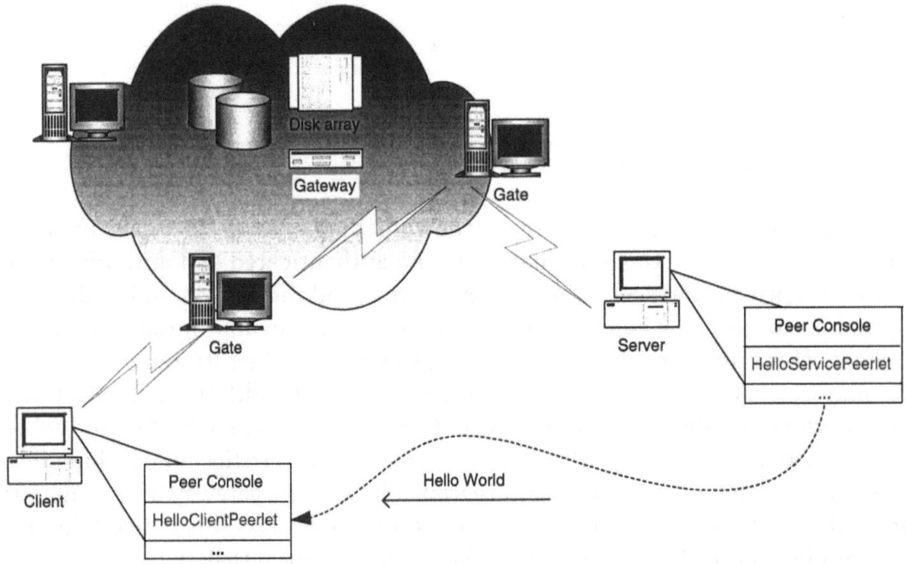

Figure 7-3: Function and Performance Unpredictable with Unconstrained Routing

The IP protocol defines "loose" and "strict" routing, with strict routing being an anachronism no longer supported, but rather generalized in IPv6 through anycast addresses. Loose routing specifies only the source and destination addresses, and can robustly follow any available path to the destination; loose routing benefits from efficient route computation through protocols such as OSPF (RFC-2328). Strict routing – which we have emphasized is typically a non-supported "feature" of the IP protocol – specifies a particular route in the IP packet; yet there is no assurance the path is even valid. It makes the unwarranted assumption that switches and routers will honor the requested route. It is inefficient as well, unable to recover gracefully from congestion or outages. Path-discovery is also a problem. Although programs such as `traceroute` can often dynamically obtain a path, routers are not required to provide this information. Cloud-centered routing needs some other method to specify an intermediate host between the source and destination.

Consider the world as seen by the peers K_1 and K_2, as shown in Figure 7-4. The peers can directly communicate *without* the cloud. This precludes K_1 (or K_2) from receiving cloud services in conjunction with the data path to K_2 (or K_1). For example, the gate can obtain callerID information from K_1 or K_2, but neither K_1 nor K_2 can directly obtain the callerID from the other. The route between them does not receive cloud mediation.

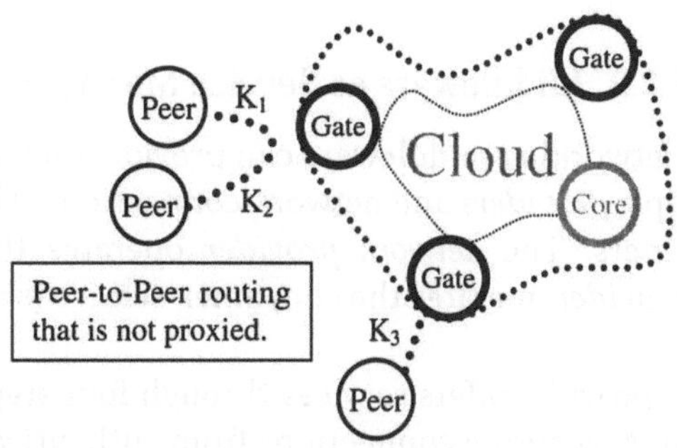

Figure 7-4: Non-Proxied Route

The reader may wonder why the Internet routers cannot simply be reprogrammed to provide this intermediate-route capability? We provide two answers:

- *Complexity.* There are potentially N^2 such routes between N clients. This gives a staggering 10^{15} routes based upon the number of Internet users in 1997
- *Security.* Each peer operates under a unique security association maintained at the edge gateway. Packets from $Peer_1$ to $Peer_2$ are transformed from the K_1 security association to the K_2 association. However, a directly shared security association (such as a symmetric key $K_{1,2}$) could defy monitoring, usage, mediation or pairwise security. The cloud might be unable to revoke $K_{1,2}$ if a peer looses its trusted status

The problem is remedied by proxitizing each of the connections to the cloud, as shown in Figure 7-5. In this case the proxy traffic will pass from a peer, to the cloud, and then to the other peer. Non-proxy data will continue to use "best effort" routing. It passes around the cloud, and does not benefit from cloud services such as security. The peer programs must distinguish between traffic they address to the proxy-address, and the traffic they address to other hosts on their network.

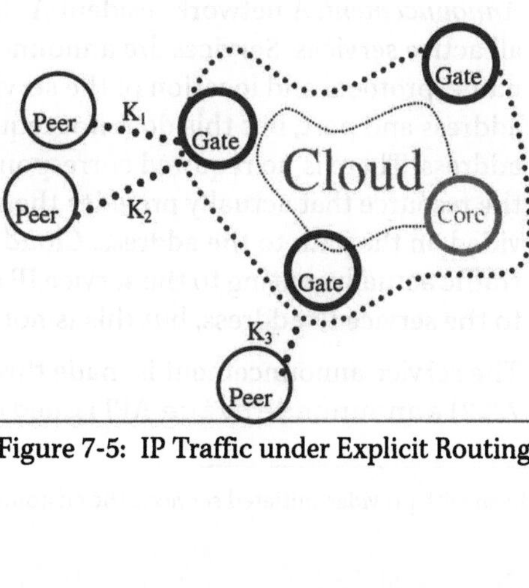

Figure 7-5: IP Traffic under Explicit Routing

Proxies provide an economical way to direct traffic through a specific host, compared to the costs of software encapsulation approaches such as L2TP or IPSec. A cloud-hosted proxy can serve as the internal end point for inbound connections. Switch based VPNs with suitable route control protocols are a developing solution that will likely provide faster service and impose less load on the end points.

7.2.2 Middleware as Service Manager: The Service Model

Networking middleware can provide a service-oriented architecture consisting of multiple *providers* and network connections. The services actually use several kinds of providers. The *network provider* operates the platform and connectivity. The *service provider* operates the consumer-service (such as a specific eCommerce application).

A provider offers services through four steps: registration, invocation, announcement, and accepting connections from authenticated and authorized customers. A customer requests the service by initiating a connection to the provider[1]. We will briefly describe these steps, and will then examine how the cloud can facilitate access to services. The basic paradigm support many variations, as determined by the particular service.

1. *Registration*: A service provider specifies the name, access policy, and the protocols required. These protocols include standard (TCP, UDP, HTTP, etc.) as well as custom protocols. The custom protocols can be intrinsic or specially built for the particular service. A provider can register the service through software that utilizes standard commands, as well by creation of a service object and storage into the domain database (see Section 8.3)
2. *Invocation*: The network-provider ensures availability of all required protocols and infrastructure, including suitable bandwidth and security. These utilize the platform features in a reusable manner, employing the trusted status of the platform as the authenticator of connections. The service provider authenticates to the cloud, activates and then verifies software which "listens" on the designated IP address
3. *Announcement*: A network resident Authenticated Service Registry (ASR) describes all active services. Services are announced into the ASR by an API that accepts name, protocol and location of the service. The location can be specified as an IP address and port, but this does not require the service is actually provided at the address. There is no required correspondence between the service IP address and the resource that actually provides the service. For example, the service can be provided on the path to the address. Cloud mediation can provide the service without traffic actually routing to the service IP address. In many cases there is a connection to the service IP address, but this is not mandatory.

   The service announcement is made through the Service Development (SD, Section 7.3.2) `announceService` API issued either from a peerlet, or through the console

1. Even with provider-initiated services, the customer must still "power on" to receive service.

commands `manageAur -e` (from the core) or the peer interface command (`pido -l announce`). The network administrator can also preload services through the `preload_aur` command

Networking clients can now attempt connection with a service. The authentication and access control software provide client-specific behavior; see "Deployment of Proxy-Enabled Services" on page 309.

7.2.3 Middleware as Manager of Global Shared State

Another area of challenge is the management of global state including system objects. Systems are composed of objects, and a state-space representation of these objects describes their essential attributes. The system regulates its activities by reference to the state space. Consider the example of a user's request for a certain service. Deciding how to process the request will reference objects that describe the user, the requested service, and system policies. The outcome might allow, disallow, or modify the users' request. Management of this state information is essential due to storage requirements as well as the latencies inherent in modification or reference to state information.

In order to operate within fixed costs, a managed platform focuses considerable effort upon the management of global state. There are costs inherent in the storage and manipulation of state, and these costs may be described in terms ranging from the physical design characteristics of storage or network components, and up through the cost a customer pays for services. Since network middleware is inherently distributed, the global state requires distribution of information to ensure the state descriptions are accurate, even when some component references the state of a distant object. It is clearly important that global objects should be available with minimal access delay, and yet the general object-synchronization problem is extremely complex.

Structure and *optimization* are two techniques that tame the complexities of managing state information. The software components therefore structure system objects in a manner that supports their intended use. Optimizations also help a system operate effectively within the multiple constraints that limit object manipulation. Of particular interest in a middleware network are the hardware devices that report and store state, as well as the transport methods that copy the state to the appropriate control point.

The physical characteristics of these devices and transports imposes delays on the propagation and synchronization of the changes. Clearly these delays cannot be eliminated. Scalable systems therefore try to avoid dependencies upon synchronized state, and when unavoidable, the systems manage such dependencies. These challenges may appear unique to networked systems, but they occur in centralized ones as well.

Networked systems work primarily with distributed information, whereas centralized systems need to structure their information for ease of access. Comparison of these two kinds of systems is highly instructive in regards to the specific middleware designs. IP networks are a prime example of distributed information. Rather than depend on global shared state or the correctness of every routing entry, IP utilizes multiple distributed information bases located at the routers, switches and end points. AS-needed computation shares information with the local neighborhood. These distributed properties facilitate large networks and global scale. However, these systems cannot easily locate specific information or control fine-grained resource allocations. Such networks require substantial extensions - such as networking middleware - to support services-specific routing or bandwidth allocations. An important challenge is support of such state-dependent services - or an approximation of them - without compromising the stateless nature of IP.

Conventional operating systems, on the other hand, retain localized and detailed information. Low-level data structures organize the information and facilitates the management of system resources, including the "virtual machine" concept. Higher-level descriptions allow exercise of very precise control over system behavior, for example by reference to a specific user's privileges. However, as the number of processes, users, and other resources increases, the maintenance of this information becomes increasingly costly. Systems therefore migrated towards distributed architectures that localize information for related tasks. Micro-kernel operating systems, for example, exploit this principle. In a similar manner, the networking middleware combines multiple systems.

This views the networking middleware as a large and distributed micro-kernel operating system. Linux is well-known for a similar approach. The power of Linux is the mechanisms to easily reconfigure the kernel while retaining Posix compliance. Linux's popularity is not due to its stability, nor to serving as an alternative to Microsoft. Rather, it is the flexibility of modular design that readily reconfigures from the smallest to the largest implementation; similar capabilities are available through commercial Unix offerings as well.

7.3 Organization of the Middleware APIs

We now shift to a specific set of communication middleware APIs that support the development, operation and management of services. These APIs are organized into general categories. These categories overlap and share common functions as required. For example, the callerID function is found in several categories.

- Proxy Development (PD) for gate and core functionality. This includes packet filter, security checks, events generation, user and service registries, as well as the proxy framework for developing new proxies. It includes a callerID capability for non-repudiable client identification even for untethered clients that do not have a fixed and unique IP address

- Software Development (SD) for peer and core functionality. This includes libraries for connections, the domain API, events, security, usage, and more features. It also includes a security framework (SF) API for credential and web authentication management
- Network Development (ND). This provides advanced firewall and QoS control through interaction with network element including the DNE
- Operations Development (OD). This supports creation and maintenance of domains.

These APIs insulate the developer from the intricacies of the networking and components. Consequently, the services built with these broad API classes (see Table 5) adhere to the platform principles and can leverage the platform optimizations. By use

TABLE 5: Network APIs and Component Availability

API Group	Purpose	Gate	Peer	Standard Browser
Routing	Secure connections at designated service levels	Yes	Partial	No
Authenticated Connections	Active registries, connection management, non-repudiation interaction including events and usage.	Yes	Yes	Yes
Access Control	User and Service access control	Yes	Yes	Use, not specify
Domain	Account hierarchy storing describing users, services	Yes	Yes	Use, not specify
Security Framework	Manipulation of user credentials and inclusion of secure methods	Yes	Yes	Use, not specify
Usage Recording and Retrieval	Non repudiation of action. Submit and retrieve usage records encapsulated in translucent cookies	Yes	Yes	Use, not specify
Naming	Directory services such as LDAP and private proxy DNS	Yes	Yes	Yes
Network Management	Log, control, and measure components. Application management. Define, publish, subscribe and receive events with descriptions	Yes	Most	Use, not specify
Name/Value pair (NVP)	Association Lists	Yes	Yes	No
Toolkits	Network Proxy framework, Service Development framework, Network Development toolkit, Security Framework toolkit	Yes	As needed	No

of the APIs one can develop any functionality and it will be reusable on many compatible architectures. One example is the SD for software development as shown in Figure 7-12. Consequently, the platform deployment is application-independent and optimized for available technologies. The ongoing developments such as OMG and JAIN may provide compatibility for even larger scale compatibility

7.3.1 PD – Proxy Development

The Proxy Development tools describe APIs, sample code, tools, and documentation to enable application developers to write proxy applications for the middleware platforms, and allows programmers to network-enabled client software. The PD describes the internal side of middleware-enabled networks, and supports full interaction with the security and service functions including access control and dynamic firewall protection. This enables the development of network proxies, allowing network mediation and enhancement of various protocols. In addition, network proxies are one technique to support scalability of various types of services, as well as fault tolerant services. These network proxies run on the gate machines in the GeoPlex Cloud. The PD enables developers to fully utilize and extend the cloud.

The proxy framework fully supports custom proxies logically placed in the data path between a client and a server, as shown in Figure 7-7. It is an integral part of the middleware platform. This allows the developer to *easily and reliably add functionality in a fully-standardized manner.* All new components share the same structure. Network proxies make use of various APIs as needed. The proxy developer can focus on the mediation facilities of the protocol, and let the rest be handled by the Development Framework. The GeoPlex PD provides the following C and C++ APIs:

- Proxy Development Framework
- Access Control, including packet filter API
- Active User Registry (AUR)
- Active Service Registry (ASR)
- Active Connection Table (ACT)
- Usage Library
- Directory Service
- Network Management Service, including monitoring and events

As a service architecture, it is important that the network provider be able to extend the cloud functionality with new network-based logic. Such custom tailoring may be designed as application level protocols that mediate data as it flows through the cloud. The proxy development framework provides managed multi-threaded support and grants such proxies the full power of the PD APIs. This includes systems management, usage recording, encryption and other security services. These APIs can run, for example, on the gate architecture of Figure 7-6 as detailed subsequent chapters.

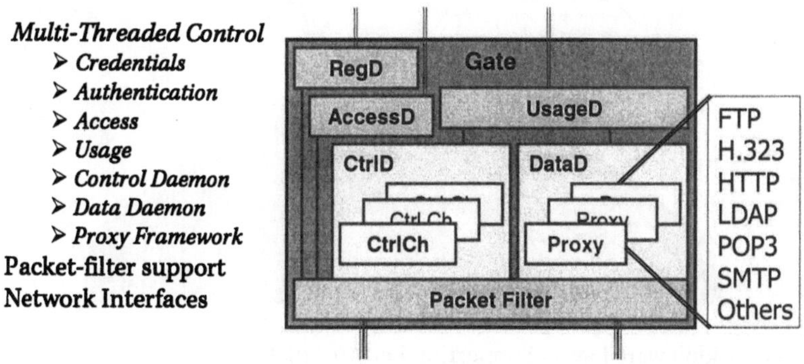

Figure 7-6: Gate Components – Network Interfaces through Application Proxies

Proxy development builds upon the firewall control and address remapping features. The development framework is programmed with the PD, and it provides access to the API sets listed above, including the packet filter, domain, and management APIs. The services are provided dynamically by a standard "plug in" process, technically dynamic load libraries. Once installed, they are protected by the network: the developer (or his company) does not have any risk of the proprietary code being copied or misused. The developer simply provides the custom proxy. The network protects this resource by restricting use of the executable. All network components, including the custom proxy code, benefit from monitoring, usage tracking, and other network behaviors.

Figure 7-8 shows the insertion of custom proxy code into the dataflow between the client-side and server side. The platform's standard proxy framework dynamically supports multiple custom proxies, for example through the data daemon (see Figure 7-6). Each proxy registers into the framework with the **proxyRegister** function. The framework then transparently places the custom code into the data flow, where it can mediate and enhance services. Proxies can register in either the "proxy" mode that interacts with two authenticated end points, as well as the "server" mode when only one end point is required. A "server" mode proxy responds directly to the client requests.

These proxies can build application-layer protocols. The protocol requirements are defined during the registration and authentication of the service. This information is stored, as one might expect, in the secured cloud storage. Specifically, the service is represented by a service object within a domain, and the protocol can be an attribute of the service object.

Application-layer protocols extend the standard protocols. This technique is known as *proxy mediation*. Proxies sit between the client and the server, for the express purpose of receiving a specific protocol and providing support. As Figure 7-7 shows, custom

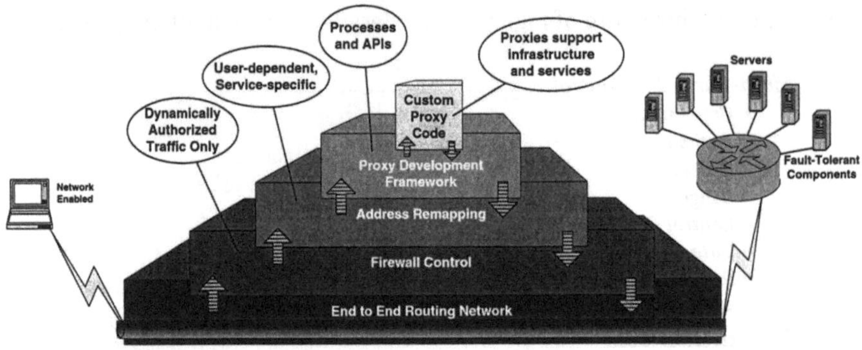

Figure 7-7: Middleware Layers Supporting End-to-End Connection

proxies build on the layered software design. The proxies can use all APIs, for example to check a user's access rights, modify the packet filter, and retrieve information from the domain API.

Every custom proxy can handle a large number of *independent* connections, each with its own "generation of storage" that remains associated with the connection for its entire lifetime. This storage is allocated to the custom proxy that mediates the connection. The proxy can selectively access or modify the storage, and does this without concern for how many other connections use the same proxy. Each of the connections originates from a unique 32-bit source IP and 16-bit port (for IPv4), with the maximum number of simultaneous connections constrained by the host operating system's capacity. While some end point devices may restrict the number of connections, it is typically not an issue for server-class machines. The new 64-bit operating systems and hardware are designed with large numbers of connections.

Data flows bidirectionally through the proxy, in keeping with the full-duplex nature of TCP service. The contents of each packet flows through the proxy framework and the

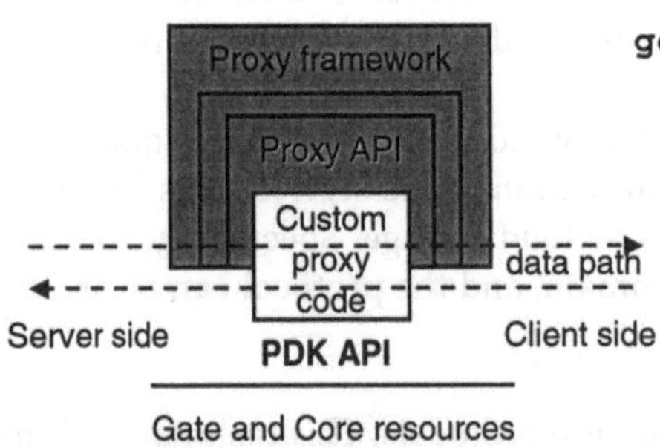


```
geoProxyRegister(
    packetHandlerFunction,
    portToProxy,
    IPPROTO_TCP,
    initializationFunction,
    PROXY);
```

Figure 7-8: Custom Proxy Code Installed with Proxy API

proxy code. The connection end points are appropriately referred to as the "connect" side and the "accept" side. The connection initially flows from the connect-side towards the accept-side, and the reply flows from the accept-side back towards the connect-side. Neither end point is constrained to a purely client or server role.

Proxies share information in several ways. Multiple instances of the same proxy can directly access global memory of the controlling process. This is useful for example to share information between distinct connections that use the same application-layer protocol. Caching is one example but other forms of shared information include read/write locks as well as other synchronization methods.

A number of tools simplify the standardized development and effective management of these mediation components. These include logging, alerting, monitoring, and online control through management interfaces. These standardized elements are automatically incorporated into all proxies thereby ensuring coordination between system components. These functions are essential to all middleware networks. Systems management and monitoring is discussed in detail Chapter 10.

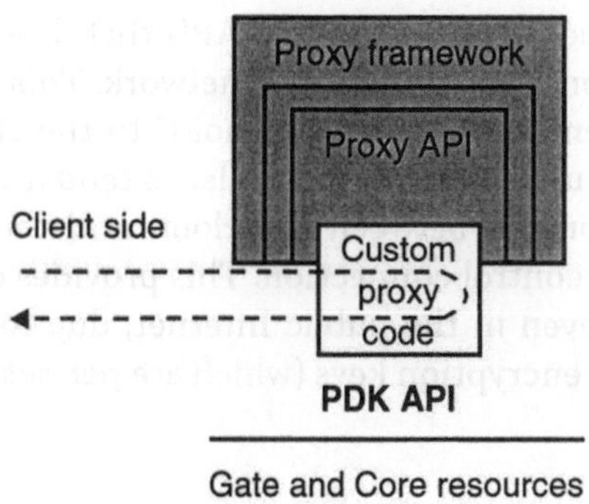


```
geoProxyRegister(
    packetHandlerFunction,
    portToProxy,
    IPPROTO_TCP,
    initializationFunction,
    SERVER);
```

Figure 7-9: Custom Server Code Installed with Proxy API

A proxy can also directly serve the connect-side requests, rather than provide the passthrough functionality just discussed. These proxies register as a "server" instead of as a proxy, as shown in Figure 7-9. This allows the custom proxy to provide all content to the client. Such proxies typically keep one or more TCP connections open to various resources. The proxy interacts with the resources on the client's behalf and provides computation and communication-based responses as required.

Proxies either modify or augment a data flow. Consider a simple proxy that resolves the problem of supporting a private password for the large number of users who can register to the cloud. The password protects some resource, for example a technical support service or a mail server. Password distribution and maintenance is error prone and difficult to control in a large open user community. Rather than jeopardize the resource, a proxy will provide the password whenever an authorized user requires it. The password can be transmitted by various means, of which a simple method is splicing it into the data stream where a dummy password occurs. A mediation proxy unlocks the resource by providing the password when required. This extends the password-based application from a closed domain to an open domain. The platform authenticates users and grants them the single-use of the password as required.

A proxy is not limited to modification of the protocol flow. Activation of secondary services can be achieved by the generation of cloud events by means of the management APIs. This can activate highly sophisticated services. They are activated by a cloud component called the `access daemon`, which modifies the firewall packet filter to map traffic to the appropriate application-level proxy. The traffic is remapped back to its original destination processing by the proxy, as shown earlier in Figure 7-7. We discuss this in greater detail later (see section 9.4.1.2 "Proxy-Enabled Service Activation").

7.3.2 SD - Service Development and Peer

The Software Development (SD) tools are composed of a set of Java APIs that developers may use to build client and server applications for a middleware network. This provides one method by which external components may gain a "toehold" to the cloud and directly request cloud services. These APIs use the SD, and can also extend a standard client-peer. Figure 7-10 shows the relationship between the cloud and the SD application. The SD supports an authenticated control connection. This provides considerable insulation against network attacks, even in the public Internet, due to the inability of an attacker to determine the proper encryption keys (which are per-session and dynamic).

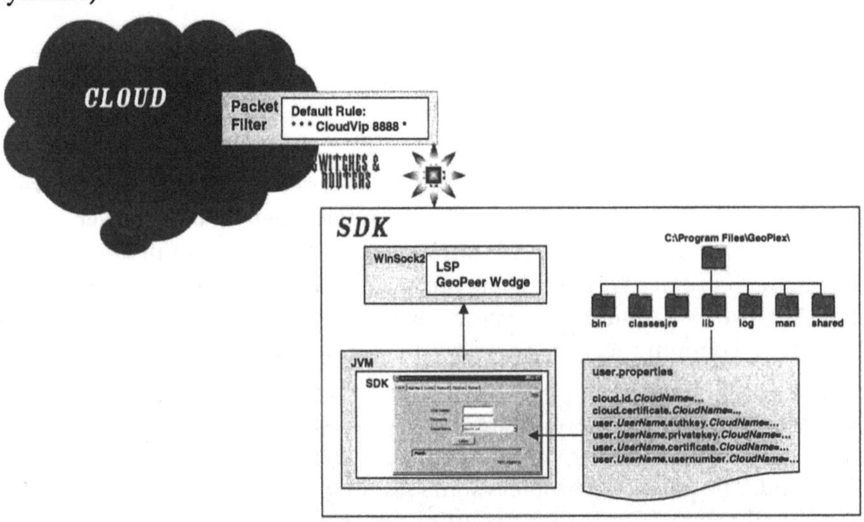

Figure 7-10: SDK Integrates Client to Cloud-Managed Network and Services

The authenticated channel allows private and verified communication between the SD applications and the cloud. They may confidently request actions, and share information. The actions are invoked subject to authentication controls as shown in Figure 7-11.

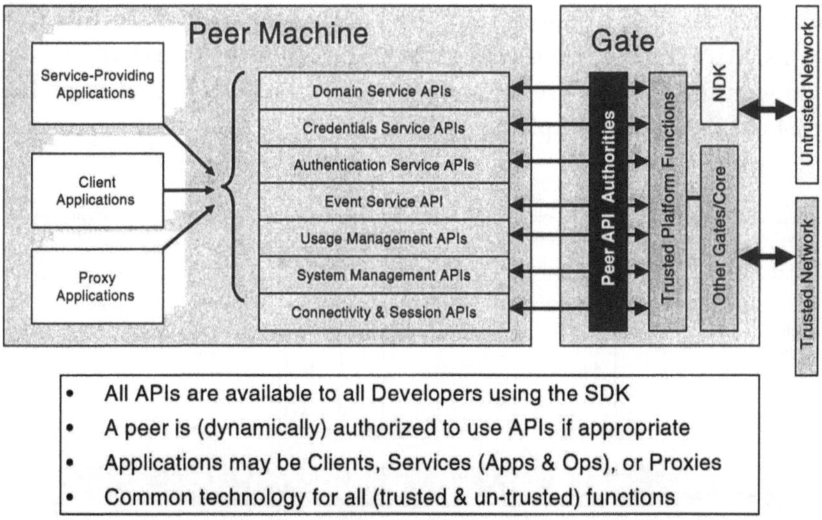

Figure 7-11: Open APIs Expose Platform Functionality

7.3.2.1 Peer Functionality

There are three primary functions of the peer, and these are available to all peer-based services:

- Establish a trust relationship between an end-point and its access Gate
- Support information privacy through encryption of network traffic
- Provide separate APIs for authentication, registration, account management, usage tracking, and the generation and reception of events on the network

The SD supports both a standard and extensible environment, known as the peer. Customized applications can be developed with the SD in accordance with the needs of specific user communities and applications. The peer functionality is mediated by the cloud as shown in Figure 7-12. Peer applications fall into three architectural models: Peerlets, Monolithic Peers, and External Peer applications. Two of these, Peerlets and Monolithic Peers, differ only in whether the application controls the Java Virtual Machine (JVM). Peerlets extend the behavior of a standard GUI peer program, whereas the monolithic peers provide interfaces. External Peer applications, on the other hand, do not run in the same JVM as the Peer, and can be written in C or in Java.

A subset of the Java-based functionality is made available for C language developers as well. It includes Peer software. This is installed on the client or server end-points of a supporting network. The Peer contains all of the Java packages and C libraries needed to support client and server applications written for the network. The SD adds documentation, C header files, examples, and the Java Development Kit (JDK) from Sun Microsystems, Inc. Figure 7-12 presents some of the clients and services that could be constructed with the SD. The user console is currently available, and several custom clients have been designed or implemented.

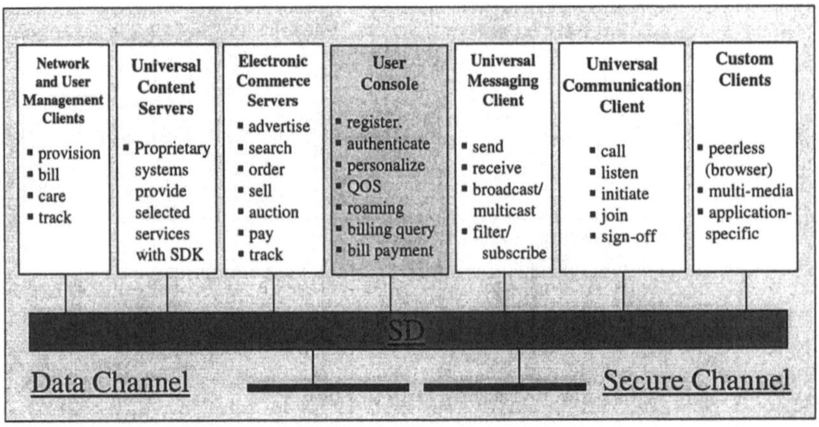

Figure 7-12: Clients Capabilities Extended through Common Platform with SD

Peer-enabled applications may use cloud functions from outside the cloud. This is a powerful method to construct integrated services. Chapter 11, "Sample Consumer Services" describes an application of "virtual worlds" that combines multiple services with the SD.

Users can authenticate to the network either with or without a Peer. If they do not use a Peer, it is referred to as "Peerless" authentication. Peerless authentication provides access to fewer cloud capabilities, and is intended for clients with web-browser access. Thus, this is not an option for developers who want to deploy a service on a supported network. Since some services may require peer-capabilities on an end-to-end basis, users who authenticate by Peerless authentication have access to fewer services than those users who use Peer-based authentication.

The SD APIs provide the following functionality:

- Peerlet management supports: starting, stopping, and communicating with Peerlets

- Connection management supports establishing authenticated connections to a network, announcing service availability (service announcements), and controlling the platform encryptor
- Registration, account management, and subscription supports registration and maintenance of user and service information that is maintained in a network
- Usage tracking supports the submission and retrieval of usage information
- Event generation and reception supports the delivery of events to and from daemons distributed across the network
- External APIs support manipulation of the Peer from an external application, via the Peer Interface

Although APIs are provided both in C and Java, the C API is restricted to the functionality available through the Peer Interface, which represents a subset of the complete support available.

7.3.3 Network Development – ND

Network Development (ND) uses a collection of APIs and tools that can be used to access the network infrastructure system. Users can access and customize the network's API to meet their own needs. It supports the following functionality

- Network measurement: resources, load, random-variable sampling
- Network Control:
  - Full QoS & MPLS network adaptation environment with network interface APIs per IP architecture
  - Multicast support
  - Extranet support
  - E-Commerce support
  - Video conferencing support
  - Fax support
- Network Interactions

7.3.4 Operations Development – OD

The Operations Development (OD) supports rapid deployment of new IP services in a secure, scalable manner. The platform also provides a means of reliably identifying both clients and servers, and a means for adding value to standard IP protocols through a proxy framework.

The platform accomplishes this by integrating a wide variety of underlying (networking) functionality into a single unified whole. Furthermore, the platform provides a unified, consistent set of interfaces for configuring and manipulating this underlying functionality. By utilizing these interfaces, anyone can effectively perform all of the necessary activities for deploying new IP services on the platform.

The platform supports three broad categories of activity:

- Activities related to controlling access to platform and service resources; this is the Domain API
- Activities related to platform and service administration; the processes that modify cloud components and accounts
- Activities related to the establishment and verification of financial responsibilities

These three categories of activity represent groupings of tasks/operations according to their overall purpose (i.e., access control, platform administration, and financial authorization) and are orthogonal to one another. Together, these three broad categories of activity effectively identify all the types of OAM&P functionality available on the platform. This book is primarily about the base technology, not the business plans that these technologies support. Consequently, we discuss only the first of the OD activities, and the reader is referred to the appendices for details on the administrative and financial capabilities of the platform.

7.4 Summary

The basic Internet Protocol (IP) based networks provide efficient packet delivery using only the Domain Name Service and routing for in-network services. All the richness and diversity of services and applications lies fully encapsulated solely in the client and server end-points. Likewise, most of the cost and complexity also lies in the end-points. Careful analysis reveals that much of the complexity is contained in the service support, and this is common to most of the clients and servers. This includes service support for registering users, their authentication, data stream encryption and compression, directory access, and usage tracking and billing. One way of reducing the cost and complexity of the clients and servers is to identify a common set of service support and embed those services in the network. These common services can be standardized and deployed through the network, where the functionality is reliable and reusable. By exposing appropriate interfaces to this enhanced network, the client and server end-points provide the same functionality as before but in a standard and simplified manner. The enhanced network forms a higher-layer of abstraction on the basic network and creates an enabling service-network infrastructure.

This enhanced network can also help solve another problem that exists in today's networks' infrastructure. Today's networks allow many hot spots and bottlenecks that increase the cost of maintaining the networks and reduce overall quality of services. Client and servers are connected to the network through POPs (Point of Presence) over a diverse set of connections such as telephone dial-up connections, ISDN lines, or LANs. The hot spots and bottlenecks can appear in the servers, POPs, and the interconnection network. In the servers and POPs, a physical limit exists on the number of connections that can be established simultaneously and on the bandwidth of the link by which the server is connected to the network. Within the network, bottlenecks can occur at the intermediate links and routers.

CHAPTER 8

Smart Network Components

This chapter gives an "inside view" of the APIs and their usage, through discussion of a reference implementation operating in a distributed environment. Beginning with a functional decomposition into logical components, the chapter subsequently discusses the layered design of these components and specific design decisions. Detailed examples describe many of the APIs with focus on their network interactions. The network interactions build upon the trusted security perimeter as safeguarded by one or more gates. Gates provide aggregate services built from reusable support components. Load balancing, scalability and manageability are inherent to this structure. The reader should not expect a "how to build it" guide, but rather an illustration of how these pieces fit together as a substrate that energizes multiple components.

The discussion distinguishes between *logical* and *physical* components. Logical components define a particular function without reference to specific hardware or software. The logical taxonomy describes *global information*, the *edge gateway*, and *monitoring/management*, as shown schematically in Figure 8-1 and enumerated below. The figure shows the architecture layers from the network interfaces up through higher level service-oriented structures. The security and information subsystems permeate all the layers and are shown at the perimeter of the diagram. Taken together, these components define the basic architecture for a large class of middleware networks.

Physical components, on the other hand, instantiate the logical components with a specific deployment or configuration. These particular deployment choices reflect the performance requirements and associated "build or buy" decisions. The core naming services, for example, combine carefully engineered and tunable custom components with suitable "off-the-shelf" components. The custom components satisfy rigorous performance requirements under conditions of rapidly changing state, and this complements the standards-driven "off-the-shelf" software components.

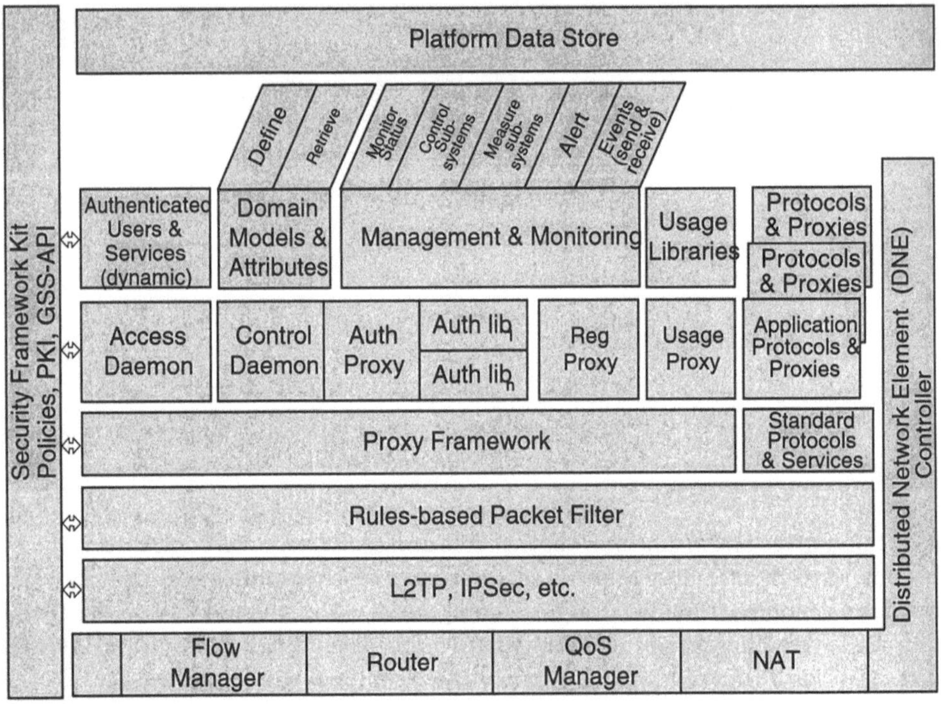

Figure 8-1: Logical Cloud: Network, Filter, Framework, Processes and Services

Most of this chapter illuminates the fundamental issues that we encountered in the design, development and evolution of the architecture. Such issues are important to application design for networking middleware, as well as forthcoming systems.

To orient the reader, we begin with the "basic anatomy" of the cloud. The following list provides the skeleton that supports detailed understanding of the cloud. The current chapter describes the use, effect and central interactions between these components. We defer discussion of the engineering, mechanisms and complexities to Chapter 9, "Mechanisms of Middleware Components".

1. Global information shared between all POP elements
   1.1. Authenticated Users and Services

   Global lists of authenticated components, addresses, and properties including security globs

   1.2. Domain Models and Attributes

   Object-oriented hierarchy of accounts, users and services providing stable store
2. Edge gateway vehicles

2.1. Security Framework

Define and enforce security methods, including Internet Protocol Security (IPSec), tunneling, and public key infrastructure (IPSec). Extensible through standard GSS API. It includes the Distributed Network Element (DNE) that defines forwarding, flow and quality of service behavior through interaction with a routed network

2.2. Secure Protocols (L2TP, IPSec)

Receive, send and forward tunnelled or secured traffic by means of appropriate security association and support appropriate interactions including PKI

2.3. Rule-Based Packet Filter/Firewall

Filter and route IP packets at local network interfaces

2.4. Authentication Proxy and Libraries

Authenticate new connection or labelled flow. Places the user into the Authenticated Connection Table (AuthConnTab). The Authentication Proxy is the custodian of authenticated users, and authentication libraries support specific forms of authentication

2.5. Control Daemon

Maintain control channel to authenticated connection or labelled flow

2.6. Access Daemon

Determine access permission for specific traffic instance (connection or labelled-packet). Update packet filter to enforce the permitted access

2.7. Data Daemon

Interface and support for custom proxies

2.8. Proxy Framework

Create and support per-connection instances of application-level protocols. Provides threaded data-driven socket interfaces integrated to gate APIs

2.9. Standard Protocols and Services

Execute standard components and protocols, including protocol wrappers

2.10. Registration Proxy and Libraries

Registration support for users and services. Create, register and store authentication credentials. Supports business offers' registration requirements through creation of credentials and interaction with domain database

2.11. Usage Proxy and Libraries

Submit and retrieve nonrepudiable usage records, both at the session level, application level, and custom levels

2.12. Application Protocols and Proxies

System components and application support that extend the platform with customized proxies

3. Monitoring and Management

   Subsystem monitors and manages components and network

   3.1. Monitor and log

        Validate component status. Support component logging and detail control

   3.2. Command and Control

        Send commands to components to start, stop, and modify behavior

   3.3. Measure performance

        Measure performance component and subsystem behavior via probes and statistical sampling

   3.4. Alert

        Recognize and generate alerts when distinguished measures of quality (DMOQ) are not met

   3.5. Event

        Generate and receive structured events with publisher/publication subscriber/subscription paradigm, including exact-once semantics and stable storage until delivery

These components provide an extensible platform that supports multiple services. Consider, for example, Voice over IP (VoIP). The gate architecture can provide trusted support for telephony protocols such as H.323 or SIP; for example, augmentation of call setup with cloud-supplied customer information. Integration of such protocols will utilize the flexible "smart controller" capability of the logical architecture.

8.1 Overview of SNode — Edge Gateway Functionality

Service nodes (SNodes) connect the external elements with the secure inner network. These SNodes support services, including transport and scalable computing. Their location at the network perimeter provides proximity to end users and thus makes the gates a logical location for intelligent functionality. This includes security services, as well as proxy-based extensions. An SNode based on the extensible architecture can have many gates, and each supports a minimum of two hardware network interfaces on different networks. The external interface supports the non-trusted side of the security perimeter, and the other interfaces supports the internal trusted network. Multiple gates provide both scaling and load balancing.

The user is, nevertheless, not tied to or limited by a particular gate. The network databases and support infrastructure are shared between them. This does not change even when load balancing uses multiple physical processors. In the current deployment, gates are hosted on large-scale UNIX machines.

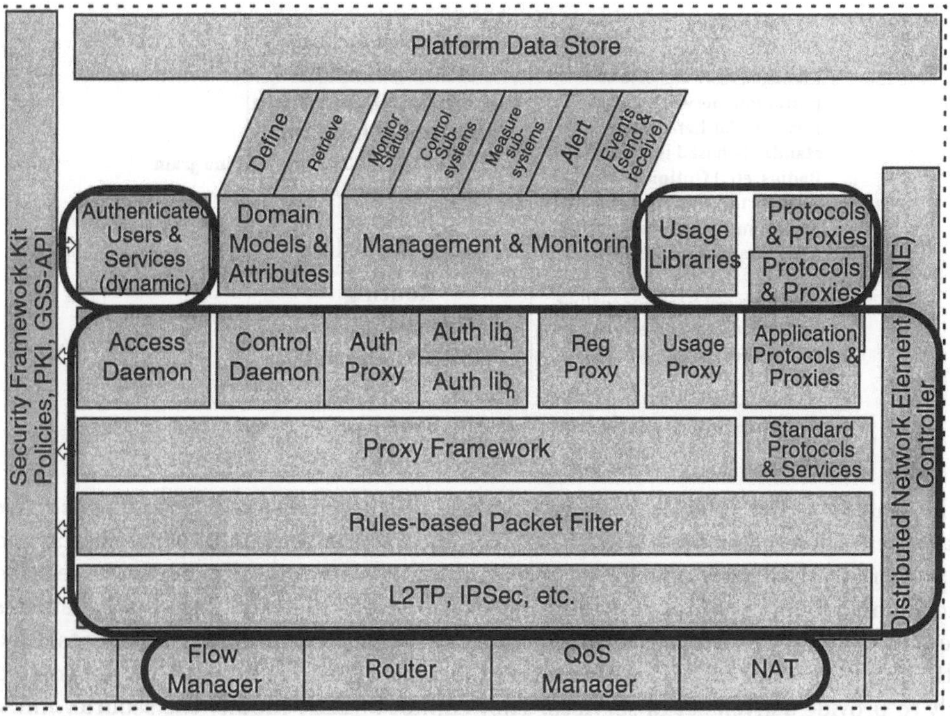

Figure 8-2: Edge Gateway: Filters and Proxies Extending Protocols and Interfaces

The gate defines a *security perimeter* and a *protocol mediation framework* for the middleware network. A dynamic packet-filter/firewall maintains this perimeter. This restricts entry to authorized traffic exclusively, and may modify the destination of any packet. The firewall provides extensible security options, and integrates multiple security packages including IPSec, low-cost web-based single-sign-on, and the proprietary peer. Data traverses the SNode perimeter only as permitted by the cloud security policy and security packages. These packages provide transformation, authentication and authorization. The combined result is *managed security* through rule-driven access policies. Enforcement of access policies is implemented at both coarse and fine granularities, as shown in Figure 8-3. The gates further support a proxy framework for service development and protocol mediation.

These powerful tools support application programming both on the gates and remotely from outside the security perimeter. The off-gate capabilities are provided by peer-based, browser-based, and proxy-enabled devices. The gates thereby become a safe haven for security information, registration information, and cloud status. This versatile architecture provides the requisite flexibility to fully and quickly leverage new standards and products.

Managed firewall secures portal into network-based services. Authentication with standards-based methods (SSL, Radius, etc.) Optional stronger security through configurable extensions. Custom peer and IPSec available as needed.	**Authentication** **Encryption/Decryption** **Distributed Caching** **Network Proxies** **Access Control** **Scaling** **Usage Recording**	Fine grain
Architectural basis for scaling, load balancing and extensibility. API support through PDK.	**Routing** **Access Control** **Packet Filtering**	Coarse grain

Figure 8-3: Gate Enforces Security Boundary

Other gates support services by accepting the authenticated connections from service machines. These gates mediate the service requests that originate with clients, and pass them to the service machines. Service machines are typically physically secured and highly reliable engines providing application-level support. The cloud insulates these machines by providing an intermediary between them and Internet clients. Nevertheless, the service machines are outside the logical trust boundary. They are trusted only to provide a given set of services. They cannot directly modify the security infrastructure or the middleware network. Rather, they provide value-added services. The service machines request cloud interactions by the use of standard APIs.

The firewall controls ingress traffic[1] through a managed service-oriented architecture. Combined with programmable APIs and toolkits, the architecture is highly extensible within the fundamental security policies. Architects and developers are completely free to add components and craft the requisite functionality. There is very little time lag involved with special purpose devices or protocols. This enables major improvements in the development cycle. Instead of working with a brittle architecture, developers build applications relatively unencumbered by the conventional complexities of system design. The open architecture supports rapid development, and the resulting designs may migrate toward hybrid architectures with better cost/performance ratio, as has occurred, for example, with managed transport.

8.1.1 Gate Capabilities

The gate software is grouped into the three layers shown in Table 6, below. The uppermost group shows the firewall through access control system. These provide substantial functionality as well as a "bootstrap" for the other components. The packet filter/

1. The firewall mechanism can also limit egress traffic, although cloud policies only limit upon entry alone. This follows logically from the concept of the cloud as a trusted intermediary.

TABLE 6: Layered Architecture Combines Firewall and Proxies

Component	Description
Firewall and Packet Filter	Admission control, classification and selective redirection. Dynamic firewall rules grouped by session. Supports multiple policies and extensible mechanisms for security and mediation. Tie-in with IPSec
Proxy Framework	Register listeners and processes for proxied connections
Authenticated Connection Table (ACT)	Cache describing active sessions. Synchronized with the packet filters and active registries (users and services)
Access Daemon	Analyze IP traffic and install rules in new, existing, or default sessions of packet filter; support access checks
Control Daemon (CD) and Authentication Proxy (AP)	Standard components for authentication and recording this information in the active registries. Supports multiple authentication protocols, encrypted control channel, and additional security requirements by means of authentication protocol and authentication libraries
Authentication Libraries	Protocol-specific components: Peer, TSL/SSL, RADIUS, NTLM, Kerberos, X.509 v3, etc.
Credential Proxies	Protocol-specific registration mechanisms for multiple devices and policies; these include web-based, peer-based, and extensions. PKI interactions
Data Daemons	Network support of advanced intelligent services and network interactions by means of *protocol mediation*

firewall inspects the IP packet headers and provides session-specific controls including rule-driven redirection. The proxy framework associates standard processes with these redirected connections.

In order to manage the multiple traffic streams, the SNode gates refer to a structure known as the authenticated connection table (ACT). This describes every valid connection, including the session's packet filter. Removal of an entry from the ACT deletes the session's rules from the packet filter thereby "shutting off" any data flow to the elements. Rules are added to the filter on an as-needed basis, through the access daemon, shown as the fourth row of Table 6. The access daemon adds rules to the packet filter in accordance with cloud access policies, as discussed in Section 9.2.4. The rules can also obtain fine-grain packet filtering by redirection of traffic to a daemon for further processing. Taken together, the first cluster of Table 6 defines a kernel supporting a powerful set of standard components.

The middle level consists of the essential cloud control programs – control daemon, authentication daemons, and credential proxies. These provide the authentication services, including control channels and secure creation of credentials. This middle layer defines how a subscriber may authenticate, and enforces the security services that maintain the integrity of the authentication. This layer also includes a registration server, and web-based peerless authentication. These use an innovative SSL Data Proxy (see Section 9.2.2 on page 294).

The control daemon and authentication proxy (AP) combine a secure control channel with a generalized authentication mechanism. Multiple methods can "plug into" the AP in the form of authentication libraries. As a custodian of security, the SNode can also issue credentials as appropriate. Taken together, the cluster supports credential formation, access control, extensible security, and advanced protocol support. The resulting gate architecture is elegant, reliable, and powerful. For example, new traffic types are directed by the firewall to the access control daemon for analysis. It decides whether the traffic should be permitted.

At the third layer, generalized data daemons support a wide range of functions. This includes HTTP support for web proxies and naming services such as DNS. Gates also support management through the GMMS subsystem and usage subsystem. Certificate authorities provide secure services to the cloud internally as well as to users of the cloud.

8.2 *Active Registries: Connections, Users and Services*

Networking middleware retains both dynamic and persistent information. The dynamic state information describes the authenticated components including active connections, services, configuration, and security contexts. The descriptions of active clients and services resides in distributed *active registries* (see Figure 8-4). Services perceive these registries as nearly instantaneous descriptions of the authenticated users and services. Optimization of the registries ensures that frequently used information is readily available at the appropriate network nodes. This exploits the locality of information access, since each edge element is primarily concerned with the connections that pass through its interfaces. A small number of transit connections may also pass through, and these are required to aggregate the traffic within the connection.

The registries are the *authenticated user registry* (AUR) that details all the authenticated users, as well as the *authenticated service registry* (ASR) with service-specific

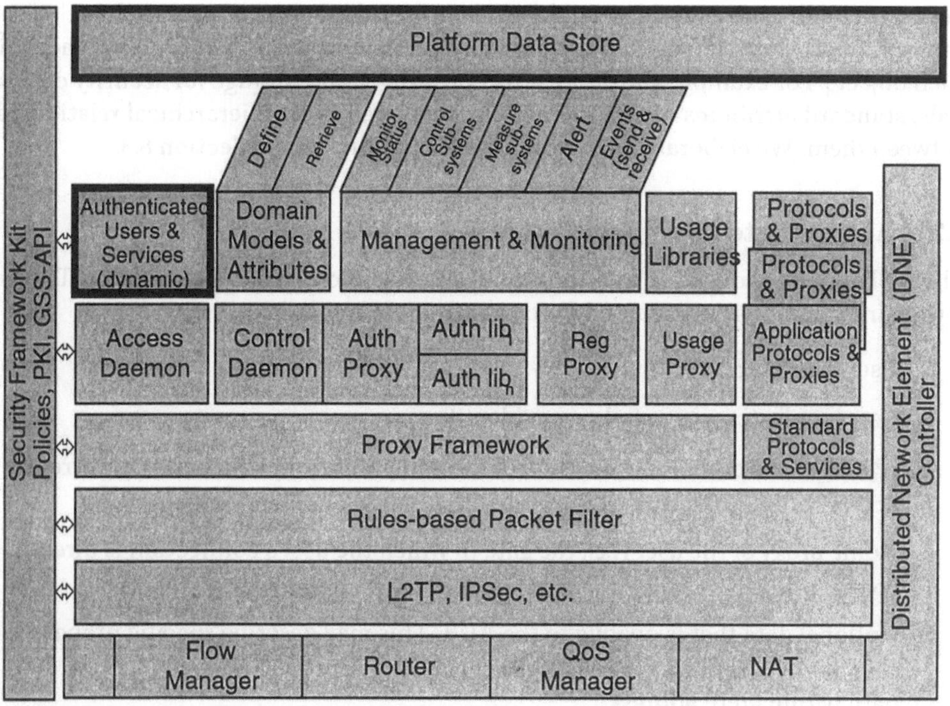

Figure 8-4: Secure Global Storage: Active Registries

information. A composite registry, known as the *authenticated connection table* (AuthConnTab, or ACT) describes every active connection including the object that owns the connection and the security parameters of the object.

These registries provide highly optimized data stores designed in view of the locational characteristics of users, services and connections. This ensures the fastest response to the most common or important events, while still ensuring correct responses for less common ones. For example, a subscriber's ingress gate stores information relevant to the subscriber and its services.

Cloud components update these registries with object-oriented APIs. As users authenticate and later terminate, session information is added and removed from the Active User Registry (AUR) and Active Connection Table (ACT). Whenever a service is announced or de-announced, the Active User Registry (ASR) is updated, and the entry records the user who made the announcement. Entries are purged when the user terminates. Service announcements occur either automatically from the client's peer software, through commands given by an administrator, or alternatively by custom code that uses the platform APIs.

Persistent information resides in the *domain database* and is accessed exclusively through the *domain API*, providing a standard method to manipulate and interact with such objects. For example, the domain API provides stable storage for security credentials, standard attributes of services and users, as well as the hierarchical relationship between them. We elaborate on persistent information later, in Section 8.3.

8.2.1 Authenticated User Registry (AUR)

The AUR can be thought of as a form of dynamic directory or login registry. The following information is maintained for currently authenticated users:

- User identifier
- User handle (i.e., a symbolic user identifier)
- IP address or other identification of the end point from which user is currently active
- Home proxy of the user (i.e., the gate to which the user's connection is directly connected)
- Optional data that is opaque to the AUR. This may describe specific properties that are relevant to a specific user, such as device properties and a unique data path within an IP address

Components that query the service registries include the Authentication Proxy, Control Daemon, Access Daemon and data proxies. Internal access control components and other cloud management/monitoring applications communicate directly with the AUR rather than with an X.500 or LDAP directory for the following reasons:

- The basic functioning of the cloud is not affected by the availability, or lack thereof, of a White Pages (directory) server. White Pages is not a core functionality of a network cloud, rather it is considered an essential service which may be tailored by the service provider. It is even conceivable that multiple White Pages servers may exist for a given cloud
- Since the AUR sits on a core subnetwork, queries to the server do not need to pass through a firewall. By contrast, the LDAP server(s) cannot sit inside the secure perimeter due to the protocol requirements. Thus, if the LDAP service is not authenticated, or that particular gate is down, no users would be able to authenticate to the cloud from any gate
- The AUR is optimized for performance based on the functionality most often used by its clients. For example, the ability to access all users that are connected to a particular gate is extremely useful when a communications failure requires the redirection of the client traffic. The affected users are easily identified through a single operation in the AUR. It might, however, use multiple operations if the information were stored in the LDAP directories described above

- The AUR information can be cached on the components that require fastest access

By providing a small and specific set of services, the AUR can be based on a lightweight protocol and operations, making it very efficient. For example, White Pages servers typically time out LDAP connections after a certain time period, causing the repeated overhead of reconnecting. The AUR, on the other hand, provides optimized services and also allows clients to remain connected as needed.

8.2.2 Authenticated Service Registry (ASR)

When a service is announced, information about the service is added to the ASR by the authentication proxy and a component known as the Control Daemon maintains an authenticated channel as required. Conversely, when the service is de-announced, the information is removed from the ASR. The ASR supplies this information to other components by providing a mechanism to search its contents. The following is some of the information maintained for currently authenticated services (henceforth referred to as active services):

- Service identifier
- Service handle (i.e., a symbolic service identifier)
- User identifier – the user that authenticated the service
- IP address of the terminal on which the service is available
- Port on which the service is available
- The TCP Protocol used by the service
- Home proxy of the service (i.e., the gate to which the service is directly connected)
- Access controls and encryption information for the service
- Information used to determine the type of proxy used by the service
- An optional glob of data that is opaque to the ASR

The information contained in the ASR is used by the Access Daemon and the Control Daemon for access control and encryption enforcement. These components enforce access policies through system-wide objects of *accounts*, *users* and *services*.

These registries support various kinds of users: both "tethered" users, who are uniquely identified by an IP address; as well as "untethered" users, who are identified through the content of the traffic. Support of untethered users includes the web proxy and peerless support. This allows a wide variety of services including web browsing, pocket phones, and other items that are granted services by an "unconventional" data stream without a dependency on a fixed IP address. Caching mechanisms ensure the system can quickly determine the status of a user or service by reference to the Active Registries. This lets the cloud know what users are logged on, the services currently active on the cloud, as well as particulars of each user. The user's device and type of authentication are of particular importance.

The middleware combines these active registries with other components and protocols. For example, a telephony application may benefit from the combination of an IP-based protocol (such as H.323 or SIP) with information on active users and services. This directly utilizes the ASR and AUR.

8.2.3 Authenticated Connections Table (ACT, AuthConnTab)

The authenticated connections table (ACT) maintains global cloud information, including descriptions of users and connections. Updates and queries satisfy the extremely stringent performance requirements, and provide the capability to manipulate connections at multiple granularities within the following hierarchy of cloud down to services and connections. The ACT uses hashed in-memory data structures supporting very fast access through shared memory, as well as through a messaging protocol. Each gate serves as the primary copy of ACT information that describes the locally authenticated connections. Gates also retain cached information describing relevant remote connections. The connection management software propagates cached information.

The ACT APIs descend the hierarchy by progressing to finer levels of detail. They can also ascend the hierarchy by identification of the users that are authenticated to a service, gate, domain or cloud.

- *Cloud.* Domains, gates, users, services, and their interconnections
- *Domain.* Gates, users, services and their connections
- *Ingress gate.* Describes the users, services and connections of the gate
- *User.* Connections from users
- *Services.* Connections to services
- *Connection.* Identification of the user that initiated the connection, the service being accessed, and the security parameters of this connection

The ACT is maintained by a communications manager located in the cloud. This enforces a the semantics of system objects and assures their correct network interactions. This guarantees that modifications originate from authorized system components, specifically the authentication libraries including peered, peerless and RADIUS authenticators. The ACT retains global state; consequently, all ACT updates are synchronized by the AP. The ACT entries are created when a client authenticates. The entries are removed – and the essential accompanying actions are performed on the firewall, usage records, and associated services of a user – when a voluntary or involuntary termination occurs.

The ACT records each client's authentication algorithm and credential type, as well as the global master secrets used by specific security methods. There are four kinds of objects:

- *Authenticated clouds.* Associated domains and routed destinations within the clouds
- *Authenticated users.* The user, the user's ingress local cloud, and the security parameters of the user. This includes the credential type such as login or RADIUS, X.509 certificate, Kerberos ticket information, or peer-based authentication key. Service-specific credentials may include PSTN phone number
- *Announced Services.* The service names, service IDs, and the user that announced the service
- *Security Information.* The master encryption secrets for peerless authentication. IPSec information is maintained separately in the SPD

Information in the ACT entries include the following, although not all fields are relevant to every connection:

- *Source.* IP address, subnet mask, port
- *Context.* Socket FD, thread ID, session ID, time stamp
- *Security information.* Encryption keys, encryption flag. These are accessed through method-specific access functions
- *User information.* Handle, ID, cloud ID, user type, indices into firewall table, service IDs
- *Cloud information.* Cloud ID, domain name, relationship, destination addresses

8.2.4 Programming the Registries – AUR, ASR and ACT

APIs provide access to the AUR, ASR and ACT. Cloud-internal processes may modify and query the registries. They should not, however, modify the ACT. A command-line interface facilitates administrative control and provides proper synchronization. The `manageAur` command, for example, permits query or adjustment to the registry.

Changes to the AUR/ASR are programmed with either Java or C++ APIs. The C++ classes **geoAsrClient** and **geoAurClient** support entry, query and deletion of registry objects, and operate upon **AsrEntry** and **AurEntry**. A query can return a set of items. Figure 8-5 demonstrates these classes. The figure initializes a **GeoAurClient** object with a connection to the AUR server at the local host; alternatively, it can use shared

```
#include "geoIncludes.h"

int main(int argc, char *argv[])
{
#define  AURSERVERNAME  "localhost"
  geoAurClient theAur;
  char *serverName = AURSERVERNAME;
  // The DNS name geoplexaur is the standard name to access AUR.
  // A parameter may specify the DNS name of the AUR server
  if (argc > 1)
  {
     serverName = argv[1];
  }

  // Connect to the AUR  server at the default port (AURSERVERPORT)
  try
  {
     theAur.connect(serverName);
  }
  catch (const GeoException& e)
  {
     cerr << "Got an exception while connecting: " << e.getMessage()
            << " (" << e.getErrorCode() << ")\n";
     return 1;
  }

  // Define the storage structure for an AurEntry entry
  AurEntry anEntry;

  // Fill in the userID, the IP addresses of the user and the gate
  anEntry.userId = 0x400001L;              // Assigned user ID
  strcpy(anEntry.userHandle, theUser); // Copy of the user's name
  anEntry.userAddress = theAddress;      // 32 bit IP address of client
  anEntry.homeProxy = homeProxy;         // 32 bit IP address of user's gate
  anEntry.proxyInstance = THISPROXY;     // Component that added the entry?
  anEntry.opaqueData = NULL;             // Optional information such as key

  // Add the entry to the AUR
  theAur.add(anEntry);
}
```

Figure 8-5: Example of AUR Update

memory instead of a connection. The process then initializes an **AurEntry** structure with client-specific update data of the user ID, name and network addresses. The client adds the information to the AUR with the **add** method. The APIs support query of the AUR in a similar manner. They may also use the Java API as discussed in Section 8.3.2.

Support of the Authenticated Connection Table (ACT) provides a more restricted API interface, as shown in Figure 8-6, and only allows read access. Updates are tightly restricted and occur only through the authentication proxy and the control daemon. There are several reasons for these restrictions, but primarily a client cannot be placed into the ACT until the firewall rules are completely built and propagated as appropriate. Likewise, removal of an authenticated connection requires coordinated purging of the users's firewall rules as well as termination of all connections to services provided by the user. The ACT methods coordinate these updates at both the local gate and other SNode elements. Such updates are therefore performed exclusively by the Authentication Proxy and libraries, as discussed in Section 8.2.4.1.

1. Define ACT pointer and entry:
   ACT_SharedMem* act = openACT();
   AuthConnTab_t act_entry;
2. Specify query by filling in keys in the **act_entry**:
   - IP address
   - subnet mask
   - network
   - userID
   - cloud ID
   - domain name
3. Issue the query for specific information:
   - Obtain a list of entries: **getACTentbyIP(act, &act_entry);**
   - Process the entries from the act_entry pointer
4. Obtain the peer authentication type:
   int geoGetPeerType(ACT_SharedMem*, in_addr);
   returns **ACT_PEERLESS ... ACT_GEOPEER**
5. Obtain the "shared secret" for peerless authentication:
   int geoGetExportedMasterSecret(ACT_SharedMem*, void *buf, int *size);

Figure 8-6: Access to Authenticated Connections (AuthConnTab)

8.2.4.1 Validation of Identity – Peer and HTTP CallerID

Caller ID is a general mechanism to identify the authenticated client who has originated a connection. It has nothing to do with POTS lines or the caller ID provided by local carriers. Rather, this allows services to verify the identity of a client. This is useful in a wide variety of services. For the example of eCommerce, the identification of a client's identity is part of securing a transaction. An IP telephony system will need to validate the client identity as well.

The cloud, authenticated peers, and general web servers can obtain the user ID of an authenticated peer at a given IP address. The Caller ID Table API is used to maintain a shared memory table to exchange session related information between different processes running on the same gate. The caller ID functionality is defined as follows: When client (peer) establishes a connection, the connection can be uniquely identified by the caller ID item represented by the triple: `(local_port, src_addr,` `src_port)`, where `local_port` is the local port (on the gate side) of the connection to the peer, and the`src_addr`, `src_port` identify the peer side of the connection. The local port is used in formation of a unique session key. Upon accepting peered connections, the server (proxy) populates the caller ID table The other processes on the same machine can use it through the common caller ID table API to store, retrieve, or delete caller ID items from the table.

The API is very simple and represented by the five functions of Table 7.

TABLE 7: CallerID Table Maintenance and Access

Name of Function	Purpose
geoOpenCIDTable	open the shared resource (caller ID table)
geoPutCIDItem	insert the caller ID item into the table
geoGetCIDItem	get the caller ID item from the table
geoDelCIDItem	delete the caller ID item from the table
geoCloseCIDTable	close the shared resource (caller ID table)

8.2.4.2 Specification of Connection Control – Packet Filter API

The packet-filter/firewall provides an essential "regulator" on traffic that passes through the network. While most of the connections are allowed by the access daemon, there are important instances where services must dynamically modify the filter. The `pf_` APIs permit programming the packet filter. Consider the support of remote procedure call (RPC). A client will typically request a service by communicating the service description to a standard well known port, often called a port mapper. This assigns an available port, and replies with a description of the port. Since the firewall never opened the port, however, the requesting client will be unable to connect over it.

This port mapper receives support of a port mapping service inside the cloud. This service monitors requests and replies. When it receives a reply message, the port mapping service matches it to a previous request, and dynamically adds this port to the appropriate connection's session table. This allows traffic to pass between the specific client/server pair. Of course, this is done subject to access controls. The port mapping service may remove this entry at any time. The access permission also closes automatically when either end point terminates the connection, when authentication is removed, upon an inactivity timeout.

The specifics of connection control are programmed by a packet filter API to pass, drop, map or check. The API operates upon distinct objects:

- *Mapping objects.* These record the original and remapped addresses for each segment of a connection, and allow, for example, restoration of the initial destination
- *Session objects.* These provide a grouping function that combines rules of a single logical connection. The full packet-filter API can define, delete or modify existing firewall sessions
- *Rule objects.* These are consulted by the packet filter to determine the correct action when unclassified packets arrive

The packet filter API provides two levels for use by new in-cloud processes. Two additional levels are preserved for internal controls such as the access control programs. The level one rules are informational only, providing status, time-out, as well as mapping between addresses.

Query packet filter status

```
int gp_pf_get_status(const char *tag, void *data,
    int length, int *actual,int*errnop);
```

Obtain default session timeout for IP protocol and action

```
ushort gp_pf_get_default_session_timeout(char_t protocol,
    gp_pf_action_t action);
```

Get real IP information from MAPPED or LOCAL packet

```
int gp_pf_get_mapped_info(const gp_pf_session_key_t *key,
    gp_pf_session_key_t *real, int *errnop);
```

Get action attribute for session defined by key

```
int gp_pf_get_session_action(const gp_pf_session_key_t *key,
    gp_pf_action_t *action, int *errnop);
```

Figure 8-6: Level-One Packet Filter API

The level two rules modify the session cache, and L3/L4 specify global filter behavior.

Add session to cache on behalf of proxy

```
int gp_pf_add_proxy_session(gp_pf_proxy_space_t
    *proxy, gp_pf_session_key_t *key, char *in_if,
    char *out_if, gp_pf_action_t action,
    ushort_t timeout, int *perror);
```

Remove session from cache on behalf of proxy

```
int gp_pf_remove_proxy_session(gp_pf_proxy_space_t *proxy,
    gp_pf_session_key_t *key, char *in_if,
    char *out_if, int *perror);
```

Figure 8-7: Level-Two Packet Filter APIs

8.2.4.3 Validation of Access Control – Access Check API

These APIs allow checking the access permission of a connection, whether it is a peer-based or a web-based connection. We will ignore the polymorphic wrapper that determines the kind of traffic, and consider two specific API calls that determine access permission.

From peer client

```
geoAccessCheck(int fd, in_addr ip, ushort_t port, int proto)
```

From web client (get uid from cookie)

```
int geoUserAccessCheck(int fd, in_addr ip, ushort_t port,
    int proto, geo_userid_t uid);
```

Figure 8-8: Access Control Validation APIs

8.2.4.4 Usage Recording and Retrieval APIs

Usage records, on the other hand, support a particular function of monitoring and tracking completed events within the system. Both accounting and performance monitoring use the usage trails. The usage records are created automatically by the cloud components to record resource usage. A redundant series of usage collectors and validation services helps to ensure that usage information will not be lost, even in the face of component faults or operator errors. The records may be retrieved by certain users such as the account administrator. These records are secure at the record level because each record is protected by a translucent storage structure called a "cookie" (these are different from HTTP cookies).

```
GeoUsageCookie cookie;
errno = geoUsageSessionCookie(userInfo->userIP,
                              userInfo->userPort, &cookie);
geoNVPInit(&nvpairs);
geoNVPPut(&nvpairs,"LOGOUT",0,userData->serviceType);
sprintf(buffer,"%d",userData->conBytes);
geoNVPPut(&nvpairs,"connectBytes",1,buffer);
errno = geoUsageSubmitRecord(cookie,
                             userData->serviceID, &nvPairs);
geoNVPDestroy(&nvpairs);
```

Figure 8-9: Submitting Usage Record

The cookie is allocated at the beginning of a session, and uniquely identifies the session. Usage content is stored into the flexible data structure of name value pairs (NVP), which can use multiple encodings. The usage records are submitted (or retrieved subject to access permissions) through the appropriate API. This is shown in Figure 8-9. The usage architecture is designed as a scalable, highly efficient, and above all, a reliable method to collect and store the critical usage information. This offers sufficient flexibility for a wide range of deployments.

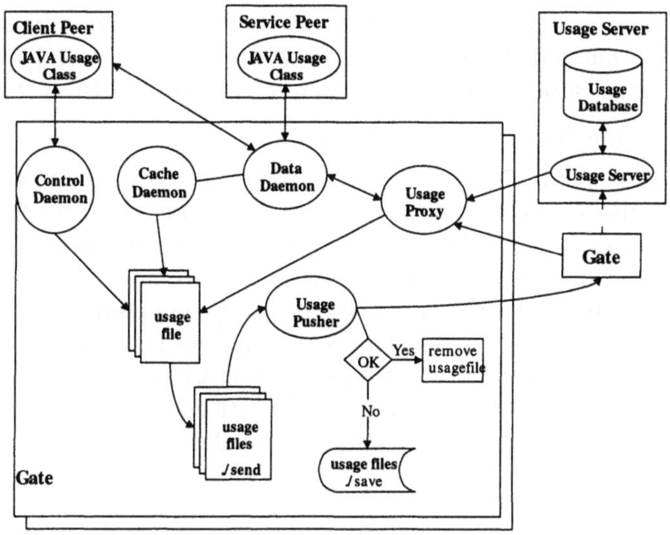

Figure 8-10: Elements and Interactions of Usage Subsystem

The usage subsystem supports the principle of "one-customer one-bill" as well as real-time billing in conjunction with suitable rating methods.

8.2.5 Summary of the Gate Architecture and Capabilities

Let's consider each of the eight design principles described in Chapter 4, "Platform Requirements and Principles", to appreciate the gate-oriented architecture:

Routability

The ability to control routing is one of the most important issues in the large, scalable Internet. A gate makes the routing decisions for all traffic that enters the cloud. For example, data passing to a gate can be monitored and routed by the gate software, as well as with special purpose switches (Distributed Network Element). This supports *per-user* quality of service (QoS) flows by means of the caller ID functionality supported at each gate. The gate decides which services the user can access, as well as the version or location of the service.

Registration

The gates support a registration service. By placing the registration support at the first network contact, the hardware design inherently supports low-cost and low-latency registration of new users. This permits them to join the network where they participate in the full range of system functions.

Coarse Grain Access Control

The hardware architecture limits service access through admission control. Unauthorized clients are refused access by the gate, and any permitted access must be mediated by the gate which provides this control.

Non-Repudiable Policy-Based Connections

The client capabilities can be determined on a per-user basis, regardless of how the users connect to the network. The gate may broadcast policy requirements in such diverse areas as security (i.e., how is the client authenticated), resource requirements (bandwidth, delay), as well as permissible content. The gate as the controlled access point is authorized to control policy settings on behalf of the client. This is possible only because the client has authenticated to the network, and, since the cloud is the contact point, this permits control. A special gate component (an access daemon) validates connection attempts and populates the policies for the user and available services.

Data Mediation Integrity

The gate machine provides the computational force for data mediation. This supports hardware routing, load balancing, and actual changes to data as required to provide advanced services.

8.3 Domains: Accounts, Users and Services

As a managed substrate of network interactions, the middleware platform constructs and represents user profiles. This supports various registration processes. However, as we have previously noted, a single API cannot address the diverse requirements of complex business issues. Registration is a particularly complex question with multiple concerns. Credential generation as we discuss it can support but not supplant resolution of such registration issues.

- Create or import secure authentication credentials
- Create or update user profiles in the domain API
- These services are deliberately "low level" and do not define the full range or user-registration services. We view registration as a higher level business process, one that is specifically oriented towards particular consumer services. Such registration services can be deployed on external servers. They may also be implemented directly on the gate machines when appropriate; for example, with a secure control channel and a cloud-resident proxy.

A second method uses an secure connection that interacts with a web server, and the web server would use APIs to register the user. A registration server receives requests to register, and selectively grants credentials to suitable clients. This corresponds to the "Peerless Reg Front-end" shown in Figure 8-11.

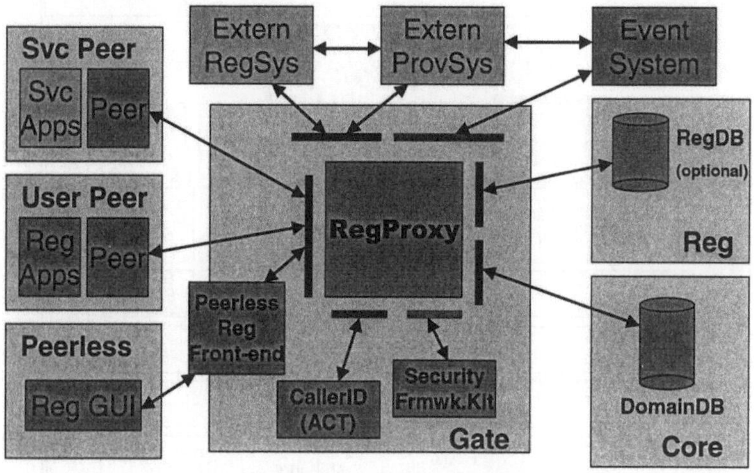

Figure 8-11: General Credential-Issuance Framework

The second major component of the networking middleware is the hierarchical active directory structure. This combines an open API, known as the domain API, with underlying implementations constructed from the "best in class" in object-oriented databases. These components are integrated into the middleware through distributed proxies, as shown in Figure 8-12.

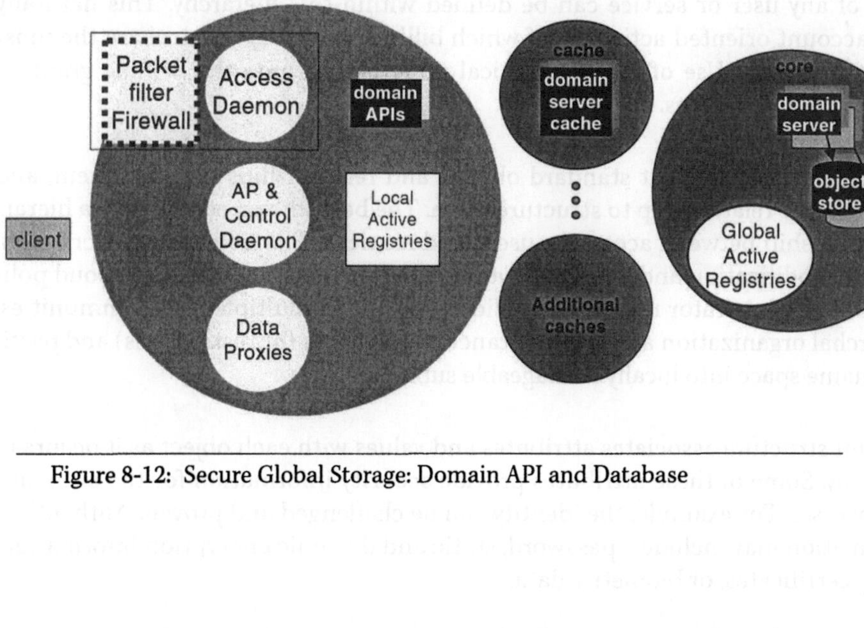

Figure 8-12: Secure Global Storage: Domain API and Database

8.3.1 Membership Structure

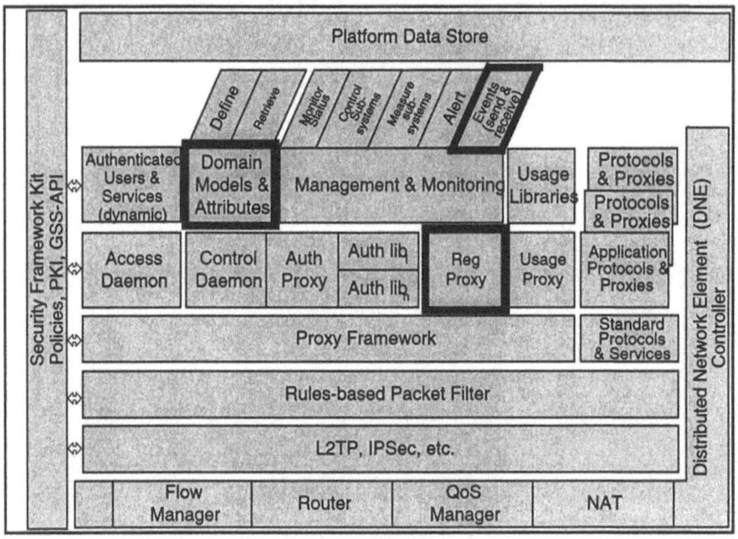

Figure 8-13: Domain Model and Attributes

The framework provides a substrate that supports all system components, as well as development kits providing an appropriate view of these components to various kinds of developers and users. The development APIs (PD, SD and ND) manipulate various objects that define a unified structure for definition and management of services. These objects are arranged in a hierarchy composed of accounts, users and services. This defines the capabilities for participants within a network cloud. The rights and privileges of any user or service can be defined within this hierarchy. This naturally supports account oriented activities, of which billing and access control are the most prominent members. Use of the hierarchical structure permits the flexible granting and revocation of privileges.

The platform should support standard objects and relationships between them, and will assume some relationship to structure them. The best-known structure is a hierarchical relationship between accounts, users and services. The objects allow creation, monitoring, modification and deletion in a coordinated manner defined by cloud policies. A cloud administrator may define policies specific to multiple user communities. The hierarchal organization allows inheritance of privileges (or restrictions) and partitions the name space into locally manageable subhierarchies.

The account structure associates attributes and values with each object as it occurs in the hierarchy. Some of these attributes provide security information for the authentication processes. For example, the identity can be challenged and proven. Authentication information may include a password, static and dynamic encryption information, public-key certificates, or biometric data.

The account structure also describes the permissions the cloud will allow to the devices or processes that act on behalf of the identity. For example, this allows subscription-based services. The domain API updates the account structure. It supports hierarchies consisting of standardized (fixed) and administrator-specific (variable) objects. The fixed objects are mandatory, whereas the variable ones reflect the information requirements of a specific administrative realm. These objects are organized into domains.

8.3.2 Domain Model

One of the most important aspects of network accounts is the concept of a domain. A domain is essentially the container which is used to hold and reference the types of entities recognized by the middleware platform (e.g., users, accounts, and services). Whenever a new entity is created, it is created within the bounds of some domain. It is created as a member of only that particular domain, and it can only be accessed as a member of that particular domain.

Domains typically correspond to some sort of natural organizational or functional groupings, and the entities contained within a domain typically correspond to the individuals and services within those groups. A domain typically corresponds to a single overarching organization or enterprise (e.g., an Internet Service Provider or a university) and typically contains information regarding all of the users, services, and administrative operators supported by that organization.

In principle, domains could be associated with smaller subsets of an organization (e.g., the sales department of a company, or the School of Engineering of a university) instead of the entire organization. However, in order to do so, any subset must satisfy the following restriction: the selected subset must represent a natural partitioning of the organization. This is because domains are mutually exclusive - domains do not overlap, and one domain cannot be a sub domain of another domain. An entity can be a member of exactly one domain and a domain can never be a member of a domain.

Figure 8-14, for example, shows two domains and the entities contained within them. Note that all of the entities in Domain A are separate and distinct from those in Domain B, even though some of them share the same (local/not-fully-qualified) name. For example, "User 1" in Domain A is a separate and distinct entity from "User 1" in Domain B. "User 1" in Domain A can only be referenced through Domain A as "A:User 1" and "User 1" in Domain B can only be referenced through Domain B as "B:User 1". Because of this restriction, domains typically map onto entire organizations. It is often easiest to partition users and services along the boundaries between distinct organizations.

Each cloud must be tied to at least one domain, and in the typical/standard configuration, a single cloud utilizes/maintains exactly one domain. In theory, multiple domains

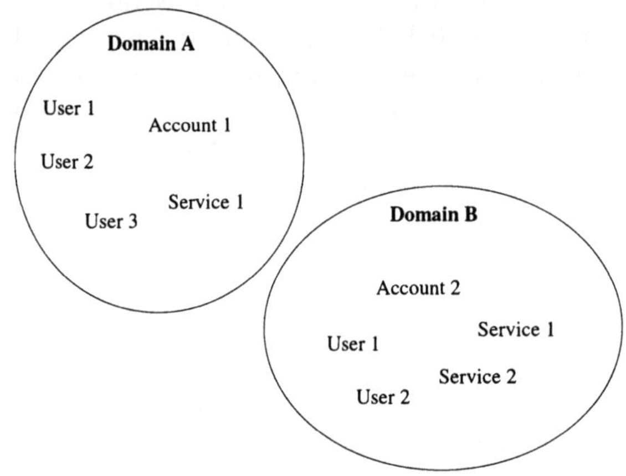

Figure 8-14: Two Independent Domains

could simultaneously be maintained on a single provider's platform, and full support for this capability will be available in the future.

Domains are identified by a globally unique name. In addition, domains also possess a "handle" attribute that is a fully qualified domain name (FQDN). This handle is currently used to find the host (or hosts) that can serve the domain and all of its associated domain objects. Finally, a domain also possesses a "certificate" attribute, which contains the platform ("cloud") certificate signed by a recognized certificate authority.

8.3.3 Domain Objects: Accounts, Users, and Services

An *account* is the root of one or more accounts, users and services. An account may have multiple descendant accounts, as well as users and services. A user is an entity that can authenticate, receive privileges, and access resources pursuant to the privileges.

A *service* is a registered provider of some value-added capability. There are many kinds of services, and they all use the cloud to obtain enhancements. For example, traffic always passes through the firewall and is subject to authentication and usage recording. Enhancements available through APIs include security services, protocol mediation, and interaction with APIs. Service composition is possible by custom codes. For example, authentication and registration are two services. Security capabilities, usage access, and Microsoft file/print are additional services.

8.3.3.1 Subscriber Management

Managed Internet platforms may choose to deliberately restrict the ability of clients to register or announce services. A prospective service provider must first be a registered user. This not only allows the network provider to bill a service provider, it also locates the service provider within a hierarchy of accounts. This account hierarchy can restrict access to the service, thereby supporting multiple views of the Internet.

The service architecture provides service-registration and service-announcement capabilities. Service registration defines the essential parameters, including location, name, access path, and protocols supported. Service announcement states availability of the service, and is required because the service might be temporarily offline.

The relationship between accounts, services and users is shown in Figure 8-15. These form a recursive structure. An account may have multiple subaccounts, as well as multiple users and services. The rights and privileges of the user or services are defined by the path from the root account to the object's parent account. This provides aggregation of multiple entities, greatly easing management. For example, when a privilege is added (or removed) from an account this affects down-level accounts, users and services.

An addition to an account structure, there are three types of service permissions. A service can be either:

- full-public
- cloud-public
- cloud-private

A full-public service may be accessed by any client, even if the client is not authenticated. This is a convenient mechanism to support registration services, for example, when users are not preregistered. A service provider can export a registration service that can be accessed even before the client is permitted to authenticate for the service. Similarly, a deprecated "free" service can be provided as a free trial that may encourage clients to register for a service.

The cloud-public service is the second kind. A client must be authenticated to the cloud but need not have any special permission to access the service.

The third kind of service is the cloud-private service. These are subscription-based services. Access to a cloud-private service is granted only when the client is both authorized and subscribed to the service. Authorization requires that the client's parent account is authorized, as are all hierarchically superior accounts.

The reader may observe that the access control requires two steps: one is authorization of the account tree, and the second is an explicit subscription action. Both must be active to allow access to an account. A user who is subscribed will not receive the service unless the user's account is authorized for the service (which requires that all ancestor accounts are allowed, as well). This simplifies the granting or denial of services to large administrative entries. Per-user control is then exercised by the subscriber paradigm. This can be seen in Figure 8-15.

In the context of a domain, a User object corresponds to a user that has registered with the network. Through authentication, users establish their identities with the network. Users who don't authenticate are referred to as anonymous users. Personal attributes of a user, such as name, address, and telephone number, are stored in User objects. Additionally, every User object has a handle and an identifier that uniquely identifies it within the domain. A user's primary use of the network is to access services. Services are applications that may be made available on the network. As mentioned before, there are three types of services in a middleware network: full-public, cloud-public, and cloud-private. Anonymous users can only access full-public services. All authenticated users can access full-public and cloud-public services, and can access private services too, provided they have previously subscribed to the service. Services are represented by Service objects in the domain, which contain the attributes that describe the service, such as name, description, and URL. As with User objects, each Service object has a unique handle and identifier within the domain.

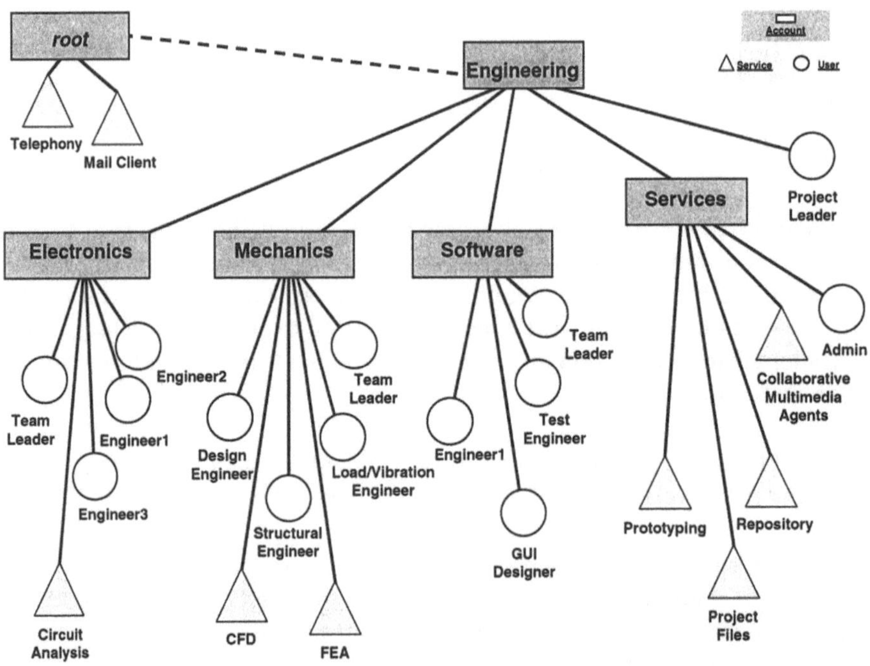

Figure 8-15: Sample Account Hierarchy for Manufacturing Domain

All User and Service objects have a single parent Account object that contains attributes that hold billing information. Each Account object can contain multiple User and Service objects, allowing for the aggregation of multiple Users and Services under a single billable entity.

Every account is controlled by an account administrator. Account administrators can add new users, services, and subaccounts to the account. Account administrators also serve as service administrators for any services that are contained in the account. A service can only be announced by its service administrators.

Accounts can also contain other accounts, referred to as subaccounts, allowing for a hierarchical distribution of users and services across the domain. When an account has subaccounts, the account administrators of the parent account are also administrators of the subaccounts. The hierarchy allows an organization's structure to be reflected in the domain, and enables policies that conform to this structure. It therefore plays an important role in the access control model, as well as the PKI model. Because of this capability, account handles are only unique within their parent account. However, like User and Service objects, accounts also have an identifier that is unique within the domain.

Accounts, users and services can be created with the registration proxies, and these in turn populate the domain database residing in the secure system core. The API supplies methods for manipulation of accounts, services, and users. The API is symmetric and allows adding, deleting, and inquiry. For example, a privilege is added to an account with the **addPrivilege** method. The privilege is added to the service with the **addAllowed**. The user can then receive the privilege with the **addSubscription** method.

8.3.4 Account Privilege List

Associated with each account is a list of privileges that the account has been granted. The users of an account are only allowed to access private services that appear in the account's privilege list. Thus, although a user may have been added to the access control list of a service, he cannot access the service unless the user's parent account has been granted the privilege to use the service.

Privileges are granted and removed by the parent account's account administrators. The account administrators can only grant privileges passed down from the parent account itself. The result of this is that a subaccount never has more service privileges than its parent account. When a privilege is removed from an account, it is also removed from all the subaccounts of that account. The methods for manipulating an account's privilege list are **getServicePrivileges(), addPrivilege(), and removePrivilege()** and can be found on the **geo.domain.Account** interface.

8.3.5 Service Access Control List

A service's access control list specifies the users that are allowed to access the service. The list is maintained as three separate lists: ALLOWEDUSERS, ALLOWEDACCOUNTS, and ALLOWEDSERVICES. The list of ALLOWEDUSERS explicitly specifies users that may access the service. The list of ALLOWEDACCOUNTS specifies groups of users to be added to the overall access control list. Any user whose parent account is in the ALLOWEDACCOUNTS list will be allowed to access the service.

A service's list of ALLOWEDSERVICES grants permissions to groups of users. Rather than specify the groups through account hierarchies, this mechanism inherits the access permission from other services. The users that have access to any related service may also access the service that lists it. This becomes clear with an example. Consider the hypothetical services PLAYMESSAGE and PRINTMESSAGE. Each services' ALLOWEDSERVICES lists a third service, ADVANCEDMESSAGES. Consequently, every user with permission to access ADVANCEDMESSAGES is also granted access to the PLAYMESSAGE and PRINTMESSAGE services. Now, suppose that PLAYMESSAGE also lists a fourth service, BASICMESSAGES. Any user who may access BASICMESSAGE will automatically be able to access PLAYMESSAGE, but requires further permission to access PRINTMESSAGE.

The lists of allowed users, accounts, and services can only be modified by the service administrator. The methods for manipulating these lists are **getAllowedUsers(), getAllowedAccounts(), getAllowedServices(), addAllowed(),** and **removeAllowed()**, and can be found on the **geo.domain.Service** interface.

8.3.6 User Subscription List

A user's subscription list contains the list of private services that the user is allowed to access. To add a service to this list, the service must be in the user's parent account's privilege list, and the user must be in the service's access control list. If either of those conditions does not hold, the subscription fails, and the service cannot be added to the user's subscription list. After the subscription has been successfully added, if either the service is removed from the privilege list or the user is removed from the access control list, the subscription is removed from the subscription list.

The subscription list can be modified directly by the user and the user's parent account administrators. The methods for manipulating this list are **getServiceSubscriptions()**, **addSubscription()** and **removeSubscription()**, and can be found on the **geo.domain.User** interface. Subscriptions can also be removed indirectly, as noted in the preceding paragraph.

8.3.7 Objects and Attributes

Domain API data can only be retrieved and modified by calling methods of a Domain API object. Data elements that are associated with objects are called attributes. The object which provides the methods to retrieve and modify the value of an attribute is called the owner of the attribute. Domain API objects can have three types of attributes:

Single-valued fixed attributes

The value of a single-valued fixed attribute can be retrieved using a `get...()` method and modified using a `set...()` method on the owner of the attribute (e.g., the user handle can be retrieved using the `getHandle()` method and modified using the `setHandle()` method of the `geo.domain.User` interface).

Multi-valued fixed attributes

The values of a multi-valued fixed attribute can be retrieved using a get...() method, which returns an iterator over the values of the attribute. Specific values can be added and removed using `add.()` and remove.() methods on the owner of the attribute (e.g., the `getServicePrivileges()` method of the `geo.domain`.Account interface will return an iterator over the list of services for which an account has privilege; the `addPrivilege()` and `removePrivilege()` methods can be used to add and remove specific services from the list).

Single-valued flexible attributes

Fixed attributes are always associated with a certain kind of domain object (e.g., users). Flexible attributes can be defined by the application and can be attached to any domain object. They can be any of the usual elementary data types (e.g., int, String etc.). The value of a single-valued Flexible attribute can be retrieved using a `get...()` method and modified using the `set()` method of the `geo.domain.FlexObject` interface. The methods of the FlexObject interface take an additional argument for the attribute name, whereas the method names of the `get...()` and `set...()` methods for fixed attributes already contain the attribute name (e.g., `getHandle()/setHandle()`).

The following sections describe in detail how to retrieve and modify these types of attributes.

8.3.7.1 Retrieving Attribute Values

In order to retrieve any attribute values, you must first retrieve the object which owns the attribute. For example, to retrieve user "`joe`" from domain `foobar.com`, you would use the code of Figure 8-16, below.

The `getUser()`, `getAccount()` and `getService()` methods of `geo.domain.Domain` have special exception behavior. These methods return objects which serve as references to domain objects. If you request a domain object which does not exist, these methods will not throw an exception – they will still return a user, account or service object.

```
Domain domain = Context.getDomain( "foobar.com" );
User joe = domain.getUser( "joe" );
```

Now you can retrieve all of Joe's attribute values:

```
int state = joe.getState(); // single-valued fixed
// single-valued flexible
String address = joe.getString( "Address" );
String phone_number = joe.getString( "PhoneNumber" );
// multi-valued fixed
ServiceIterator si = joe.getServiceSubscriptions();

Service service;
while ( si.hasNext() )
{
  service = si.nextService();
  System.out.println( service.getHandle() + " : "
    + service.getString( "Protocols" ) );
}
```

Do not rely on the fact that if you retrieve the same domain object more than once, the objects will be the same Java objects, although you can compare them using the `equals..()` method:

```
Domain domain = Context.getDomain( "foobar.com" );
User joe = domain.getUser( "joe" );
User joe_again = domain.getUser( "joe" );
// Following is guaranteed by Domain API
if ( joe.equals( joe_again ) )
// Following is NOT guaranteed by Domain API

if ( joe == joe_again ))
```

Figure 8-16: Retrieval of User Joe from Domain foobar.com

If you call any method on this object, the method will throw `DomainObjectNot-FoundException`. If you pass the object as an argument to a method of another object, this method will also throw `DomainObjectNotFoundException`.

If you want to make sure that a domain object exists when you call `getUser()`, `getAccount()` or `getService()`, you can use the `has...()` methods of `geo.domain.Domain`:

```
Domain domain = Context.getDomain("foobar.com");
User joe = null;
// this will always call the remote server
if (domain.hasUser("joe"))
joe = domain.getUser("joe"); // joe certainly exists
now
else
... // joe does not exist
```

The `has...()` methods will always make a call to the remote server to check if the domain object exists or not. The following example illustrates the reason for this behavior. If you call a method that takes a domain object as its argument, you often write code like this:

```
Domain domain = Context.getDomain("foobar.com");
Account foo_account =
domain.getAccount("foo_account");
Service foo_service =
domain.getService("foo_service");
foo_account.addPrivilege(foo_service);
```

This code will add the privilege for service "`foo_service`" to account "`foo_account`". If `foo_service` does not exist, you would expect `getService()` to throw HandleNotFoundException. However, in order to determine if `foo_service` exists, Domain API would have to make a call to a remote server. Then, if `foo_service` does exist, Domain API would have to make a second call to the remote server to add privilege for `foo_service` to `foo_account`. So for increased efficiency, Domain API does not call the remote server to check if `foo_service` exists. Instead, the `getService()` method always returns a service object which you can use as a reference to service "`foo_service`". When `addPrivilege()` is called, Domain API will make the call to the remote server. If it turns out that `foo_service` does not exist, `addPrivilege()` and not `getService()` will throw `HandleNotFoundException`.

8.3.7.2 Retrieving Multiple Attribute Values in One Network Call

The Domain API obtains information from the primary repository, and this typically runs on a remote server. Network interaction and concomitant delays may be incurred upon attribute retrieval, specifically when you invoke the `get...()` methods. As an optimization, the Domain API can retrieve several attributes with a single call to the remote server. This is substantially more efficient because it avoids the network delays. This allows the application to run much faster. In order to take advantage of this feature, you have to specify which attributes you want to retrieve when you retrieve the owner of the attributes.

The attributes are retrieved in one call, and subsequent requests for the attributes will return the statically stored local copy:

```
static final String[] ATTR_NAMES =
new String[] {User.STATE, "Address", "Phone Number"};
Domain domain = Context.getDomain("foobar.com");
User joe = domain.getUser("joe", ATTR_NAMES);
// single-valued fixed
int state = joe.getState();
// single-valued flexible
String address = joe.getString("Address");
String phone_number = joe.getString("Phone Number");
// Following retrieves identical static local value
String address2 = joe.getString("Address");
```

For user "`joe`", the Domain API will retrieve state, address and phone number from the remote server at the time when you call `getUser()`. It does not have to make additional calls to the remote server when you call `getState()`, `getString("Address")` and `getString("Phone Number")`. If you omit attribute names when you call `getUser()`, you will incur a network interaction upon each `get...()` method to retrieve an attribute. *The network calls occur only the first time that you retrieve the attribute.*

If you retrieve an attribute a second time (e.g., when you call `joe.getString("Address")` the second time in the previous example), Domain API will not make a call to the remote server. Instead, the API will return the same value as the first time when you called the method (i.e., in the previous example, `address2` will always be equal to `address`). This assumes you do not need a fresh value.

8.3.7.3 Value Refresh

In order to force Domain API to reread current attribute values from the remote server (e.g., because they may have been changed by someone else in the meantime), you simply retrieve the owner of the attribute again (e.g., by calling `domain.getUser("joe")` in the previous example, or by using any other Domain API method that returns a user object). Subsequent `get...()` calls on this object will retrieve updated attribute values from the remote server.

Iterators are a second technique to obtain fresh values. When you request an iterator over the values of a multi-valued attribute, you can also specify the names of the attributes that you want to retrieve from every element in the iterator. Domain API will use this information to optimize the number of calls to the remote server.

For example:

```
static final String[] ATTR_NAMES =
new String[] {Service.HANDLE, "Protocols"};
ServiceIterator si =
   joe.getServiceSubscriptions(ATTR_NAMES);
Service service;
while (si.hasNext()) {
   service = si.nextService();
   System.out.println(service.getHandle() + ": "
   + service.getString("Protocols"));
}
```

When you request an iterator a second time (e.g., if you called `getServiceSubscriptions()` again in the previous example), Domain API will always make a call to the remote server. The iterator does not lock the record; you may get different values in the second call than in the first call if someone has changed the values in the interim.

In order to modify attribute values you must first retrieve the owner of the attribute in the same way as described above. For example:

```
static final String[] ATTR_NAMES =
    new String[] {"Phone Number"};
Domain domain = Context.getDomain("foobar.com");
User joe = domain.getUser("joe", ATTR_NAMES);
String new_phone =
    changePhoneNumber(joe.get("Phone Number"));
// single-valued flexible
joe.set("Phone Number", new_phone);
// single-valued fixed
joe.setState(User.INACTIVE);
// multi-valued fixed
joe.addSubscription(domain.getService("foo_service"));
joe.update();
```

Figure 8-17: Modifying Attribute Values

For efficiency, you can specify the attribute names when retrieving the user object, so Domain API can retrieve the user object and the attribute values in one network call. After all modifications to a domain object have been made, you must call `update()` on the domain object to make the changes permanent. If you do not call `update()`, your modifications will be lost.

8.3.7.4 C++ Example Running as Proxy Code

Figure 8-18 combines the network thread API with the domain API. Taken together, this provides the user identity of the active thread, and then retrieves essential domain elements. This example runs within the proxy framework. This demonstrates the retrieval of user information from the domain database, and the subsequent use of this information. This code can run as a proxy process and is written in C++

8.4 Service Development

Services benefit substantially through adherence to the design principles described in Section 4.5. Such services exhibit well-defined characteristics including manageability and extensibility. Rapid and reliable compliance with these design principles enhances the service development process by standardizing the network interactions, as well as through common features, easily and reliably invoked. Existing applications receive benefits through a software peer, thus attaching the application to the network. New applications obtain full benefit through the platform Software Development (SD) APIs.

Rather than reinvent from "the ground up", the SD provides managed interfaces that operate independently of location, hardware or interface capabilities. This "toehold

```
// Initialize for usage system
  GeoUsageCookie cookie;
  errno = geoUsageSessionCookie(userInfo->userIP,
                                userInfo->userPort, &cookie);
  // Invoke network thread API to obtain user number of this connection.
  GeoUsr geoUsr;
  GeoNetworkThreadToInit.geouserinfo(geoUsr);      // Get user info
  userData->geouser    = geoUsr.geouser;           // Retain Geo user number
  // Prepare to use the domain'API for detailed information
  DomainContext *dc; User *u; Service *s;  Domain *d;  Account *a;

dc = new DomainContext();
try { domain = dc->getDomain(); }
catch (DomainException &de)
     { fprintf(stderr, "fail getdom obj");
       de.print(stderr);
       exit(1); }

// Retrievable flexible attributes are defined in .../GeoDefs/names,
// The will be cached locally by getUser.   The cached values are strings.
String items[] = {GEO_NVPNAMES_USER_X509_CERTIFICATE,
                           GEO_NVPNAMES_ACCT_NUMBER
                           GEO_NVPNAMES_USER_HANDLE};
int itemLen = 3;
u = domain->getUser(geoUser.geouser, items, itemLen);  // Returns user object

// Retrievable fixed attributes are defined by specialized methods in the API.
// These methods return objects.
userData->geoHandle = u->getHandle();  // This object happens to be a string
u->getId(); // Get the integer ID;     //  This object happens to be an int
a=domain->getAccount(u);               //  And this object has methods
```

Figure 8-18: Network Thread API Combines with Domain API

into the network" firmly establishes a trust relationship and identity through authentication with the cloud. Applications benefit from managed network interactions that provide security, resource allocation, and usage tracking. Network interactions build upon a bundled collection of objects active in the peer. Runtime support makes use of development components that satisfy the principles given in Chapter 4, "Platform Requirements and Principles". Thus, a service utilizes the SD on a peer, while providers enhance cloud functionality with the PD on the gates. This section describes the SD peer APIs for service development and deployment.

8.4.1 SD APIs for Service Development and Development and Peer

Service development and delivery – the sole purpose of the platform – utilize the SD to efficiently provide services that may leverage the cloud environment. There are several special properties of the SD, and these resolve many costly issues of ensuring a common behavior. The underlying control channel coordinates network behavior and interactions. This channel distinguishes the SD applications. These realize the *service model* of Section 7.2.2 through this channel. This extends the basic network through the attachment of the service to the network. The SD guarantees the identity and secure interactions between any authenticated component and the service that is active on the peer. As such, the physical peer location is immaterial to a consumer of the peer's services. The peer also receives network services without regard for the physical location of these services. This insulates each peer from maintenance issues such as the distribution of software updates, and enables network-managed resources. Interactions are mediated by the cloud. These interactions can be custom-tailored to attributes that are specific to the peer's identity; for example, account membership and accompanying privileges.

Each SD application runs in a peer. This receives an appropriate level of trust depending on whether it has authenticated to the cloud. The SD and peer establish and maintain an authenticated connection to the cloud. Access to the APIs and services may be based on the user/service trust relationship. The following APIs require prior authentication: connection management, domain database, event management and usage recording. The SD supports development in Java or C++. The Java APIs correspond to these categories, specifically:

TABLE 8: SD Java Classes and Purpose

Class	Purpose
Geo.peer	Peer class and peerlet management
Geo.connection	Connection management, including remote user identification through caller ID. The class `Connection` contains the methods used to establish and disconnect an authenticated connection between a peer and a supported network. It also provides initial access to many of the networking APIs, including the domain API, the usage API, and the event API. It can be used to determine the identity of a remote user accessing a service (caller ID)
Geo.dom, geo.domain.util	Domain API (stable store). Registration, account management, and subscriptions (directory services)
Geo.security	Manipulation of user credentials
Geo.usage	Submission and retrieval of usage records
Geo.event	Generation and reception of events to and from the network
Geo.defs	Internationalization support
Geo.util	Utilities
Geo.peer.pi	Application management, including control of the peer from external applications

Let's briefly discuss the primary APIs in each of the major classes, and then view a few simple examples.

Peerlet management

Provides installation, invocation, and termination of nearly independent programs into a specific peer. Each program runs as a separate thread of control within the peer, which allows a high degree of concurrency between these programs. These programs are called "peerlets" because they are active within a single peer and share resources as defined by the peer. They receive runtime support from this peer, specifically the remaining categories of activity listed below

Connection management

Provides control and information for the network connection. This includes providing a secure control channel, authentication of the peer to the network, definition of per-connection encryption to the cloud, as well as announcement of active services. Authentication is the essential prerequisite for network interaction, although specific interactions can be permitted to unauthenticated clients. Rather than assume the security of the network connection, a platform encryptor controls encryption on a per-connection basis. SD APIs specify encryption requirements on a per-connection basis where necessary to communicate with nonencrypted devices or systems. Nonencrypted connections rely on the network, rather than peer encryption, for transport security.

The connection class supports single-sign-on by providing services with the ability to determine the identity of remote users using the services. This is essential to services that implement native access control or provide client-specific behavior. Nonrepudiable client identification is strictly more powerful than simple knowledge that a client is authenticated. This works through a mechanism known as *callerID*. One mechanism supports peer request for the remote identification, and a second supports legacy HTTP servers' requests for the remote identification.

Both the SD and the PD support `geoPeerGetCallerID` returning the caller ID information of a user, purportedly authenticated from a specific IP address and port. It is required that the peer be authenticated with the cloud to perform this operation successfully. This function utilizes the cloud's Caller ID table to obtain the ID of the user authenticated at the given address. The cloud authentication mechanisms must ensure the accuracy of this information. We have previously discussed the gate's role in maintaining this table.

When a service receives a new socket connection from a remote user, it can use the IP address and port of the remote user to determine the identity, or caller ID, of the user. This is done using the `getCallerID` method of the Connection interface. The `getCallerID` method returns a `geo.peer.CallerID` object that contains the user handle and numeric identifier of the user, as well as the handle and identifier of the cloud that the user is authenticated to. If the user if not authenticated to a middleware-supported network, an exception is thrown.

The caller ID function also supports CGI programs by including a mini web-server in the peer package. A "legacy" web server can query the peer and obtain its caller ID information. The caller ID "wedge" is a preinstalled peerlet that is deployed with the peer and operates as service from each peer instance. This service should be announced on the port the wedge is listening on so that the HTTP traffic is sent to the wedge when a client makes an HTTP request. The wedge inserts the caller ID cookie and forwards the request to the actual web server at serverhost:serverport. This HTTP "wedge" is shown in Figure 8-19:

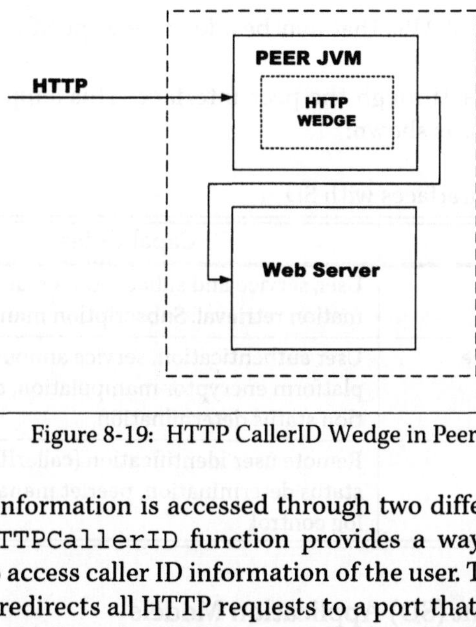

Figure 8-19: HTTP CallerID Wedge in Peer

Caller ID information is accessed through two different APIs. The `geoPeerGetHTTPCallerID` function provides a way for (http) web-based services to access caller ID information of the user. The peer software intercepts and redirects all HTTP requests to a port that provides caller ID, and adds a "cookie" to the HTTP request before handing it off to an HTTP server. A CGI program subsequently extracts the cookie via a CGI environment variable and uses GetCallerID API.

Domain database

Interface to persistent store for user, account and service information. This includes declaration of the names and parameters of the services hosted on the peer machine. It also describes availability of the services. A peer places services into the domain by authenticating as the administrator of an account. It then creates the service object through assignment of a name and appropriate parameters. The parameters include protocols (both transport and application protocols), access controls, the IP ports providing service, and additional service-specific parameters

Usage tracking

Submission and retrieval of usage records. Such records support fine-grain tracking of peer activities and thereby ensure nonrepudiation of action. Usage tracking provides important management support through profiling of usage patterns

Event Generation and Reception

Definition, generation and receipt of events through the publish/subscribe paradigm. These events provide a distributed systems-level communication of exactly-once semantics providing structured messages to subscribed components. It utilizes stable storage to ensure event reception even by components that are unavailable at the time of event generation

External APIs

Interface to additional APIs that may be added for a specific application.

The SD API supports C/C++ through the peer interface. This supports a substantial subset of the SD Java classes, as shown:

TABLE 9: C/C++ Interfaces with SD

Interface	Capabilities
Domain Interface	User, service and subaccount creation. Information retrieval. Subscription management
Connection Interface	User authentication, service announcement, platform encryptor manipulation, connection status determination
Peer Interface	Remote user identification (callerID), peer status determination, peerlet management, log control

8.4.2 Service Development (SD) Application Models

There are three programming models for peer activities: peerlet, monolithic peers, and the external model. These share the common software base of a software peer that interacts with the cloud network. The peerlet and the monolithic peer use the Java language and Java APIs; and the external model supports other languages or applications through peer-resident capabilities.

Peerlets run under the control of a precompiled peer running in a Java virtual machine. The peer provides the execution environment and support. Peerlets are precompiled and then loaded into the peer, which invokes them as distinct threads. Monolithic peers use the peer software as a library, but provide a main program that invokes the peer's initialization functions. Indeed, the peer itself is a monolithic program that can load and invoke peerlets. The peerlet and the monolithic peer models both run a single process containing the SD control and the application logic.

External applications run in their own process and communicate with an existing peer through a peer interface. Existing applications, or programs written in C/C++, interact with middleware APIs through the interface channel to the running peer.

8.4.3 Peerlets

SD programs use either of three models – the peerlet described currently, as well as monolithic peers or external models, which provide varying amounts of structure to the developer. The greatest structure is provided with the so-called *peerlet* model. Collections of functions pertaining to a single purpose are compiled into an archive that can be installed as a complete peerlet. This runs as a thread within the peer, technically by extending the *geo.peer.Peerlet* class.

The peerlet therefore is controlled by the peer, and must be installed into the peer. This provides a module method for distribution of prepackaged functionality. A peerlet is relatively unconstrained by the peer environment, and may access the execution context and command-line arguments as needed The peer runs many peerlets with resource allocation under the control of the Java virtual machine.

```
package samples.sdk.peerlets;
import java.awt.*;
import java.awt.event.*;
import javax.swing.*;
import geo.peer.*;

public class HelloWorldPeerlet extends Peerlet {
    private JFrame _frame;

    public void run() {
        _frame = new JFrame( "Hello World Peerlet" );
        _frame.addWindowListener( new WindowAdapter() {
            public void windowClosing( WindowEvent we ) {
                getPeerletContext().firePeerletStopped();
            }
        } );
        _frame.getContentPane().add( new JLabel( "Hello World",
                                                  JLabel.CENTER ),
                                     BorderLayout.CENTER );
        Dimension prefSize = new Dimension( 250, 60 );
        _frame.getRootPane().setPreferredSize( prefSize );
        _frame.pack();
        _frame.setVisible( true );
    }

    public void cleanup() {
        _frame.dispose();
    }
}
```

Figure 8-20: The "Simplest" Peerlet

Peerlets may not provide a `main()` method, and must provide a `run()` method. They should not invoke the `System.exit()` method since this terminates the entire process. Instead, they invoke the `firePeerletStopped()` method of their runtime context, `getPeerletContext()`. This allows the peer to reclaim resources. Peerlets are, in essence, prepackaged routines stored as Java archives. The peer methods support loading, starting and stopping of peers.

Figure 8-20 shows a simple peerlet. The reader may notice this code is nearly indistinguishable from a well written Java module. This peerlet, when invoked, displays a popup window that displays the time-honored welcome text of any first program, "Hello World". Lines 1 through 4 define the package and import standard `java.awt` and `javax.swing` providers of graphics and popup windows. Line 5 imports the `geo.peer` class that defines the interfaces for the peer. Lines 7 through 29 implement the `HelloWorldPeerlet` class. Line 7 defines this class, and in particular the class extends the `peerlet` class. This uses the libraries that we imported back in line five. The class defines a private graphics frame at line 8.

Line 9 departs from an ordinary Java class, and provides the mandatory method `public void run()`. All peerlets must have a `run` method. This serves as the entry point when the peer invokes the peerlet. The peerlet also calls the `getPeerletContext().firePeerletStopped();` The body of this method defines what the peerlet does; this example creates a suitable graphics frame and displays Java code that defines and displays a window, as well as a resource deallocation routine (lines 27-28). The peerlet is compiled, packaged for distribution, and installed through tools included with the SD.

8.4.4 Monolithic Peer Application Model

Monolithic peers define a main() method and call the geo.peer.Peer.init() method to initialize the SD. This provides full access to all SD APIs, including the ability to load and invoke peerlets. Rather than define a standard runtime environment, it grants greater freedom to the developer who develops the service or application.

The sample program of Figure 8-21 also creates a popup window that displays the time-honored welcome text of any first program, "Hello World". The simplest monolithic program includes the same application logic as the peerlet model. However, several significant differences change it from a peerlet into a monolithic program. The class definition that line 7 provides no longer extends the `Peerlet` class, and instead the monolithic example provides a `main()` method rather than the `run()` line of the Peerlet. Line 9 (which was intentionally left blank in the Peerlet) now initializes with `Peer.initialize()`. Upon completion at line 13 it terminates with `System.exit()` whereas the peerlet signalled completion with `getPeerletContext().firePeerletStopped()`.

```
package samples.sdk.external;
import java.net.UnknownHostException;
import java.io.FileNotFoundException;
import java.io.IOException;
import geo.peer.pi.*;
import geo.util.GeoException;

public class AuthenticateExternal {
   static private void usage( )
   {
     System.err.println( "usage: AuthenticateExternal " +
                         "userHandle cloudName passPhrase" );
   }
   static public void authenticate( String userHandle,
                         String cloudName,  String passPhrase )
   {
     try {
      String deploy = System.getProperty( "GEOPLEX_DEPLOY" );
      PIConnection piConn = new PIConnection( deploy );
      ConnectionHandler conn = new ConnectionHandler( piConn );
      conn.login( userHandle, passPhrase, cloudName, "PropertiesFile" );
         }
    catch ( Exception ge )
         {
      System.err.println( ge.getLocalizedMessage() );
         }

static public void main( String argv[] ) {
    if ( argv.length != 3 )
         { System.err.println( "Incorrect number of command " +
               "line arguments provided: " + argv.length );
                usage();   System.exit( 1 );
          }
    authenticate( argv[0], argv[1], argv[2] );
    }
}
```

Figure 8-21: Simples Monolithic Peer without Authentication

There is one more, somewhat hidden difference. The peerlet ran in the context of its peer, and the peer interfaced directly with the cloud. The peer supported authenticating and other cloud interactions through a GUI. On the other hand, the simplest monolithic program merely initialized the peer, but never authenticated it. We need to enhance the program through several internal changes and an additional 20 lines of Java program, shown in Figure 8-22.

8.4.5 Connection Objects Independent of Domains and Locations

The very significant security implications of mobility, peering, and other issues require careful consideration of the client's identity, as well as the network connection and authentication. The program networking APIs therefore provide a general framework available through abstract APIs that leverage the specifics of the client, local devices, networking or remote capabilities. These capabilities utilize the connection, security and utility classes imported at lines 2 through 4 of Figure 8-22. Note in particular that the connection object (line 28) does not specify what it is connecting to. Rather than constrain the connection to a single cloud or domain, the API supports a variety of domains, peering and roaming arrangements. This example provides specific values as program parameters (lines 24, 25 and 26 access `argv[]`), though in practice the authentication passphrase cannot be a simple stored `String`.

```
1   package samples.sdk.mono;
2   import geo.peer.*;
3   import geo.connection.Connection;
4   import geo.security.Credentials;
5   import geo.util.*;
6
7   public class AuthenticateMPeer {
8
9       static private void usage( ) {
10          System.err.println(
11              "\nusage: samples.sdk.mono.AuthenticateMPeer " +
12              "userHandle cloudName passPhrase\n" );
13      }
14
15      static public void main( String argv[] ) {
16          Peer.initialize();
17          Log log = Peer.getDefaultLog();
18          if ( argv.length != 3 ) {
19              log.log( Log.ERROR, "Incorrect number of command " +
20                      "line arguments provided: " + argv.length );
21              usage();
22              System.exit( 1 );
23          }
24          String userHandle = argv[0];
25          String cloudName = argv[1];
26          String passPhrase = argv[2];
27          try {
28              Connection conn = Peer.getConnection();
29              Credentials cred =
30                  conn.createCredentialsObject("PropertiesFile");
31              cred.setUserHandle( userHandle );
32              cred.setCloudName( cloudName );
33              conn.authenticate( cred, passPhrase );
34              System.out.println( "Authentication succeeded!" );
35          } catch ( GeoException ge ) {
36              log.log( Log.ERROR, ge );
37              log.log( Log.ERROR, ge.getKeyword() );
38              System.err.println( ge.getLocalizedMessage() );
39              System.exit( 1 );
40          }
41          System.exit( 0 );
42      }
43  }
```

Figure 8-22: Monolithic Peer with Authentication Code

The credential object (line 29) provides a structured container for the various credentials or algorithms that may be required to establish and protect the connection. These include X.509 certificates as well other security information described in Section 6.3. This information is too voluminous for most people to remember, and hence it must be stored on a hardware device. The `conn.createCredentialObject()` specifies a source, which in this example (line 30) it is a `propertiesFile` stored in partially encrypted form on the local disk. The specific user and cloud are placed into the object (lines 31, 32), but the "unlock key" is not placed into the object. The program specifies values including the subscriber's home cloud, user name, and authentication information appropriate for the activities the subscriber requires of this object (lines 31, 32), and then authenticates over the connection. The credentials can be constrained by the

```
1   package samples.sdk.mono;
2   import java.awt.*;
3   import java.awt.event.*;
4   import javax.swing.*;
5   import geo.peer.*;
6
7   public class HelloWorldMPeer {
8       static public void main( String argv[] ) {
9           Peer.initialize();
10          JFrame frame = new JFrame("Hello World Monolithic Peer");
11          frame.addWindowListener( new WindowAdapter() {
12              public void windowClosing( WindowEvent we ) {
13                  System.exit( 0 );
14              }
15      static public void main( String argv[] ) {
16          Peer.initialize();
17          Log log = Peer.getDefaultLog();
18          if ( argv.length != 3 ) {
19              log.log( Log.ERROR, "Incorrect number of command " +
20                      "line arguments provided: " + argv.length );
21              usage();
22              System.exit( 1 );
23          }
24          String userHandle = argv[0];
25          String cloudName = argv[1];
26          String passPhrase = argv[2];
27          try {
28              Connection conn = Peer.getConnection();
29              Credentials cred =
30                  conn.createCredentialsObject("PropertiesFile");
31              cred.setUserHandle( userHandle );
32              cred.setCloudName( cloudName );
33              conn.authenticate( cred, passPhrase );
34              System.out.println( "Authentication succeeded!" );
35          } catch ( GeoException ge ) {
36              log.log( Log.ERROR, ge );
37              log.log( Log.ERROR, ge.getKeyword() );
38              System.err.println( ge.getLocalizedMessage() );
39              System.exit( 1 );
40          }
41          System.exit( 0 );
42      }
43  }
```

Figure 8-23: External Application Model

local connectivity; for example, an office provides a private physical network, whereas a "road warrior" or telecommuter may access a specialized local access through information defined in the credentials.

The program provides a `main()` method (line 15), initializes the peer and sets up a standard log (line 16), and verifies the parameters (lines 18-23). It then creates a connection object (line 28) thereby enabling the IP connectivity, and specifies a source for the credentials that will be needed to authenticate (line 30). The user's name (line 31) defines identity for this connection. The identity is unique within a domain as defined through the setCloudName method (line 32). Authentication of the connection is then requested (line 33), at which time the volatile "unlock key" or passphrase must be provided. The remainder of the program handles errors and terminates with an appropriate return code.

8.4.6 External Peer Application Model

.External applications are more loosely integrated with the peer. They control an independently executing Peer using a Peer Interface (PI), and can be written in any supported languages such as C, C++ or Java. However, access is limited to the networking services and SD APIs. It is best used for legacy applications, but may also be useful for applications that specialization to Java virtual machines makes difficult to achieve under the peerlet or monolithic models. This is shown in Figure 8-23.

8.5 Summary

We have presented a reference implementation for network middleware. This defines and explains essential components including active registries, dynamic directories, and access control models. These components provide APIs that describe, at an abstract layer, the activities necessary for service development and deployment. Middleware components provide these services in keeping with the platform design principles, and thus the polymorphic APIs may specify "why" rather than "how". The middleware can deploy the APIs through various mechanisms that leverage the most appropriate technologies available.

CHAPTER 9

Mechanisms of Middleware Components

This chapter explores the form and function of the middleware components, with emphasis upon what they can do and how they work. Starting with the selective admission of IP packets through the firewall, Section 9.1 describes a full range of functionality that subsumes the enforcement of security policy. The firewall directly supports a framework for managed security (Section 9.2) through dynamic binding of secure modules, thereby integrating standards-based security components into a manageable structure. Extensibility leverages a generalized proxy framework, as described in Section 9.3. We then present several examples, including customizing the standard domain name service (DNS) protocol, network-based extensions of the hypertext transport protocol (HTTP), and the Common Internet File System (CIFS) protocol ubiquitous to Microsoft networking. The latter example enables "software leasing", a model recently identified by the Application Service Provider (ASP) industry as it evolves from the Internet Service Provider (ISP) model.

9.1 Rules-Based Packet Filter Firewall

Firewalls typically serve exclusively as a security component, while ignoring the higher-layer application semantics and lower-layer network behaviors. This narrow expertise sustains highly efficient performance with minimal delay and maximum safety. Consequently, we partition the firewall into separate control and action components. The control portion maintains a structured rule base that quickly locates the appropriate rules. Several structuring techniques organize the rules according to the static hierarchy of users, services and sessions. Dynamic data structures maintain per session rule caches for fast runtime lookup. Machine specific parameters configure the specific sizes of these dynamic structures, although this tuning question is beyond the confines of the current work.

Rapid execution by a powerful firewall engine enforces the rules at low cost, and eliminates dependence upon either extensive runtime state or expensive algorithms. This follows directly from the logical decomposition into a specialized rule component, plus a refined engine that executes the rules. Reliability also improves because each component is smaller and hence easier to test, validate and refine. The composite rules-base and programmable firewall protects the SNodes from invalid traffic, while also adapting to new traffic patterns.

Positioned as the physical mediator of all network traffic, the firewall aptly enforces a broad range of system behaviors that extends beyond security. Rather than confining the firewall to security enforcement alone, the architectural partitioning between rules and engine extends naturally into a more capable view of the firewall. This synergistic result arises from the design requirements of highest attainable throughput, and the consequent engineering of a highly efficient and streamlined engine. Reuse of the component does not in any way diminish its efficiency, but rather reinforces its centrality to the SNode design.

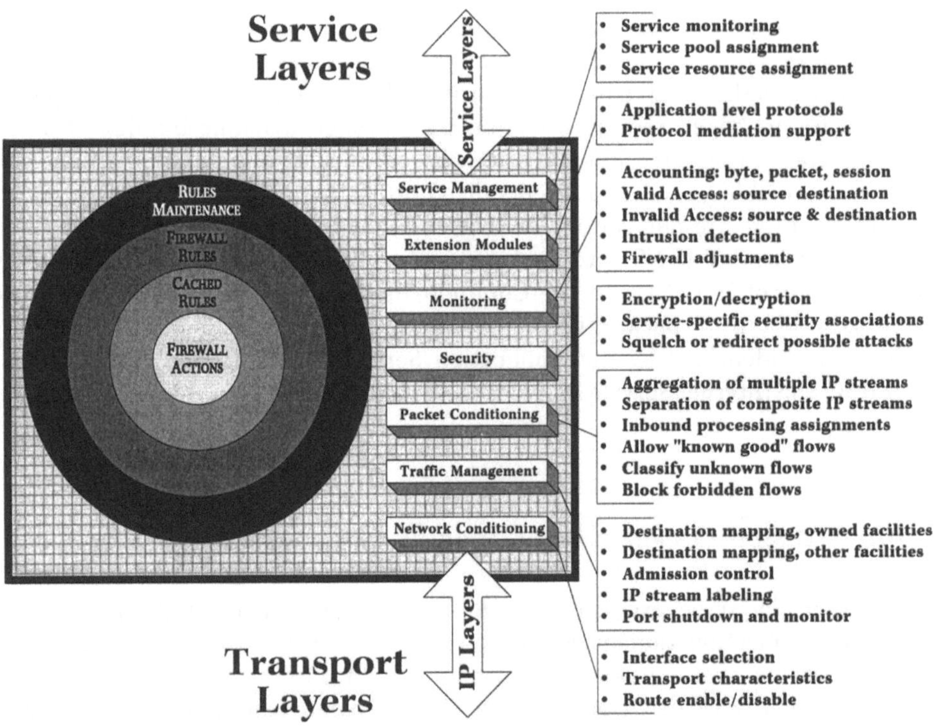

Figure 9-1: Firewall Integrates Transport Features with Service Requirements

SNodes deploy two or more network interface cards (NIs) that constitute the physical connection between multiple networks. All information passed into the SNode enters through these NICs and encounters the firewall. When filtering at a coarse granularity and acting upon packet-header information through cached rules, the filter does not impose a significant computational burden. The filter selectively activates fine granularity processes only when necessary. It is interesting to note this coarse-to-fine approach arises as the preferred solution in other complex processes as well. The SNode also provides a routing function as it receives packets that are destined for various IP addresses - not only the local IP address.

The dynamic firewall interposes as a mediator between IP networking and higher layer services, and thus preserves the rich capabilities of the higher and lower layers, as shown in Figure 9-1. The dynamic firewall is constructed from five primary components:

- Packet filters that define the behavior of IP connections ("Managed Firewalls" on page 180)
- Encryption modules that recover inbound data and protect outbound data ("Authentication and Session Layers" on page 165)
- ACT APIs that modify the firewall rule cache as client authentications change ("Active Registries: Connections, Users and Services" on page 246)
- Authentication proxy that validates client credentials and indicates when a client is authenticated ("Security Framework: Authentication Proxy and Agents" on page 290)
- Access daemon that maintains the firewall rules to the firewall rule cache ("Firewall and Access Control - Access Daemon" on page 297)

The firewall can perform any of four actions upon a packet, and makes this determination through the packet's source/destination IP address and port. These actions are: PASS, DROP, LOCAL and MAP (see Table 3 on page 182). These methods support both coarse-granularity and fine-granularity access control. At the coarse granularity level, the PASS action allows direct IP routing to the destination IP and port, whereas the DROP action discards the traffic. This may squelch certain cyber attacks such as denial of service, at least when there is a rhyme or reason to the targeted addresses and ports. Traffic flow and function are modified through the MAP action, as this redirects traffic to another address. The LOCAL action activates a local process, and it is through such local actions that fine-grain access control is enforced. The LOCAL action also supports protocol mediation.

The architecture runs multiple and simultaneous copies of the firewall (each copy running within its own gate). Additional servers can run duplicate copies of the gate and firewall software that is brought online as the volume of network traffic increases.

These components support a flexible security system while also preserving the rich capabilities unique to both upper-layer services and the lower-layer networking:

Security System

The packet filter allows the rules to be changed dynamically by the authentication system. This is capable of creating independent sets of rules or rule bases and combining the changes with an authentication system. These rules sets can be tuned to the needs and service demands of a particular session without affecting the service relationship of any other session. For instance:

- When a host authenticates to the network, a rule base can be loaded into the packet filter defining which packets will be allowed to pass from and/or to that host, thereby defining one aspect of access control and security for the host
- Adding fortification to the security of a specific session or service. The security configuration may be modified; for example, to enable or disable integrity checks or heartbeat signals. This balances the costs and benefits of such integrity checks
- Similar methods facilitate custom monitoring tools and proactive responses to possible intrusion, through methods to prevent damage from service attacks by restricting packet flows

Services Layer

Rule sets can be allowed to evolve as new network services are added, or experimental services are tested. These rule sets grant privileged peers special access without affecting other components or clients. The behavior of network services can be influenced in several ways, for example:

- Coarse granularity access control uses firewall rules inserted into the session cache by the access daemon. These rules support services by passing traffic to an appropriate service instance; the rules can even drop the traffic under overload conditions
- Services can be easily switched on or off based on the time of day or network load. To ensure a high quality of service, the firewalls can be adjusted to temporarily deny or limit access to services that are in high demand but have low priority during known time periods
- Network services can be throttled back when server and network load exceeds acceptable maximums. To prevent network congestion, automatic limit switches can use firewalls to reduce the load. In a similar manner, rule sets can be equipped with time locks, allowing network operators to offer limited "trial periods" of services
- Network operators can move a peer from one service pool to another by adjusting the peer-specific firewall rule sets

Network Layer

The firewall can modify egress (outbound) packets to use specific NIs or to redirect specific packet classes to other networks. This can support roaming agreements and redirection to alternate switching locations. Proxy processes such as the DNEAPI directly affect network elements such as switches and routers.

Early packet filters, when properly configured, were an effective first line of system defense – they accepted authorized traffic without restriction but excluded all other packets. However, sophisticated services need more support, including routing and mediation. Therefore, the rules-based packet filter integrates with a service model and supports the protocol mediation principle. Multiple application-specific protocols are supported without the requirement of any change to the client's operating environment.

9.1.1 Rules Management: Unambiguous Caching of Dynamic Entries

The firewall programs ensure the accuracy of firewall rules and caches. These programs respond dynamically to the changing network traffic. This traffic consists of valid traffic interspersed with erroneous or fraudulent traffic. Clients and services receive services as they authenticate, invoke packet filter APIs, dynamically modify the firewall behavior, and exit. Intruders should not disrupt this, although proactive countermeasures must be imposed through the firewall rules. These complex interactions interact with many firewall capabilities, and in particular:

- Rule lifetime
- Rule ambiguities
- Cache management
- Number of rules

The first of these – rule lifetime – manages the introduction and removal of rules from the packet filter. It maintains a session cache of per-peer information that can be quickly removed from the firewall. The immediate expunging of irrelevant rules is essential to avoid "stale" rules that could be exploited by clever hackers. By managing the rules we can immediately flush selected rules when needed, either to protect against an attack, or merely because a user logged off the network.

The second – rule ambiguity – must address conflicts between rule actions. Suppose one rule allows a user access, and another denies the access? The rule manager maintains these rules along the principle of maximal security, thereby imposing the maximally restrictive actions.

The packet filter maintains two rule bases, as previously described in Section 6.6. First are the global rules that affect all the hosts on a network. These are partitioned into global pre-rules and global post-rules. Second are the peer rules that affect a particular subscriber. These are partitioned into an in-rule base for packets travelling toward the peer, and an out-rule base for packets travelling away from the peer.

Rule management begins when a subscriber authenticates to the network. The in-rule base and out-rule base are retrieved from the subscriber's entry in the domain database. Dynamically allocated packet filter memory stores these rules, and backpointers to these allocations support fast access by hashing the peer's identity or IP address. This is required, for example, to remove rules when a peer voluntarily cedes its authenticated status; disconnects abruptly; or when an intrusion is detected.

Thus, we encounter the third element in rules management. The session cache stores the actively referenced rules, and thereby ensures the firewall can run very quickly. This cache holds the "drop" rules that block invalid traffic, as well as the recent peer rules that permit the traffic. The cache uses a strict timeout algorithm. A rule is placed into the cache with a given timeout value. This value decrements once per second, and resets upon each access to the rule. A rule is purged from the cache when its timeout value is non-positive.

Allowing dynamic changes to the rule bases causes entries to remain in the session cache, which may not be accurate because of a change to a rule base. This occurs when an entry is placed in the session cache and the rule base(s) from which that entry is derived is removed or modified.

To ensure consistency, the session cache may use either of the following methods:

- Remove all the entries in the cache whenever a rule base is added, modified or removed. This is unreasonably costly
- Associate version numbers with each rule base. The version number increases whenever a change is made to the rule base, at which time the current version number is copied into the session cache entries that are derived from the rule base. The rule base and session cache entries match when their version numbers are equal. This technique is described in Section 6.4.1

While it might seem contradictory to let a crucial piece of the system's "armor" be programmable though an API (and an open one at that!) it actually makes good sense. The platform is designed to support services, including, of course, someone provisioning a service (the "service provider"). Hence, the ability to self-provision by managing the firewall traffic to his or her own site (only) is a reasonable extension of platform capabilities. The API requires that a client first authenticate, at which time the client permissions propagate to cloud elements as needed. The propagation occurs within the trusted security perimeter, thereby granting limited access to firewall capabilities. This enforces sufficient and clearly defined safeguards. Automatic programming of the firewall is actually a process of examining and modifying user-specific rules, which are used to determine permissible access. These rules, loaded when a user authenticates to the system, are consulted the first time the user attempts access to any service. This is done by a combination of the packet filter and a special access control daemon.

9.1.2 How to Build a Packet Filter

Packet filters, once a Frankenstonian technology of the research laboratories, are now available for many operating systems. Sun Solaris®, for example, can be extended to support packet filtering. This exploits the implementation, in which each protocol or layer provides an interface. One such interface is sockets to make the traffic available through a file descriptor (`fd`).

As an engineering decision on Solaris and other System-V derivatives, this flow is encapsulated as a logical sequence known as a *stream*. The stream interacts with the Solaris TCP stack shown in Figure 9-2. Solaris supports modification of the stream flow by adding streams modules. This provides a powerful API to modify data flow and thereby capture the raw data beneath the IP layer within the kernel. Prior to modern UNIX systems such as Solaris, HP-UX and others, such changes would have required relinking the kernel. Packet filtering is available under Linux as well, through `ipfilter`.

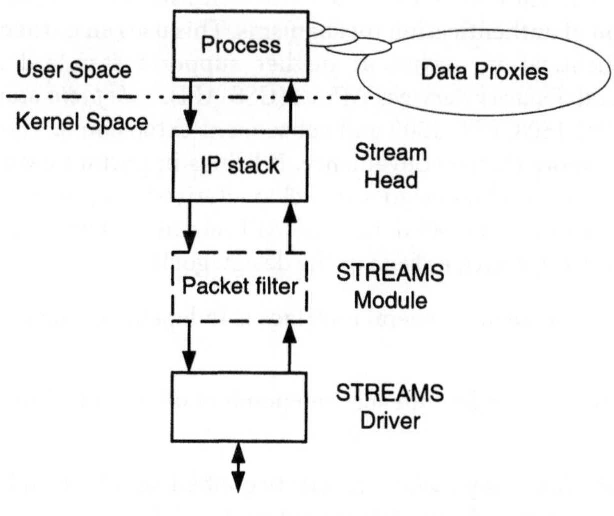

Figure 9-2: Streams-Based Packet-Filter

The stream-based filter supports a kernel layer mechanism to intercept the data before it arrives at the IP layer. A firewall exploits this architectural feature; it simply captures every packet, determines if it is well-formed, and decides what should happen to the packet. The IP header contains the protocol, source address/port, and destination/port. The firewall logic compares these values with the packet filter rules and selects the appropriate rule. Rules can specify:

- Drop the packet
- Pass it unchanged
- Remap to a new IP/port
- Introduce traffic mediation in this connection; the packets of this connection will pass through the mediation process *en route* to the client-specified destination

Traffic mediation introduces application-layer protocols that mediate existing streams. Traffic maps to a new port, and a listener on this port receives the packets, modifies them, and then forwards them as necessary. The various mechanisms of standard listeners, maps, etc. are provided by the proxy framework, thereby supporting a well-integrated methodology of proxy processing.

9.2 Security Framework: Authentication Proxy and Agents

The security framework (SF) provides an extensible and standards-based structure for the secure definition of authentication mechanisms. This uses an authentication proxy supported by authentication agents. It further supports standard security APIs, including the General Security Services API v2 (GSS-API), a *de facto* standard security services API (see RFC-1508, RFC-1509 and subsequent extensions). The use of a standard security API is more than a convenience. It brings important assurances regarding the completeness and solid design – two characteristics of particular importance for security. As discussed in [Oppl96], the GSS API retains maximum freedom for the deployment of effective security, as seen in the design goals:

- *Mechanism independence*: general interface is independent of particular mechanism
- *Protocol environment independence*: independent of communications protocol suite
- *Protocol association independence*: security context should be independent of communication protocol association context
- *Suitability to a range of implementation placements*: clients should not be constrained to reside with a trusted computing perimeter

Data transformation services, including encryption or security contexts, are registered internally through the GSS-API. The services are subsequently available to both authentication and session transport. The modular architecture enforces a single point of authentication (the authentication service), and provides extensibility. Despite its value as a standard, GSS-API is not universally deployed, and several major software suppliers have developed similar but syntactically incompatible APIs. This presents a challenge that middleware easily accommodates. For example, the model discussed in this text uses an Authentication Proxy (AP) providing a security framework which can load libraries that implement the authentication mechanisms. As a standardized security service, it provides a single control point, and furthermore this decreases operational expenses. It may be viewed as:

```
AuthProxy  +  AuthAgentLibrary  =  AuthMechProxy
```

The AP implements the AuthProxy API, the exclusive communication between the AuthAgent and AP. This API allows verification of a user's credentials and subsequent granting of network access. An AuthAgent cannot directly authenticate a client, but must instead communicate through internal AuthProxy and AuthAgent APIs. The AP also hosts add-on authentication components that are specialized for specific security extensions. The AP is an efficient multi-threaded and distributable component. An AP configuration object contains the parameters of an installation's security options and extensions.

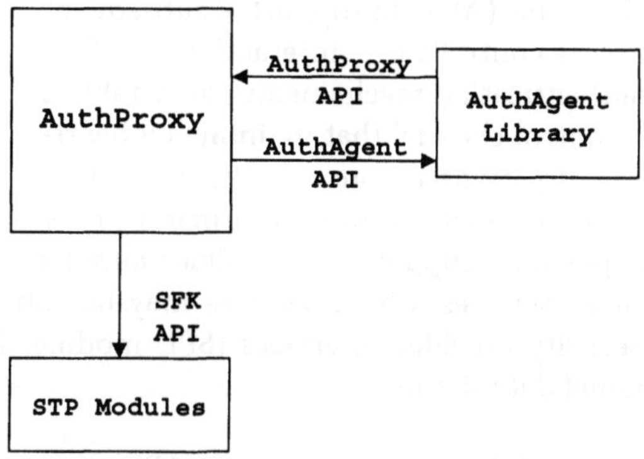

Figure 9-3: Authentication Structure

The two-phase agent/proxy architecture supports multiple authentication protocols without jeopardizing security. The AP is a highly trusted component. It is not restricted to any specific authentication protocol. Instead, the AP communicates with protocol-specific software by means of the authProxy and authAgent APIs. The details of a specific protocol are encapsulated within *authentication agents.* Agents support, for example, the proprietary peer, SSL-based with cloud-supported single-sign-on, and RADIUS.

These agents interact with the AP thereby enforcing cloud-specific requirements. The agents and AP negotiate the client's authentication over the authProxy API and the authAgent API. The typical outcome of the negotiation is authentication of client traffic. Another outcome can be limited access, for example to specific sites or by means of a data filter. The authentication agents support the major forms of authentication: proprietary peer-based, open web-based with explicit login, open web-based with implicit login, as well as others. The authentication proxy may also validate the authentication agents.

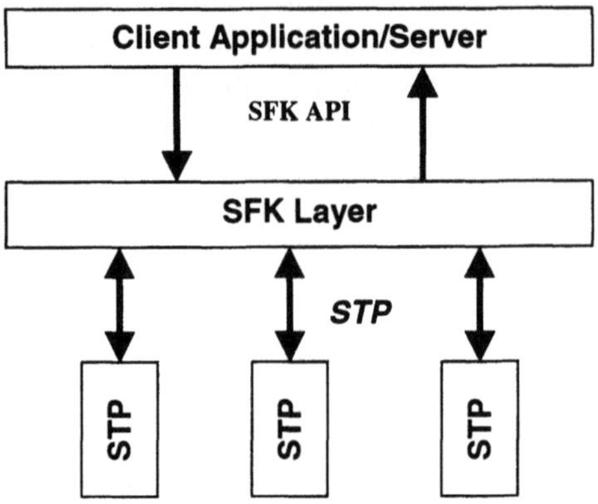

Figure 9-4: Service Provider Interface

The authentication agent supports mutual authentication between the client and cloud, with the client proving identity through appropriate credentials as required by the agent. The authentication agent negotiates with the AP on the client's behalf, specifically to present the credentials. Upon satisfactory "authentication dance" the AP may create an authenticated connection. This places the client into the Authenticated Connection Table (ACT) in support of subsequent access-controlled interactions. The authentication mechanisms can establish a control channel that maintains a heartbeat to validate connectivity, as well as state information. State information must include encryption keys, and may include application-support as well. Once authentication is complete, the client may request cloud services. Client services may be subsequently transformed as needed by the Security Provider Interfaces (SPI) module. The transform modules support bidirectional data streams.

The AuthProxy and AuthAgent APIs negotiate through a series of request/reply calls. These APIs also permit dynamic installation of callback functions. The callbacks establish a security context and activate agent-specific heartbeat functions. The AuthAgent must initialize before accepting any connections. The initialization grants secure resources to the agent, while also providing validation information to the AuthProxy. Validation information establishes the permitted activities of the authAgent as well as shared-secret information. This information can be changed at any time; for example, to synchronize the AuthAgent and the AuthProxy.

An initialized AuthAgent receives requests from external hosts or devices. These requests may arrive on a new IP connection, and interestingly they may also arrive on an active IP connection. A single IP connection carries secure traffic for multiple clients, provided the payload can be associated with a specific client. For example, the peerless web-based agent (see Section 9.2.2) accepts multiple clients over a single connection, thereby effectively multiplexing multiple clients that are distinguished through unique HTTP cookies.

Authentication requests may be encrypted; for example, through SSL/TLS. The AuthAgent obtains identification and security credentials from the client, and may interact with the AuthProxy to refine specific requirements of an authentication. The AuthProxy references master secrets and security transforms in deciding how the client must complete authentication. AuthAgent transfers the login credentials to the

AuthProxy for validation. The AuthProxy may then call a protocol-specific function, thereby authenticating the user to the cloud; this updates the AUR and ACT entries. Since the AuthProxy alone may modify the ACT, this retains a single source of active authentications. The AuthProxy then reports successful authentication through a callback function, thereby notifying the AuthAgent. AuthAgents can also "fortify" a secure connection through API calls that specify mandatory channel maintenance such as periodic challenge/response or CBC-mode "heartbeat" signals (see Figure 9-6). These serve as "heartbeat" signals that monitor the connection through bidirectional protocols that detect tampering on the communication channel.

Considerable care has been taken to protect privilege information even within the secure domain. At no time are protected resources simply decrypted into cleartext. Instead, the AuthAgent and AuthProxy interact with the GSS-API through protected (hashed) pointers that indirectly share security context. The AuthAgent and AuthProxy cannot obtain the referenced data. The callback can also return information to the agent, thereby supporting supervised "need to know" access to security keys. For example, such information is also protected through security contexts that must be passed along with the data. Making this concrete, we can observe the integrated security architecture shown in Figure 9-5.

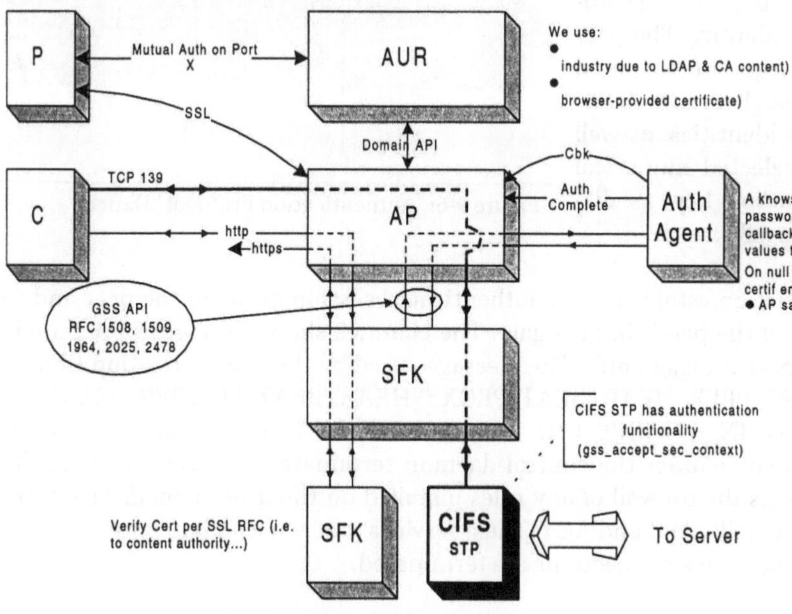

Figure 9-5: Integrated Security Architecture

Authentication agents support multiple authentication methods. Browser-based access supports login passwords, authentication certificates, or a trust relationship with a hosting domain. Password authentication will validate the password supplied by the user. Certificate authentication uses an X.509 certificate for mutual authentication. Clients can either register an existing certificate for the purpose of cloud authentication, or they may request a cloud-sponsored certificate. These specific security implications of these issues are discussed in Section 6.7.2.

We now examine several security components in detail. We will study the access control daemon, the control daemon, several protocol-specific authentication components, and a prototypical registration daemon.

9.2.1 Authentication Agent – Control Daemon and Peers

Managed network connections become established through the authentication server at an appropriate port. Authentication proceeds over a secure channel to *mutually* prove the identifications of the client and the cloud. The client will not authenticate unless all components satisfy a cryptographic proof of identity. The peer and the cloud negotiate a shared session key through secure bilateral exchange of identities, as well as a randomly selected numerical basis for the session key, as discussed in Section 6.3.1.

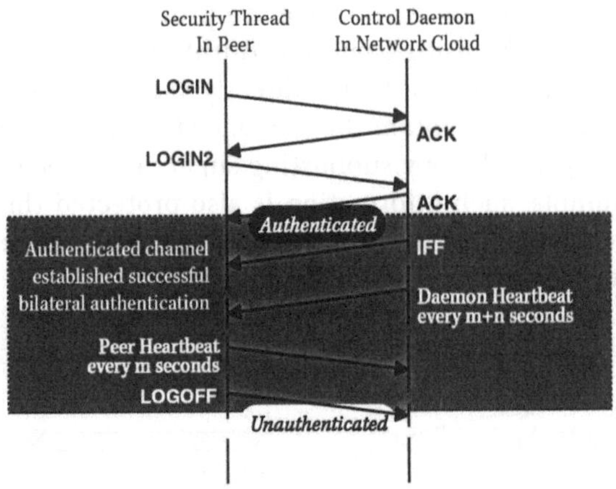

Figure 9-6: Authentication Protocol "Dance"

Successful negotiation establishes an authenticated session between the peer and the control daemon of the peer's ingress gate. The channel, shown in Figure 9-6, remains active until the peer is logged off. The messages used by the Authentication Channel are IFF, ENCRYPT, PEER_HEARTBEAT, PROXY_HEARTBEAT, LOGOFF, USAGEREC, AURLOOKUP, LOGIN, LOGIN2, CID_REQUEST. If the heartbeat signals are not received in a timely manner the control daemon terminates the user's session. This immediately purges the firewall of any rules installed on the user's behalf. The user is removed from the AUR, ASR and ACT. Thus, services that the user had announced are de-announced, and active connections are terminated.

9.2.2 Authentication Agents – Data Proxy and Secured Web "Logins"

Web authentication supports SSO with secure and personalized content. Authentication uses the AuthProxy and an HTTP-based AuthAgent that we collectively refer to as AP. Content services utilize a Data Proxy (DP) that supports all HTTP/HTTPS requests and requires specially encrypted HTTP cookies. This section describes behavior and interactions of the AP and DP; the cryptographic properties are described in Chapter 6, Section 6.7.1. The current section discusses these components from the perspective of Alice, a remote web user who is purchasing desert wine from `NinoVino.com` (which recently took over the `DandelionWine.com`; see Pages 9 and 91 for discussion of these services).

Alice authenticates *exactly once* through her web browser over a secured SSL connection (step one of Figure 9-7). An authentication data exchange validates her identity by means of a previously enrolled certificate, or through a user name with password. Bilateral authentication ensures the veracity of the cloud identity, based on the cloud certificate previously downloaded. Assuming that Alice is a legitimate user, the AP will add Alice's user ID to the ACT (Authenticated Connections Table, step two of the Figure). Before finalizing Alice's login, the AP creates a new SSL connection and popup window on Alice's browser; these support control functions such as logout, as well as dynamic refresh of the authentication information.

Alice's authentication should persist over many HTTP requests within the domain, and yet HTTP does not directly support a user "login". Rather than repeat the authentication, the AP provides Alice's browser with special authentication tokens. Encrypted through a time-sensitive algorithm, these tokens cannot be recovered after expiration. The AP generates authentication tokens for each web service protected by the network. Each one contains her unique user ID, the token's expiration-time, and service-specific information. These cookies may be restricted to secure web services (i.e., services that require use of the `HTTPS` protocol) through the appropriate attribute.

The cookies are received into Alice's computer through the SSL connection established during authentication, and are installed by the browser into its cookie database. All standard browsers send the correct (i.e., domain matching) cookie each time Alice visits a web site. Since the cookie database is shared by all instances of the web browser on Alice's machine, the cookie is automatically sent to the appropriate site whenever Alice visits it. The cookies are protected through time-sensitive encryption (Section 6.7.1.1 discusses the cryptographic techniques that protect cookies, as well as domain-matching). These steps proceed automatically without Alice's intervention.

Alice directs her browser to a network-protected web site such as `HTTPS://portal.domain.com/server`. Her browser augments the request message with the domain-specific cookie (step 4). Since the service is protected, the request is redirected to the data proxy (DP). DP extracts the cookie from the Alice's request, and tries to decrypt its content; the decryption can only succeed for legitimate and non-expired cookies. DP verifies the cookie, extracts the user ID, and verifies Alice's ACT entry (step 5).

If Alice uses an `HTTPS` connection, finding Alice among active users gives the DP the assurance that the authentication token is not being replayed. Unprotected `HTTP` con-

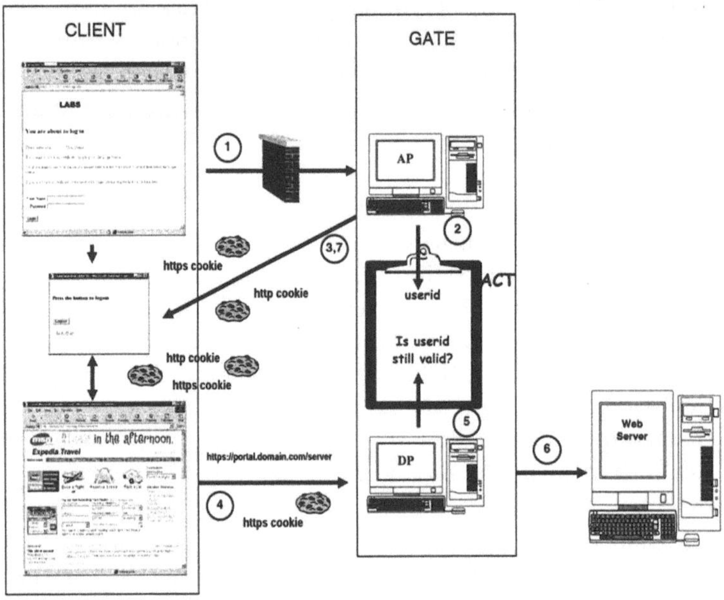

Figure 9-7: Time-Varying Encrypted Cookies Securing Identity

nections, however, strictly require fortification to protect their content. The tokens sent by Alice over an unprotected HTTP connection may be captured and replayed by malicious users who share Alice's IP address. The limited lifetime and specificity to Alice's ACT entry provide substantial fortification. Given the expense required to intercept Alice's network traffic, the transient nature of the tokens, and the fact that those tokens are rejected by DP on the HTTPS connections, the loss of resources as the result of such attack is negligible (see "Encrypted Cookies from Authentication to Termination" on page 204).

After the DP has finished the verification procedure, it contacts the content server through a secure proxy connection on Alice's behalf. The content is returned to Alice's browser. Thus, the middleware supports the most common Internet protocol – HTTP – through combination of multiple standards and improvements built on them. The example of browser login uses the globally accepted standards for HTTP, HTTPS and HTTP-state (cookies). Security vulnerabilities are closed through specific encryption schemes that protect system resources and prevent misuse of the accounts of web-based clients. Details of the actual cookies are described in Section 6.7.1

9.2.3 Authentication – RADIUS Dial Support and Session Control

A third important example is RADIUS authentication (RFC-2138, RFC-2139). This is a supported standard often used within inbound dialup modem pools. The RADIUS server, operating at the modem pool, receives credentials from the user. These credentials could be specific to the modem pool, or they could be part of the middleware network. The first situation may arise when an enterprise chooses to administrate its uses with a private domain. Such enterprises can broker the requests over a private tunnel connection to the middleware. In such uses the enterprise retains responsibility for user actions, except when the user negotiates a secure SSL session with a service end point. In such cases, the RADIUS authentication agent enforces server-specific policies. The agent directly supports requests that originated from a modem pool or other ingress network, and negotiates the AuthProxy API. These methods standardize the interaction with the cloud, simplify development, and guarantee that authentication occurs only through a common and controlled framework.

The second situation allows access to direct subscribers of network middleware. The dial platform essential becomes a tunneling pass-through. For these users the requests are passed directly to the middleware for validation, with appropriate encapsulation in `PPP`, `L2TP` or other protocol [Shea].

9.2.4 Firewall and Access Control - Access Daemon

The access daemon (AD) maintains the firewall rules. This enforces service and security policies by classifying the first packet of any new IP connection or "stale" existing connections not recently used. AD accepts a raw IP packet, analyses the packet, modifies the dynamic firewall according to cloud policies, and sends the packet back to the firewall. Packets arrive at the AD due to previously installed rules in the packet filter. All valid rules sets include a terminating LOCAL rule directing unprocessed packets to the AD, thus ensuring AD will receive the packet.

The new rule specifies appropriate processing for the original packet, as well as management information such as the rule inactivity lifetime, and optionally the associated user or service. The association with a user or service ensures the rule's annulment upon termination of the user or service; this mechanism utilizes the ACT interfaces of the ACT. The rule is also removed upon inactivity. This aging of rules resembles similar time-outs in paging caches found on modern operating systems.

The additional rules directly support higher-level services, either as IP pass-through, redirection to a service, invocation of a mediated service, or fine-grain access control. Rules can also provide a "circuit breaker" against many kinds of cyber attack by instructing the network to immediately drop similar packets.

Looking more deeply into the rule modification, each new rule must specify one of the permitted actions (PASS, DROP, LOCAL or MAP), along with any modification to the destination address (see Section 6.4 for details on the firewall actions and modifications). The rule also includes management information. Suspected security intrusions are handled differently through proactive measures not discussed here; interested readers may contact the authors. The standard actions are include:

- Allow the source IP/port to reach an authentication agent
- Allow the source IP/port restricted access to a fully public service through an address defined by the access daemon; this may be either the requested destination or an alternate address
- Activate an application-layer protocol
- Direct the packet to the data proxy (DP) or other HTTP server
- Drop the packet

These activities "bootstrap" the service model. The AD receives raw packets as provided by the firewall engine. It classifies and determines the appropriate rule through reference to the cloud's current state. This includes peer rules, authenticated users, announced services, protocol definitions, type of network connection, and internal policies.

The classification process defines attributes, and then applies logic tables that produce the correct action. The attributes include:

- Whether the packet sources is an authenticated entity
- The access control rights of the authenticated entity
- The access control requirements of the requested service
- The strength of the authentication method
- The capabilities of the end point devices
- Declarations of security requirements of any connection that may be established (either proxy or to a server)

The access daemon attempts to identify the owner of the traffic; for example, by reference to the packet header. This allows reference to the access rules specific to both the service and the client identity, which of course must be irrefutable. Anonymous traffic, which does not provide an identity, utilizes the service's "anonymous" rules. These rules are flushed when the supporting connections cease to be authenticated and announced. Browser-based traffic utilizes HTTP-centric rules including use of the DP for protected sites.

Consider how a client can gain access to the cloud. New client traffic is completely unknown to the packet filter, and cannot even reach the authentication proxy! The packet is redirected to AD. The AD classifies the packet, selectively installs a firewall rule into an appropriate rule base within the packet filter session cache, and then sends the packet back to the firewall. The authentication daemon can then negotiate an authentication with the client.

The access daemon enforces policies before installing firewall rules. These policies consider the permissions of the connection source, including its authentication status. This supports the access control activities such as permitting or denying a connection to the port associated with a service. Since services have unique ports, the access daemon allows the connection only if a client is permitted access to the service at the given port.

The access daemon places rules into the session cache, and then returns the packet to the firewall. It must validate the request to determine the proper action. The access daemon validates the request in several ways. The destination IP/port must identify a previously announced service, as recorded in the ASR. The originator of the request must also own an access control entry for the requested service. For peer-based requests, the source IP/port identifies the originator through the authenticated user registry (AUR). For other clients – such as web-based – the IP packet contains identifying attributes such as authentication tokens.

The access daemon decides whether to install a DROP or a PASS rule based on the above information. When there is an announced and authorized service the access daemon installs a PASS, LOCAL or MAP rule. Otherwise, it installs a DROP rule. A PASS rule is suitable when no protocol mediation is required. A LOCAL rule activates protocol mediation at the local gate, and a MAP rule reroutes to receive services. The PASS, LOCAL and MAP actions are provided for full-public services; for cloud-public services when an authenticated client attempts access; or for cloud-private service when an authenticated client is subscribed to the service. Access is forbidden in all other situations, and a DROP rule is placed into the session cache to block any attempt

The access daemon obtains the new port for LOCAL and MAP (if any) by consulting the Active Service Registry (ASR) to obtain the service type that corresponds to the destination IP and port (as specified in the original IP packet). The daemon then examines data from /etc/GeoParams to obtain the new port corresponding to the service type. The redirection parameters are now known to the access daemon. It updates the firewall session cache and routes the packet back to the firewall. This mechanism is independent of the proxy framework. Section 9.4.2 shows a detailed example.

The access daemon returns the packet back to the firewall after installing a rule into the session cache. In this manner, the packet arrives at the firewall at most twice. The double-arrival occurs only on the first packet of any connection, and subsequent packets are described by the session cache. The packet can be IP routed as soon as the firewall specifies the destination IP and port. The session cache entries are duration limited and are purged upon inactivity. The access daemon will refresh the cache if a packet fails to be recognized due to recent purging of the cache entry.

The firewall's redirection and proxy support are also harnessed to combine multiple interacting clouds, as shown in Figure 9-8.

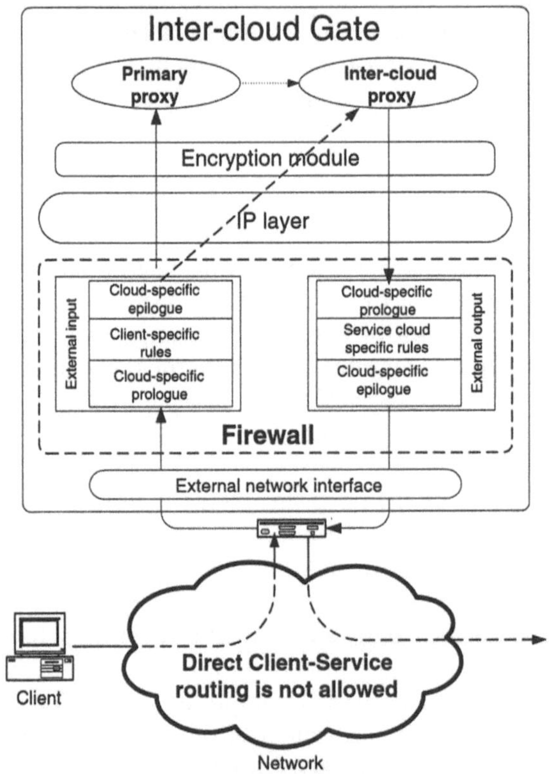

Figure 9-8: Multiple Cloud Firewall

9.2.5 Middleware-Based PKI and PKI Management

The mechanisms and deployment of middleware Credential Proxy (CP) controls all the credentials related mechanisms in the platform. This handles the generation/issuance, revocation and update of credentials. A Credential Management API supports the administrative management of credentials and is subject to standard middleware access control checks.

This gives a user the ability to access all the services provided by the platform with a standard web browser without the need for any additional client side software.

- Use of certificates issued by certificate authorities external to the platform – a commercial CA service, Intranet hosted CA, etc.
- Integration of CAs systems offered by different vendors
- Multiple CAs from multiple vendors serving the platform users

- CAs in unlimited hierarchy configuration
- Life-cycle Management (issuance, revocation, expiration, etc.) of certificate and CAs hosted by the platform
- Account hierarchy based certificate configuration, and CA trust policies

9.2.5.1 PKI as Basis for Wide Scale Single-Sign-On

Client certificates are a starting point for a specialized vision of single-sign-on (SSO) known as single-credential-sign-on. This exploits the standard certificates conforming to the X.509 v3 specification. All such certificates include a name field that is consistent with the X.500 directory structure of the issuing authority or third party certificate issuer service, such as Verisign Inc. Several vendors have demonstrated different approaches for enabling single-sign-on using client certificates. Many of them use a directory as the repository for user information, with certificates directly coupled to it for authentication purposes. Since, the Subject Name field of the certificate must – for all compliant implementations – correspond to the Distinguished Name of the X.500 directory, this appears at first as the most logical choice.

However, this tight coupling also has its drawback in terms of making it very difficult to change or manage the certificates, directory tree, and user accounts as the practical demands of business, and frequent changes, take place. It is also problematic for a service provider in the business of offering hosting services to existing VPNs, Certificate Authorities, and users. It is therefore advantageous to decouple the SSO notion from a traditional directory structure. While the X.500 directory structure may hold a user's information, it is not the sole repository of account and authentication information.

A provider can find greater flexibility with a domain database that includes an account tree of user authentication, access control and other information. This tree is consistent with the service provider's requirements and models of domains, accounts, sub accounts, users and services. Multiple certificates can be associated with any item in this tree.

Each certificate is identified through a numerical thumbprint. This is simply a message digest computed from appropriate certificate fields. A certificate becomes associated with an account through an enrollment process. This computes the thumbprint of the certificate, and associates it with the specified user account in the tree. The thumbprint provides a reliable and trustable association between the certificate and a user object within the account tree. The user object can be identified upon subsequent presentation of the certificate through a simple indexed lookup keyed from the thumbprint. Of course, enrollment and usage are subject to standards-compliant verification.

User-initiated authentication commences with a standard certificate-based authentication. This proves the presenter posses the private key. The platform then computes the thumbprint. The thumbprint identifies at most one user object in the account structure through a simple index lookup. This lookup obtains the unique user object that was created during user registration, and which was associated with the certificate during certificate enrollment. The platform may now authenticate the entity and grant access to the specified user object. This grants all privileges of the user object.

This method works for several simple reasons. It is *reliable* due to collision-resistance of the thumbprint function. It is *trustable* because the issuing CA is accredited by the platform. It is *secure* because the certificate subject must first authenticate by standard protocols that require the user hold the private key corresponding to the public key included in the certificate.

There mechanisms also allow the association of many certificate thumbprints with one account, as well as one thumbprint to many accounts. This provides the capability of providing different features and functionality to each user, giving a much broader SSO capability than use of a single certificate. A user may have multiple accounts in different roles, may authenticate from different platforms, and yet have a single-sign-on experience in terms of service accesses. These extensions require the user specify the name of the account that the user wishes to use. This architecture also allows for greater flexibility in certificate revocation and expiration management. We discuss the pieces of the structure in the following sections.

9.2.5.2 Credential Generation - Accreditation of Authorities

Protection against non-accredited CAs is essential given the relative ease of establishing a new, but possibly untrustworthy CA. Indeed, a rogue CA could easily obtain a wealth of personal information under the guise of low-cost or value-added certificates. In addition to securing a system against rogue CAs, there is also a necessity to ensure compliance with local requirements for certificate contents. Certificates should conform to appropriate configurations including certificate extension fields that may be unique to a specific CA. These are defined by administrative controls, and then are refined by the user preferences.

Certificate generation begins with the selection of an internally accredited CA. The user and middleware then provide the information to be written onto the certificate in accordance with policies regulating the CA. The middleware mediates the certificate content by control of data passing into the certificate request; this includes permitted, forbidden and required certificate extensions, as well as validity dates and algorithms. The middleware translates the user request to the specific form required by the CA. The middleware then supervises the secure request and import of the certificate and associated keys.

9.2.5.3 Credential Enrollment – Importation of Certificates

Credentials can be enrolled by a user for multiple purposes. The enrollment process first requires proof that one is the certificate owner. A representation of the certificate may then be entered into the domain database. When a new certificate is enrolled by a user, the credential management system computes two thumbprints, also known as message digests. A full certificate thumbprint is based on the complete certificate, and is appropriate for authentication. A partial certificate CRL thumbprint supports the revocation of third party certificates, and includes only the issuer name and serial number. This CRL thumbprint and the corresponding user account mapping are stored in the local CRL service. The subject name is neither needed nor stored.

9.2.5.4 Credential Revocation – Invalidation of Thumbprints

Revocation of a certificate takes immediate effect through the removal of the certificate thumbprint from the core database. The certificate thumbprint was initially generated when the user registered the certificate with the platform. Without the presence of the certificate thumbprint, a user will not be able to authenticate to the platform.

Removal of a thumbprint is the only function that is performed for third party (CAs not hosted by the platform) issued certificates. However for a platform hosted CA, a revocation request is also propagated to the CA simultaneously. This is managed by the Credential Management System that provides an uniform interface to the user or to the administrator for managing revocation of certificates for the platform.

The platform also uses CRLs crafted especially for third party CAs (not hosted by the platform) for managing revocation. The CRL management service on the platform periodically retrieves the CRLs from the directory locations specified by each of the third party CAs. The retrievals interval is specified in each CRL. A revocation service maps the information in the CRL to the local store of registered certificate CRL thumbprints and account associations. All matching CRL thumbprints are removed from the core database for user accounts. The certificate can no longer be used for authentication purposes.

The CRL service management also includes an interface to the standard Online Certificate Status Protocol (OCSP, RFC-2560) for certificate status queries by any middleware service. This service is also used by the Credential Management service to check the CRL before registering a certificate. The components are designed with appropriate abstraction of the interfaces, and this ensures a convenient migration path. Thus, if an OCSP service comes into existence for all CA services, or a future status checking mechanism is invented, the CRL Management Service could be easily changed to accommodate it.

9.2.5.5 Examples of PKI Management and Revocation Services

In conclusion of the discussion about PKI, the following shows several examples of a platform PKI integration service. This service is capable of supporting the services we have discussed above.

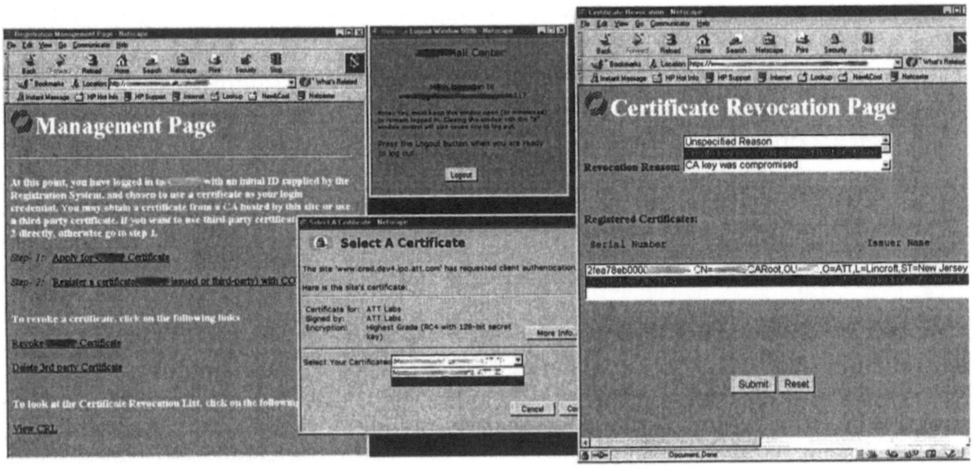

Figure 9-9: User-Managed Certificate Selection and Revocation

9.3 *Proxy Framework*

The second mechanism we discuss, namely the proxy framework, builds upon the packet filter of Section 9.1. The proxy framework provides a structured mechanism for definition, registration, activation and control of new components. The framework is specifically designed to accept the redirected connections of the packet filter firewall. Using multi-threading technology, it can support large numbers of simultaneous mediation processes. Since it is multithreaded, each client connection can be configured with private data storage; or, multiple clients can share a single thread. In either case, the new components, called data proxies, register to receive particular kinds of data traffic. The gate security architecture sends authorized data to appropriate data proxies. The proxy may utilize all gate capabilities. Proxies typically restore the original destination to each packet, with the option to forward the connection to other IP address, or to directly serve a client's request.

Some of the things we have done with the proxy framework include:

- *Security Extensions.* Support access to the security systems of third party systems, such as Microsoft file and print services, and integration of the Microsoft

Commercial Internet Service (MCIS) by means of common protocols such as LDAP (see Section 6.7.2.4)

- *Smart HTTP support.* Caching middleware is controlled through user-specific and account-specific monitoring of the hypertext, thereby enhancing the user experience (see Section 9.4.3.2)
- *Load balancing to multiple servers.* Both round-robin and feedback-based methods work to funnel traffic from a gate to the correct server
- *Multiple cloud interactions.* Support interactions and trust relationships between multiple clouds, as shown in Figure 9-8

9.3.1 Proxy Framework Mechanisms

A new runtime thread supports each new connection into the gate for a given proxy type. Data is decrypted as necessary upon entry into the gate. It then passes to the proxy framework. The framework receives each packet of data and may modify the data as needed. The proxy may invoke any API call, and can modify the traffic flow. Data then IP-routes between the ingress gate and the egress gate without undergoing encryption within the cloud. At the egress gate the data may be re-encrypted as required by the connection, and subsequently routes to the destination. A second proxy can optionally intercede on the data when required for specialized services.

Per-connection threading provides a robust method and highly capable development tool. The framework maintains limited local state information, thereby alleviating the otherwise *ad hoc* methods that would complicate development and maintenance. Client status is associated with the thread. For example, it can interact with the packet filter, support load balancing, and invoke multiple management functions. Per-connection threading is an appropriate mode of operation when providing sophisticated services.

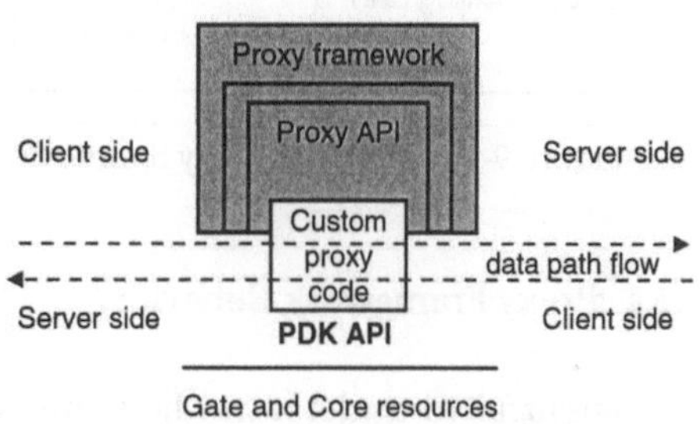

The proxy mechanism supports a general technique called *protocol mediation* where an IP connection may receive enhancement or modification as necessary. Network middleware enhancements can be constructed and fully integrated with other frameworks (such as security, usage, and event recording) by use of APIs to interact with the gate, core and network layers. These capabilities allow the cloud to deploy intelligent services. This builds on the bidirectional flow of data as it passes from the client to the server, and returns toward the client. This data passes through the proxy, as shown earlier in Figure 7-8 and repeated above.

A proxy can be easily developed and deployed into the gates. The simplest proxy is shown in Figure 9-10. The program consists of standard **include** statements, a proxy routine named **int sampleproxy**, and an entry point **void sampleinit()** that registers the sample proxy.

This **sampleproxy** is a trivial example that shows the basic features of the proxy framework. It provides a simple "pass-thru" proxy. The proxy code is invoked every time the gates authorize a specific kind of packet, as we will discuss shortly. The pass-thru example does not manipulate the data or invoke any network functions. The routine simply returns the **GEOERROR_PDK_OK** value, thereby allowing the proxy framework to resume control of this instance of the proxy. The framework writes the packet to the server side of the connection.

```
#include <stdio.h>
#include <stdlib.h>
#include <dlfcn.h>
#include <netinet/in.h>
#include <geoProxy.h>

#ifdef __cplusplus
extern "C" {
#endif
void sampleinit();
#ifdef __cplusplus
}
#endif

int sampleproxy(GeoProxyNetworkThread &thread, const int client_fd,
   const int server_fd, GeoConn side, GeoProxyMsg **buf, void *control)
{
  return GEOERROR_PDK_OK;
}

void sampleinit() {
#define PORT 2000
#define PROTO IPPROTO_TCP
  try {
         geoProxyRegister(sampleproxy, PORT, PROTO); }
  catch (xmsg &e) {
         cerr << e.why() << endl; }
}
```

Figure 9-10: Simplest Proxy Source Code

9.3.1.1 Proxy Framework Behavior

It is insightful to understand how and when the proxies are invoked. The following questions discuss the these issues.

When does the framework invoke the proxy?

Assume the **sampleproxy** is already installed as a custom proxy. The gate receives a packet from an authenticated peer, provides security services as required, and passes the packet to the custom proxy code, **sampleproxy** in this case. The proxy is now ready to run. It may call any of the proxy APIs; for example, to modify the packet, interact with the firewall, etc. The proxy completes its processing and returns **GEOERROR_PDK_OK**. The proxy framework now ensures the packet will route to the server side of the connection. From there it routes to the destination. Technically, the proxy framework uses highly efficient primitives of the underlying operating system to support a large number of proxies with extremely low overhead.

How does the proxy API specify what traffic should be sent to the proxy?

The proxy framework dynamically loads proxies and invokes their initialization handler. The initialization handler of our example was called **sampleinit()**. The initialization handler must always register at least one proxy. In our example the **geoProxyRegister** call specifies three parameters: the entry point of the proxy (**sampleproxy**), the port where the proxy should listen (`2000` in this case), and the protocol that the proxy will process (`TCP` in this case).

How many copies of each proxy are running?

The third question concerns the number of copies of the proxy. The framework creates a new thread for each active connection. A connection is a five-tuple `(Clientip, Clientport, Serverip, Serverport, Protocol)`. Thus, if one IP address contacts the port 2000 from five different source ports, there will be five threads. If a second IP address contracts port 2000 there will be a sixth thread, even if this reuses one of the source ports of the first IP address.

Once the proxy is compiled and linked into a relocatable shared library, it is dynamically loaded by the proxy framework.

How does one proxy support multiple independent connections?

The process is constructed with the proxy-framework that invokes POSIX threads to listen on the port specified by the proxy registration function (**geoProxyRegister**). When the listener accepts a new connection, the framework spawns a new listener thread, supporting subsequent connections. The previous thread opens a new connection to the connection to original service IP (step 5). Data will be written to this destination IP.

Once the connection is complete, the proxy framework waits for traffic by use of a blocking `pollfd` system call. It polls the `source fd` and the `destination fd`, and then reads from the first `fd` that unblocks the poll. The framework reads and buffers the data. The framework then starts the proxy function, passing it a pointer to the proxy instance, the two `fd`'s, the direction of data flow (i.e., an indication of the `fd` that received the data), and buffered message data. Upon return from the proxy function, the framework writes the data to the corresponding output `fd`. The sequence repeats as:

1. Create thread that makes a socket, binds and listens
   1.1. Thread will accept a connection from a client
   1.2. Thread executes initialization function
   1.3. Thread completes the connection to the server
   1.4. Thread yields
2. Poll, waiting for any the proxy's file descriptors (two thread)
   2.1. Find the matching thread
   2.2. Read the data
   2.3. Invoke the thread
   2.4. Write data back
3. Return resources when connection terminates

9.3.1.2 Summary of Proxy and Component Interactions

The cloud components communicate over IP connections. Static port assignments provide the simplest configuration; an example is shown in Table 10. These ports to support both standard and custom application-layer protocols. When necessary, the platform extends standard protocols such as `HTTP` or `HTTPS` and thereby simplifies the interaction with common services. One example of is secure formation of credentials, as well as authentication. A mini-HTTP server supports specialized client requests, and issues API calls to the authentication (and registration) components. These components interact with the domain API and the active registry API. In this manner we assure that content is served exclusively to authorized users (see Section 9.2.2, "Authentication Agents - Data Proxy and Secured Web 'Logins'").

TABLE 10: Commonly Used Ports

Purpose	Port
Authentication server	2113
Core server	2114
AUR service	2221
ASR Service	2223
HTTP caller ID	7000
Peer caller ID	9000
Control Daemon	41512
Peerless Proxy	41515
Peerless Certificate	41517
RADIUS Server	1812
Router Server	41507

The firewall and proxy mechanisms provide a layered and structured software architecture that supports the proxies and daemons needed at service nodes. Some of these proxies support the middleware infrastructure such as registration, authentication, and access control. Other proxies support IP services built upon TCP, UDP and other protocols within the TCP suite. These IP services are often referred to as *application protocols* to distinguish them from transport protocols. The application protocols range from simple (such as SMTP and POP3) to complex (such as H.323). The protocols may benefit from enhancements by protocol mediation, as well as "hardware assist" in the form of a protocol gateway. The proxy structure is designed to support both kinds of protocols in an API-driven manner. These integrated functions are shown in Figure 9-11.

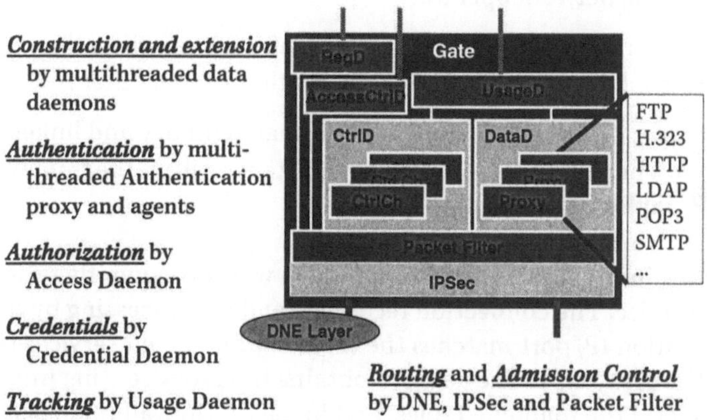

Figure 9-11: Packet Filter Protects Gateways and Supports Proxie

9.4 *Proxy Design, Deployment and Methodology*

Consider, for example, a new service we wish to add with a name (or "handle") of MYSVC. Proxitization of this service requires several steps: listing the service in the domain database; announcing the service; updating the system configuration; and installation of the software modules that provide the service. The access daemon will subsequently redirect the MYSVC traffic to a new IP address, which is most efficiently a different port on the local ingress gate. The SNode supports a multithreaded proxy framework that defines and operates multiple proxy instances.

9.4.1 Deployment of Proxy-Enabled Services

In order to define a proxy-enabled service, the administrator assigns an attribute known as the proxy type. The proxy type identifies one of the proxies previously installed into the network by the network operator. An administrator then associates the proxy type with the service object.

- The domain database describes the service object. This description contains a service ID that identifies the service, and is now updated to include the proxy type (also known as the protocol). The domain database describes the registered services, though they may not all be active
- A service announcement indicates that a service is now active. The announcement specifies the service ID, the proxy type, the service IP address (this can be implicit when announced from a peer), and the service port. The proxy type

identifies the application layer protocol. This can be standard protocol such as `TCP`, `UDP` or `HTTP`. Additional application-layer protocols are defined and installed by the network operator

- The system configuration file `/etc/GeoParams` describes the available application protocols, proxy types and the ports that support them
- The proxy was previously compiled into a shared library and linked to the proxy framework. The proxy was registered as a listener within the framework by use of the **GeoProxyRegister** function

Service requests – in the form of IP connections – will subsequently receive mediation *en route* to the service. The connection receives standard processing by the access daemon. The destination IP/port matches the table of announced services (i.e., the ASR), and identifies the proxy type. The daemon obtains the proxy routing information from GeoParams, updates the mapping tables, and installs a firewall that remaps the traffic the proxy. In-memory routing occurs when the proxy runs in the same memory space as the firewall, as typically occurs. These steps are subject to access control and other validity checks.

9.4.1.1 Proxy-Enabled Service Definition

This section expands on the example given above (Section 9.4.1), and shows the detailed service deployment that combines a server with an application-layer proxy.

An administrator initially creates a service object in the domain, thereby obtaining a cloud-unique `serviceID`. Services can run either on an existing IP protocol such as TCP, or a new application-layer protocol that runs on top of either TCP or UDP. The protocol name, identifying the application-layer protocol, must be defined in the system configuration parameters (`/etc/GeoParams`). The example below uses IP address 135.197.81.45 with a TCP application layer protocol named `MYSVC`.

An *announcement* later indicates the server is ready to receive traffic. The service provider advertises the service at the service port, for example 5556, and provides service by listening on the local IP address at this port. The service subscriber can use the service through a connection to the given IP/port.

The registration and announcement may specify an application-layer protocol, for example `MYSVC`. This ensures the connection will receive mediation services by the `MYSVC` protocol, which can be implemented as a proxy. The client connection steps are:

1. Client connects to the service IP/port
2. Middleware accepts the connection, and provides the application-layer protocol at the protocol port
3. Middleware either serves the request, or completes the connection to the service IP

4. This protocol may run on either the announced service port, or on its own unique port (called the proxy port). The middleware software will "detour" the connection to the proxy port
5. Client connects to the service IP/port
6. Middleware accepts the connection, and reroutes it to the proxy IP/port. This can be completely different from the service IP/port
7. Proxy provides application-layer protocol
8. Proxy completes connection to the service IP/port

For example, this could announce the service as:

```
IP=135.197.81.45
TYPE=MYSVC
ID=serviceID  (as assigned during the registration)
PORT=5556
```

The client connection for `135.197.81.45/10121` receives service at a cloud IP address at the port where the protocol is active, in this case:

```
ProxynnType=MYSVC
ProxynnPort=10121
```

This example can be implemented by an administrative update of the GeoParams configuration information, followed by a service announcement with the `manageAur -e` to activate the service IP/port. The announcement can also be accomplished with the SDK connection management APIs.

9.4.1.2 Proxy-Enabled Service Activation

Assuming a registered and active service, a proxy-based service can be activated by service-announcement with associated protocol and address information. Figure 9-11 shows all steps and traffic flows in detail. The example shows a service called the `michahsvc3`, for the purpose of example, running a proxy that supports an application-layer protocol (called `michah001`). The proxy runs on port 10121 of the firewall machine, and the service runs on port 5556 on the `store17.dom19.com` facility.

The steps are:

1. The service provider initializes the service with a service-specific command. This example uses the application-specific `Server` command with suitable options
2. The service provider's administrator announces the service, giving the service name (`michahsvc3`), protocol (`michah001`) and local address (`port 5556`)
3. The client requests the service by name. Naming services, including proxy DNS (see Section 9.4.3.1) resolve the name to an IP address; and advanced routing, where available, defines a suitable path to the service. This path may depend on the client and server access permissions

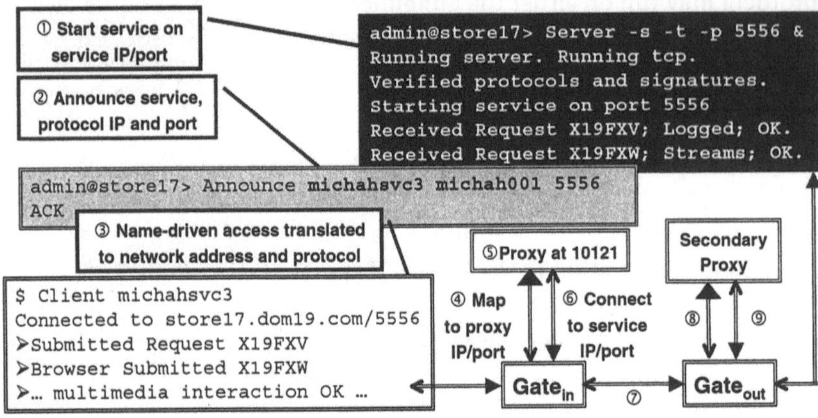

Figure 9-12: Announcement and Cloud Mediated Access

4. Client directs packets towards the service. In this example the service runs on store17.dom19.com port 5556
5. The firewall rules remap the packets to the `michah001` protocol that is active at port 10121. The proxy, active at port 10121, handles the request through a new or existing thread of control, as necessary
6. The framework remaps the proxy output to the service address
7. Secured communication between gateways
8. Optional proxy support at the egress gate
9. Connection routes to server, in this case store17 and port 5556

9.4.1.3 Proxy-Enabled Traffic Flow for Gate-Deployed Mediation

Port-specific processing of data permits construction of services upon the redirected IP traffic. The processing is provided by a proxy function, and the proxy function requires a framework to provide standard processing in a reliable manner. The traffic flow is shown in Figure 9-13. The proxies listen on the ports that the **GeoProxyRegister** function specified. This occurs regardless of the access daemon's activity. This is the natural behavior of the proxy framework or other listener-based process. The firewall, however, will not pass any data to the port unless a rule permits. A rule could be specified statically (for example by the rules.pre file) or dynamically (by the access daemon or an API call such as **gp_pf_add_session**).

When traffic arrives (step 1), the firewall checks for a packet filter rule that matches the protocol, source IP/port and destination IP/port. The packet filter does not pass unknown traffic: the firewall rules must contain instructions for the protocol, IP and port. Unknown traffic is sent to the access daemon, which installs a DROP, PASS or MAP rule (step 2). The daemon evaluates the security-related and service-related observables, including the type of authentication, the client identity, and the service requirements. The daemon constructs the appropriate access rule, which is then installed into the packet filter and the session cache. The daemon then sends the packet back to the firewall for reevaluation. For example, the access daemon could install a DROP rule, and the firewall would subsequently drop the traffic.

In the MYSVC example, the connection, destined for 135.197.81.45/5556, will be redirected to the access daemon. The access daemon finds that the destination IP/port must use the MYSVC application protocol. The daemon issues a lookup to the cloud configuration and obtains the ProxynnPort corresponding to the MYSVC protocol. The daemon installs the MAP, and sends the traffic back to the firewall.

The traffic will now match the packet filter. Figure 9-13 shows the destination IP change from $\texttt{Service}_{\texttt{ip,port}}$ to $\texttt{proxy}_{\texttt{ip,port}}$ (step 1). The traffic skips the access daemon (step 2), and proceeds up the IP stack to the TCP layer. Selected traffic may receive security services at the top of the TCP stack; for example, decryption (step 3). The TCP layer will direct the packet to a process that listens on the modified IP/port. The proxy framework provides one such process, one that conveniently creates a new thread for the connection (step 4), connects to the service address (step 5), and invokes the proxy functionality (step 6). The modified data is written to the service address and routes to the appropriate interface (step 7).

9.4.2 Proxy Design and Development Methodology

The network middleware provides functionality either with classical server-based components, or with the network-based components. Thus, the service of Figure 9-12 can be provided either at an end point (such as a server-farm identified by store17 in Figure 9-13), or in the network (such as proxy at 10121). The development and deployment decision requires understanding of performance trade-offs that are specific to each application.

9.4.2.1 Proxy Affinity and Server Affinity

Balancing these trade-offs can begin with analysis of target service or suite of applications. This arrives at a distinction between functionality and implementation. Various alternatives can be evaluated for their affinity to specific deployments. Components may benefit from proxy-deployment when they have any of the following characteristics. Each characteristic increases the *"proxy affinity"*. Some of the characteristics are:

- *Security.* The cloud defines a logical security perimeter. It is also physically securable. This protects resources such as data, programs and configurations. Elements within the cloud receive guaranteed access policies because there cannot be "back door" access

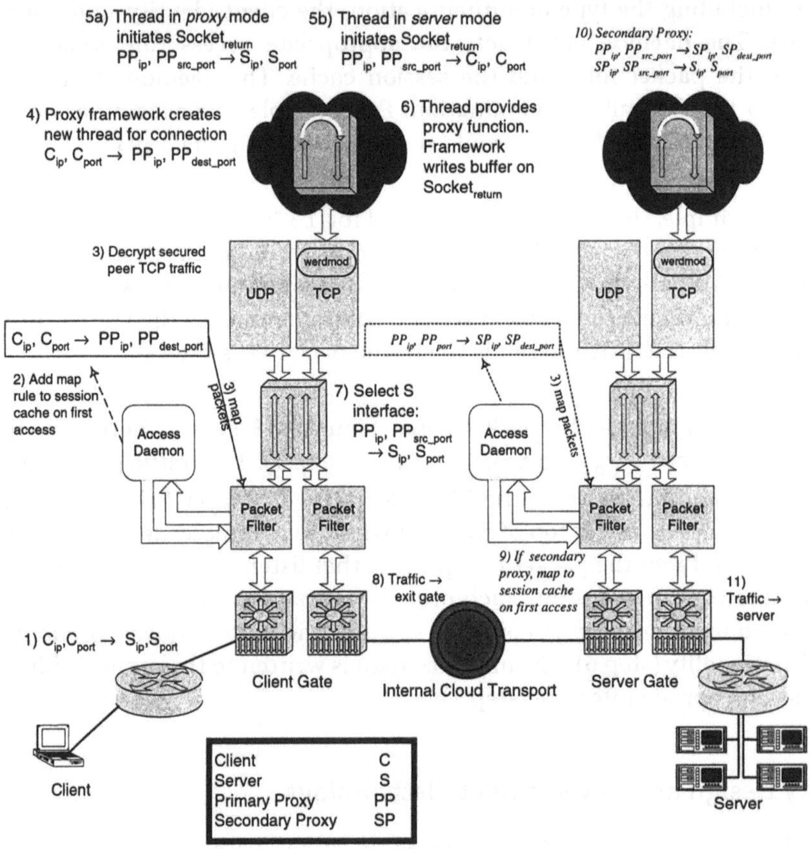

Figure 9-13: Detailed Traffic Flow from Client to Proxy and Service

- *Resource availability.* Cloud-centric resources may be more reliable, efficient or flexible from inside the cloud. For example, clustered computing elements adjust to specific load conditions
- *Path reduction.* The route to service may be improved by providing service at a cloud element
- *Composition.* Interaction between multiple external elements can be mediated through the cloud
- *Reusability.* Multiple services can use the same proxy component, and independent services' use is tightly controllable if required. Application layer protocols invoke these proxies as described above.

Designers may consider other characteristics that suggest deployment through the SDK rather than a proxy from external deployment in other situations. Characteristics that increase the "*server affinity*" include the following:

- *Size.* Very large databases reside on specialized servers
- *Existing applications.* It is easier to integrate an existing application to its own platform
- *Simplicity.* Externally-deployed elements, unlike proxies, may be designed and operated with fewer constraints

9.4.2.2 Examples of Proxy Affinity and Server Affinity

Security services, such as single-sign-on (SSO) are highly suitable for development as cloud services. These processes secure information, and are integral to overall resource management. SSO services are reusable by any external domain that chooses to allow access to cloud-authenticated users.

As a second example, consider a subscription-based virtual private network (VPN). A cloud could provide different VPN services, to accommodate both bandwidth-hungry demands of transport-VPNs as well as dynamic route encapsulation of private tunnel VPNs. Each service includes a *configuration* component and a *transport* component.

The configuration VPN has a large proxy affinity. It works with secure information such as the subscriber and service information. It directly affects resources, and should be available at low delay. The configuration component also interacts between multiple external components. Provisioned as a network proxy, this is an application-layer protocol available to authorized VPN providers.

Turning to transport, a VPN may be viewed either as a pure transport mechanism, or alternatively as a service access method. Transport subscribers require low delay with high bandwidth. They have little affinity for a proxy during the transport phase. On the other hand, service access VPNs may benefit from cloud-hosted features. Consider, for example, a managed VPN with the ability to terminate the VPN from within cloud.

A third example, the processing of a large database site, is left as an exercise for the reader. While the database might appear to have little proxy affinity, transaction processing (TP) introduces time-critical communication for record locking, concurrency control, and atomic commit. Thus, the TP applications can benefit from network assists including proxy support.

9.4.3 Enhancement Examples – DNS, HTTP and CIFS

Protocol enhancement and service support may occur either in the network or the end points, as discussed previously. We now present several examples of each kind of enhancement. The first, DNS, runs at a system end point. The next two – HTTP and CIFS – run in the network.

9.4.3.1 DNS: End-point Enhancement for Names and Services

When networks were small it was possible to assign a unique IP port to each service, and a unique IP address to each provider. However, IP addresses were intended to describe hosts, rather than services. This situation persists with naming services. The Domain Name Service[1] (DNS, RFC-1035) provides a highly robust and distributed lookup facility that resolves symbolic names to the provider's IP address. DNS was intended to define the mapping between host names and the corresponding IP addresses, or "provide a mechanism for naming resources in such a way that the names are usable in different hosts, networks, protocol families, internets, and administrative organizations" [RFC-1035]. DNS was not intended as a general directory service for service location, and is not subject to client authentication or access control. The X.500 directory, and the derivative Lightweight Directory Access Protocol (LDAP), attempt to resolve these naming issues. Newer protocols will likely provide a better solution; for example, the Service Location Protocol (SLP, RFC-2165).

A partial resolution of these challenges uses a technique of virtual IP addressing. The cloud can protect internal services by the selective routing of traffic to the appropriate internal service element. The external DNS identifies these services with the name `cloudvip` (for *cloud virtual IP*), along with an IP address on the cloud-internal sub-network. Internet routing protocols will then obligingly route the service-bound traffic to the cloud. The ingress gate then makes access control decisions and reroutes such traffic appropriately. The gate selects the best location to provide service. For example, an authenticated user may receive service at one destination. An unauthenticated user can be remapped to a different location. This affords the cloud considerable flexibility. Indeed, a similar approach is seen at the routing layer, where IP addresses can be associated with localized cache content or other replicas.

A second solution uses protocol enhancement of the actual DNS protocol. This occurs at the end point that provides service, or it can occur in the network. As such, it contrasts with the typical DNS caching that provides the global name at the end point that requests the service. The protocol supports the open distribution, maintenance and translation of host/address pairs, as well as associated information about the hosts. While the Internet owes its success partially to the effectiveness of DNS, the unprotected access raises privacy related issues.

A secure system requires selective export of names, and may also require variations on name resolution in accordance with subscriber access permissions. The end point mediation provides three overlapping name spaces:

---

1. DNS is defined by RFC-1034 and RFC-1035. Newer naming services extend the concept of naming, for example X.500, LDAP, and service location protocol (SLP, RFC-2165) that combines a service name with a set of attributes.

- *Externally visible name space.* This stores the NIC-registered domain names and network numbers. Connected peers are given the legal public IP address
- *Internal name space.* This stores internal protected resources, such as the addresses that implement the protected core network. Proxies redirect appropriate inquiries to the internally supported DNS server. The DNS protocol assures proper handling of external names
- *Proxy name space.* DNS running as a protected service resolves names on a per-client basis, and can further use the network middleware to enable routing for these clients as required

The middleware network intercepts DNS requests that are bound for the hosts in its address space. The DNS responses are generated selectively depending on the requestor's status. Naming is partitioned into internal and external names, with an additional proxy-based capability of selective response to external DNS queries. One solution is protection of internal cloud components by means of an *internal* DNS. This supports name lookups for private addresses within the middleware network.

Extending the idea of an internal DNS is an additional proxy DNS[1]. This provides selective responses that depend upon the client's identity and service profile. A conventional external DNS provides the standard functionality and resolves public addresses through the standard reference mechanisms. The internal and proxy DNS can be extended to support firewall-mapping, caching and routing as necessary.

The proxy DNS provides user-dependent responses. This enforces per-user limited views of the name space. The user-specific views adhere to the access control policies defined in the domain database. Reference to the user's service profile allows customizing responses to name queries. The proxy intercepts the DNS requests for names that are within the protected middleware network. The proxy can selectively respond to these requests, or alternatively forward the request to an external name server. For example, an authenticated user will succeed in name resolution for a cloud-public service, but an anonymous user will not.

9.4.3.2 HTTP: Web Development Framework

Every web browser has its origins in the hypertext transfer protocol, HTTP[2]. This general distributed request/reply protocol lets clients `get` or `post` information, and a server responds with HTTP headers or documents. The protocol supports the storage and transfer of state information (RFC-2109) through domain-specific storage called cookies. HTTP/1.1 supports persistent connections and defines caching behaviors

1. Steve Bellovin of AT&T Laboratories, for example, developed a proxy DNS for such purposes.
2. RFC-1945 describes HTTP/1.0, and RFC-2616 describes HTTP/1.1

including cache correctness[1, 2]. The Web Development Framework insulates services from variations in the HTTP version, changes in the security framework, and extensions such as XML pages.

The HTTP framework supports authentication, plug-ins, caching, and standard adapters. Conceptually, this monitors HTTP traffic, and executes system callbacks upon occurrence of specific detailed events; these events include appropriate headers. We find it useful to interact with client's HTTP requests at distinct points: upon the acceptance of a connection, upon receipt of a complete request, just prior to issuing a connection, upon the completion of a data transfer, or just prior to closing a connection. The action that occurs in each situation can be defined by a "plug in" code tailored to the design of the reply-request cycle.

The mechanisms can substantially extend the security and performance of the HTTP traffic. For example, this includes inherent support for secure transactions thus insulating software developers from the security layer. Consider an HTTP server or client that is protected by a secured connection to the network middleware. This could be an SSL, IPSec, or other protected connection. HTTP requests must be translated from the incoming security association into the outbound association. This allows each component to select its security method, and utilizes the network middleware as a "trusted broker" between the associations.

The second use of these data path enhancements improves service by selective redirection or caching. Load balancing translates the client requests into references to replicas of the required content. These replicates are provided either through explicit caches such as the Internet Object Cache (Squid) or advanced commercial caches. Such caches are often deployed as part of the network switching structure, where these data path enhancements can become fully integrated into the network.

9.4.3.3 CIFS: Data Path Enhancement for File and Print Services

Network enhancement can also extend security-aware protocols. Consider the Common Internet File System (CIFS, see RFC-1001 and RFC-1002) protocol. This permits access to file and print services on a Microsoft domain. It provides a measure of security through a challenge-response protocol in which the server enforces the domain's access control mechanisms. This requires that the client own an identity on the Microsoft domain, which can impede scaling and sharing of resources. CIFS' other fea-

---

1. We note that RFC-2616 discussion of cache behaviors cannot anticipate all future applications, and does not compel compliance by all Internet components. Indeed, content management is a complex area. A substantial component of Internet traffic carries the NO-CACHE tag to ensure correct content delivery.
2. Caching in the Internet is a major and complex topic, and the subject of many interesting patents (see for example Srbljic *et al.* in US Patent 5,933,849 "Scalable distributed caching system and method").

tures include multiplexing of multiple users over one TCP connection, as well as various kinds of file locking.

GeoCIFS maps the user, service registration and access control model into the NT domain and security models. This enables NT and CIFS servers, provided they are in domains that trust a GeoCIFS NT Domain Controller, to validate and control access for users. The GeoCIFS proxy (running at a gate) modifies the CIFS identity and credential information that users pass to GeoCIFS servers, thereby securing and tracking GeoCIFS usage. A user on a Windows 95 client running both the peer and Windows Explorer accesses shared files held on an NT server named \\SOFTWAREMART. The CIFS traffic between these is proxitized by the GeoCIFS proxy running on the gate. The 'soft_dom' NT Domain that \\SOFTWAREMART belongs to has an NT trust relationship with the 'geodev4_dom' NT domain. This allows \\SOFTWAREMART to both validate users from the geodev4 cloud, and also to use NT global groups of those users for access control.

The resulting coupling of platform with Microsoft networking provides enhanced user management, user authentication, service provisioning, and access control:

- GeoCIFS enables network operators and vendors to offer typical LAN-sharable applications to subscribers
- GeoCIFS offers a flexible service model enabling the CIFS server to support a variety of access models, including duration-based and time limited access to shared resources. These leverage the underlying CIFS/NT access mechanisms
- GeoCIFS supports advanced sharing of files and directories, enabling sophisticated multiuser applications, such as databases
- GeoCIFS supports advanced sharing of printers

It combines a peer-enabled account manager on a Microsoft domain, plus a network proxy that provides service to authenticated members of the network middleware. The account manager receives significant events from the network, and then modifies the Microsoft domain's account structure accordingly. For example, the account manager receives notification when a network user registers to use a Microsoft domain. The manager is notified whenever the subscription status of the client changes. Upon initial registration, the account manager creates an authorized login account on the Microsoft domain. Subsequent subscriptions affect the Microsoft domain as changes in NT global group memberships.

Now, when traffic arrives destined for the Microsoft domain, it will not have valid credentials to support the challenge-response protocol. These credentials are provided by the network proxy. Since the client identity is available within the network, the corresponding credential is provided on the client's behalf. The traffic may now route to the Microsoft domain and receive appropriate access.

GeoCIFS integrates Microsoft's NT Networking with a non-Microsoft network to enable use of Microsoft Windows NT networking by users. This provides seamless access to the shared network drives and printers on Windows NT Servers and other CIFS-compliant file servers. The initial deployment of GeoCIFS focused on the specific functionality of file-server and print-server access, with 100% integration between the user and the Windows NT security, and Microsoft's NT Networking, which uses Server Message Block (SMB) protocol.

Microsoft has published the SMB specification under the name Common Internet File System (CIFS) and has submitted a specification to the IETF for standardization. Numerous CIFS-compliant servers are available, including offerings from Microsoft (NT Server), AT&T (Advanced Server for UNIX Systems), Samba, SCO (VisionFS), and SUN (Syntax1 SMB server). The CIFS protocol builds on the services of NetBIOS. NetBIOS can run over NetBEUI, IPX, and TCP (using RFC-1001 and RFC-1002). Since the Internet supports IP-based service, GeoCIFS supports the NetBIOS-over-TCP, known as NBT (described in RFC-1001 and RFC-1002).

NBT traffic supports name services on the NAME_SERVICE_TCP_PORT (137 decimal) and the NAME_SERVICE_UDP_PORT (137 decimal). It supports session services under SSN_SRVC_TCP_PORT (139 decimal) and datagram service under DGM_SRVC_UDP_PORT (138 decimal).

By offering a service that exposes shared network disk drives that are accessed via CIFS protocols, service providers can offer subscribers access to virtually any application that can be shared over a LAN. In addition, subscribers benefit from file and resource locking capabilities supporting multiuser collaboration on databases, documents, and other file-based objects without risk to data integrity. Each shared network drive or file server can be treated as a service, and access to shared drives can be tracked by means of usage recording as appropriate.

GeoCIFS maps the user, service registration and access control model into the NT domain and security models. This enables NT and CIFS servers, provided they are in domains that trust a GeoCIFS NT Domain Controller, to validate and control access for users. The GeoCIFS proxy (running at a gate) modifies the CIFS identity and credential information that users pass to GeoCIFS servers, thereby securing and tracking GeoCIFS usage.

An essential component of the GeoCIFS is the account daemon. This is a peer application written with the SD. This component leverages the reliable event mechanisms of the platform. These capture significant events, and the daemon acts upon them. It can thereby maintain user accounts in the trusted CIFS domain. Whenever a client registration event occurs, the event is received by the account daemon. This daemon has a trust relationship with the domain controller of the hosting CIFS domain.

The GeoCIFS proxy provides enhanced services beyond the "mere" maintenance of credentials and passing of NetBIOS traffic. In particular:

- *Secure Connectivity Services.* The GeoCIFS proxy refuses to pass traffic from users to NetBIOS Application Services that they are not subscribed to
- *Advanced Name Resolution Services.* The GeoCIFS proxy's name service can consider a variety of factors when deciding which IP address to return to a client peer. Potential considerations include:
  - *Active Service Registry (ASR) integration.* The GeoCIFS proxy name service can resolve service names directly from the ASR database and return the IP address from the ASR
  - *WINS support.* Additional naming logic is added by proxy services, which build upon the standard WINS support provided with Microsoft products
  - *Localization.* Directing a peer to the GeoCIFS server that offers localization in their preferred language. For instance, \\SOFTWAREMART can maintain one server with English software, another with French software, and a third with German software. When a user tries to find \\SOFTWAREMART, the GeoCIFS proxy checks with the registration database to determine their preferred language, and returns the IP address of the server hosting the correct software localization
  - *Load balancing.* Intelligently distributing clients over an array of GeoCIFS servers, or directing them to the 'closest' server. This maps a name onto one of several IP addresses
  - *Fault tolerance.* Not directing clients to a failed GeoCIFS server, and use of backup domain controllers and WINS capabilities
- *GeoCIFS Group Membership and Client Authorizations*

  When a client wants to access a service in a Windows NT-based service, the GeoCIFS proxy performs two validation checks:

  1. The service must have been previously announced and is represented in the ASR
  2. The user must have subscribed to the service

     If either one of these is false, the connection is rejected

     If the conditions are satisfied, the GeoCIFS proxy will use the credentials <NT user name, domain, hashed-authenticator> to access the requested Windows resource. Because the user has previously subscribed to the service, the cloud passes traffic to the destination. Access will succeed only if the security descriptor of the target object grants access to the user.

     Because of the trust relationship between soft_dom and GeoDev4_Dom, \\MASTERPDC will authenticate "Fred". The \\SOFTWAREMART will accept Fred's request in accordance with the ACL entries of the object that Fred is attempting to access

- *Authentication by Credential Replacement*

  Security in GeoCIFS builds upon the secure middleware environment. The system identifies each user to the GeoCIFS server by a username, domain, and authenticator. The user name is generated from the user ID with a suitable masking option when client anonymity is required

1. The client machine of authenticated user Fred sends a request SMB with SMB_COM_NEGOTIATE in the Command field to the target Windows NT Server \\SOFTWAREMART in the resource domain. The message is intercepted by the GeoCIFS proxy at gate A
2. The GeoCIFS proxy forwards the message to the target server
3. The target Windows NT server responds with a session key in the return message. The return message is intercepted by the GeoCIFS proxy at gate A
4. The GeoCIFS proxy saves the session key and then forwards the message to the client machine
5. The client machine sends a session-setup request SMB to the target server, which is intercepted by the proxy
6. Assuming that Fred's user ID is 1234 and the name of the master domain is geodev4_dom, the GeoCIFS proxy forms the triple <1234, geodev4_dom, hashed-authenticator> and sends the SMB to the server in the resource domain
7. Note that the user already has an account in the master domain, since the account daemon created this on the user's behalf. The account creation occurred when the daemon, running as a trusted program on the PDC, received a "user registration" event. By combining APIs with the Win32 APIs it can create NT accounts and global groups, as well as maintain appropriate membership in NT global groups. The daemon is an SDK application that uses the event store feature of the Global Management and Monitoring Systems (GMMS) to receive notification of relevant events. After registering to receive notification of user registration events, as well as subscription to private services, the daemon processes these events and issues the appropriate Win32 APIs
8. Since \\SOFTWAREMART is not a member of geodev4_dom, it must forward the credentials to a domain controller in geodev4_dom for validation. This connection is proxitized by gate B
9. The GeoCIFS proxy forwards the request to the master domain PDC. The credentials pass unmodified through the cloud to the PDC, since the credentials at this point are encoded within a Microsoft RPC request
10. The master domain PDC authenticates the user against its own accounts database and sends the user's SID and the SIDs of all global groups in the master domain of which the user is a member, via gate B
11. The GeoCIFS proxy forwards those SIDs to the server

12. The server in the resource domain augments the packet of SIDs that it received from the master domain by adding the SIDs of the appropriate local groups from the resource domain. This augmented set of SIDs forms the core of the token that represents the authenticated user on the server in the resource domain.
13. The server in the resource domain compares the SIDs with the ACLs of the object that the client is attempting to reference. Access is granted if an ACE permitting the access is positioned before an ACE denying the access. Access is now complete. The server in the resource domain responds to the user's session setup SMB, via gate A
14. The GeoCIFS proxy sends the session setup response back to Fred. Moreover, the resource domain authenticates Fred, and authorizes his session. Thus, GeoCIFS is one part of SSO.

We note that rental of business software is a commercial reality through widely advertised sites on the Internet. This motivates another important service, real-time video on demand. Integration method using current technology can combine high-layer middleware with lower-layer network communications, as we now discuss.

9.5 Programmable Interfaces for Networks (PIN)

Thusfar we have presented the various roles of networking middleware, as well as some of the details behind its operation. We can now describe a specific application that leverages multiple network layers through middleware. This includes the negotiation of ATM flows through an IP service platform that integrates multiple transport mechanisms in a smart middleware network. The middleware provisions services with the transport mechanisms that are best suited for specific activities. In particular, secure transfers at low data rates have little concern with the underlying transport mechanism, although the transport properties may affect the cost of securing the traffic. On the other hand, high-speed isochronous traffic is sensitive to the transport properties; for example, ATM specifically was designed to support the QoS requirements of streaming video. While both traffic types can run on IP, the underlying transport makes a significant difference to the customer experience. The dynamic selection of appropriate transport is one advantage of smart networks.

Middleware networks are smarter, more active and yet less complex than either the intelligent PSTN or the "dumb" Internet. Rather than impose intelligence upon a existing infrastructure, middleware networks are constructed from the "best in class" standards, protocols and technologies. These are structured into layered interfaces, thus partitioning the network into separate and independent subspecies. This major design advantage contrasts with earlier systems that had to leverage existing physical infrastructure and optimize specific service requirements.

9.5.1 Edge Gateway Architecture and Distributed Network Element (DNE)

The proliferation of IP applications suggests an ever-increasing demand for end-to-end Quality of Service (QoS) increase. One viewpoint suggests these complex and interacting goals can be achieved through a Programmable Interfaces for Network (PIN), thus reducing the complexity into manageable components. The IEEE, for example, developed a PIN reference model that defines the vertical layers shown in Figure 9-14. Specialized networking groups continue to refine this model, thereby incorporating various perspectives on hardware, programmable switches, and protocols.

One model derived from IEEE PIN is the IEEE P1520. This defines specific interfaces at each layer, and the interfaces support containers for multiple QoS mechanisms. These include standards-based models (IntServ, DiffServ), as well as routing algorithms and flow-layer protocols. Each of these has a mapping to IP routing through the IEEE PIN model. The full model is described by [P1520].

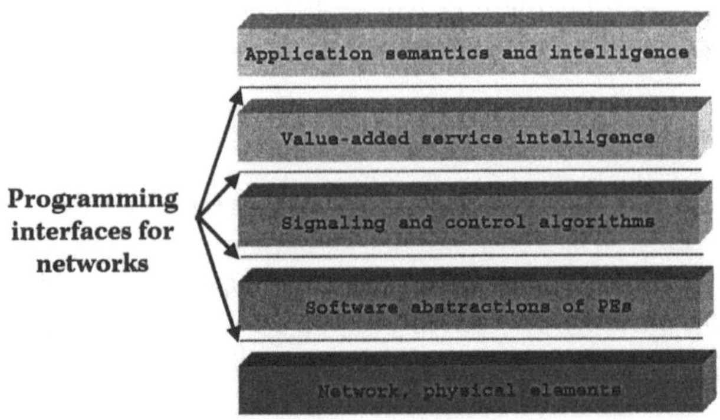

Figure 9-14: IEEE Programmable Interfaces Networks (PIN) Reference Model

The upper layers mesh with the high layer middleware services such as authentication, access control and naming (see Table 5 on page 227). Networking middleware interacts with the broadband network through for a generalized discussion of these issues.

9.5.2 Broadband Network Reference Implementation of PIN

Much like the first cross-continental railroad, the networking middleware meshes with the upper layer (management) interfaces in the networking stack. Following the IEEE PIN model, the feature set includes IP-based signaling and service creation through a open programmable network. This supports multimedia applications through appropriate underlying transports. The multiple abstractions in the underlying PIN models simplifies the combination of different technologies such as ATM with IP. The integration technologies provide solutions for important challenges in open networks:

1. Open programming interfaces
2. Support for Quality of Service
3. Programmable transport protocols.

Rather than exhaustively describe every DNE interaction, we present two examples that illustrate some of these capabilities. The first example leverages a broadband network of heterogeneous switching hardware pioneered by Xbind, Inc.; a prototype realization of the xbindIP stack shown in Figure 9-15. The second realization is the Distributed Network Element (DNE) that builds on standard APIs and hardware; see Section 5.5.2 for the introductory concepts, and Section 9.5.1 for details on the programming and internal models.

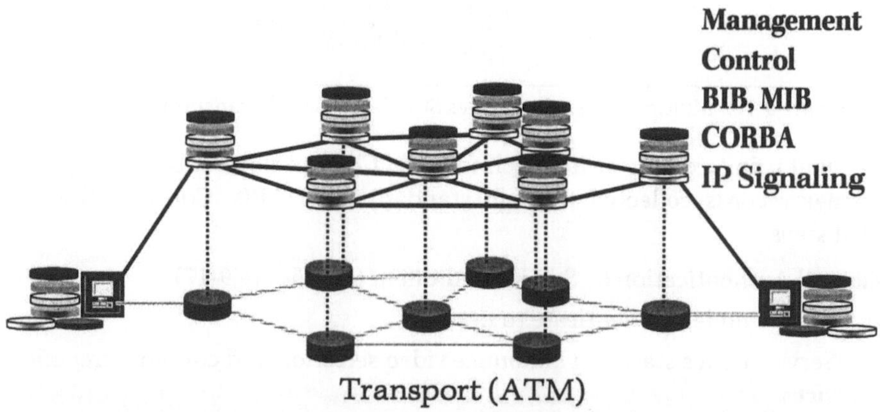

Figure 9-15: PIN Model Realization of Managed IP Over ATM

The xbindIP [LAZA97] provides service over a hybrid of IP control with ATM transport. IP connectivity maintains a flexible service-oriented network that leverages the full suite of middleware, thus leveraging the substantial IP infrastructure.

Selection and display of streaming video is one application that can use this multi-level structure. Figure 9-16 shows IP control through a cloud, with lower-level ATM switching fabric for content-delivery. This uses a mediating layer, in this case xbindIP between the underlying high-speed transport and the upper-layer control functions. At the lowest layer, a fully general transport system provides highly efficient delivery with well-engineered standards-compliant components. This was demonstrated at OpenArch-99 using hardware from multiple manufacturers including Cabletron Systems, Fore Systems, Hitachi and NEC (see http://comet.columbia.edu/openarch).

Services can use this structure in several ways. Consider purchase of media through the secured link by means of an HTTP web site. This requires authentication of all clients and peers thereby allowing capture of nonrepudiable usage information. The video service then invokes the mediation level to establish a high-speed transport link

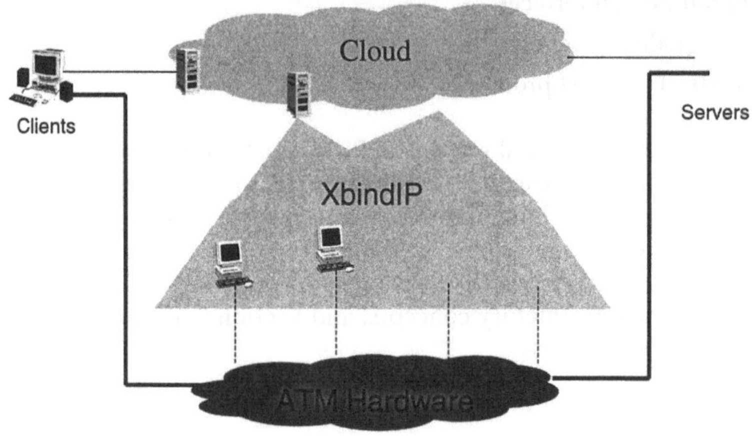

Figure 9-16: Multiple Layers Integrates Standards-Based Transports

to the client using existing switch technologies. Content flows subsequently, with suitable usage records collected through standard open APIs. Consider the following detailed steps:

1. Bilateral Authentication by Service and Client (see Figure 9-17)
    1.1. Service nodes authenticate to network
    1.2. Service nodes start and announce video selection and content streaming services
    1.3. Client node authenticates to network

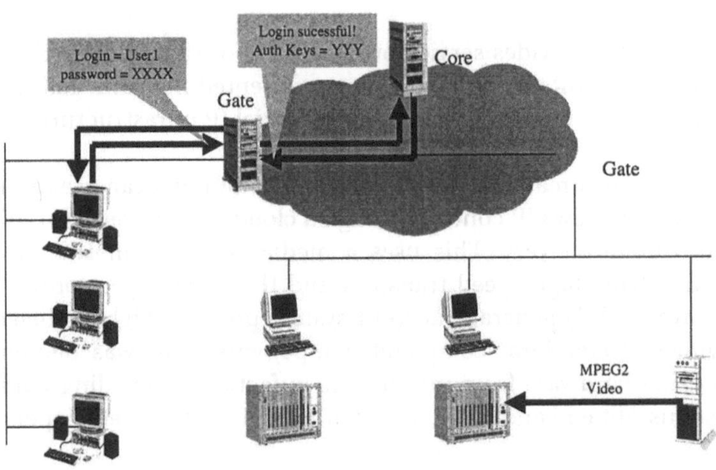

Figure 9-17: One-Time Secure Authentication Allows Client to Request Content

2. Client node visits URL and requests content
3. Service Delivery through Managed Transport (see Figure 9-18)
   3.1. Service node receives request and submits usage record
   3.2. Network elements negotiate connection to the client
      - The negotiated connection provides the appropriate Quality of Service (QoS) in keeping with the level service agreements between client, network and service
      - In this example this defines an ATM connection at a bandwidth that corresponds to the detail level requested by the client
   3.3. Content streams to client
4. Stream completes or connection-termination event is generated by an end point or an administrative component
5. QoS connection terminates
6. Service node submits total usage records

These capabilities are harnessed, for example, to securely establish a client identity and then provide an ATM session that streams video to the client.

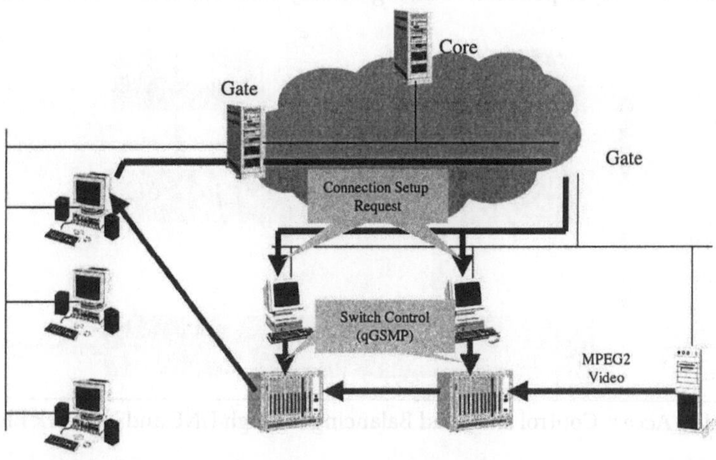

Figure 9-18: Client IP-Based Request with Delivery over High-Speed Transport

9.5.3 Distributed Network Element - DNE

To address such issues we devised an edge gateway architecture that is based on a Distributed Network Element (DNE). The defining feature of a DNE is the *flow separation*. Flow separation allows the small-volume control flows to be routed through the gate and the proxies, and the large-volume data flows to be routed directly through the elements. Flow separation can lead to a significant performance improvement while keeping the improved control over the network traffic expected in a service network. The DNE can be configured as a logical extension of the gate architecture, thereby enhancing the scalability and efficiency.

Within the network node (i.e., the gate), the Network Element Adaptation Layer provides a uniform abstraction of the Network Element. This defines, for example, the buffers, policies, and other behaviors that are enforced by the switches outside the SNodes. In general, any gate process should be able to access and control the network element. A client program may access and control the DNE through an API layer, known as the DNE Control Daemon (DNECD).

The DNECD implements methods that communicate with the network elements using well-defined control protocols, and interacts with the access daemon (AccessD) and the load balance daemon (LoadBalD), and thereby defines routing policies. The supported features include the network layer resource allocation and scheduling, and this allows the development of highly efficient components. The lowest layer consists of a driver that is implemented as a dynamically loadable module. The module implements methods that communicate with the network elements using well-defined control protocols, and interacts with gate functions such as access control and load balancing, and thereby defines routing policies. It is implemented as a dynamically loadable module running as a user layer process running on any host machine with a valid TCP/IP stack.

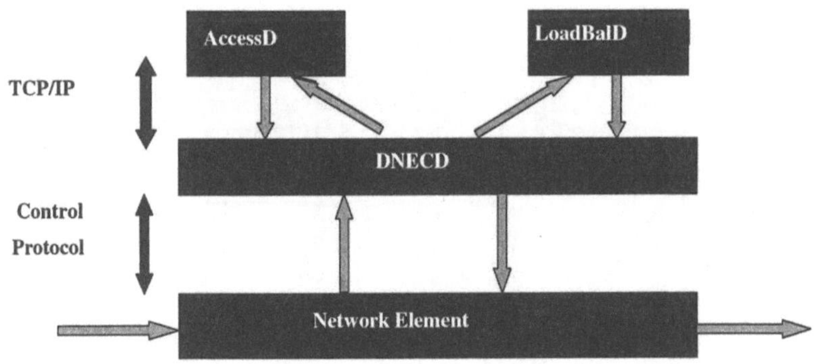

Figure 9-19: Access Control and Load Balancing through DNE and Network Elements

In addition to DNECD, the Network Development APIs (DNEAPI) support increased integration of the software-defined gate architecture as it interacts with the DNE hardware and switch-defined network infrastructures. The DNEAPI is provided in C++, CORBA and Java; there is also a GMMS interface for relatively static management and monitoring of the DNE. Its functionality includes:

- Quality of Service
- Routing/Address remapping
- Packet Filter

- Firewall/Security
- Control and Management
- Flow Separation
- Monitoring

The API obtains the requisite functionality through underlying data structures. These describe *flows* and *rules*. Flows are stored in `FlowDB`, a hashtable keyed on the 5-tuple (source IP, source Port, destination IP, destination Port, protocol ID). The table describes all specific flows, and does not have any flow with wildcard attributes. `RuleDB` contains general rules. It has the same structure as FlowDB, but supports wildcards in the FlowSpec. Access-policy objects describe the composite flows, flow-bundles, listener addresses, and actions, shown below.

```
FLOW a,b,c;
a.ACTION=PASS;
a.SPEC={*,*,135.197.25.94,*,*};
FLOWBUNDLE x;
a.BUNDLE=x;
x.SETBUNDLE;
b.ACTION=PASS;
b.SPEC={135.197.25.94,*,*,*,*};
```

By establishing a privileged control plane to modify these two DBs, the DNE provides highly secure network control. The `RuleDB` structure defines network-layer access controls and paths, forming the basis of securable IP networks. Data flows can be enabled or stopped through the definitions in FlowDB and RuleDB.

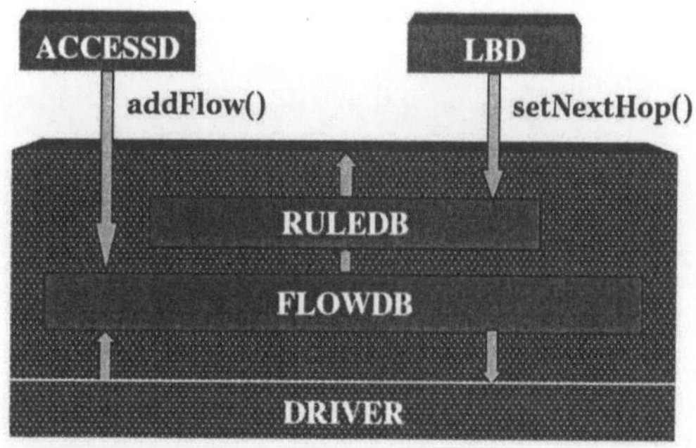

Figure 9-20: DNE Data and Control Structures

The Network Element Adaptation Layer provides a uniform abstraction of the Network Element. This architecture is highly scalable for multimedia applications and avoids an important bottleneck for high bandwidth traffic – the network node. The dual system containing the network node and element behaves like a single virtual network element but with its functionality implemented in a distributed manner. It promotes a new concept through which using open and dynamic API and standard protocols, the network elements and nodes constitute a tightly coupled dual system.

9.6 Summary

This chapter presented a wide range of mechanisms that support reusable software in a distributed environment. The idea has been to "factor out" the common features and form a standardized "substrate" that supports the development of new and varied components. These components can easily obtain services from the substrate through the common APIs, including authentication, access control, extensibility and security. These APIs allow development of reusable software components that draw upon these middleware-enabled capabilities.

The mechanisms are network-aware and enforce the platform principles. This supports standard behaviors that leverage the network as a source of managed capabilities. Thus, internationalization happens at the client SNode easing the entry of a service to new markets. Security is customized and adjustable in accordance with the safety of the physical connectivity and demands of the application.

These activities all occur in a managed framework. This management system is the topic of the following chapter.

CHAPTER 10

Systems Management and Monitoring

A given cloud based on an IP service platform is a distributed system with hardware components such as servers and routers and software components seen as processes that function as proxies, relays, monitors and servers. From the operational viewpoint all these components need to be constantly monitored and managed to maintain a smoothly running cloud.

In this chapter, we look at how these hardware and software components are monitored and managed. We base the software management on the GeoPlex Management and Monitoring System (GMMS). We base the hardware and network management on some third party SNMP-based tool (NMS). This chapter offers a detailed look at GMMS and offers a detailed view of its event notification and alerting system that have proven useful for operations, accounting and maintenance (OA&M).

When confronted with a combined software and hardware management challenge, most operators resort to an SNMP-based solution for the hardware and network management as well as a solution for the software management. This well developed solution is appropriate in a hardware and network-oriented operation in which the software components are light and easily managed. In a software-oriented environment, such as a cloud relying heavily on an IP service platform, this is not such a great solution; here, the software management part can greatly benefit from the GMMS approach where only the hardware and network components are left to the third party network management system, while the software components are managed by GMMS. Additionally, GMMS ties the entire system together into a single managed space as seen by the system administrators. This provides greater resistance to difficulties inherent in SNMP, including its separation from the specific service requirements, as well as sometimes creating network problems[1]. It also eliminates much of the inherent complexity of attempting to overload SNMP with general software management tasks for which it does not offer an elegant, simple, and general solution.

Lets look at two well-known commercial products, one from SUN, called the Enterprise Management System (Sun EM); and the other from HP, called OpenView/ITO (HP IT/O). Both have two parts. One is related to hardware (SNMP compliant). The other is related to software. The software processes are managed with non-SNMP methods based on Remote Procedure Calls (RPC). For SUN it is EMS using ONC-RPC (Open Network Computing); for HP it is DCE-RCP (a version taken by Microsoft and bolted onto NT). In either case, the software parts are not SNMP compliant and they are too complicated and cumbersome (a similar fate plaguing RPC in general).

SNMP-2.0 was supposed to solve this problem, but with too many companies adding their requirements, it got way out of hand, leading to a nonstandard set of competing products. In the case of HP, SNMP was scrapped and replaced by a pure RPC control. Consequently, to run HP IT/O, one needs HP machines and a special version of Oracle to get the entire OpenView/ITO operational. Furthermore it offers authentication, in the form of Kerberos, a security system used by DCE-RPC. Although this is a viable solution in itself, its use would require a complete bypass of the clouds authentication method if implemented without Kerberos. Again, to integrate the two authentication methods this would require additional effort and could even eliminate the single-sign-on feature offered by a cloud.

Interestingly, even if the cloud was to add SNMP-capable MIBs for all its software components, it would still require the implementation of agents as well as GUI management applications using the third party vendor APIs. This would lead to the vendor specific implementation. While this may not be a bad solution for any one particular deployment of a cloud, it is not a viable solution in general. Each cloud's management and monitoring system would subsequently have to customized for the underlying network infrastructure and its supporting third party NMS.

As such, our approach is to leverage any third party network management solution such as the HP IT/O or SUN's EM to monitor and control the health of hardware and network infrastructure, including any of the third party software middleware components that are SNMP compliant. However, for monitoring and managing the software components that make up the cloud's IP service platform, we require a general solution that is third party NMS independent.

For this, we propose a system such as our GMMS. This dual approach offers the greatest flexibility for the cloud operators that may want to use their third party NMS tools, yet require the complete control over the IP service platform. By offering the platform with an inherent ability to monitor and manage itself, it becomes a simple matter to tie the software platform and the underlying hardware infrastructure together. Without the inherent self-management and monitoring of the software platform, having to inte-

1. Cite "Network Storms" in *Distributed Systems.*

grate the management of the software components into the third party NMS could be extremely costly if not outright impossible.

From the software management point of view, a cloud consists of many interdependent processes running on gates, core, and store machines, interconnected over both the internal and the external networks

Fundamentally, GMMS is a hierarchical distributed event system with embedded agents (as shown in Figure 10-1). The GMMS architecture consists of a single system monitor (SM), subsystem monitors (SSM) and management agents (GeoMAs). These logically form a tree with the SM as the root, the SSMs as the internal nodes, and the agents as the leaves. The nodes communicate with simple text-based protocol that allows the recipient (SM, SSM, or GeoMa) to execute commands described by a simple text-based command line syntax. The syntax originated from an early interpretation of these commands in the Tcl language. The protocols also allows for general text-based replies and alerts. The whole system is then accessed from web-based GUIs running on remove peers or consoles connected directly to the core machine.

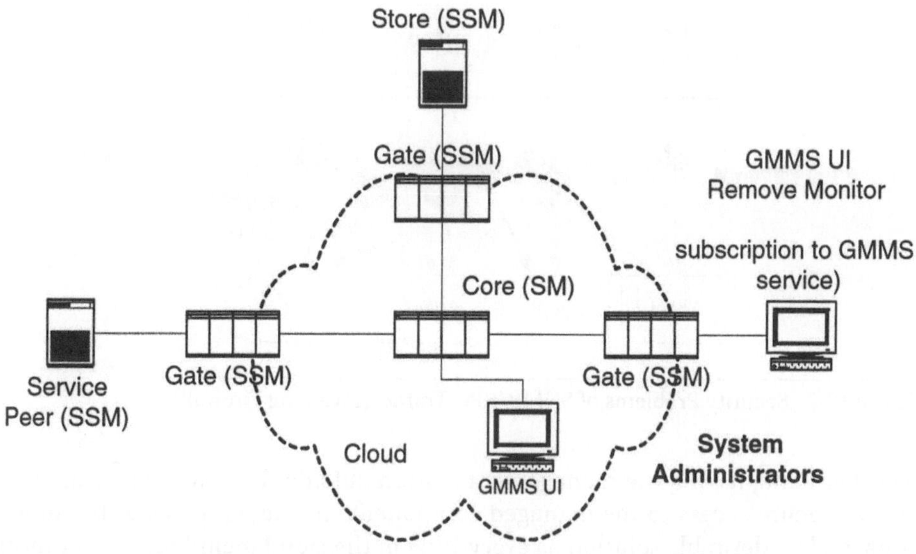

Figure 10-1: GMMS Web GUIs for Remote Management of All Components.

There is a GeoMA for the Java language, and also for C/C++. Gate components such as the control daemon, the data daemon, the cache, the usage daemon, and the active user directory are linked to GMMS through their GeoMAs. This offers system level logging, and built-in commands such as manipulating the log level, measuring cpu and memory usage, or obtaining version numbers. In addition, control commands can be issued directly to these daemons through the GMMS console.

10.1 Third-party Network Management System

Given that it is essential to support third party NMS for the hardware and network infrastructure, it has always been a controversial issue as to where to place it in relation to the cloud. Placing the management station (of an HP IT/O, as an example) inside the cloud security domain raises the issue of allowing access to operators in a secure manner across the firewall. Also, devices such as routers and modem racks that are outside the cloud have to be accessed for monitoring and management. Recall that using a system like HP IT/O uses SNMP and RPC. Here, opening up the cloud's firewall for SNMP and RPC traffic raises security issues. Figure 10-2 highlights the problem of managing external SNMP enabled devices from inside the cloud, if this requires that the administration open a number of permitted connections through the cloud firewall for SNMP traffic.

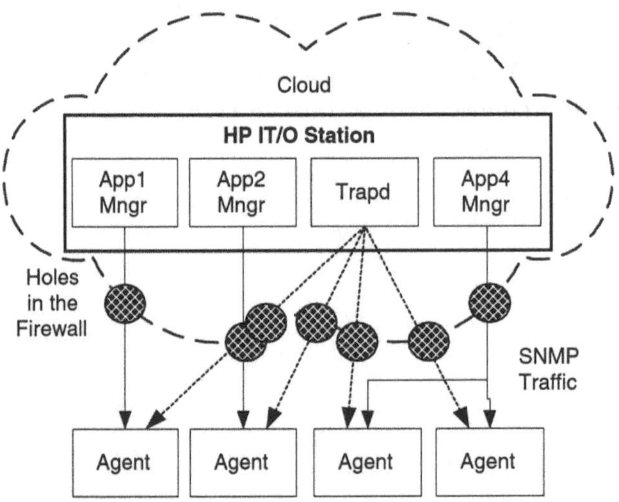

Figure 10-2: Security Problems of SNMP/RPC Traffic Traversing Firewall.

On the other hand, having the management station outside the cloud raises the issue of effective, secure access to the managed components inside. From security point of view, this is a less desirable solution as everything in the cloud including the bordering edge gateways need to be secured. Putting the station outside is like placing the king outside the castle to conduct the battle.

Although this may be a preferred configuration in certain deployments, a general recommended and tested configuration is to place the NMS station inside the cloud and then solve the issue of how to manage components outside and how to offer remote monitoring. The solution to the problem is to have an intelligent firewall and an SNMP proxy at the gates. The proxies filter SNMP traffic according to the policies and rules of the cloud. Alarms can be raised and automatic intrusion-prevention mechanisms

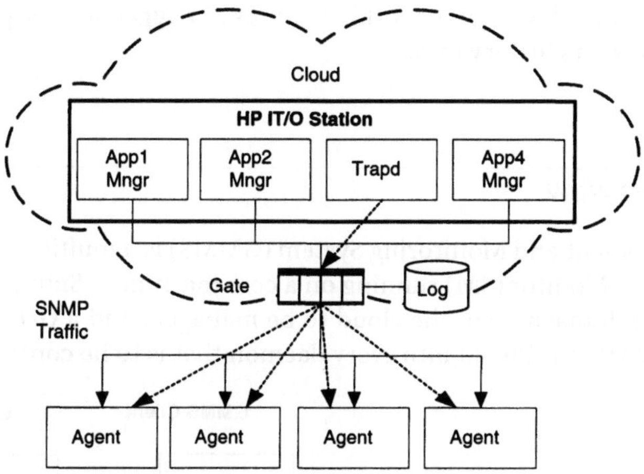

Figure 10-3: Firewall/SNMP-Proxy Solution

imposed if certain configured thresholds are reached. This solution is shown in Figure 10-3. This is a general solution that can be used for other services and legacy systems. The whole nature of the platform, as based on the design principles, offers a general mechanism for mediating protocols; in this case SNMP.

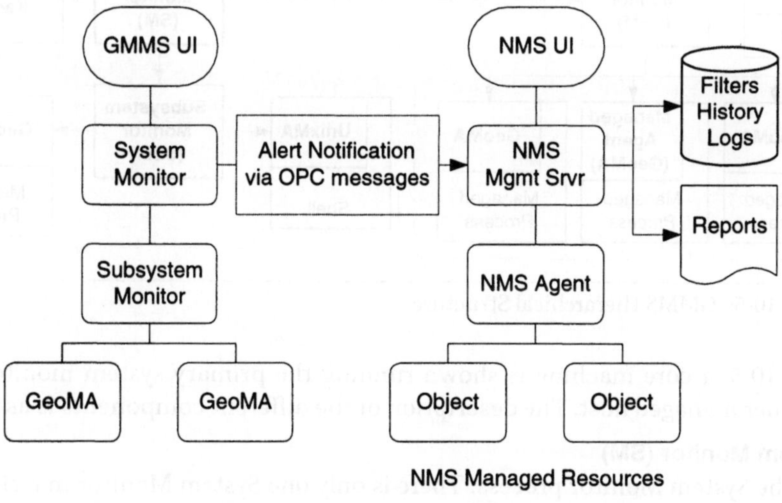

Figure 10-4: GMMS and NMS Integrate Application Management

With GMMS in place it can be easily integrated with the infrastructure NMS, such as HP IT/O, as shown in Figure 10-4. GMMS feeds alert messages into the NMS from the system monitor by mapping GMMS alerts to OPC messages via an OPC agent. This also allows the entire system to leverage the NMS's features to trigger alarms, perform automatic actions, or utilize its history logs.

10.2 GMMS Overview

The GeoPlex Management and Monitoring System (GMMS) is a multilayered hierarchy composed of a System Monitor (SM) running on a core machine, a SubSystem Monitor (SSM) running on each machine of the cloud to be managed, and a GeoPlex Management Agent (GeoMA) that is linked into every daemon that is to be controlled.

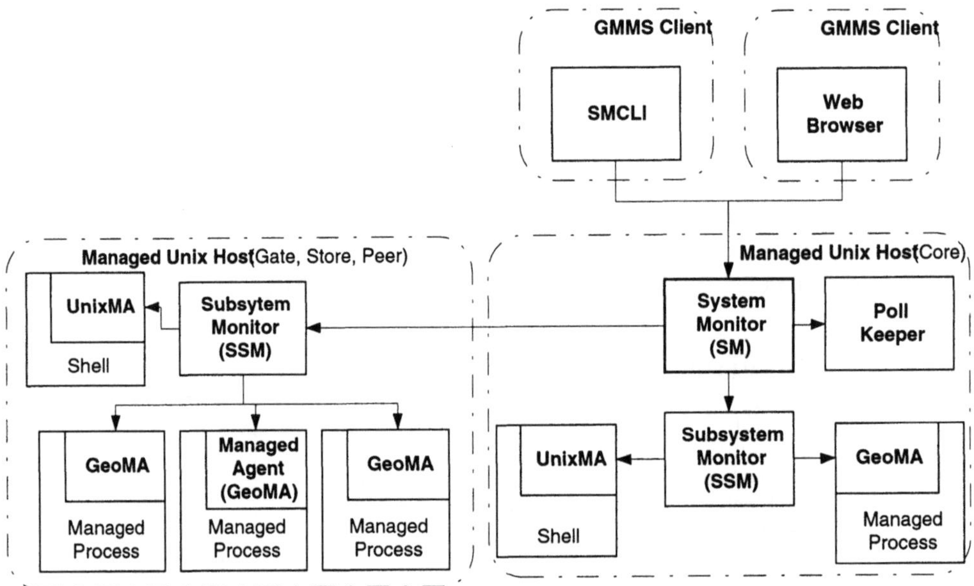

Figure 10-5: GMMS Hierarchical Structure

In Figure 10-5, a core machine is shown running the primary system monitor along with another managed host. The description of the different components is as follows:

System Monitor (SM)

The System Monitor process. There is only one System Monitor in a cloud. Once started, it listens for SSMs to connect to it. Of course it can explicitly start or restart specific SSMs. When the System Monitor starts, it initiates a Poll Keeper process alerts

SubSystem Monitor (SSM)

This is the SubSystem Monitor daemon. There is one SSM for every host in a cloud. When started, the SSM tries repeatedly to connect to the cloud's SM. Through the SSM the system can then reach the host's local daemons via their GeoMAs. The SSMs are responsible for monitoring the health of the network and the local daemons

GeoMA enabled processes
are linked to the GeoMA library. They execute GMMS commands and generate GMMS alerts. The UNIXMA is a special agent that allows an operating system level control over the host. The GeoMA daemon runs even if its SSM fails or is not present. In this way, the entire SM/SSMs hierarchy can be stopped, restarted, or turned off completely without affecting the normal operations of the cloud. Of course, without the GMMS the administrators are blind and would have to resort to standard means of monitoring the system such as open a TELNET or SSH connection to a host and executing administrative scripts by hand

UNIXMA (and WinMA)
is a GMMS daemon that exports shell commands to the GMMS system. It facilitates access to UNIX shell commands. Typically, one UNIXMA process runs on each UNIX machine and is associated with that host's SubSystem Monitor. The same holds for a Microsoft's Windows NT machine running a WinMA

GMMS clients
are applications, such as an Internet browser or the System Monitor Command Line Interface (SMCLI), that connect to and communicate with GMMS

GMMS commands
are issued by GMMS clients and delivered to the System Monitor, SubSystem Monitors, or GMMS daemons. GMMS commands result in replies to the issuing client. Replies may be in the form of error messages if the command execution failed

GMMS alerts
are messages generated by the System Monitor, SubSystem Monitor, or GMMS daemon and delivered to all GMMS clients

GMMS is registered as a private service. Administrators can authenticate from any peer, establish an encrypted connection, and use a browser to access GMMS. Each SSM listens on port 2016 to locally running daemons with their embedded GeoMa's. The SM listens on Port 2015 for SSM's and 2014 for UI's (Java). SSMs' on stores (peers) connect to SM though gates after they are registered and authenticated. So network management runs as a standard service on a cloud and relies on the same security measures offered to all other services. That is, encryption form store machines is standard peer encryption.

Most of the software components in a cloud connect to GMMS. This provides a way of accessing each component's state and controlling its operations. Components connect to GMMS through an API provided by the GeoMA library. However, daemons can be controlled in two ways: directly through a link in the GeoMA library, or externally through a UNIXMA process that contains the GeoMA library. Using a UNIXMA process, an administrator can check process status, read data files, or perform almost any task that could be accomplished at the system console.

A GeoMA API allows one to dynamically define new commands. For example, to initialize, run, or export commands. With initialize and run, GeoMa links to the system. With export one can creates new commands accessible through GMMS. These commands can then be invoked by the GUIs to access certain specific functionality in a given component. There are a few standard ones.

There is also a poll keeper that initializes pollers in the UnixMAs. Polling is used to ping the status of noncompliant daemons. As we already indicated, most of the components that are integrated into the cloud are compiled with a dedicated GeoMA that can asynchronously alert the system of events that need management. However, not all daemons are extended with a GeoMA interface. There are components, such as third party or legacy daemons that cannot be so extended. In these cases, an external mechanism needs to be set up to handle these functions. Typically, this is done with some command line scripts running under a UnixMA. Very much like the Unix Cron, the poller runs these periodically to sense the status of the components. When you start GMMS, it starts the poll keeper, SM, and one UnixMa. The poll keeper reads the configuration of the system, and for each component it runs a dedicated pollers. These are applets that get downloaded from a web server running on some core machine.

10.3 Event System, An Overview

An event system provides a way of interconnecting components in the system that need to exchange relatively small amounts of data (e.g., control messages, or events, notifying each other of significant changes in the system). Components that generate events do not need to know about recipients of the events; and similarly, components interested in notifications about significant changes in the system do not need to know which components generate the events. The event system works in such a way that even when a component is offline, for a limited amount of time, events are delivered to the components that subscribe to those events upon the components' activation. Components make use of a simple API to interact with the event system.

Two examples of component interconnections that use the event system are:

- Notify system components of updated configuration, so these components will refresh
- Notify system agents of changes to the domain database, so these agents can alert and adjust third-party systems accordingly

10.3.1 Event System Concepts

Event producers generate events of a specific event type. Events in addition to event type include event priority and event data. Event type has to be registered with the event system, or more specifically with the EventStore daemon. Each event type is associated with the event queue size limit and the event storage time limit (or ttl). Event consumers subscribe to specific event types, and each event producer and consumer has to register with the event system, i.e., with the EventStore daemon, through the event system administrative APIs. The gmms command is perhaps the most convenient way of accessing the administrative API. It can be however also accessed through the geo.sysmon package; i.e., through the GMMS client API. Components are uniquely identified with their GMMS names and the physical location where they run, e.g., Aur/coredb, ControlDaemon/gate2, peer/mail, EventStore. This allows multiple and selective naming of the events.

If a component is accessing the event system from outside the cloud trusted domain, a user on whose behalf the component executes has to ensure access privilege and subscription to the GMMSstore service. GMMS subsystem has to be running on a machine for events to reach components on that machine. A more comprehensive access control mechanism will be provided in the future.

Components make use of simple event client APIs to send and receive events. The APIs include both synchronous and asynchronous APIs for sending and receiving events. The APIs are provided in Java and C within the gate development (GD). A component may miss an event if the component is offline for too long. The number of events a component missed can be found through the administrative API mentioned earlier.

10.3.2 Implementation

The event system is implemented using C and Java programming languages, with GMMS as transport mechanism. Main components of the implementation are EventStore daemon, administrative APIs, C client APIs, and Java client APIs. The event system implements "at least one" delivery semantics. Events can be repeated very seldom, thus the semantics are very close to "exactly one". Implementing "exactly one" delivery semantics was highly impractical. The EventStore daemon runs on the core machine and acts as a GMMS daemon connected directly to SM; i.e., at the level usually inhabited by SSMs. EventStore is implemented in Java. It uses PSE Pro 3.0 database from ObjectStore to store event type, component, subscription and undelivered event information. EventStore accepts events on TCP port 2017, and delivers events to components through GMMS. There are two main threads in EventStore. The accepter thread accepts events from components and stores them in memory, after which they are acknowledged to the components. The deliverer thread takes events from memory, stores them in the database, and continually attempts event delivery. As events expire, or exceed the allowed space, deliverer thread removes them from database and accounts for missed events with the relevant components. (The current implementation has the deficiency of keeping events in memory for a short time. This trade-off between performance and reliability was made to improve performance of event generation, and reliability will be improved in the future by storing events temporarily in a file.)

Administrative API is implemented in EventStore as a set of GMMS commands. These commands provide capabilities of creating, updating and deleting event types, subscribers, and subscriptions. The commands can be sent to EventStore using gmms(1) shell command, using geo.sm.Sm class; from Smlet GMMS client applet; or from any other GMMS client through the geo.sysmon GMMS API. The administrative API is described in detail on the gmms(1) man page.

The C API is implemented on top of a layer of reliable GMMS protocol. Reliable GMMS implements retransmissions, acknowledgments, duplicate message handling, transparent connection establishment and reset, etc. There is a queue of events between reliable GMMS and C API. GMMS deposits events in the queue. C API removes events from the queue and acknowledges event reception after its processing. This means that event is acknowledged as soon as the geoEventRecv() function returns, in case of synchronous event receive, and after the callback function completes, in case of asynchronous event reception. If the asynchronous receive API is used, then there is a event processing thread in C API code which invokes the callback functions. The C API determines the class of machine it runs on, and establishes a channel directly to coredb:2017 when inside the cloud trusted domain, and cloudvip:2017 when outside the cloud. The API implementation generates a lot of log entries at high trace level, which can be observed by raising traceLevel log parameter to 200 or higher.

Java API is implemented on top of C API through the use of Java Native Interface functions. Thus, most of the discussion about C API above applies to Java API as well.

10.3.2.1 Requirements

Event polling mechanism provides the support for communication between the registration process and user/service/account aware components of the system. For example, mail and directory service subscribe to registration events. Registration service stores events and delivers them on demand by consumers. Consumers poll for new events periodically (e.g., every few minutes).

A general event mechanism, decoupled from any service, would be useful to other components. Initially, it would give more flexibility to registration service, where its Oracle database could be easily substituted with other databases.

The event system should include the following capabilities:

- Publish/subscribe paradigm, where event producers can produce only events that are already published or registered with the event system. The process of registering event types is an administrative/management operation. Consumers can receive only those events to which they are subscribed. Subscription is also performed through the management interface, at the level of daemons

- Reliable event delivery, with "exactly one" semantics, even when some or all subscribers are not active
- Persistent storage for undelivered events to subscribers, such that no events are ever lost, even when a subscriber is not running. However, there will be a limit to how many events can be kept undelivered before issuing an error to the producer, giving the producer a signal that not all subscribers are receiving data. Events would also have a limited time to live and be deleted once they expire. The time limit and size of persistent queues would be configured through management API and they would be attributes of each registered event
- Simple APIs, for the producers and consumers. Management/administration APIs include comprehensive set of capabilities for manipulating event type registration, attribute inspection and modification, event subscription management, persistent queue management, event type(s) to service(s) mapping, etc.
- Management/administration APIs that would allow for inspection and management of the event storage, published event types, event subscriptions, etc.
- Access control for who can send what event and who can receive what event, at the level of users or accounts and event pseudo services. This is done through the regular account/user/service subscription mechanism

10.3.2.2 Architecture

There are three entities in the event mechanism:

- *Producer.* Any daemon or program that sends events
- *Consumer.* Any daemon or program that is interested in receiving specific types of events
- *Event storage and transport* infrastructure. This entity is responsible for permanently storing events until delivered to all subscribers. It provides reliable transport, "exactly one" semantics

The event transport and storage infrastructure is built on GMMS. GMMS already provides a communication infrastructure that spreads throughout all of the GeoPlex system. A GMMS daemon can use the new event APIs to send and asynchronously receive events it is subscribed to. GMMS itself keeps track of what events are published; what are their mappings to services; which daemons are subscribed to which events; and what events have been delivered to which subscribers. GMMS dynamically updates the persistent information to ensure minimal disk space consumption; i.e., it removes events that have been delivered to all subscribers and events that have been in the storage longer than a predefined limit. Furthermore, GMMS provides a scalable communication infrastructure for an event mechanism, since only one event is generated by producer and sent to SSM/SM, and only one event is sent from SM to each SSM, to finally be received by multiple subscribers. This is in effect an application level multicast communication structure.

Producers are able to generate events with a simple API call. Status of the API invocation indicates the status of event delivery to GMMS, and is further described under APIs below. Producer does not know who the recipients are. It simply generates an event for which there may be subscribers. GMMS may drop the event if it knows for sure that there are no subscribers for that specific event.

Consumer starts receiving events in the order in which GMMS receives them, as soon as consumer initializes GeoEve library. The consumer is responsible for providing the event processing function during its initialization. If the consumer does not specify from whom it wants to receive events, it receives all events to which it is subscribed regardless of who sent the event. Consumers receive the information about the producer of an event. The consumers also receives information about how many events it has missed since last connected to the event system.

The order of event delivery is guaranteed to be that of the order of issue; from one producer, however, there are no guarantees regarding ordering among events from multiple producers. For example, if two producers send one event each, e.g., e1 and e2, then two different consumers could receive them in either order, e1 e2 or e2 e1.

Event are described through an internal event type, event source, i.e., the producer name, event data, and event attributes (e.g., length of validity, size of permanent queue, access control information, etc.). Some of this information is relevant to event type only, while other pertains to individual event instances. All event components are ASCII strings, making it easy to map event messages onto current GMMS protocol. In addition to producer and consumer APIs, the event mechanism includes management interface exposed through GMMS. Through the management interface, a management application can perform all necessary management operations.

Security aspect of the event mechanism consists of two parts:

- Security
- Event mechanism access control

Security provides for control of who can connect to GMMS. Only a machine inside a cloud or authenticated machines that are subscribed to GMMS service can connect to GMMS. Access control provides finer level of control, described below.

Access Control

Access control provided by the event mechanism allows for control of who may send or receive events of specific type. The granularity of the access control is that of a user and pseudo service corresponding to the event type of interest. For a related set of event types, there is a service corresponding to the send operation on this set of event types and another service corresponding to the receive operation on this set of event types, registered through usual service registration mechanisms. Users that need to send events must be previously subscribed to the corresponding service(s). The event mechanism performs the necessary access control based on the relation of the users, accounts and event type services obtained through the core API.

Event mechanism management interface provides means for examining and modifying the mapping between event types and event type services.

10.4 Summary

GMMS provides an integrated monitoring and management solution. This combines the myriad components of multiple vendors, thus enabling fully interoperable systems. This grants increased flexibility to utilize the most functional components – including the monitoring systems from vendors of infrastructure hardware and software. Our experience in dynamic systems management has demonstrated this as an essential capability of large scale managed systems. In particular, the ability reliably monitor and modify system function *remotely* under *all circumstances* is an essential capability. The distributed yet secure components allow GMMS perform this.

CHAPTER 11

Sample Consumer Services

Middleware service platforms are about *services*, and in particular ones that offer concrete value to the end users. As mentioned in the introduction, this book does not discuss any AT&T consumer-oriented services. We discuss instead a number of original and innovative middleware services and extensions designed by the graduate students enrolled in "Programming and Design of Modern Internet Service Platforms," given during the Fall of 1999 through the Computer Science Department of Columbia University[1]. Approximately 50 students completed this course, which was based on an earlier version of this book. These students are not networking experts or experienced service builders. Rather, they are bright yet overworked young men and women who carry full-time academic loads. The course increased their workload through a required semester project using shared computing facilities, somewhat in contrast to the usual Industry model. The students completed design, prototypes, documentation and demonstration, but did not fully integrate their work with the middleware infrastructure.

Virtually all the students immediately understood the advantages of common APIs on a managed network-integrated platform. The resulting projects demonstrated a wide range of ideas, yet shared the common theme of reusability. About half of the projects looked at issues in eCommerce. Of these, several groups developed electronic shopping malls, and investigated reusable features such as a uniform payment gateway that provides a single "virtual checkout line". One eCommerce project developed an application portal that customized the user's environment through dynamic monitoring of actions, and the construction of individualized shopping malls that cater to a customer's shopping preferences. A stock service agent provided multiple classes of accounts, with purchase, sale, portfolio and pricing services.

1. The course home page at http://www.cs.columbia.edu/~lerner/CS6998-03 includes full project reports.

TABLE 11: Student Projects during Fall 1999 Developed Innovative Services

Category	Project	Summary
Electronic Commerce	Micro cent payment Systems	Allows making purchase for goods or services which cost only a few cents, or even less
	EasyMeal Food Ordering Service	One-stop shopping for food ordering. Order food and have it selected locally and charged to your credit card or GeoPlex account
	Stock Service Agent	Full featured and secure stock service agent supporting purchase and sale of online stocks, and online portfolio, prices and account information
	Virtual Retail System	Portal for sales in a virtual shopping mall
	Student Registration	Workflow service for student registrations
Gateway	More KidsVille	Extended a network-enabled "virtual world"
	Interpeer Communications	Secure and reliable inter-peer communication through a secure channel in the middleware
	Remote Peer Administration	General and scalable method for administering multiple distributed peers
Quality of Service (QoS)	Unified programmable QoS API	Based on IEEE P1520 Reference Model
	Differential Services simulation	Experimental scheduling algorithm for DiffServ model and performance measurements
Network Enhancements	Application Translation Service	Language translation of applications between languages
	Customer Profile Exchange	Marketing-oriented customer profiling through collection of actions for customized services
	User Profiler and Merchant Portal	Portal gathers information on a users' usage; constructs a customized virtual mall of online stores and services
	ThingServer	Generalized object repository attaches user-defined metadata to chinked distributed store with shared caching and object lookups
Database	Transaction Processing Support	Distributed commit combines multiple databases through managed replication and synchronization
	Optimized Multi-Inventory & Manufacturing System	OMIMS provides geographically distributed manufacturing through managed network connections for ordering of composite systems

In addition to eCommerce, several students investigated network-based issues, in particular the ideas of APIs for DiffServ, and simulation of DiffServ methods. This produced a high-quality conference paper on the topic of DiffServ APIs. A cousin project simulated the scheduling of multiple traffic queues within each gate as a pragmatic technique for DiffServ; for example, to support both text-based and isochronous multimedia over the same connectivity.

11.1 *KidsVille*

One student project extended an existing application known as KidsVille, written by Steve Klinkner *et al.* in 1997. KidsVille is a multimedia service that combines visually appealing graphics with network-based services. Authenticating and service access use the middleware facilities to access chat, mail, and other forms of communication. Network-based services are invoked through stylized icons; for example, one reads e-mail by clicking on a mailbox to open it. The virtual reality application is active at the client end points, shown to the left of Figure 11-1 as Andrea, Anya, and Julian. These clients

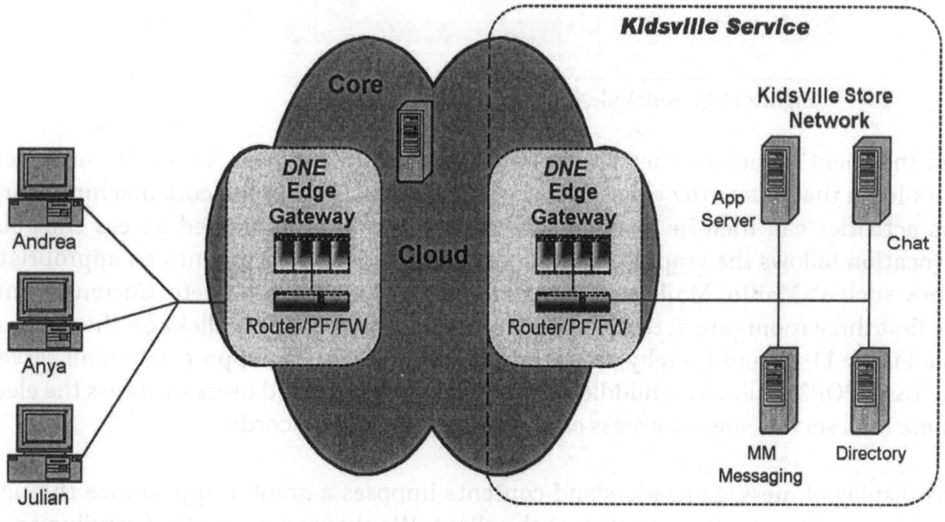

Figure 11-1: Conceptual Diagram of Subscribers Access to Service

access the KidsVille service through the edge gateway into the cloud. This gateway requires authentication and enforces the service model. Similar controls must be adhered to by the KidsVille services, shown on the right of the cloud. An authenticated administrator needs to announce the various services before the cloud will permit users to see service on them. This protects the client, the service provider, and the network provider, since they receive platform monitoring and maintenance services.

Authentication begins with a login screen (Figure 11-2) through which the client enters login credentials. The client and cloud negotiate their bilateral authentication,

Figure 11-2: KidsVille-II Login Screen

and the client's machine then shows the image of a *HomeRoom*. This achieves a network login that enters the client into the AUR maintained on the core machine. Various activities can then be invoked subject to the cloud-maintained access controls. Invocation follows the graphical metaphors by moving the mouse into an appropriate room, such as MailIn, MailOut, Chat, Phone room, JukeBox room, etc. Currently, only the first three rooms are active. To check electronic mail the user clicks on the mailbox (see Figure 11-3), and thereby activates the Java code for the appropriate mail server, such as a POP3 mailer. The middleware only allows authorized users to access the electronic mail service, and all access can be subject to usage records.

The display of message headers and contents imposes a graphic appearance through graphics rendering software active at the client. We show an example of sending an e-mail in Figure 11-4. Assuming that SMTP is a cloud-public service, it can be accessed only by authenticated users. Since the KidsVille user previously authenticated, he can send an e-mail. In similar fashion, the "chat room" can talk to specific chat servers that are enabled for the client login. Figure 11-5 shows an Internet chat server with access from the graphical world. The server itself is registered either as a public or private service, depending on the service model for Chat. This supports all the standard chat features, including an *Audience* list for displaying active users of the channel.

The students extended KidsVille by addition of the chat room and other middleware services. Whereas chat servers traditionally maintain their own client list, the middleware network provides an authenticated user registry (AUR) and an authenticated

Figure 11-3: KidsVille-II Homeroom Displays Services with 3D Graphics

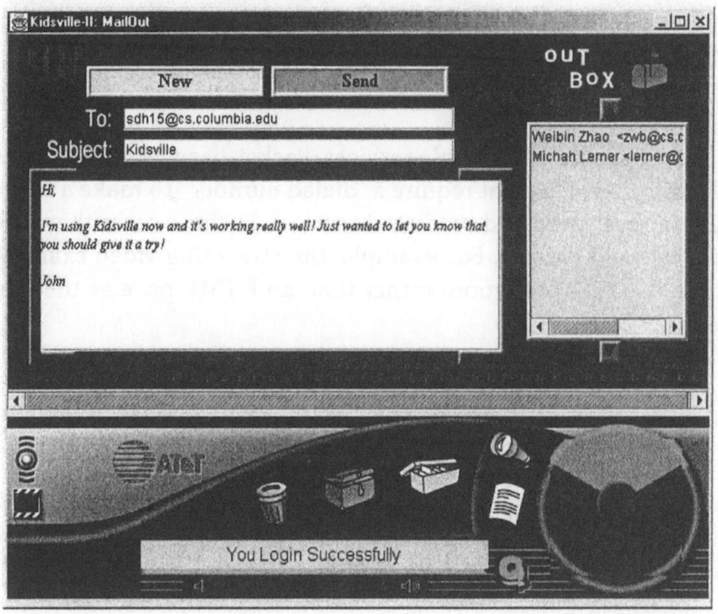

Figure 11-4: KidsVille-II Sending E-mail Through Secure Server

connection table (ACT). These improve the ability to *monitor* and *maintain* the chat service. Likewise, service features such as notification ("Tell me when Marshall enters the room") can be provisioned through the event mechanisms common to the middleware, rather than specializations unique to a particular chat protocol.

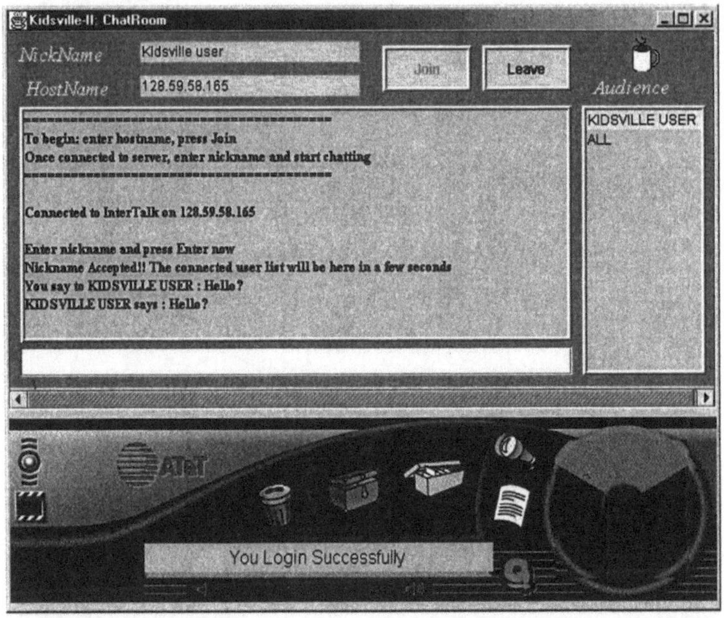

Figure 11-5: Chatting with Friends On KidsVille-II

It should be clear these are only simple services. Packet-based video and audio services, as well as telephony services that require a "dialed number" to make a connection, can use the same interface and cloud-mediated services. In these cases they would actually activate network-based objects. For example, the streaming video example discussed on page 293 can use the video room rather than an HTML page as the selector of the video service.

CHAPTER 12

Conclusion: Future Directions

In today's fiercely competitive global marketplace, a network provider must gain technological advantage; for example, by efficiently integrating voice and data. Only then will network carriers be able to join fellow carriers around the globe to offer worldwide deployment of essential new services – thereby demonstrating ubiquity among separately owned network infrastructures. *This clearly is the future!*

These challenges can be largely addressed today through a common, "intelligent" infrastructure within the existing network environment. This infrastructure – described in detail in this book – has a unified distributed architecture that efficiently fuses the resources of many networks and machines. Common capabilities such as information retrieval, security, usage recording and access control are fully integrated by this infrastructure. Such an approach far excels the global "dumb transport" network operating as a pure "best-effort", uniform priority, packet delivery means. Such networks force themselves into a commodity position by providing only the raw wiring, without processing support for signaling or management. They follow the model of a simple LAN interconnecting multiple PCs.

For all practical purposes, corporate extranets and the Internet backbone more closely resemble an "intelligent network" than a "dumb network". If you peek under the hood of any of the systems supporting our networks, you will observe many different kinds of middleware at work. Every system has some middleware even though this fact may not be advertised. All vendors – from network to ISV to ISP and Telco – have heard the jest:

Nowdays, someone's middleware lies above
and others' lie below;
one industry's middleware is someone else's underware
and someone else's outerware

If the mere abundance of middleware is not the source of the Intelligent network, then what is? In actuality, the intelligence is obtained through interoperability between various system layers, each one cooperating with the others. These interactions also introduce some limited stateful information. There can be repercussions of pulling inappropriate stateful information into a large network. Indeed, there are good reasons why the Internet transport does not depend upon stateful information - scalability and reliability being the most widely cited. Nevertheless, substantial state has become associated with the Internet. Applications and services require more than a "best effort" transport. Over-engineering is neither an economical nor practical solution in the long run. Thus, IETF models such as DiffServ and IntServ have begun to force a reevaluation of the totally "stateless" position. In many cases, limited stateful information augments the transport and services, while the basic IP transport remains stateless.

DiffServ, in particular, recognizes the requirement to localize such state information *at the edges of the network*. The concepts discussed in this book share a similar approach. By admitting stateful information into the network view, yet confining it to the edges, it becomes possible to efficiently communicate the necessary state changes between edge components. This is likely to prove more effective than forcing it outside of the network view completely. And yet, it preserves the stateless characteristics currently required for very high speed transport and unconstrained scalability. Indeed, SS7 switching maintains separate control and data channels; still, it can share a common and configurable transport fabric.

It was such observations that impelled us in 1995 to establish a common service platform thus leveraging the growing presence of network middleware, and extending the provider's network. Much like the early rocky and uncertain path to the wide acceptance of the Java platform today, the notion of an IP service platform has begun to take hold in key communities including the ASPs, ISPs and Telcos. Witness the recent movement towards Application Service Providers (ASPs) and their business of Web Application Hosting (WAH). Front page news proclaims "Internet as Platform" for services and ASPs [INFO2000].

If we look at the recent growth of ASPs and compare it to the growth of ISPs that started back in the mid-1980's, we see that ISPs have been steadily adding value to their service offerings and reinventing themselves as ASPs, as shown in Figure 12-1. Much of the ASPs' growth, as well as realignment of the ISPs core values, emerges in direct response to the appearance, availability, and deployment of viable service middleware and the con-

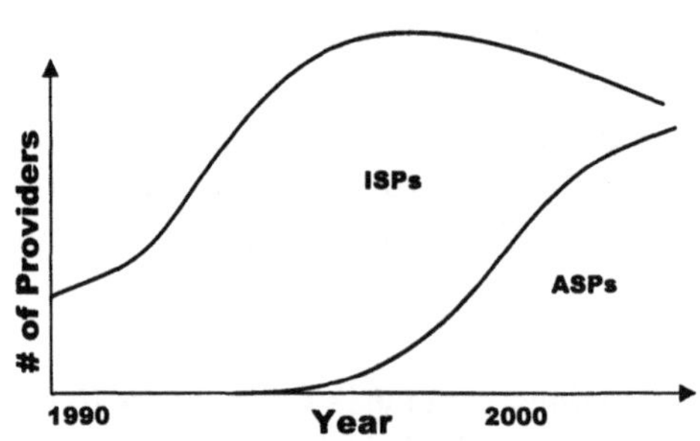

Figure 12-1: The Merging of ISPs and ASPs.

comitant restructuring of the service providers. Looking back over the history of ISPs and service providers, we can identify four distinct phases related to this latest trend.

These four phases are:

1. First generation of lightweight clients, with a dumb network – essentially only a copper interconnect – and a heavy backhaul to the mainframe
2. Proliferation of heavy, more functional, clients: PCs or workstations. However, their interconnectivity is limited and interactions are not well integrated
3. Aggregation of common capabilities that can interact in forceful ways, but at relatively high cost and without 7x24 reliability
4. The carriers and ASPs currently improve on the third generation

As we conclude the book, we take a closer look at the structure of these ASPs as they relate to IP Service platforms, and demonstrate the ideal position for the network middleware outlined in this book.

12.1 Application Service Providers

At the end of 1998, Web Application Hosting (WAH) emerged as a powerful new force in the marketplace. WAH offers customers access to fully supported applications *online.* Rather than license, install and support applications in-house, customers can simply pay a recurring fee to access applications via the public Internet and VPNs. Offering software solutions as a *service* instead of as a product met wide acceptance.

In 1999, worldwide revenues generated by ISVs from hosting services totaled about $77 million. This market is expected to exhibit a cumulative annual growth rate (CAGR) of 153 percent in Western Europe; 157 percent in Japan; 108 percent in the Asia/Pacific region; and 80 percent in North America[1]. This adds up to about $8 billion by the end of year 2004[2]. About 66 percent of this business will be Web hosting and eCommerce, while the rest will go to front- and back-office support, including application hosting[3].

An Application Service Provider (ASP) is a company that operates a hosting center for on-line applications owned by other businesses. These businesses outsource their application services to the ASP, which operate and manage them. The ASP Industry Consortium defines an ASP as:

1. International Data Corporation (March 1999).
2. According to ARC Advisory Group's new Web Application Hosting Worldwide Outlook.
3. The Yankee Group (August 1999).

An ASP manages and delivers application capabilities to multiple entities from a data center across a wide area network.

ASPs offer multiple advantages. Information Technology (IT) costs decrease as the client company outsources its own information technology to an ASP facility. IT quality improves too, as the ASP can offer a single bill and single point of contact. The ASP's full range of services may more readily accommodate changing market conditions and technologies. Corporate resources, thus freed from the IT concerns, can be refocused on the company's strategic projects and core values.

Of course, this assumes that an ASP can demonstrate their facility and support staff are capable of handling all the business customer's IT service needs. To do so requires a first-class, well-staffed facility supporting the following services and responsibilities:

- Ability to prepare and manage the infrastructure, connectivity, security, and applications necessary for enabling the delivery of services
- Mechanism for accepting orders from customers, implementing the applications, and training end users
- 24x7 support of network connections and applications for customers

The ASP market is growing quickly and absorbing other specialties. One example is the ongoing redefinition of the traditional network providers (Telcos). Ongoing developments impel the Telcos towards closer association with content providers, as well as the essential industries of service providers, systems integrators, consultants, outsourcers, and independent software vendors (ISV), as shown in Figure 12.2. This is fueled by new entrants that can start off without any legacy infrastructure to revamp or depreciate; these originators are depicted as the "Pure Play" in the figure. The software vendors and the hardware suppliers are also relabelling themselves as ASPs. In general the title is appropriate for anyone who owns a customer relationship and the service level agreement (SLA).

The highly diverse ASP market continues to define new segments. Nevertheless, these ASPs can be categorized on the basis of the different classes of applications and services they provide[1]. This categorization reveals that ASPs tend to use each other's complementary services to offer composite solutions to their customers; thus ASPs have defined specific core competencies forming a cooperative (*sic.*) symbiosis:

Collocation Providers

These firms lease technical facilities including servers and Internet access to clients; these clients then host their own application software on the leased facilities. This arrangement is ideal for companies that want to

1. From December 1999 article in the SummitVision newsletter.

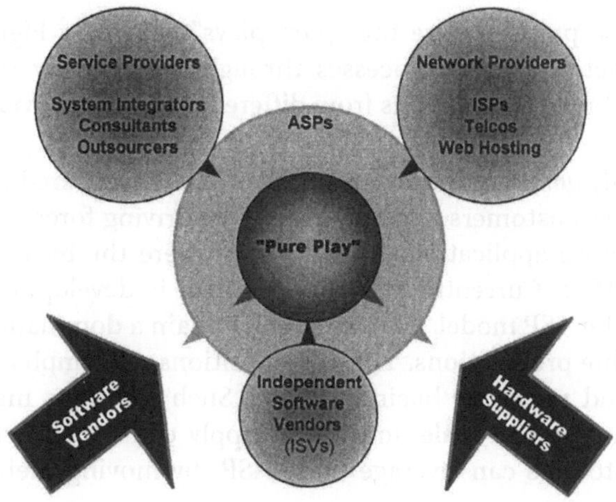

Figure 12-2: ASP Players (International Data Corp., 1999)

retain full control over their *software* while leveraging the specialized expertise of hardware management and maintenance provided by the collocation vendor.

Wholesale Service Providers

These firms develop and operate large data centers. The data centers are typically optimized for ISVs and ASPs that want to host applications software in such centers. Two of the larger players that fit this category are Intel and Digex.

Managed Application Providers

These ASPs specialize in customizing and managing specific enterprise-class hosted applications. This includes enterprise resource planning, sales force automation, eCommerce and customer relationship management. By operating their own data centers or renting space from a wholesale service provider, these ASPs offer a complete solution for enterprises that need to completely outsource these services. USinternetworking and Pandesic are well known in this field.

Rentable/Instant Application Providers

These firms offer application software that customers can rent on a short-term basis and access instantly through the Web. Some of the companies that offer this are Interliant and Netledger.

Business Service Providers

These firms offer their applications software as business services. Good examples are On The Go Software and Works.com.

Business Process Providers

Finally, these providers are the "pure plays" shown in Figure 12-2. They offer complete business processes through the Web by integrating the best-of-the-breed applications from different software providers.

The ASP market only gelled in the later part of 1999, and garnered phenomenal interest amongst business customers and end users. The driving force is the business customer's ability to move applications to the ASPs, where the businesses leverage the economies of the ASPs. Currently, almost every firm is developing or realigning its strategy in light of the ASP model. As change will remain a dominant market force, the ASPs hone their value propositions. These propositions will emphasize solutions that support multiple and malleable business needs. Such solutions must be highly efficient, through economies of scale, improved supply chains, and customer relationships. Business customers can leverage these ASPs by moving their processes to the ASP.

With the presence of ASPs, customers will have the luxury to ignore the details of the software applications, hardware platforms and the underlying middleware technologies, and instead focus on the business values. This is one hard lesson that the telecommunication industry has recently learned: customers do not want to know nor do they care about middleware and platforms – but the industry does indeed care, in as far as it forges an enabling infrastructure for their core assets. This lesson translates to a strategy that targets the end-user applications while internally developing the necessary platforms.

12.2 ASPs and IP Service Platforms

For over 20 years businesses have been building and optimizing their internal operations, processes and networks, creating substantial LANS, WANs and data services. These efforts developed specialized networking systems built upon private and managed resources. Simultaneously, the Internet grew in size, reach and bandwidth, providing ubiquitous service. This was nearly unnoticed at first, since it was perceived as merely a "best effort" system supporting only the most essential services such as DNS. Somehow this somewhat primitive Internet began to outstrip many of the dedicated packet switched solutions.

Proliferation of the Web-based services impelled IP towards its current role, the "king" of data networks. ISPs and Telcos have started offering online services. These services are in many ways similar, as each is constructed from the same basic IP protocol, with similar switching and control mechanisms. Despite these similarities, each service started out with unique mechanisms for access, authentication, authorization, roaming, directories of names or services, as well as unique usage collection and billing.

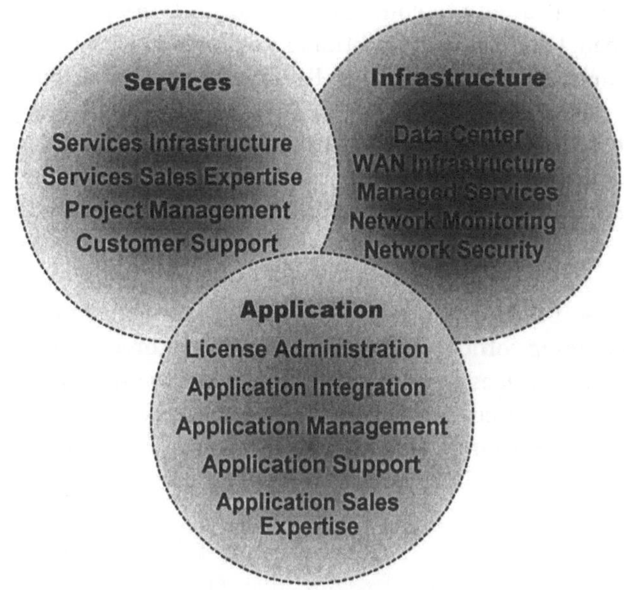

Figure 12-3: Taxonomy of ASP Businesses

The Telecom industry realized these duplications were costly to business and confusing to customers. To operate effectively and efficiently, the Telecom industries require an administrative service infrastructure incorporating registration, authentication, customer care and billing. Yet today, there still exists no such "off-the-shelf" platform. Furthermore, network-enabled online services lack the necessary integration with consumer telephones to offer seamless interoperable multimedia services. These challenges become increasingly important as new services supporting video, unified messaging and bandwidth-on-demand add to the complexity of the network. In addition, network-enabled online services must operate at "carrier grade" levels of nearly 100% reliability while scaling to profitable volume.

The Telecom developments have not been ignored by other business. Corporations and private companies continuously look towards options for their traditional cost centers, including communications. The public data networks became a viable alternative to the expensive private WANS with their insatiable appetite for bandwidth. External providers developed the necessary expertise in communications, and encouraged outsourcing of communications services. This placed the Network service providers (NSPs) under ever-increasing pressure to replace the depleted POTS market, and to offer service level agreements (SLAs), thereby creating a contractual commitment for specific service levels. These providers began to compete fiercely, as their niche of protected services no longer provided a safe haven of secure revenue. The "king", namely IP, had levelled these distinctions.

The NSPs perceived the ability to combine communication-based SLAs with information services. Indeed, the Telecoms traditionally innovated with computers as a means to manage the communications network. By shifting this expertise into traditionally computational services, their customers could obtain "one stop shopping" through an aggregate service rather than separate computational and communication services. Driven by such compelling business reasons, NSPs deployed vastly increased capacity, and sought to manage this resource exceedingly well. Integrated middleware functionality satisfied these requirements, placing middleware directly into the network.

This trend continues. Businesses now outsource many data and communication items. For example, messaging, office automation and sales force automation are viewed nearly as commodity services to be contracted at the lowest standard bid. The trend even affects human resources and financial business processes. Thus, the NSPs are now starting to deliver corporate applications services as network-resident functionalities. What started with pure IP transport is now pervading the processes that run on the transport.

12.3 Summary

An important aspect of the NSPs' economic survival depends upon efficiently providing computing-based applications as a fundamental part of the networks. They are building up the general purpose computing capabilities within their networks to host these applications. The NSPs aspire to manage the complex interactions between the myriad businesses that increasingly interconnect through shared information: financial, inventory, engineering, reference, distance conferences, as well as the automation of office, sales and financial processes. These applications are both computationally intensive as well as communications intensive. Well coordinated management of such resources must occur to efficiently operate the networks that are intended to support these applications.

Efficient operations calls for common features at the enterprise scale. Without generalized yet secure access, there cannot be authentication of users, machines, or automatic agents. Authorization becomes increasingly critical to ensure that information cannot be incorrectly accessed, either through error or intent. Accounting for these resources – from usage recording through the generation of bills – occupies another shared role that is inherent to all such business processes.

Finally, the mere availability of service is of little benefit. The services must be provisioned to customers in a timely manner that provides both what they want and what they need. Thus, the services must be easily extensible and customized as needs change. Such flexibility indeed characterizes the IP transport, and the successful IP services that we have today provide a malleable structure. There is no longer tolerance for brittle applications returning an "`error 222`", "`Segv`" or "`General Protection Fault`". Neither can they tolerate the costs of inefficient security systems, redundant billing systems, or manual processes. Rather, these services must be reliable and standardized, yet flexible; this not only means they work flawlessly, but they must also adapt to changing resources, support network-wide monitoring, and integrate with multiple systems for management and control.

Which brings us back to middleware – a standard way to provide common functionality that is ubiquitous to all networked applications.

The rest, as they say, is history ...

Glossary

AMPS
Advanced Mobile Phone Service is the mobile phone system equivalent of POTS making up PSTN.

API
Application Programming Interface

ATM
Asynchronous Transfer Mode

BGP
Border Gateway Protocol

CHAP
Challenge Handshake Authentication Protocol

CORBA
Common Object Request Broker Architecture

DEN
Directory Enabled Network

DNE
Distributed Network Element

EAP
Extensible Authentication Protocol

FDDI
Fiber-Distributed Data Interface

FTP
File Transfer Protocol

GSMP
General Switch Management Protocol

GUI
Graphics User Interface

HPC
High Performance Connections

HTTP
Hyper-Text Transfer Protocol

ICMP
Internet Control Message Protocol

IMAP4
Internet Messaging Access Protocol a mail protocol with MIME integration, folders, shared mailboxes and more, that is better than POP3.

IP
Internet Protocol (see IPv4)

IPv4
Internet Protocol version 4

IPv6
Internet Protocol version 6

IPSec
IP Security is an IETF security protocol that offers authentication and encryption.

ISDN
Integrated Services Digital Network

JAIN
Java Advanced Intelligent Network

Java Language
Sun Microsystems object-oriented language for the Internet.

KERBEROS
A system that authenticates users, developed by MIT.

L2F
Layer 2 Forwarding is a Cisco protocol that has been combined with PPTP to form L2TP.

L2TP
Layer 2 Tunneling Protocol is an IETF tunneling protocol that was formed from L2F and PPTP.

LAN
Local Area Network

LDAP
Light-weight Directory Access Protocol

MIME
Multipurpose Internet Mail Extensions is an ASCII encoding of non-text files with an ASCII header used by mail and web technologies.

NAT
Network Address Translation

NCSA
National Center for Supercomputing Applications for high-performance computing that is located on the University of Illinois in Urbana-Champaign, Illinois.

NGI
Next Generation Internet

NIST
National Institute of Standards and Technology, previously known as the National Bureau of Standards (NBS)

NSF
National Science Foundation

OSS
Operations Support System

POP
Point of Presence, usually ran by ISPs, is the local exchange consisting of RAS's and other network equipment through which users access the Internet or other networks.

POTS
Plain Old Telephony Service as relating to the PSTN.

POTS
Plain Old Telephony Service as relating to the PSTN.

PPP
Point-to-Point Protocol

PPTP
Point-to-Point Tunneling Protocol is a Microsoft tunneling protocol that encapsulates other protocols and encrypts the tunnel with RSA.

PSTN
Public Switched Telephone Network is the worldwide voice telephone network, now almost entirely digital except for the analog lines connecting most homes and the central offices.

PVC
Private Virtual Circuit

QoS
Quality of Service

POP3
Post-Office Protocol 3.

RADIUS
Remote Access Dial-In User Service

RAS
Remote Access Service is a computer at the edge of a network that terminates dial-up or ISDN connections and offers network access to remote users.

RSA
Rivest-Shamir-Adleman is a public-private cryptography method.

RSVP
Reservation Protocol

RTP
Real-Time Protocol

SET
Secure Electronic Transaction

SSL
Secure Sockets Layer

SMTP
Simple Mail Transfer Protocol

SNMP
Simple Network Management Protocol

SS7
Signaling System 7

STAR-TAP
Science, Technology and Research Transit Access Point located in Chicago

TCP
Transfer Control Protocol

TINA-C
Telecommunication Information networking Architecture Consortium

UCAID
University Corporation for Advanced Internet Development

UDP
User Datagram Protocol

URL
Uniform Resource Locator

vBNS
The very-high-performance Backbone Network Service is an IP-over-ATM network over Sonet, OC-12 (622.08 Mb/s infrastructure).

VPN
Virtual Private Network

WAN
Wide Area Network

References

[ARNO98]

K. Arnold and J. Gosling, *The Java Programming Language, Second Edition*, Addison-Wesley, 1998.

[BIDZ97]

D. James Bidzos, *Digital Signatures: the Key to Identification and Authentication in a Digital Age*. Testimony before the House Committee on Science; Subcommittee on Technology, October 28, 1997. See http://www.house.gov/science/bidzos_10-28.htm.

[BISW99]

J. Biswas, J-F. Huard, A. Lazar, K. Lim, S. Mahjoub, L-F. Pau, M. Suzuki, S. Torstensson, W. Weiguo and S. Weinstein, *White Paper on Application Programming Interfaces for Networks*, Working Group for IEEE P1520, January 1999. See also, http://www.ieee-pin.org.

[BLAC98]

U. Black. *The Intelligent Network, Customizing Telecommunication Networks and Services*, Prentice Hall Series, Upper Saddle River, New Jersey, 1998.

[BLAC2000]

U. Black. *Voice Over IP*, Prentice Hall Series in Advanced Communications Technologies, Upper Saddle River, New Jersey, 2000.

[BOUM98]

F. Boumphrey, et.al., *XML Applications*, Wrox Press, Birmingham, UK, 1998.

[BRET98]

E. A. Bretz, *The Internet*, IEEE Spectrum, pp. 32-42, January 1998.

[BUSH98]

D. Bushaus, *Who Knows?*, TeleDotCom, May 1998.

[CALV98]
K. L. Calvert, S. Bhattacharlje, et al. *Directions in Active Networks*, IEEE Communications Magazine, pp. 72, October 1998.

[CHES94]
W. Cheswick, S. Bellovin, *Firewalls and Internet Security: Repelling the Wiley Hacker.* Addison-Wesley Publishing, 1994.

[COUR98]
T. Courtois, *Java Networking & Communications*, Prentice Hall PTR, Upper Saddle River, NJ, 1998.

[DEPR93]
M. De Prycker, *Asynchronous Transfer Mode*, 2nd ed., Ellis Horwood, Ltd., 1993.

[DIFF76]
W. Diffie, M. Hellman, New Directions in Cryptography, *IEEE TRansactions on Information Theory*, 22; 1976.

[DODD99]
A. Z. Dodd, *The Essential Guide to Telecommunications*, Second Edition, Prentice Hall PTR, Upper Saddle River, NJ, 1999.

[DORA99]
N. Doraswamy, Dan Harkins, *IPSec: The New Security Standard for the Internet, Intranets, and Virtual Private Networks,* Prentice Hall 1999.

[ENGL97]
R. Englander, *Developing Java Beans*, O'Reilly & Associates, June 1997.

[FEGH99]
J. Feghhi, I. Feghhi, P. Williams, *Digital Certificates: Applied Internet Security*, Addison Wesley, 1999.

[FRA86]
N. Francez, *Fairness*, Springer-Verlag, Sept. 1986.

[GARE97]
R. Gareiss, *Is the Internet in Trouble?* Data Communications, pp 36-50, September 21, 1997.

[GARF97]
S. Garfinkel and G. Spafford, *Web Security & Commerce*, O'Reilly & Associates, 1997.

[GBAG99]
C. Gbaguidi, J-P. Hubaux, M Hamdi, and A. N. Tantawi, *A Programmable Architecture for the Provision of Hybrid Services*, IEEE Communications, July 1999.

[GEOP97]
GeoPlex Project, http://www.geoplex.com, AT&T Labs, IP Technology Organization, San Jose, CA, 1997-1999.

[GIGAET]
Gigabit Ethernet Alliance, http://www.gigabit-ethernet.org.

[GOLL99]
D. Gollman, *Computer Security*, John Wiley and Sons Ltd. (West Sussex, England), 1999.

[GONC99]
M. Goncalves and K. Niles, *IPv6 Networks*, McGraw Hill, 1999.

[GREE99]
E. Greenberg, *Network Application Frameworks: design and architecture*, Addison Wesley, 1999.

[HALA97]
J. Halamka, P. Szolovits, D. Rind, et al. "A WWW implementation of national recommendations for protecting electronic health information." J Am Med Inform Assoc 4(6): 458-464 (1997). See http://www.medg.lcs.mit.edu/people/psz/secman.html

[HAMD99]
M. Hamdi, O. Verscheure, J. P. Hubaux, I. Dalgi, and P. Wang, Voice Service Interworking for PSTN and IP Networks, To appear in IEEE Communication Magazine, 2nd Quarter 1999.

[HARVST]
Harvest: A Scalable, Customizable Discovery and Access System, Technical Report CU-CS-732-94, Department of Computer Science, University of Colorado - Boulder, Revised March 1995.

[HOWE97]
T. A. Howes, and M. C. Smith, *LDAP: Programming Directory-Enabled Applications with Lightweight Directory Access Protocol*, MacMillan Technology Publishing, 1997.

[HUIT95]
C. Huitema, *Routing in the Internet*, Prentice Hall, 1995.

[INFO2000]
Info World, *Internet as platform*, February 7, 2000 (page 1).

[JAIN]
Java Advanced Intelligent Network, http://www.sun.com.

[JAMI98]
J. Jamison, R. Nicklas, G. Miller, K. Thompson, R. Wilder, L Cunnigham, and C. Song, vBNS: not your father's Internet, IEEE Spectum, July 1998, pp. 38-46.

[KAUF2000]
E. Kaufman, A. Newman. *Implementing IPSec: Making Security Work on VPNs, Intranets, and Extranets*. Wiley, 2000.

[KRAU99]
J. K. Krause, *How AT&T got the Internet,* The Industry Standard, pp 88-102, August 16-23, 1999.

[KUJU98]
L. Kujubu, *Can IP answer AT&T's call?* InfoWorld, May 1998.

[LAWS98]
S. Lawson, *AT&T Plans migration to IP,* InfoWorld, Vol 20, Issue 20, May 1998.

[LAZA97]
A. A. Lazar, *Programming Telecommunication Networks,* IEEE Network, Sept/Oct 1997.

[LIU94]
C. Liu, J. Peek, R. Jones, B. Buus, and A. Nye, *Managing INTERNET Information Services,* O'Reilly & Associates, 1994.

[MESS96]
D. G. Messershmitt, *The Convergence of Telecommunication and Computing: What are the Implications today?,* Department of Electrical and Computer Sciences, University of California, Berkley, 1996.

[MESS99]
D. G. Messershmitt, *Networked Applications: A Guide to the New Computing Infrastructure,* Morgan Kaufman Publishers, February 1999.

[MCIS98]
Microsoft Commercial Internet System (MCIS), http://www.microsoft.com/mcis/default.asp.

[METZ99]
C. Metz, *IP Switching: Protocols and Architectures,* McGraw-Hill, USA, 1999.

[NEWT98]
H. Newton. *Newton's Telecom Dictionary,* 14th Edition, Flatiron Publishing, March 1998.

[NEWM96]
P. Newman, et. al. *General Switch Management Protocol Specification,* Ipsilon Networks Inc, Palo Alto, Inc, CA, March 1996.

[NORM98]
D. A. Norman, *The Invisible Computer, (Why good products can fail, the personal computer is so complex, and information appliances are the solutions),* The MIT Press, Cambridge, MA, 1989.

[OPPL96]
R. Oppliger, *Authentication Systems for Secure Networks* Artech House, Norwood MA, 1996.

[PARL]
PARLAY working group, http://www.parlay.org.

[REGL99]
W. Regli, Y. Shapirshteyn, V. Zaychik, GUNet Applications: *Active User and Active Service Registry,* AT&T Labs IP Technology Organization, Geoplex University Network, http://www.gunet.net, August 1999.

[RFC]
See http://www.ietf.org for the RFCs referenced throughout this book.

[RIVE92]
R. Rivest, The MD5 Message-Digest Algorithm, IETF Network Working Group, RFC 1321.

[RUMB99]
J. Rumbaugh, I Jacobson, and G. Booch, *The Unified Modeling Language Reference Manual,* Addison-Wesley, 1999.

[SCOT99]
C. Scott, P. Wolfe and M. Erwin, *Virtual Private Networks,* 2nd Edition, O'Reilly & Associates, 1999.

[SEIF98]
R. Seifert, *Gigabit Ethernet: Technology and Applications for High-speed LANs,* Addison-Wesley, 1998.

[SERA99]
D. Serain, *Middleware,* Springer-Verlag, London, 1999.

[SOFTS]
SoftSwitch Consortium, http://www.softswitch.org.

[SSWW99]
K. Arnold, A. O'Sullivan, R. W. Scheifler, J. Waldo, and A. Wollrath, *The Jini Specification,* Addison-Wesley, Reading MA, 1999.

[STAF99]
A. Staff, *"Making Sense of Middleware",* Application Development Trends, Volume 6, Number 5, May 1999.

[STEV94]
W. R. Stevens, *TCP/IP Illustrated, Volume 1,* Addison-Wesley, 1994. Additional volumes in the *TCP/IP Illustrated* series.

[TANE96]
A. S. Tanenbaum, *Computer Networks,* 3rd Edition, Prentice Hall PTR, Upper Saddle River, NJ, 1996.

[TINAC]
Telecommunication Information Networking Architecture Consortium, http://www.tinac.com.

[TRIP98]
M. V. Tripunitara, S. Rajamani, and N. Mihai, Security Policy Communication in a Distributed Network Element, International Conference on Advanced Communication Technology (ICACT'99), 1999.

[UCAID]
University Corporation for Advanced Internet Development, vBNS, Abileen, and Internet2, http://www.ucaid.org.

[UDUP96]
D. K. Udupa, *Network management Systems Essentials*, McGraw-Hill Companies, 1996.

[VALE99]
T. Valesky, *Enterprise JavaBeans: Developing Component-Based Distributed Applications*, Addison Wesley Longman, 1999.

[VANE98a]
G. Vanecek, *21st Century Advanced Network Services Platform: a Technology Overview White Paper*, AT&T Labs, Internet Platforms Organization, April 1998.

[VANE98b]
G. Vanecek, D. Vrsalovic, N. Vidovic, and T. London, *Universal Service Platform*, Proceedings of IWS'98, Tsukuma Center, Japan, March 1998.

[VANE99a]
G. Vanecek, N. Mihai, N. Vidovic, and D. Vrsalovic, *Enabling Hybrid Services in Emerging Data Networks*, IEEE Communications, July 1999.

[VANE99b]
G. Vanecek, *Enabling Smart Networks through IP Service Platforms*, Web Techniques, April 1999.

[VRSA98]
D. F. Vrsalovic, *Intelligent, Stupid, and Really Smart Networks*, ACM Communications, May 1998. NOTE: This was written as a rebuttal to David Isenberg's article on dumb networks.

[WACL98]
J. G. Waclawsky, *Connectionless Network Prioritization: Is It Real?* NCP and 3745/46 Today, Fall 1998.

[WILS98]
C. Wilson, GeoPlex: *AT&T's Bid For IP Power*, Interac@ctive Week, May 26, 1998.

[WONG99]
C. Wong, S. Lam, *Digital Signatures for Flows and Multicasts*, IEEE/ACM Transactions on Networking, August 1999, Pg 502-515.

Index

V

W

X

MIX
Papier aus verantwortungsvollen Quellen
Paper from responsible sources
FSC® C105338

If you have any concerns about our products,
you can contact us on
ProductSafety@springernature.com

In case Publisher is established outside the EU,
the EU authorized representative is:
Springer Nature Customer Service Center GmbH
Europaplatz 3, 69115 Heidelberg, Germany

Printed by Libri Plureos GmbH
in Hamburg, Germany